Cambridge Texts in the History of
Political Thought

KANT
Political Writings

Cambridge Texts in the History of Political Thought

SERIES EDITORS

RAYMOND GEUSS *Columbia University*

QUENTIN SKINNER *Christ's College, Cambridge*

RICHARD TUCK *Jesus College, Cambridge*

The series is intended to make available for students the most important texts required for an understanding of the history of political
thought. The scholarship of the present generation has greatly expanded our sense of the range of authors indispensable for such an
understanding, and the series will reflect those developments. It will
also include a number of less well-known works, in particular those
needed to establish the intellectual contexts that in turn help to make
sense of the major texts. The principal aim, however, will be to produce
new versions of the major texts themselves, based on the most up-to-
date scholarship. The preference will always be for complete texts, and
a special feature of the series will be to complement individual texts,
within the compass of a single volume, with subsidiary contextual
material. Each volume will contain an introduction on the historical
identity and contemporary significance of the work or works concerned, as well as a chronology, notes on further reading and (where
appropriate) brief biographical sketches of significant individuals
mentioned in each text.

For a list of titles published in the series, please see end of book.

KANT
Political Writings

EDITED WITH AN INTRODUCTION AND NOTES BY

HANS REISS
Professor Emeritus of German, University of Bristol

TRANSLATED BY

H. B. NISBET
Professor of Modern Languages, University of Cambridge

SECOND, ENLARGED EDITION

The right of the
University of Cambridge
to print and sell
all manner of books
was granted by
Henry VIII in 1534.
The University has printed
and published continuously
since 1584.

CAMBRIDGE UNIVERSITY PRESS

CAMBRIDGE

NEW YORK   PORT CHESTER

MELBOURNE   SYDNEY

Published by the Press Syndicate of the University of Cambridge
The Pitt Building, Trumpington Street, Cambridge CB2 1RP
40 West 20th Street, New York, NY 10011-4211, USA
10 Stamford Road, Oakleigh, Victoria 3166, Australia

© Cambridge University Press 1970, 1991

First published 1970
Reprinted 1971
First paperback edition 1977
Reprinted 1979, 1980, 1983, 1984, 1985
Second enlarged edition 1991
Reprinted 1991, 1992

Printed in the United States of America

British Library cataloguing in publication data
Kant, Immanuel, *1724–1804*
Kant's political writings. – 2nd ed. – (Cambridge texts in
the history of political thought)
I. Title   II. Reiss, Hans
320.01

Library of Congress cataloging in publication data
Kant, Immanuel, 1724–1804
[Selections. English. 1990]
Kant's political writings/edited with an introduction
and notes by Hans Reiss; translated by H.B. Nisbet. – 2nd ed.
(Cambridge texts in the history of political thought)
Includes bibliographical references.
1. Political science – Early works to 1800.   2. Kant,
Immanuel, 1724–1804 – Contributions in political science.
I. Reiss, Hans Siegbert.   II. Title.   III. Series.
JC181.K29513   1990
320'.01–DC20   90–1453 CIP

ISBN 0 521 39185 7 hardback
ISBN 0 521 39837 1 paperback
ISBN 0521 07717 6 hardback first edition
ISBN 0521 29212 3 paperback first edition

To Thomas, Richard, Arnold and Marcus

Contents

CONTENTS

Preface to the Second Edition

The Cambridge University Press and the editors of the new series of Cambridge Texts in the History of Political Thought have kindly invited me to produce a second edition of *Kant's Political Writings*, of which the first edition first appeared in an earlier series almost twenty years ago. They also agreed that the volume might be enlarged by three additional texts. To decide on the most suitable texts presented me with anything but an easy choice. The three suitable pieces chosen, the reviews of Herder's *Ideas on the Philosophy of the History of Mankind*, *Conjectures on the Beginning of Human History* and *What Is Orientation in Thinking?*, are not 'political' writings in the narrow sense of the word. They do, however, supply a context for the strictly political writings published in the first edition; for all of them illustrate Kant's critical approach to reasoning and his attitude to the public use of reason without which political justice could not, in his view, be achieved. *What Is Orientation in Thinking?* does so particularly clearly. It also introduces the reader to the moral basis of Kant's politics, while the other two texts illustrate Kant's conception of history, another pillar of his political thought. I greatly regret that there was no space to include the other pieces relating to politics mentioned in the preface to the first edition. Perhaps one day the constraints on space will be less pressing and all writings by Kant which refer to politics, including the whole of the *Theory of Right*, can be printed in a later edition.

In order to keep down printing costs and make the volume affordable by students the text of the first edition could not be substantially altered. For this reason, it has unfortunately not been possible to revise and enlarge my introduction itself. I have, however, been able to add a postscript in which I take up issues raised during the discussion of Kant's political thought over the past two decades. I have also provided a more extensive bibliography and a new index.

My thanks are due to Barry Nisbet for translating the additional texts and for giving me invaluable help by commenting on and checking my manuscript. I should like to thank Jeremy Mynott of the Cambridge

PREFACE TO THE SECOND EDITION

University Press and the editors of the series for asking me to produce the volume; and also Richard Fisher and Susan Beer for seeing the manuscript through the Press. I am also indebted to University of Bristol colleagues William Doyle, Stephan Körner and Niall Rudd, to Peter Nicholson (University of York), Onora O'Neill (University of Essex) and Lewis White Beck (University of Rochester) for their helpful advice. The German Academic Exchange Service provided me with a grant to work in the libraries of Heidelberg University, for which I am duly grateful. I am also conscious of my debt to the whole corpus of Kant scholarship, and I regret that I have been able to acknowledge only some of the many writings on Kant in the notes and bibliography. For all shortcomings I myself am alone responsible.

Bristol/Heidelberg   H. S. REISS
Autumn 1989

Preface to the First Edition

This volume, to the best of my knowledge, is the first in English to contain all the political writings of Kant which the author himself had published. There have been earlier translations of almost all the pieces which make up this volume; Dr Nisbet has asked me to acknowledge his debt to these, particularly to Professor John Ladd's translation of *The Metaphysical Elements of Rights* (*The Metaphysical Elements of Justice*, Indianapolis, New York, Kansas City, 1965). The aim of this volume is to introduce English-speaking readers in general and students of political theory in particular to Kant's Political writings. The bibliography in the present volume may serve as a guide for further reading. For a general introduction to Kant, the student can do no better than read Stephan Körner's *Kant* (Penguin Books, Harmondsworth, Middlesex, 1955), easily available in a pocket edition.

Only those writings which deal explicitly with the theory of politics and which were published by him have been included. I have omitted other essays, such as the *Conjectures on the Beginning of Human History* (*Mutmasslicher Anfang des Menschengeschlechts*), *The End of All Things* (*Das Ende aller Dinge*) and Kant's review of J. G. Herder's *Ideen*, which touch only marginally on politics. I have, however, included a brief but essential passage from the *Critique of Pure Reason* (*Kritik der reinen Vernunft*). In accordance with the aims of the series, I have not included any extracts, unless they form self-contained wholes. A few passages in other writings published by Kant are excluded, since they do not add anything of substance to his theory of politics. I decided to include the first part of *Theory and Practice* (*Über den Gemeinspruch: Das mag in der Theorie richtig sein, taugt aber nicht für die Praxis*), which is devoted to ethics. Since this volume does not set out to be a definitive critical edition of Kant's political writings I did not follow this precedent in the case of *The Metaphysics of Morals* (*Die Metaphysik der Sitten*) and *The Contest of Faculties* (*Der Streit der Fakultäten*). To print both works in full would inevitably have distracted attention from the main purpose of this volume. I hope that the brief summaries of what was omitted will give the reader some means of orientation. Except for the appended passage from the *Critique of Pure Reason*, I have also excluded all passages on politics from any other of Kant's larger works, such as the *Critique of Judgement* (*Kritik der Urteilskraft*) and *Religion within the Limits of Reason Alone* (*Religion innerhalb der Grenzen der blossen Vernunft*). I have even excluded a brief appendix attached to *The Metaphysical Elements of Right* (*Die metaphysischen Anfangsgründe des Rechts*). In neither case is anything of substance omitted. Kant is simply repeating points which he has made elsewhere. Those readers who wish to study the omitted parts of *The Metaphysics of Morals* should consult John Ladd's commendable translation in *The Metaphysical Elements of Justice*. For the second part of *The Metaphysics of Morals*, *The Metaphysical Elements of Virtue* (*Die Metaphysischen Anfangsgründe der Tugendlehre*), they should consult the German text, which they will in any case have to do for *The Contest of Faculties*. To consult the original is naturally always the best course, even if it involves learning German; for all translations fail, in some degree or other, to do justice to the original.[1] I also decided not to include either Kant's preliminary studies for his published works on politics as found in volumes XXII and XXIII of the *Akademieausgabe* of his works and in *Kant-Studien* LI, 1959/60, or his notes on politics and law, as found in volumes XIX and XX of the above edition. These writings were published posthumously and Kant did not intend them to be published. They do not offer anything substantially different from what is found in his published writings. They are often repetitive since many of them are rough notes, comments on the textbook which he was using for lectures on the theory of law (Gottfried Achenwall's *Ius naturae*, Göttingen, 1755–6) and notes for lectures or (probably) later publications. It will always be difficult to decide how much weight should be given to material of this kind; for it could easily contain views later rejected by an author on mature consideration. In Kant's case, the notes may occasionally clarify some of his views. Furthermore, they can give us some insight into the origin and development of his political thought. This latter aspect has been exhaustively discussed by Georges Vlachos in his full-length study of Kant's political theory (*La Pensée Politique de Kant. Métaphysique de l'ordre et dialectique du progrès*, Paris, 1962, pp. xx and 590). However, the development of Kant's political ideas will always

[1] The translations in this book follow the style and substance of the original texts as closely as possible, except that we have not reproduced the indentation (possibly used for emphasis in the original texts) of some passages on pp. 135, 138–140 and 164.

present problems; for although the work of the editors of the *Akademieausgabe* has been dedicated and painstaking, they have found it difficult to date many of the notes exactly.

Finally, I should like to thank all those friends and colleagues who have helped or encouraged me in my work for this volume. I am indebted to my former colleagues and friends at the London School of Economics and Political Science: Ernest Gellner, Morris Ginsberg, the late Harold Laski, William Pickles, Julius Gould, Donald Macrae, Michael Oakeshott, Sir Karl Popper, the late William Rose, K. B. Smellie and J. O. Wisdom. I have profited considerably from the advice of Stephan Körner and Peter Bromhead of the University of Bristol, who were good enough to read the introduction. David Eichholz of the same University kindly translated Kant's Latin quotations for me. I have also greatly benefited from conversations on Kant with Dieter Henrich of the University of Heidelberg. I have to thank Denis Donoghue of University College, Dublin, Irvin Ehrenpreis of the University of Virginia, Raymond Klibansky of McGill University, George Levine and Irving Massey, both of the New York State University at Buffalo, and Philip Harth of the University of Wisconsin for generously helping me to trace some quotations. Above all I must thank Dr H. B. Nisbet, who not only undertook the formidable task of translating Kant, but has also spent much time in checking the notes and bibliography and has offered many valuable suggestions on scrutiny of my introductory essay. He has also helped me in seeing the whole manuscript through the press. I have in turn scrutinised his translation. Mrs M. L. Taylor, Mrs Rosemary White and Miss B. Gertsch have had the unenviable task of typing the manuscript, for which we owe them sincere thanks. Much of my work on Kant was done when I had a year's leave of absence from McGill University in 1962–3 on award of a grant from the Rockefeller Foundation. I am grateful to both institutions for making it possible for me to have leave in Europe for the purpose of study. It is a happy coincidence that, as I conclude my work on this volume, I am once again at McGill, this time as Visiting Professor on leave from the University of Bristol.

For any errors that remain I am alone responsible.

H. S. REISS

Hugessen House
McGill University
Montreal
Autumn 1968

Abbreviations

AA	Immanuel Kant, *Gesammelte Schriften* (generally called *Akademieausgabe* since first published by the Prussian Academy of Sciences), Berlin, 1900ff.
AIKK	*Akten des 4. Internationalen Kant-Kongresses in Mainz 6.–10. April 1974*, ed. Gerhard Funke. Berlin and New York, 1974.
APP	'La Philosophie de Kant', *Annales de Philosophie Politique*, IV, Paris, 1962. Published by the Institut International de Philosophie Politique.
CLR	*Columbia Law Review*.
EGerr.	Gerresheim, Eduard (ed.). *Immanuel Kant 1724/1974. Kant as a Political Thinker*. Bonn–Bad Godesberg, 1974.
JHI	*Journal of the History of Ideas*.
KS	*Kant–Studien*.
KSE	*Kant–Studien*. Ergänzungshefte.
RdA	*Rechtsphilosophie der Aufklärung* (Symposium Wolfenbüttel 1981), ed. Reinhard Brandt. Berlin and New York, 1982.
SW	Johann Gottfried Herder, *Sämmtliche Werke*, ed. Bernhard Suphan. Berlin, 1877–1913.
PTh	*Political Theory*.
ZwBat.	Batscha, Zwi (ed.). *Materialien zu Kants Rechtsphilosophie* (suhrkamp taschenbuch wissenschaft, 171). Frankfurt/Main, 1976.

Introduction

I

Immanuel Kant was born on 22 April 1724 in Königsberg (now Kaliningrad) in East Prussia which, except for occasional journeys into the immediate vicinity, he hardly ever left during the whole of his long life of almost eighty years. Königsberg in the eighteenth century was a lively city which, owing to its flourishing trade, was by no means isolated from the world at large. Kant, who was anything but a recluse, enjoyed social life and intelligent conversation. He was friendly with many Königsberg merchants, among whom there were also Englishmen, two of whom, Green and Motherby, were particularly close friends. Although he was meticulous and regular in his habits, punctual to a fault, he was also a man of urbanity and wit.

Kant's parents were not rich. His father was a harness-maker who lived in Königsberg. His family was steeped in Pietism, the Protestant religious movement which stressed emotional religiosity and the development of the inner life. The pietistic atmosphere of his parents' household was a formative influence in his childhood, and he was particularly impressed by his mother's simple piety. After the early death of his parents (his mother died in 1738, his father in 1746), Kant's relations with his family were not very close.

Kant's outstanding intellectual gifts were recognised at school. It was made possible for him to enter the University of Königsberg, where he was a brilliant student. In 1755 he was granted the right to lecture as *Magister legens* or *Privatdozent*, i.e. as an unsalaried lecturer who depended on his lecture fees for his income. Since his lectures were popular and since he gave a large number of them—twenty a week at least—he was able to eke out a meagre living. He lectured on many subjects—logic, metaphysics, ethics, theory of law, geography, anthropology etc. He began to make his name as a scholar and scientist by his writings. In his *General History of Nature and Theory of the Heavens* (1755), he put forward a highly original account of the origin of the universe similar to the one later elaborated by the French scientist Laplace. It is now generally called the 'Kant-Laplace' theory. Kant thus started his academic career by discussing a scientific problem, i.e. he sought to vindicate Newtonian science philosophically—an attempt which later gave rise to his critical philosophy. But it was not until 1770 that he was appointed to the chair of logic and metaphysics and at last found economic security. When his fame spread, his stipend was considerably increased. He was Rector of the University on several occasions.

Kant was a stimulating and powerful lecturer. His students were struck by the originality and liveliness of his observations, which were seasoned with a dry ironic humour.

He was also a prolific writer. His really decisive breakthrough as a philosopher came only in 1781 when he published the *Critique of Pure Reason*. For him, this work initiated a revolution in thought realistically compared by himself to the Copernican revolution in astronomy. In fairly rapid succession, the other important works followed.

The publication of *Religion within the Limits of Reason Alone* (1793, 2nd ed. 1794) offended the then King of Prussia, Frederick William II, who (contrary to Frederick the Great, his predecessor) did not practise tolerance in religious matters. Frederick William II ordered his obscurantist minister Wöllner to write to Kant to extract a promise that he would not write again on religion.[1] Kant reluctantly agreed with their request, which amounted to a Royal command, implicitly qualifying his promise by saying that he would not write again on religious matters as his Majesty's Most Loyal Subject. After the King's death, Kant considered himself to be absolved from this undertaking and explained that his pledge applied only to the life-time of Frederick William II, as this phrase 'Your Majesty's Most Loyal Subject'[2] indicated. He explained his attitude fully in the preface to his *Contest of Faculties*,[3] in which, by implication, he attacked Frederick William II who had died the year before.

Kant was obviously not easy in his mind about this decision. In an unpublished note, he explained his conduct: 'Repudiation and denial of one's inner conviction are evil, but silence in a case like the present one is the duty of a subject; and while all that one says must be true, this does not mean that it is one's duty to speak out the whole truth in public.'[4]

Kant gradually retired from the university. His mind slowly declined,

---

[1] Cabinet order of Frederick William II, King of Prussia, of 1 October 1794; *AA* VII, 6; *AA* XI, 506 f.
[2] Letter to King Frederick William II, 12 October 1794; *AA* VII, 7–10, particularly p. 10; also *AA* XI, 508–11, particularly p. 511; cf. also *AA* XII, 406 f.
[3] *AA* VII, 7–10.   [4] *AA* XII, 406.

his memory gave way, and he had to abandon lecturing. In 1800, his pupil Wasianski had to begin looking after him. Other pupils began to publish his lectures from notes which they had taken down. In 1803, he fell seriously ill for the first time. His mind became more and more clouded. He finally died on 12 February 1804, a few months before the end of his eightieth year.

II

Kant, at least in English speaking countries, is not generally considered to be a political philosopher of note. Indeed histories of political thought do not give him pride of place, but generally mention him only incidentally, if at all. Historians of political thought ignore him, however, at their peril. Only too frequently, he is merely seen as a forerunner of Hegel. The reasons for this neglect and misunderstanding are not hard to discover. Historians of philosophy, even Kant scholars, have neglected his political writings because the philosophy of his three critiques has absorbed attention almost entirely. And historians of political thought have paid little attention to him, because he did not write a masterpiece in that field. *The Metaphysical Elements of Right* has interested legal historians rather than historians of political theory. Furthermore, the very fact that Kant's great works of critical philosophy are so formidable makes his less exacting political writings appear very much less weighty. It also encourages the belief that they are not central to his thought. This assumption, however, is greatly mistaken. While it would be going too far to see in them the ultimate end of his thought, they are not an accidental by-product. Indeed, they grow organically out of his critical philosophy. In fact, Kant has rightly been called the philosopher of the French Revolution.[1] There is, indeed, an analogy between the spirit of Kant's philosophy and the ideas of the French and American revolutions: for Kant asserted the independence of the individual in face of authority, and the problem of human freedom was at the very core of his thought. Similarly, the revolutionaries of 1776 and 1789 believed that they were attempting to realise the rights of man. Besides, the events of the American and of the French Revolution greatly excited and preoccupied him and he sympathised with the aims of the revolutionaries. He did so although he was a man of conservative disposition who refused to countenance revolution in politics as a legitimate principle of action, and certainly did not

[1] Cf. Heine, *Sämtliche Werke*, ed. Ernst Elster, Leipzig and Vienna, n.d., IV, 245; also Karl Marx/Friedrich Engels, *Historisch-Kritische Gesamtausgabe* (Frankfurt/Main, 1927), I, 254.

3

advocate revolution in his native country, Prussia. But his approach to politics was already shaped well before 1789, as his essays of 1784 reveal. It is possible that the French Revolution may have stimulated him to continue writing on the subject. But the example and influence of Rousseau must not be underrated. Rousseau had taught him to respect the common man;[1] he was for him the Newton of the moral realm.[2] Rousseau's portrait was the only adornment permitted in his house, and when reading *Émile* he even forgot to take his customary afternoon walk, allegedly the only deviation ever to occur from a daily custom followed with clock-like regularity. Kant's views are also, in many ways, close to the aspirations of the French revolutionaries, but in his demand for perpetual peace he goes further. Here he takes up ideas first put forward by Leibniz and the Abbé de St Pierre, but develops them in a novel, original and philosophically rigorous manner.

If it is correct to infer this link between Kant's philosophy and the ideas of the two major eighteenth-century revolutions, the significance of Kant's political thought becomes clear; for the American and French revolutions constituted an open break with the political past. An appeal was made to a secular natural order and to the political rights of individuals for the purpose of initiating large-scale political action. The revolutions, of course, arose from the political, social and economic situation in America and France, but the beliefs of the revolutionaries were not intended as a smoke-screen designed to mislead the public. They depended on a political philosophy in which a belief in the right of the individual would be guaranteed. This attitude was new. In earlier revolutions, even in the English civil war and in 1688, Christian theology had still played an important part in shaping revolutionary thinking in the West. The realities of a revolutionary situation are, of course, always complex. It usually presents a pattern of ideology and political practice which is difficult, if not impossible, to disentangle. Kant did not set out to provide a blueprint for revolutionaries or a theory of revolution. On the contrary, he wanted to arrive at philosophical principles on which a just and lasting internal order and world peace could be based. He wanted to provide a philosophical vindication of representative constitutional government, a vindication which would guarantee respect for the political rights of all individuals.

To understand his political thought, it is necessary to see it in the context of eighteenth-century thought, and against the background of his own general philosophy. The American and French revolutions had,

[1] *AA* xx, 44.   [2] *Ibid.* p. 58.

to some extent, been prepared for by the ideas of the Enlightenment, the intellectual movement which dominated so much of eighteenth-century thought.[1] Incontestably, the revolutionaries largely used the vocabulary of the Enlightenment, which had created a climate of opinion in many ways favourable to revolutionary action. In Kant, many of the intellectual strands of the Enlightenment converge. He presents a culmination of this intellectual movement, but he is also one of its most thoroughgoing critics. Kant himself characterised the Enlightenment (*Aufklärung*) as a dynamic process. It was not a static condition, but a continuous process leading to further self-emancipation. The age was not yet enlightened, but still in the process of becoming so. *Aufklärung* meant liberation from prejudice and superstition. It also meant the growing ability to think for oneself. This observation echoes Lessing's famous dictum that what mattered most was not to possess the truth, but to pursue it.[2] In Kant's view, man was to become his own master. In his special function as officer, clergyman, civil-servant etc., he should not reason, but obey the powers that be, but as a man, citizen and scholar, he should have 'the courage to use his own intelligence'.[3] This is the translation which Kant gives to the watchword of the *Aufklärung*, *Sapere Aude*, expanding its meaning for his own purpose. Indeed, this Horatian tag was so popular that it had been inscribed as a motto on a coin struck in 1736 for the society of Alethophiles, or Lovers of Truth, a group of men dedicated to the cause of Enlightenment.[4]

Kant, in his essay *What is Enlightenment?* (*Was ist Aufklärung?*), outlines his view of the major tendencies of his age. The Enlightenment has frequently been called the Age of Reason. One of its most striking characteristics is, indeed, the exaltation of reason, but the term 'Enlightenment' (or *Aufklärung* or *les Lumières*) covers a number of ideas and intellectual tendencies which cannot be adequately summarised. A brief characterisation of this movement, as of any other, must needs remain incomplete. For this movement, like all intellectual movements, is made

[1] For thorough general discussions of the Enlightenment cf. *inter alia* Ernst Cassirer, *Die Philosophie der Aufklärung* (Tübingen, 1932) (*The Philosophy of the Enlightenment*, trs. Fritz A. Koelln and James Pettegrove, Princeton, N.J., 1951); Paul Hazard, *La pensée européenne au XVIIIième siècle. De Montesquieu à Lessing*, 3 vols. (Paris, 1946) (*European Thought in the Eighteenth Century*, trs. J. Lewis May, London, 1953); Jack F. Lively (ed.), *The Enlightenment* (London, 1966); Fritz Valjavec, *Geschichte der abendländischen Aufklärung* (Vienna, 1961).
[2] Gotthold Ephraim Lessing, *Werke* (ed. Julius Petersen and Waldemar von Olshausen), Berlin, Leipzig, Vienna, Stuttgart, n.d. XXIII, 58 f.
[3] *AA* VIII, 35.
[4] Cf. Elizabeth M. Wilkinson and L. A. Willoughby (ed. and trs.), Friedrich Schiller, *On the Aesthetic Education of Man, in a Series of Letters* (Oxford, 1967), LXXIV ff.

up of a number of various, and often conflicting, strains of thought. What binds the thinkers of the Enlightenment together, however, is an attitude of mind, a mood rather than a common body of ideas. A growth of self-consciousness, an increasing awareness of the power of man's mind to subject himself and the world to rational analysis, is perhaps the dominant feature. Reliance on the use of reason was, of course, nothing new, but faith in the power of reason to investigate successfully not only nature, but also man and society, distinguishes the Enlightenment from the period which immediately precedes it. For there is a distinct optimistic streak in the thought of the Enlightenment. It springs from, and promotes, the belief that there is such a thing as intellectual progress. It is also revealed in the increasing and systematic application of scientific method to all areas of life. But there was by no means agreement on what scientific method was. Newton's impressive scientific achievement dominated eighteenth-century thinking on science. One school of thought interpreted his work as a great attempt, in the wake of Descartes, to systematise scientific knowledge, whereas another school was struck rather by his emphasis on observation and experiment.

Voltaire, in his *Lettres Philosophiques* or *Lettres sur les Anglais* (1734) (English translation *Letters concerning the English* 1733), popularised Newton and English science in general. He also praised English political life, not only English constitutional arrangements, but also political theory as represented by Locke. Locke's ideas of government by consent and the toleration of different religious and political views appeared to Voltaire in particular and to the thinkers of the Enlightenment in general as exemplary.

These ideas sounded revolutionary in the atmosphere of French politics. Here Church and State resisted change. On the other hand, they persecuted or suppressed heterodox political and religious thought only intermittently. Many thinkers of the Enlightenment believed not only that politics could be subjected to rational scrutiny, but also that political arrangements and institutions could be reconstructed along rational lines. The sceptical refusal to accept traditional political authority is consonant with scepticism towards authority in general. This critical attitude towards authority led to an incessant questioning of all accepted values, particularly those of religion. Revealed religion was scrutinised; in fact, it was put on trial.

The secularisation of accepted beliefs and doctrines is an important process in the development of the Enlightenment, whether it be in the field of religion, science, morals, politics, history or art. Contrary to medieval custom, the individual spheres of human experience were isolated from religion. The basic intellectual position, then, was anthropocentric. And for the purpose of our enquiry into Kant's politics, it is particularly important to note that the realms of morality and law, politics and history were seen in a secular context. Although these spheres were separated from religion, the view prevailed in the Enlightenment that, for each of them, universal laws could be established.

The tone of the Enlightenment in Germany was somewhat different from that prevailing in Britain and France. On the whole, considerably less emphasis was laid on empiricism than in Britain. The German thinkers were more erudite, but also more abstract and professorial than their English and French counterparts; and they were frequently more heavy-handed. The absence of a metropolitan culture militated against certainty of style, while the parochial politics of the many petty principalities and comparatively small free Imperial cities were not conducive to the rise of lively political discussion. Unlike Britain, Germany offered virtually no opportunities for the intellectuals to take part in politics. Frederick the Great was, of course, an intellectual, but an absolute monarch anyhow presents a special case.

It is characteristic of this political stagnation that the political event which most affected eighteenth-century Germany took place in France: the French Revolution aroused German political thought from its somnolence.[1] Nonetheless, modern political thought in Germany virtually began with the impact of 1789. Many thinkers, in Germany as elsewhere, welcomed the revolution at first and believed it to be the dawn of a new age. But disillusion began to set in with the outbreak of the Terror. The revolution in practice spread only to those territories occupied by the French revolutionary armies. Revolutionary sentiment in Germany was a tender plant capable of blossoming forth only under the stimulus of force.

Kant and Goethe, the two leading German minds of the age, assessed the political situation correctly. Both recognised that while in France the revolution had answered a great political need, the political situation in Germany was not at all ripe for revolutionary activity. In Germany as in England and France, the rise of the bourgeoisie was noticeable, but the German bourgeoisie had not become emancipated from the dominance of the princes and the aristocracy. It did not possess the self-confidence

[1] Cf. Jacques Droz, *L'Allemagne et la Révolution Française* (Paris, 1949), pp. 154–71; G. P. Gooch, *Germany and the French Revolution* (London, 1920), pp. 160–82; Karl Vorländer, 'Kants Stellung zur französischen Revolution', *Philosophische Abhandlungen Hermann Cohen gewidmet* (Berlin, 1912); for a full discussion of Kant's attitude to the French Revolution.

of its French and English counterparts. Germany was a much poorer country than either Britain or France, and a rising self-confident class which is prevented from giving free expression to its political ambitions is much more likely to take revolutionary action than a weak and unsure one. There was little scope for political freedom in Germany. Even in the Prussia of Frederick the Great, freedom of speech, according to Lessing, meant only the ability freely to criticise religion, but not the government.[1] In addition, the small size of most German principalities permitted a much closer supervision of the subjects by rulers than in larger countries. The growth of bureaucratic control also impeded economic development and was another operative factor in sapping the self-confidence of the German bourgeoisie.

Given these political, social and economic conditions, it is not surprising that the Enlightenment in Germany was different from other Western countries. German philosophy, unlike British philosophy for instance, continued in many ways to resist the impact of empirical aspects of science. Rationalism dominated the outlook of German and French universities, but the style of German philosophical writing was, on the whole, much less urbane than that of its French counterpart.

In setting Kant against this background, it must not be forgotten that the Enlightenment was only one body of thought in the eighteenth century, even if it was the dominant one. There were other strands. Criticism of the Enlightenment arose not merely in its decline, but accompanied its rise and predominance. In Germany, and not only in Germany, the eighteenth century saw the spread of scientific ideas through the thinkers of the Enlightenment, but it was also characterised by a religious way of life centred on the emotions and inward experience. In Germany, Pietism stressed the cultivation of the inner life and fostered an emotional approach to religion. (It was not without its counterparts elsewhere—e.g. Methodism and Quietism.) Kant's fervent conviction of man's inward sense of morality may well have been rooted in that particular soil. Furthermore, persistent criticism of the Enlightenment came not only from the orthodoxy of established religion and from privileged or traditional political interests, but also, as the century progressed, from various new irrationalists. It came from those who preferred intuition to reason, the perception of genius to common sense, and spontaneity to calculated reflection. They tended to base their understanding on the individual instance and example rather than on the universal rule, and even on poetry rather than on science. Their attitude to science was, at

[1] Letter from Lessing to Friedrich Nicolai, 25 August 1769.

its very best, ambivalent. One of the ironies of history is that Königsberg harboured at the same time the most potent champion of the Enlightenment, albeit a most critical one, *and* its most original opponent, viz. Johann Georg Hamann. The seminal critic of the Enlightenment, Johann Gottfried Herder, the mentor of the German literary school of the *Sturm und Drang* (Storm and Stress), also spent some time in Königsberg and became a friend of Hamann and a pupil of Kant. Hamann and Herder criticised the claim of the Enlightenment to discover universally valid principles and to see history and society in terms of uniform regularity. For them, the individual instance was more revealing and could not readily be subsumed under general laws. In a particularly incisive and outspoken review of Herder's main work, *Ideen zur Philosophie der Geschichte der Menschheit* (*Ideas on the Philosophy of the History of Mankind*) (1785), Kant took issue with Herder.[1] He apparently sensed that here was not only the decisive issue that separated his approach to knowledge from Herder's, but that it was also the watershed between those who wish to understand the world principally in terms of science and logic and those who do not. Consequently, he mercilessly exposed the logical flaws in Herder's argument. Herder, in turn, reacted with unforgiving bitterness.[2] Indeed, there can be no bridge between Kant's method and an approach to knowledge primarily based on intuitions of poetic truth and emphasis on the individual example.[3]

In the sphere of political thought, the differences between Britain and France on the one hand, and Germany on the other, were as marked as they were in any other area of life. There was no single dominating school of political thinking in Germany prior to Kant. There were many people who wrote about politics, and some of their writings were distinguished. The school of Natural Law forms one strand, the cameralists another. In addition, there were a number of publicists, such as Schlözer and the two Mosers, father and son. The most important, perhaps, and certainly the best known political thinkers, were Leibniz and Frederick the Great. Political theory was not central to the activity of either: general philosophy absorbed Leibniz's interests, and government, war and the administration

---

[1] *AA* VIII, 43–66, *Rezensionen von J. G. Herders Ideen zur Philosophie der Geschichte der Menschheit*, first published in *Allgemeine Literaturzeitung*, IV, No. 271 (Jena, 1785).
[2] *Metakritik zur Kritik der reinen Vernunft* (1799) (Johann Gottfried Herder, *Sämtliche Werke*, ed. B. Suphan, Berlin, 1877–1913, XXI).
[3] For a general account cf. Alexander Gillies, *Herder* (Oxford, 1944); cf. also H. B. Nisbet, *Herder and the Philosophy and History of Science* (Modern Humanities Research Association Dissertation Series, 3, Cambridge, 1970) for a thorough account of Herder's approach to science.

of his country the Prussian king's. The thinkers of the school of Natural Law,[1] indeed, propounded political theories of great importance, and even laid the foundation for revolution, but their style of thinking was not itself revolutionary. Nor was it specifically German. It continued, modified, and even changed a great tradition. The modern representatives of that school—men like Althusius, Grotius and Pufendorf—had continued to uphold an immutable standard of law which was to determine the positive laws enacted by the state and to regulate the conduct of its citizens, but they had liberated the philosophical study of law and politics from its dependence on theology. Its German practitioners dominated the faculties of law in German universities and German jurisprudence in general. Their works were, like many of the philosophical writings of the *Aufklärung*, abstract and dry. It was the accepted doctrine; it is therefore not surprising that Wolff, the leading philosopher of the *Aufklärung*, wrote a treatise on this subject. Not even Leibniz or Frederick the Great brought about a revolution in political thinking in Germany. It needed perhaps both the events of the French Revolution and the radical reorientation of thought promoted by Kant's philosophy to set in train a new mode of political thinking.

Kant assimilated or criticised the political ideas of many great thinkers, such as Machiavelli, the theorists of the school of Natural Law, Hobbes, Locke, Hume and Rousseau. Of these, only Hobbes was singled out for attack (in *Theory and Practice*), a fact which calls perhaps for comment. The political theories of the two philosophers, of course, differed greatly. Kant rejected Hobbes' authoritarian view of sovereignty, his rationalism, his attempt to apply the methods of geometry to human and social affairs and his explanation of society based on a psychological assumption, that of the fear of sudden death. Yet the basic political problem is the same for both: to turn a state of war into a state of order and peace. Law is a command and has necessarily to be enforced. Sovereignty is indivisible; the individual's status as an independent rational being can be safeguarded only in a civil state. Finally, despite all radical differences in method and conclusions, both thinkers are exemplary in their attempt to develop a rigorous, consistent and coherent argument based on an appeal to reason, unhampered by tradition or any other form of tutelage. In contrast to Hobbes, Kant is indebted to the school of Natural Law and believes in an immutable standard of right. He was, however, much more radical than

[1] See A. P. D'Entrèves, *Natural Law* (London and New York, 1951); cf. also Otto von Gierke, *Natural Law and The Theory of Society* (ed. and trs. Ernest Barker), 2 vols. (Cambridge, 1934).

the traditional proponents of that school; for he mapped out a theory of politics independent of experience. Another patent influence was Rousseau,[1] but Kant differed from Rousseau in his interpretation of nature and of the general will. Above all, whereas Rousseau is frequently ambiguous, he is clear.

As a thinker, Kant was adventurous and differed courageously, though tacitly rather than explicitly, from his king. He differed from Frederick the Great's view that the king was the first servant of the state and that the state should be run on the patriarchic lines of benevolent despotism. Not only did he oppose Frederick's doctrine of enlightened autocracy (admittedly not always followed by the Prussian king in practice), but he also rejected cameralism, the doctrine that politics is a mere exercise in statecraft. And he also argued against the Machiavellian view that political actions arise solely from egotism. To emphasise the need to obey the law, as Kant did, could imply a bias in favour of authoritarianism.[2] In Germany his theory has, indeed, been invoked to strengthen the executive prerogative in carrying out the law, the *Obrigkeitsstaat*, the state in which obedience to political authority is writ large. In fact, his outlook was liberal. The citizens of Königsberg, his native city, knew it well; when he died they followed his coffin because they saw in him a great champion of human freedom in an age in which benevolent dynastic despotism was the prevailing mode of government. But Kant's influence has been greatest in shaping the doctrine of the *Rechtsstaat*, the state governed according to the rule of law. It has been the ideal to which at least lip-service has been paid during most of the nineteenth and twentieth centuries in Germany, though there have, of course, been significant and disastrous deviations from this ideal in practice.

Kant is in fact the fountain-head of modern German political thought. Political thinkers who followed him differed from him in profound respects, but his political thought was for many either the starting-point of their own enquiries or he was an opponent against whom they pitted their strength. Kant's political writings appeared when his reputation was established. His views rapidly commanded attention. They were challenged by men like Justus Möser,[3] who, from a conservative standpoint,

---

[1] Cf. Ernst Cassirer, *Rousseau, Kant, Goethe* (History of Ideas Series, No. 1), Princeton, N.J., 1945, for a penetrating study of Rousseau's influence on Kant.
[2] G. Vlachos, *La Pensée politique de Kant. Métaphysique de l'ordre et dialectique du progrès* (Paris, 1962), *passim*, argues that Kant's political theory favours the state against the individual. He calls it *étatiste*. I cannot accept this interpretation.
[3] Cf. Hans Reiss, 'Justus Möser und Wilhelm von Humboldt. Konservative und liberale politische Ideen im Deutschland des 18. Jahrhunderts', *Politische Vierteljahresschrift*, VIII (1967).

rejected Kant's approach. Möser believed it was wrong to theorise from lofty presuppositions, and political practice and experience mattered considerably more than abstract liberal ideas. On the other hand, many German thinkers disagreed with Kant's conservatism; to respect law and to reject the right of rebellion was, in their view, mistaken. Among them Rehberg and Gentz sought to defend the prerogative of the individual confronted by tyranny.[1]

On a more profound level, two thinkers sought to follow and improve on Kant's liberal approach to politics; Friedrich Schiller[2] and Wilhelm von Humboldt.[3] For Schiller, the Kantian approach to politics was inadequate, because Kant did not pay any attention to the psychological basis of our political decisions. Schiller wanted to show that it is not enough to obey the dictates of duty; that men are able to live a harmonious moral life only if they act in accordance with nature. In order to bridge the gulf between instinct and reason, between will and knowledge, a third mode of experience, the aesthetic mode, is necessary. In his major work on the relationship between aesthetics and politics, *On the Aesthetic Education of Man, in a Series of Letters* (*Über die aesthetische Erziehung des Menschen in einer Reihe von Briefen*) (1795), Schiller delineated an approach which, while respecting the tenor of Kant's political thinking, would be capable of taking account of the whole complexity of man's involvement in the political process. It should, so to speak, map out the interrelations between the aesthetic response to life and political practice. Schiller's political writings, profound and interesting as they are, have not attracted much attention. The first truly exciting and subtle attempt to put across his message and to spell out its cogency and significance in terms of our own age is very recent indeed.[4] Schiller has been influential as a political thinker only indirectly, through his dramas, whose political import has only too frequently been misunderstood.

Schiller's friend, Wilhelm von Humboldt, also felt that Kant's political theory needed to be supplemented by an awareness of man's character. His theory of politics, as expressed in his treatise *The Limits of the State*

[1] Cf. Dieter Henrich, Introduction to *Kant. Gentz. Rehberg. Über Theorie und Praxis* (Frankfurt/Main, 1967).
[2] Cf. Wilkinson—Willoughby's edition of Schiller's *Aesthetic Letters*; cf. also H. S. Reiss, 'The Concept of the Aesthetic State in the Work of Schiller and Novalis', *Publications of the English Goethe Society*, XXVI (1957).
[3] For an account of Humboldt's political thought, and references to further secondary literature, see Reiss, 'Justus Möser und Wilhelm von Humboldt', *Politische Vierteljahresschrift*, VIII (1967).
[4] Elizabeth M. Wilkinson's and L. A. Willoughby's profound analysis of Schiller's *Aesthetic Letters* appeared only last year (1967); cf. above, p. 12, n. 2.

(1793),[1] sought to safeguard the creative power and cultural development of man.

Kant's impact on German legal history was profound, but the rise of nationalism prevented his work from being the dominant force in German political thought during the nineteenth and early twentieth centuries which it might easily have been. For the Romantic mode of thought introduced into German political thought a note of irrationalism which permeated almost all areas of German thinking for a century and a half between the Napoleonic wars and the end of the Second World War.[2] The Romantics' rejection of Kant's cosmopolitanism in politics meant that, with his death—followed a year later by that of Schiller—(most of von Humboldt's political writings were only published many decades later)—the climate of opinion changed drastically. It no longer mattered much whether the individual was politically free. The organic theory of the state, which subordinated the individual to the community, prevailed.

For the German Romantics, Kant was an arch-enemy; for he embodied for them the characteristics of the *Aufklärung* which they fought so vehemently. Fichte, who started as a self-professed disciple of Kant and who even, in a private letter to Kant, claimed to be his successor, developed a theory of politics diametrically opposed to Kant's.[3] Fichte paid lip-service to Kant's method, but his political theory can be interpreted as an attempt to supersede Kant's political thought. In Fichte's view, freedom is no longer to be seen in negative terms, but becomes a positive force to be utilised by the initiated, who alone can interpret the collective will. Whilst Schiller, in contrast to Kant, had sought to explore the relationship between art and politics, seeking to preserve a careful balance between the two realms, Romantics such as Fichte, Novalis, Schelling and Adam Müller sought to see life and politics from an aesthetic point of view. This method of reasoning is, on the whole, anti-Kantian, but they discernibly write in the shadow of his work. Only too frequently they are, one feels, either seeking to escape from his dominance or implicitly repudiating his method and thought. They base their principles of politics on feeling and intuition, a mode of thought rejected by Kant as a 'lawless use of reason'.[4] The historical approach to politics and law, too,

---

[1] The exact title is *Ideas towards an Attempt to Delineate the Limits of the Activity of the State* (*Ideen zu einem Versuch, die Grenzen der Wirksamkeit des Staates zu bestimmen*).
[2] Cf. Reiss, *The Political Thought of the German Romantics* (Oxford, 1955), and *Politisches Denken in der Deutschen Romantik* (Munich and Berne, 1966), for further literature on German Romantic political thinkers.
[3] Cf. *ibid.*
[4] *What is Orientation in Thinking?* (*Was heißt: sich im Denken orientieren?*) (1786); *AA* VIII, 145.

is fundamentally different from Kant's own mode of thinking. It cul-
minated in the thought of Hegel, which, like that of early adherents of the
historical approach such as Herder[1] and Savigny,[2] becomes fully intelligible only if set against Kant's philosophy. (Hegel's approach to political
philosophy is, of course, profoundly different from that of Kant.) Through
Hegel, Kant affected Marx, and the impact of Marx on modern political
thinking has been powerful, to say the least. Much of modern political
thinking thus continues the revolution begun by Kant, just as the
American and French revolutions, whose ideas Kant vindicated, set a
movement afoot which has shaped much of modern European political
history.

Kant's influence on Hegel and his successors is frequently more general
than specific. There were, of course, many thinkers who specifically
sought to elaborate and apply his political ideas. Jakob Friedrich Fries[3]
is the most prominent among them, and his ideas were taken up again
a century later by Leonard Nelson[4] who founded the so-called Neo-
Friesian school. Or we might mention Sir Karl Popper,[5] on whose conception of the open society the imprint of Kant's political thought can be
discerned. But to single out any specific instances is perhaps less worth-
while than to note the impact of his general philosophy on Western
thought through which modern political thought has been affected more
profoundly than is sometimes realised. It is the touchstone of a great
thinker that he not only makes us view the thought of those who have
gone before him in a different light, but that subsequent philosophy, too,
is affected by him.

Kant's ideas have thus been a significant political force. But they have
also been attacked and modified, sometimes beyond recognition. In any
case, they are ideas that look ahead into the future. But more than that:
Kant's theory of politics philosophically justifies man's right to political
freedom, the view that he should no longer be considered to be under
tutelage. Man's growing political and intellectual maturity must be recognised. According to Kant, man is in the process of becoming enlightened.

---

[1] Cf. F. M. Barnard, *Herder's Social and Political Thought: From Enlightenment to
Nationalism* (Oxford, 1965).

[2] *Of the Vocation of our Age for Legislation and Jurisprudence* (*Vom Beruf unserer Zeit
für Gesetzgebung und Rechtswissenschaft*) (Heidelberg, 1814).

[3] Cf. Jakob Friedrich Fries, *Vom deutschen Bund und deutscher Staatsverfassung.
Allgemeine staatsrechtliche Ansichten* (Heidelberg, 1816); *Politik oder philosophische
Staatslehre* (ed. E. F. Apelt) (Jena, 1848).

[4] Cf. Leonard Nelson, *System der philosophischen Rechtslehre* (Leipzig, 1920), for
example.

[5] Cf. Karl R. Popper, *The Open Society and its Enemies*, 2 vols. (London, 1952).

Man has both the opportunity and the responsibility to make use of his mind in the spirit of criticism. Such is the temper and the message of the Enlightenment as understood by Kant.

III

Kant had been thinking about political theory for many years before he first published any of his views on this subject. His notes, published posthumously and never intended for publication, reveal his continued preoccupation with and interest in political ideas. The first extant notes probably date from the 1760s when he was studying Rousseau and Natural Law.[1] Kant gave his first lecture-course on the Theory of Right in the summer term of 1767, a course which he repeated twelve times. The kernel of his political philosophy, however, is summed up in a passage from the *Critique of Pure Reason* of 1781 in the section entitled 'Transcendental Dialectic I'.[2] It is the first substantial account of his political thought, but the first writings published by Kant which explicitly deal with politics, the two essays *What is Enlightenment?* and *Idea for a Universal History with a Cosmopolitan Purpose* of 1784, were written after the publication of the *Critique of Pure Reason* (1781), while the later writings, *Theory and Practice* (1792), *Perpetual Peace* (1795), *The Metaphysical Elements of Right* (1797) and *The Contest of Faculties* (1798) follow the publication of the *Critique of Judgement* (1790). But we do not know whether he ever planned a comprehensive treatise on politics. Whether he did or not, his intellectual vigour gradually began to wane in the last decade of his life, and he never produced a work in which he summarised his philosophical discussion of politics. But the political events which really stirred him occurred relatively late in his life. He was over fifty at the outbreak of the American Revolution and in his mid-sixties at the beginning of the French Revolution. He was sixty when he published his first political essays, and he was in his seventy-fifth year when he published his last piece on this subject. We thus have to turn to these scattered political writings for his views.

Kant's standing and influence as a political philosopher would indubitably have been greater if he had left a more highly organised comprehensive work on politics. His style did not increase his popularity. The reader should not, however, be put off by his relatively unattractive

[1] Cf. *AA* XIX, 334; 445 ff. These entries date from approximately 1766–8. Cf. also Georges Vlachos, *La Pensée politique de Kant*, pp. 20 ff., who argues that we can date Kant's reflections on politics only from 1763 onwards.
[2] *AA* III, 247 f.; *AA* IV, 201 f.; cf. p. 191 below.

manner of writing. His political essays do not in fact require the same extreme intellectual effort as the *Critique of Pure Reason*, although this does not mean that they do not tax the mind. Except for *The Metaphysical Elements of Right*, they are not written solely for the technical philosopher, but also for the educated general public. The essays belong to his so-called popular writings. He did not, however, claim to be able to master so 'subtle and at the same time so attractive'[1] a manner of writing as Hume. Indeed, he wrote when German was still emerging as a literary language.[2] Heine, a brilliant stylist himself, called Kant's mode of writing 'a grey wrapping-paper style'.[3] He accused him of 'being afraid to speak in an easy, pleasant and gay manner'[4] and of thus being 'a philistine'.[5] According to Heine, the effect of Kant's manner of writing was highly detrimental to the development of a clear and elegant philosophical language in Germany. He writes in the *History of Religion and Philosophy in Germany* (*Geschichte der Religion und Philosophie in Deutschland*): 'by his awkward, heavy style...he [Kant] did much damage. For the unintelligent imitators aped him in this externality and the superstition arose that one could not be a philosopher if one wrote well.'[6] Nonetheless, Kant's political writings, though far from elegant, are not always cumbersome, and are at times vigorous and characterised by a dry irony. Although the structure of his sentences is frequently complicated, memorable key-sentences occur. And there are impressive passages.[7]

IV

To understand Kant's political thought it is necessary to see it in the context of his general philosophy. His writings on politics correspond with the period of his critical philosophy. They were all written after the completion of the first critique, the *Critique of Pure Reason*, in 1781. Ideally, I should first give a summary of his critical philosophy but it is virtually impossible to summarise! It must here suffice to indicate the trend of his critical thinking, though this will necessarily be somewhat misleading.[8]

Both rationalism and empiricism appeared to him inadequate modes of

---

[1] *AA* IV, 262 (preface to *Prolegomena for any Future Metaphysics that may be given the Status of a Science*).
[2] Cf. Eric A. Blackall, *The Emergence of German as a Literary Language, 1700-1775* (Cambridge, 1959).
[3] Heine, *Sämtliche Werke*, ed. Ernst Elster, IV, 251.
[4] *Ibid.*   [5] *Ibid.*   [6] *Ibid.* p. 252.
[7] Cf. S. Morris Engel, 'On the Composition of the *Critique*. A Brief Comment', *Ratio*, VI (1964) for a discussion of Kant's style.
[8] For the following account I owe much to Stephan Körner's fine analysis in his *Kant* (Harmondsworth, Middlesex, 1955).

explanation to account for mathematics and science, particularly New-tonian science. Hume had convincingly refuted the possibility of philo-sophically justifying induction, the method of establishing necessary universal laws proceeding from individual instances; for him causality was only the result of a habitual association of the mind. Hume's writings roused Kant from his 'dogmatic slumber'.[1] In order to refute Hume and to vindicate science philosophically, he found it necessary to start his enquiry not from objects of experience, but from the mind. For him, the laws of nature were not inherent in nature, but constructions of the mind used for the purpose of understanding nature. We can never explain the world as it appears to us merely by reference to experience; to do so we need necessary principles logically prior to and independent of experience. Only then can we see any order in nature. In fact, uniformity, coherence and order are imposed on nature by our minds. In other words, we cannot know the world other than as it appears to us, for we must see it within the framework of our mind. The world of appearance is thus conditioned by being located in the particulars of space and time and ordered by *a priori* concepts of our understanding or categories such as causality. The world as it really is, the noumenal world or the world of things-in-themselves, is unknowable. We can apprehend only the world of appear-ances. This does not mean that the external world is a world of mere appearances or illusions—on the contrary, Kant had the greatest respect for empirical fact and had been a scientist of note—but rather that the world of appearances or the phenomenal world is not self-sufficient for the purpose of explanation. For this purpose it is necessary to have *a priori* principles and ideas of reason. Kant expresses this problem, which is for him *the* philosophical problem of epistemology, in the question: How are synthetic *a priori* judgements possible?—i.e. how can we formu-late propositions which are necessary, universal, logically independent of sense experience and capable of being contradicted? Kant's critical method thus seeks to establish a system of synthetic *a priori* principles for the purpose of understanding the external world. This emphasis on the function of the mind in ordering scientific experience Kant called, with just pride, the Copernican revolution in philosophy, and his achieve-ment, argued and elaborated in the *Critique of Pure Reason*, has always been hailed as a landmark in philosophy.

The *Critique of Pure Reason* deals with the problem of how we can understand science, but there are other realms of human experience which are not scientific—moral experience, for example. In order to

[1] *AA* IV, 260.

understand its character we must follow a method similar to that delineated in Kant's account of theoretical scientific enquiry; that is to say, we can understand moral conduct only if we discover rules or principles which are logically independent of experience and which are capable of contradiction. Kant calls such rules 'practical synthetic a priori judgements'. He believes that they underlie all moral decisions and are inherent in all arguments about moral issues. To justify these rules we must suppose that man is not only a phenomenal being, subject to strict causal laws, but also a noumenal being who is free. For moral decisions are possible only if the will is assumed to be free to act. Each man has a will. This will alone can make a moral choice. To will is to decide on action. An action, however, is moral only if it is done for the sake of duty. In a case of a conflict of interest this criterion allows us to distinguish between actions which are right and those which are not. It allows us to distinguish between duty and desire. Kant calls the general moral law the 'categorical imperative'. It categorically enjoins us to act in accordance with morality. A hypothetical injunction, on the other hand, cannot carry this universal and necessary force, for it merely commands us to follow a course of action if we wish to attain a particular end. The categorical imperative in its basic formulation tells us to act according to that maxim which we can at the same time will should become a universal law.[1] A maxim is a subjective principle of action. It is, in fact, a general rule which we choose to follow. 'To choose maxims is to choose a policy.'[2] The test of the morality of a maxim is whether or not it agrees with the moral principle of the maxim becoming a universal law.

For Kant, the categorical imperative is the objective principle of morality. The statement that the will of the rational being is subject to the categorical imperative is an a priori synthetic proposition. It is also practically necessary. This is so because man is not only a means for the arbitrary use of this will or that, but as Kant says in the Groundwork of the Metaphysics of Morals 'he must in all his actions...be regarded at the same time as an end'.[3] From this postulate follows the second formulation of the categorical imperative which says: 'Act always so that you treat humanity whether in your person or in that of another always as an end, but never as a means only.'[4] Although this formulation is 'at bottom one and the same thing' as the first one,[5] it is, in another sense, already an application of the supreme moral principle; for it indicates to us what kind of maxims could be willed as universal laws. We thus learn what

[1] Ibid. pp. 437 f.   [2] Körner, Kant, p. 134.
[3] AA IV, 428.   [4] Ibid. p. 429.   [5] Ibid. p. 438.

right actions are, whether in morality or politics; for they involve our not using ourselves or others as means to our subjective ends. Man should not merely be subject to another will, but he should be his own law-giver. This view leads to another formulation of the categorical imperative: 'Act always in such a way as if you were through your maxims a law-making member of a universal kingdom of ends.'[1] To act for the sake of duty is thus to act in order to conform to some self-imposed law. This last formulation of the categorical imperative also implies an affinity between morals and politics, for man's actions, it suggests, do not take place in a vacuum, but always in relation to other men—thus implicitly suggesting a theory of politics, a system of principles governing organised human relations.

Kant's principles of morality are formal. Their very generality means that they do not say anything about the content of an action, but they supply rules to which we can appeal if we wish to judge actions and if we wish to decide what action is moral in the case of a conflict of interest. They rule out reference to, or regard for, the consequences of our actions, such as concern for the attainment of happiness. If the pursuit of happiness is made the maxim of our actions, the will is not autonomous. It does not then live under self-imposed laws, but follows heteronomous principles on which, in Kant's view, a sound moral theory cannot be founded. 'A practical law of reason', on the contrary, is 'the principle which makes certain actions a duty'.[2]

Such is Kant's view of the character of morality. Because of his approach to knowledge, be it in science or morality, Kant did not work out a system of nature nor did he set out to provide a complete system of morality which would take account of 'empirical diversity'.[3] A complete account of moral practice in all particular instances where the concept of morality can be applied is impossible. What Kant wishes to provide is an approximation to such a system, elaborating the relevant *a priori* principles. An attempt of this kind Kant calls a metaphysics, which, for him, is a set of the fundamental *a priori* principles of a particular discipline. According to him, all propositions of right are *a priori* propositions; for they are laws of reason. It can often be a matter for discussion whether some sentences stating such principles are to be interpreted as synthetic *a priori* propositions, or as analytic *a priori* (i.e. where the meaning of the sentence is contained in the term and does not permit contradiction) or synthetic *a posteriori* propositions (which are logically dependent on experience).

[1] *Ibid.*
[2] *AA* VI, 225.
[3] *Ibid.* p. 205.

The line between one and the other is not always easy to draw,[1] but the case for a Kantian approach to morality—and thus also to politics—is not refuted if any one sentence (or indeed any number of sentences) can be interpreted as not being a synthetic *a priori* proposition.[2] It suffices if some of them are of that type—and clearly the categorical imperative and its various formulations and immediate derivations are. This presupposes Kant's view that a metaphysics of morality is at least possible. For Kant, a theory of politics (which, for him, amounts in the main to a metaphysics of law) is inevitably a part of a metaphysics of morality. This is so because politics deals with the question of what we ought to do in our social and political context, or in other words, it is concerned with establishing criteria by which we can settle public conflicts of interests. The principle of universality demands that our social and political relations should be governed and our public conflicts settled in a universal manner. This requires the existence of law. The principles of morality would, in one way, go beyond purely legal questions; for they affect private inner decisions by men which can neither be regulated nor enforced publicly. Law deals only with what remains once such inner decisions have been subtracted. It is the outer shell, so to speak, of the moral realm. And a theory of law is that which can be necessary and universal in the realm of politics. A metaphysics of law is thus all that a metaphysics of politics can ever amount to. Such a metaphysics will set out the *a priori* principles of reason according to which we can judge the lawfulness of any given positive laws and thus of any form which political action may take. Kant's political theory is thus closely bound up with his ethics, though this is not its only affinity; for it is also closely connected with his philosophy of history. On the one hand, ethics and politics overlap. On the other hand, moral and political duties are clearly different. Political duties are not perfect duties towards oneself, but only what Kant calls perfect duties towards others, whose non-performance is wrong and whose performance may therefore be enforced. Kant here rules out from consideration all actions which merely concern oneself. He also does not consider those actions which are imperfect duties to others, i.e. actions involving the choice of one person and the mere aims and wishes of another. For instance, he does not prescribe acts of benevolence as legal duties. Perfect duties to others are therefore an object of law and thus of

---

[1] According to Mary J. Gregor, *Laws of Freedom* (Oxford, 1963), pp. 4 ff., Kant does not distinguish very clearly between pure knowledge and *a priori* knowledge. The former does not contain any empirical elements, the latter presupposes concepts of sensuous origin.

[2] I owe this observation to Stephan Körner.

politics; for law is *the* universalised expression of politics. In other words, an action is a moral action only if the maxim on which it is based agrees with the idea of duty; morality is therefore concerned only with subjective motives. Law, on the other hand, is concerned with the actions themselves, i.e. with objective facts. Moral actions can thus only be commanded; legal actions, however, can be enforced.

V

If politics results in law, what then, are Kant's principles of politics? They are substantially the principles of right (*Recht*). The philosophical enquiry into politics must establish which political actions are just or unjust. It must show by what principles we can establish the demands of justice in a given situation. Justice must, however, be universal, but only law can bring it about. A coherent political order must then be a legal order. Just as in Kant's ethics actions ought to be based on maxims capable of being formulated as universal laws, so in politics political arrangements ought to be organised according to universally valid laws. Political action and legislation ought thus to be based on such rules as will allow of no exception. Kant's principles of politics are normative. They are applications of principles of right to experience.[1] Right, in a succinct phrase of Kant's, 'ought never to be adapted to politics, but politics ought always to be adapted to right'.[2]

There is, of course, no reason whatsoever to believe that Kant was not aware that the details of the political situation always vary. His aim, however, was to discover the philosophical foundations on which political actions could, and ought to, be based. Right is to be found only in external relations which are the proper business of politics. External relations are relations which arise because we have possessions, 'an external mine and thine' as Kant calls it. He here uses the terminology of Roman Law for the concept of 'mine and thine' (*meum et tuum*).[3] These relations have to be placed under rules. Politics, as Hobbes had argued, belongs to that sphere of human experience in which man's will can be coerced by another will; for like Hobbes, Kant reduces all action to the will. If coercion is exercised according to a universal principle, it is law. Thus, law is conceived as 'a coercive order'.[4] Legality is therefore the decisive

---

[1] *On an Alleged Right to Lie for the Sake of Philanthropy (Über ein vermeintes Recht aus Menschenliebe zu lügen)* (1797), *AA* VIII, 429.
[2] *Ibid.* [3] *AA* VI, 245 ff.
[4] John Ladd, introduction to *Immanuel Kant. The Metaphysical Elements of Justice* (Indianapolis, New York and Kansas City, 1965), p. xviii.

principle in the sphere of politics. The moral decision of the inner man finds outward expression in legality, i.e. in an action conforming with law. But man's inner life must not be subject to coercion. Because we cannot know for certain anything about another person's inner life, it ought not to be the task of political action or legislation to change or in any way to condition another person's thought. As men we are free. Our freedom implies that we have a hypothetical right to acquire anything in the world of a nature which we are potentially capable of acquiring.

Not only any one particular individual, but all individuals have this right of acquiring possessions. It is the expression of their freedom. Collision between the freedom of one individual and that of others must, however, be avoided. Otherwise there would be chaos and constant strife. The freedom of each individual has consequently to be regulated in a universally binding manner. Thus, external freedom is freedom from any constraint except coercion by law, a freedom which allows each individual to pursue his own ends, whatever they may be, provided that this pursuit leaves the same kind of freedom to all others.

Acquired rights do not, however, belong to us merely by virtue of our humanity. They can be regulated or even curtailed by law. The act of acquisition establishes the right to property. It does not necessarily mean physical possession, but rather an intelligible or noumenal possession independent of time. In order to distinguish my possession from that of others, it is necessary that the choice of others should agree with my own. This condition is only possible under a law regulating possessions. But such a law is not possible in a state of nature, only in a civil society. From the principle that everyone has a right to acquire external possessions, therefore, there arises the command that everyone ought to act in such a way that everyone is able to acquire the external 'His' (or his external possessions). This in turn amounts to a command to enter civil society, to become a member of the state. Or, in other words, when a conflict about external possessions arises, as it inevitably does, a right exists to compel the other person to enter civil society.

In establishing this view of right, Kant is again not concerned with delineating the content of relations between individuals (i.e. the ends which they desire or ought to desire), but only with the form. What matters is the arrangement which establishes that the free actions of one individual 'can be reconciled with the freedom of the other in accordance with a universal law'.[1]

From this conclusion, the universal principle of right can be deduced.

[1] *AA* VI, 230.

It runs: 'Every action which by itself or by its maxim enables the freedom of each individual's will to coexist with the freedom of everyone else in accordance with a universal law is *right*.'[1] This universal principle of right imposes an obligation upon us, but it does not expect, let alone require, us to act in accordance with it. It tells us merely that if freedom is to be restricted in accordance with right and if justice is to prevail it must do so in accordance with this universal principle of right. To restrict freedom in this manner does not entail interfering with the freedom of an individual, but merely establishes the condition of his external freedom.

The universal principle of right is basically only an application of the universal principle of morality, as laid down in the Categorical Imperative, to the sphere of law, and thus also to the sphere of politics.[2] But since it is morally necessary to realise external freedom, we can be compelled by others to carry out our duty of entering civil society. But we do not have to become morally better to enter it; for the political problem must be capable of solution not only by good men, but even by 'a nation of devils (so long as they possess understanding)'.[3]

To restrict freedom except on the basis of the universal principle of right is wrong. It is not only wrong, but will also lead to strife, and thus is self-defeating. He who restricts freedom otherwise, i.e. arbitrarily, violates the freedom of another and abuses his own. To use constraint against anyone who violates the freedom of another is, however, right. The principle of right implies analytically the authorisation to use coercion by means of or on the basis of law against anyone who violates freedom illegitimately.

If this principle is applied to politics it is necessary that there should be established: 'A constitution allowing the *greatest possible human freedom* in accordance with laws which ensure *that the freedom of each can coexist with the freedom of all the others*'.[4] Kant elaborates this principle by saying that it is 'a necessary idea which must be made the basis not only of the first outline of a political constitution but of all laws as well'.[5] This fundamental principle could, by way of analogy, be called the universal principle of political right, although Kant himself does not use this term in the *Critique of Pure Reason* where he discusses it.

From these elementary principles, all other Kantian principles of politics follow—Kant's approach also makes it clear that, for him, the philosophical problem of politics is virtually that of Hobbes, viz. the

[1] *Ibid.*; cf. p. 133 below.
[2] Gregor, *Laws of Freedom*, p. 13.
[3] *AA* VIII, 366; cf. p. 112 below.
[4] *AA* III, 247; *AA* IV, 201.
[5] *AA* III, 247 f.; *AA* IV, 201.

transition from a state of war to a state of peace and security.[1] But Kant's solution is different.

What further principles did Kant then formulate which ought to govern external relations among men? A state is a union of a group of men under laws.[2] Since laws must then be based on the principle that we ought to be treated as ends and not as means, and since we must be considered as our own law-givers, we should be asked to consider as right only those laws to which we could agree or ought to have agreed if we had been asked to do so. 'For so long as it is not self-contradictory to say that an entire people could agree to such a law, however painful it might seem, then the law is in harmony with right.'[3] An important corollary of this principle is the necessity that all laws be public laws. Any legislation based on a maxim that needs publicity to achieve its end is just.

The sovereign has not only rights, but also duties. He thus has not only the right but also the duty to coerce his subjects by the giving of laws; it is, however, his (moral) duty to treat his subjects as ends and not as means. Kant here is not entirely clear. It is not at all certain whether he refers to the sovereign (legislature) or to the ruler (executive). The sovereign (according to him) can never do wrong;[4] whatever the laws given by him are, they have to be obeyed. But the positive law which is given has still to be judged by the standard found in the principles of right. The ruler cannot be judged by the sovereign since if this were done the legislature would usurp the power of the executive or judiciary which is self-contradictory and thus not right.

The problem of sovereignty, in fact, greatly occupied Kant; for he reverts to it again and again in his unpublished notes.[5] His discussion is not without occasional contradiction, as might be expected from a philosopher wrestling with a problem which he had not solved entirely to his satisfaction. The whole trend of Kant's thinking as revealed in these notes, makes it, however, abundantly plain that, according to him, sovereignty resides or originates in the people[6] which ought to possess legislative

[1] Cf. Pierre Hassner, 'Situation de la philosophie politique chez Kant', *Annales de philosophie politique*, IV (Paris, 1962), 77 ff.
[2] *AA* VI, 313; cf. p. 138 below.
[3] *AA* VIII, 299; cf. p. 80 f. below.
[4] Cf. for example *AA* XIX, 515 No. 7782; 566 No. 7965; 572 No. 7982.
[5] Cf. for instance *AA* XIX, 414 No. 7494; 480 No. 7660; 498 No. 7713; 499 No. 7719; 515 No. 7781; 549 No. 7905; 555 No. 7921; 555 No. 7922; 561 No. 7941; 563 No. 7952; 567 No. 7971; 572 No. 7982; 575 No. 7991; 582 No. 8016; 582 No. 8018; 584 No. 8020; 593 No. 8049; to mention only some of the more important reflections on this question of sovereignty and its implications.
[6] Cf. *AA* XIX, 503 No. 7734.

power.[1] However, a monarch could possess it as a representative of the people in a derivative form. Yet Kant appears convinced that if the monarch is to exercise this power together with executive powers, his rule is despotic.

It is also the sovereign's (moral) duty to give just laws and to introduce constitutional reforms so that a republican constitution can be established. (The term 'republican' in Kant's writings could be interpreted to represent what nowadays is generally called parliamentary democracy, though it does not necessarily have this connotation.) But the subject cannot coerce the ruler (or sovereign) to exercise these duties. They are therefore not legal, but moral duties for the ruler.

All this also implies that men have inalienable rights. In a state of nature, the war of all against all may prevail, but in a state where men live under law it is different. Men are free, equal and self-dependent. This statement is derived from the idea of freedom. For if all individuals are free, they must necessarily be equally so; for the freedom of all individuals is absolute and can only be universally and equally restricted by law. Each free person must also be self-dependent. The idea of freedom entails the individual's autonomy, for it postulates the individual's power of exercising his will independently, uninhibited by improper constraint.

Kant thus starts his enquiry into politics from the standpoint of the individual. This view reflects his emphasis on the need of the free individual to make decisions, a view which he had propounded in his writings on ethics. The political freedom of the individual can, as we have seen, be understood only in terms of legal arrangements guaranteeing the freedom of all individuals.

But Kant states the political problem in a negative manner. He does not consider it to be the purpose of politics to make people happy. Happiness is subjective. He thus strongly condemns utilitarianism in politics, just as he objects to utilitarianism in pure ethics. This argument, of course, does not mean that he does not wish people to be happy. It only means that political arrangements should not be organised in such a way as to aim at promoting happiness, but that they should permit men to attain happiness in their own way. He thus rules out benevolent despotism as practised, and defended in his writings on politics, by Frederick the Great.

Kant realises, indeed, that it is necessary for the ruler to give such laws and act in such a manner that the subject will not seek to destroy the state

---

[1] Cf. Gierke, *Natural Law and the Theory of Society*, p. 153, who maintains that the principle of popular sovereignty is for practical purposes 'a mere idea of reason'. Gierke, in my view, overstates his case.

and to overthrow the system of laws. For this purpose, men must be treated as ends and not as means. A genuine paradox, the paradox of political freedom, appears to arise. Man's freedom can be safeguarded only by his submitting to coercion; for law presupposes coercion, and thus an infringement of the individual's freedom. Rousseau saw this paradox clearly when he stated at the very beginning of the *Contrat Social* 'Man is born free, and everywhere he is in chains'.[1] He blamed society for this state of affairs. Kant agrees with him in considering this act of coercion to be a result of man's membership of civil society, of his citizenship of the state, but he solves the paradox by seeing it as a necessary condition of civilisation. He resorts to the following explanation. We are free only in so far as, in the case of a conflict of interests, we obey the law to which we would have agreed, i.e. we submit only to coercion which is legally exercised, on the basis of public law given by the sovereign authority. The sovereign ought thus to be obliged to respect the laws which he has given. Kant here differs from Hobbes for whom the sovereign is above the law; law is the sovereign's command to the people. Man, according to Kant, preserves his freedom by remaining his own law-giver. In principle, every subject thus participates in all legislation as a fellow-legislator, and the ruler when legislating ought to respect this right of his subjects. This solution ensures freedom and security for all. Political freedom, then, is independence from coercion by another will.

If freedom is the first principal right of a citizen in a state, equality is the second. Men must be equal before the law; legislation must not make an exception nor must the law be administered so as to allow for exceptions. Kant attacks the entire heritage of feudal privilege, a foremost contemporary issue. He also rules out in principle slavery or any inferior political status for a citizen. But he thinks of political equality only, and does not at all consider the question of economic equality. He does not, however, ignore economic issues entirely. He asserts the right of man to own property. He even goes further; for he makes economic independence a criterion for active participation in political affairs.

The third principal right, independence (or *Selbständigkeit* as Kant calls it), requires that each citizen must have a right to participate in the government. He ought to do this not directly, but indirectly by the exercise of the vote. Each citizen must have one vote, however large his estate may be. No one must, by statute, have more legislative power than has been agreed to by a law concerning the delegation of legislative power.

---

[1] Jean Jacques Rousseau, *The Political Writings*, II, ed. C. E. Vaughan (Cambridge, 1915), II, 23: 'L'homme est né libre, et partout il est dans les fers'.

But while every one is free and equal and ought to enjoy the protection of law in these respects, not every one has a right to participate in the making of laws. Kant, if judged by modern criteria, here appears to depart from his own enlightened standpoint. Although in many ways he was ahead of his time, he was not so in all respects. He is still, not surprisingly perhaps, profoundly steeped in eighteenth-century traditions. He may be the philosopher of the American and French revolutions, but it should not be forgotten that the former was essentially a revolution of landowners and the latter a revolution of the bourgeoisie. So Kant, perhaps understandably, differentiates between men of independence and those who have none. He classes those who are independent as *active* citizens and those who are dependent as *passive* citizens. Only active citizens have a right to vote and to legislate. Women are, on principle, disqualified. But any legislation should always be enacted and carried out as if the passive citizens too were participating, for, inherently, they have the same political right as active citizens. The requirements for independence are, for him, partly economic. A man must not be dependent on any one else economically, as a servant or as an employee, for otherwise he cannot freely and independently take part in politics. No self-dependent citizen untainted by crime or insanity can abdicate the duty of participating in legislating. He cannot relinquish this duty even if he were mistakenly to find the spectacle of politics abhorrent and beneath his dignity. For while no one has a right to coerce others except by a public law executed by the sovereign, no one can divest himself of this right either.

These three rights of freedom, equality and self-dependence show that, in a properly organised state, men can find security and justice. Kant differs from Rousseau, since he believes that the state of nature is not a state of innocence. Thus, man is not corrupted by society. On the contrary, society has civilised him. Kant rather agrees with Hobbes that the state of nature is the state of a war of all against all.

What is therefore needed is a will that binds every one equally, i.e. a collectively universal will that alone can give security to each and all. Consequently, everyone has to restrict his freedom so as to make possible the establishment of such a supreme power and to avoid collision with the freedom of others. Kant, following the tradition of his age, uses the analogy of the social contract to explain this existence of the state governing a people by a system of civil law. For Kant, however, the social contract must not be considered a historical fact. On this point, he is quite unambiguous. Any such conception would be fraught with peril; for it is likely to encourage disobedience of, or even active rebellion against, the prevailing law. The social contract must therefore be seen as a practical Idea of reason. (An Idea, for Kant, is not found in experience and can thus be neither proved nor disproved by scientific enquiry, but is a regulative principle of Reason in the light of which experience can be given order and unity, which it would otherwise lack.) It is a practical Idea of reason in so far as it can be applied to the world of practical affairs or to experience, i.e. the phenomenal world; for it allows us to say something about the kind of state which ought to exist, i.e. the state which ought to be established in accordance with the principles of right. The social contract is thus a criterion of political judgement, but it should not lead us to go into historical reasons for the purpose of drawing practical conclusions. The Idea that men have made a contract to establish the state means rather that they have been prepared to submit their own personal will in matters external to them to a universal will. This universal or general will is, of course, the will of reason. It is not the united will of all, even if this were to be found so in fact, nor is it the will of the majority. Kant is again close to Rousseau, but again, where Rousseau is ambiguous, he is decisively clear. He transfers the conception of the general will, which might be embodied in the government, to an Idea of reason which entitles the government to exercise the power of political action, to coerce others according to universal law. He differs cardinally from Hobbes, who ruled out the question as to whether the sovereign could make just or unjust laws as illegitimate; for in Hobbes' view, there can be no such moral yardstick to measure existing laws.

For Kant, the Idea of the social contract also implies the necessity of a civil constitution. While it is necessary and obligatory, as he believes, to establish a civil constitution, it is also the greatest practical problem for mankind to attain this end; for only in a civil society, universally administering right according to law, can freedom exist. Only then does the freedom of one co-exist with the freedom of others. But to find a just government ruling according to a just constitution is not easy. For who is to safeguard the rights of the individual in face of authority? Who will see to it that a just constitution is established and that the government will act in accordance with the principles of right?

There is no perfect solution to the old problem *quis custodiet ipsos custodes?* This means that 'only an approximation to the idea'[1] of a just constitution and a just government is given to us by nature.

According to what principles, then, should a rightful government be organised, even if completely just political arrangements can never be

---

[1] *AA* VIII, 23: cf. p. 46 below.

attained? Kant differentiates between the republican form of government, where the executive is separated from the legislature, and the despotic, where it is not.[1] Republican government is impossible in a democracy; for a 'democracy' is necessarily despotic. A power is established where all rule. It means that all take decisions about all and also against any one who decides to differ from the prevailing majority view. It would in fact be a contradiction of the universal will with itself and with freedom.

Republican government, however, is rightful government. A republican constitution is established in accordance with the principles of right if powers independent from one another are set up. First, there is the sovereign, in the person of the legislator who represents the united (or general) will of the people, which, in theory, is the will of reason. The ruler (or regent), i.e. the government or the executive, cannot be the legislator. Finally, neither the legislator nor the ruler can be the judiciary. For interpreting the law and for making individual judgements, an individual justice is required. For this function, a special representative of the people—a court of law or a jury—has to be appointed.

The legislative sovereign power, according to Kant, ought to be vested in the people. He also states that, in practice, the idea can only be approximated to. The most that we can hope for is that this power will be exercised indirectly by representatives of the people.[2] It cannot be expected that all should give laws and agree on legislation. All that can be attained is apparently a representative assembly which will legislate for all. The people as a whole must be expected to agree to this procedure and accept the legislation. They are, of course, bound by it.

Kant does not specify in detail how the representatives of the people ought to exercise their power, nor does he say according to what principle they should be chosen. He does not advocate the rule of the majority, and certainly not its unfettered power to legislate, which would have appeared to him only another form of the arbitrary will in action. He does, however, state explicitly that all should combine to give laws[3] and that legislation is to spring from the united will of all.[4] But he criticises the constitutional practice prevailing in eighteenth-century Britain.[5] For British constitutional monarchy appeared to him merely as a device designed to cloak an autocratic rule. He warns that the danger of a monarch becoming a

---

[1] Unfortunately he does not always appear to use his terms consistently. Indeed, he makes the distinction only in later writings, such as *Perpetual Peace* and *The Theory of Public Right*. Even then, when he speaks of the ruler, he sometimes appears to mean the sovereign legislative assembly, but at other times he appears to mean the executive of the government, which on other occasions again is described merely as an organ of the legislative.

[2] Cf. *AA* VI, 341.   [3] *AA* VII, 90 f.

[4] *AA* VI, 313.   [5] Cf. *AA* VII, 90; *AA* XIX, 606.

despot is particularly great, because one man is more easily tempted to become a tyrant. But he also states that where the government is in the hands of the smallest number of people and the representation is at its widest, republican rule will be most easily assured. He even appears to prefer a monarchy to an aristocracy. Yet he appears to be somewhat obscure on this point. The general drift of his argument is clear, however; his use of the term 'republican' shows us that he is basically anti-monarchic. And because he knew of the dangers of one man abusing his power, he, like Rousseau, did not believe that the united will of all could well be represented by one man. There can also be no doubt as to his basic plea for separation of powers and his conviction that the sovereign authority should rest in the people or its representatives. And he is equally clear in his demand that the sovereign must not own any private property so that he may be unable either to exercise private power or to be affected by private interest.

The fundamental element of any republican constitution, however, is respect for law. The subjects as well as the ruler and the sovereign must possess this respect. In the last resort, the subject can be expected to respect those laws in the giving of which he has participated as fellow-legislator. But the subject or citizen must neither rebel against the laws which the sovereign has made nor against the regent who carries them out, whether he likes the laws or approves of the regent or does neither. This attitude is perhaps surprising, especially if we consider Kant's attitude to the French Revolution.[1] It follows, however, from Kant's general conception of the supremacy of law, for to rebel against the supreme power would amount to disregarding, or even overturning the law. This is evil. Kant is most outspoken on this point.

His favourable view of the French Revolution, however, complicated his argument.[2] He tries to give legal status to the revolution by saying that it was not in fact a revolution at all in the legal sense; for the king had surrendered his sovereign power to the Third Estate. This is a dubious contention, though admittedly Louis XVI had abandoned absolute monarchy when he called the States-General.[3] It is, however, doubtful

---

[1] See the titles listed under p. 7 above, n. 1, for discussions of Kant's attitude.

[2] Cf. H. S. Reiss, 'Kant and the Right of Rebellion', *Journal of the History of Ideas*, XVII (1956), 179–92 for a discussion of these difficulties.

[3] Cf. Alfred Cobban, in his *History of Modern France* (London, 1962), I, 138 for instance, who writes: 'The calling of the States-General was undoubtedly the critical step, for it meant the abdication of absolute monarchy': cf. Kant's comments on this very theme in one of his notes (*AA* XIX, 595 No. 8055) where he expands his contention that by asking the States-General for assistance to solve the financial problems of France, he did in fact surrender his sovereignty.

whether he relinquished sovereign power. Kant's argument on this point remains controversial, to say the least, and does not carry much conviction. According to Kant, the case against rebellion is unambiguous. The people cannot possess a right to rebel. There can be no power to determine what constitutes the right to rebel. Rebellion would upset the whole system of laws. It would create anarchy and violence. It would also destroy the civil constitution which the idea of the social contract demands. For if a constitution contained an article permitting a people to rebel or to depose a sovereign, a second sovereign would thereby be established. This event would be a contradiction. It would, in fact, require a further, third sovereign to decide between the two, which is absurd. There cannot therefore be in a constitution a clause giving any one a right to resist or to rebel against supreme authority.[1] The idea of the civil constitution must be sacred and irresistible. To overthrow the sovereign or the ruler is not only wrong but will also fail to achieve its end; for it does not produce a true reform of thought.

But once a revolution has taken place, attempts to undo it and re-establish the old order are just as wrong, for it is men's duty to obey as citizens. If a government is newly established, as in England in 1688, it has to be accepted and obeyed. On the other hand, there exists no right to punish the ruler for deeds committed as ruler, for the ruler's deeds, in principle, are not subject to punishment. The sovereign cannot be punished for issuing unjust laws or for committing unrightful political actions; for such an endeavour would amount to rebellion while he is in power, and would violate the same principle after he had been deposed.

The sovereign has the right to dismiss the ruler, but he has no right to punish the dismissed ruler for actions committed as ruler. Judicial action against, and punishment of, the ruler are worse than the assassination of a tyrant. In fact, the judicial punishment of a (sovereign) ruler, such as the regicide of Charles I or Louis XVI, is the worst crime imaginable. It is a perversion of the Idea of the law itself.

[1] There is, of course, the possibility of passive resistance or disobedience to a government. While Kant unambiguously rules out active rebellion and states that we should not reason about the origins of the supreme power with a view to action, he suggests in his treatise *Religion within the Limits of Reason Alone* that passive resistance or passive disobedience by not carrying out the decrees of a government may be legitimate. He argues there that the verse 'we ought to obey God rather than men' (Acts v. 29) means that when men command what is evil-in-itself, i.e. what runs directly counter to the moral law, we ought not to obey (*AA* VI, 99). But it should also not be forgotten in this context that this passage, as well as a similar one from the same treatise (*AA* VI, 154), cannot nullify Kant's general hostility to the right of rebellion which necessarily rules out civil disobedience.

Kant, however, demands from the sovereign that he should promote a spirit of liberty. Only if it prevails is it likely that the coercive ends of the ruler will not be defeated. The rulers are, in fact, aware of the desire for liberty; for no ruler dares to say that he does not recognize any rights whatsoever in the people, that they owe their happiness exclusively to the government, and that any claims of the subjects to have rights against him are a punishable offence. Rulers dare not say this because a declaration of this kind would make the citizens band together in protest. Yet even if citizens conclude that their happiness could be taken away, they have no right to rebel. Obedience, however, does not mean silence. What must and does remain for the people is the right of public criticism, i.e. not only freedom of the press, but the right of open criticism of the powers that be. Following Voltaire, Kant believed that '*Freedom of the pen* is the only safeguard of the rights of the people'.[1] This is tantamount to demanding an open society, a society which seeks to carry on government and to give laws by a process of free rational discussion.

The right to criticise in public ought, therefore, to be guaranteed by the republican constitution. This right is restricted only by 'respect and devotion towards the existing constitution'[2] of the state in which it is exercised.

To qualify the right of public criticism by the proviso that it should be resorted to only if respect for the republican constitution is not infringed implicitly establishes the principle of the limits of tolerance. This principle amounts to saying that all views must be tolerated provided that they are views which involve the toleration of the views of others. Or, in other words, only those views ought to be tolerated which do not advocate the overthrow of the constitution established according to the principles of right. For anyone publicly to advocate views calculated to overthrow the republican constitution amounts to a demand for violating the principles of right and thus the freedom of others. It is, therefore, legitimate to frame laws which restrict the freedom of the pen in this respect, but in this respect only. Such a law can be made universally applicable. If, on the other hand, violation of a republican constitution and of the principles of right and thus of the freedom of others is advocated, a demand of this kind cannot be given the form of a universal law. For if such a violation were to prevail, chaos, and with it the erosion of all laws, would ensue. A law permitting violation of the constitution and thus of the system of laws itself would amount to a law contradicting itself, which is absurd. It must, however, be made equally clear that this restriction is the only

[1] *AA* VIII, 304; cf. p. 85 below. [2] *Ibid.*

possible one. To restrict public criticism in any other way would amount to violating the principles of right and thus of freedom. And this limitation of public criticism must not be construed to mean that the government has a right to suppress public criticism as such, but only public criticism which has no respect for the constitution (i.e. criticism which amounts to advocating, or involves violation of, a republican constitution). Kant does not lay down the exact limits beyond which it is not legitimate to criticise a constitution publicly. The phrase 'respect' should not be taken to mean that it could be illegitimate to discuss the principles of right and their application in practice in a philosophical manner. But it does suggest that an unreasoned or forcible attack upon a republican constitution and any attempt to establish a rule which does not permit public criticism can, in principle, be legislated against. For such attacks do not carry respect, while a philosophical enquiry into the constitution and the principles underlying it does.

Unfortunately, Kant does not elaborate on this point. He was much more concerned with the problem of his age, with establishing the right of public criticism in face of a paternalistic ruler, and much less with problems of modern liberal democracy, the need to limit this right and to define the limits of tolerance so as to avoid destruction of public freedom by excessive liberality in tolerating views hostile to free public criticism and thus to freedom itself. The limits of public criticism are thus the defences which must needs be erected against those who wish to destroy it, from whatever quarter they may come; but this is the only frontier which requires protection.

VI

Right, however, cannot possibly prevail among men within a state if their freedom is threatened by the action of other states. The law can prevail only if the rule of law prevails in all states and in international relations. Only then are all individuals free; only then does right prevail everywhere. Clearly, the very universality of the demand that right should prevail makes it imperative that it should apply to all men and provide legal protection against all kinds of violence. This is possible only if war is abolished as a means of politics and peace is established and safeguarded on earth according to the principles of right. This is the ultimate problem of politics. Kant had predecessors in this view of international politics, but once again the rigour of his argument and the relentless search for philosophical vindication are unprecedented.

In Kant's view, right can be jeopardised by war or by preparations for war. As he writes in his essay *Conjectures on the Beginning of Human History* 'We have to admit that the greatest evils which oppress civilised nations are the result of *war*—not so much of actual wars in the past or present as of the unremitting, indeed ever-increasing *preparation* for war in the future.'[1] Neither a republican state (however just its legal arrangements are) nor its citizens are safe unless they avoid conflicts with other states. The only way to do so is by establishing peaceful relations between independent states according to the principles of right. Kant realises, as his ironic preamble to his treatise *Perpetual Peace* indicates, that the ultimate alternative to this view is the graveyard, the death of all, a possibility which has become only too real in this nuclear age of ours.

It is a duty to work towards the establishment of a cosmopolitan society. A world state would be the ideal solution, but states are not likely to agree to a complete surrender of their sovereignty, nor is the territory of the world compact enough to permit control by one supreme authority. (Modern technology has, so to speak, made the world shrink since 1795, but there are still almost insuperable barriers to effective control of the globe by a world government, owing to the diversity of nations.) This positive solution is therefore unrealistic; a negative solution must suffice. As war becomes more and more expensive and as the peoples (not the sovereigns) will have to bear the burden, they will not desire war any more. Necessity will bring about this state of right; for the balance of power is too precarious. Indeed, Kant harshly attacks the concept of the balance of power because it cannot lead to perpetual peace. This state of affairs can be brought about only gradually. It needs a nucleus of republican states. To have a world republic is impossible unless all nations agree to it, which is not very likely. Kant admits that, on the analogy of individuals uniting to form a state, all states might be compelled to unite into a world state governed by law. He points out that states would not wish to abandon their sovereignty. In his view, so it would seem, they are intrinsically incapable of doing so.[2] This is surprising, since for him, as distinct from Fichte or the Romantics, states do not have an unalterable traditional, natural or linguistic basis. Since the states persist, a world state would create only the semblance of public international law; it would, in fact, be likely to result in a particularly oppressive despotism.

What could be brought about is a federation of states which are opposed to war. Again the *a priori* principles of right decide the issue. War is not the right way of settling disputes between nations. Nor is war invigorating

---

[1] *AA* VII, 121; pp. 231 f. below.   [2] Cf. *ibid.* p. 357; *AA* XXIII, 169.

or noble. Kant's principles of right demand that the nations agree to laws capable of settling disputes between them and that they be prepared to submit to arbitration according to law. The respect for law which prevails in a republican state makes it incumbent upon its citizens and its government to establish a similar system of law in international affairs.

Kant was thus well aware of the role of power in politics. He was certainly not so naïve as to believe that it would be sufficient to proclaim such rules in order to bring about perpetual peace. But in Kant's view, the sense of right is all-pervasive; for even the mighty tend to appeal to right when they violate law. It is an observation which Machiavelli, though from a completely different standpoint, had also made. Kant therefore thinks it imperative to make men aware of the principles of right and accept the rule of justice.

Kant expressly rejects the rule of expediency in international politics. Men who espouse expediency, however, also have principles, principles which are derived from the view that might is right. Kant shrewdly analyses them. He was indeed aware of customary political practice and he acutely discerned the arguments usually put forward to deceive political opponents.

Kant considers it essential to demonstrate that perpetual peace cannot be established by following the doctrines of expediency which are: *fac et excusa, si fecisti nega* and *divide et impera*.[1] These principles are not objective *a priori* principles of right on which men can agree and act. They involve considering the consequences of one's action and not the maxims of one's action. They are therefore heteronomous, i.e. uncertain and imprecise. It is impossible to agree on them by the use of reason. They do not allow of a philosophical enquiry into politics, nor do they afford points of orientation for rightful political action.

VII

Just as Kant did not write a single masterpiece on political philosophy, he did not write a single comprehensive work on the philosophy of history. We have to turn to the essays *What is Enlightenment?* and *Idea for a Universal History with a Cosmopolitan Purpose* of 1784 and to a section of *The Contest of Faculties* of 1798. What then is his view of history?

First of all, Kant asks whether we can formulate laws in history, just as we can formulate laws in nature, so that we can understand history in the

---

[1] Cf. p. 120 below.

way in which we understand nature. In his view, it is difficult to detect these laws, but perhaps biography—and Kant here takes up a point frequently raised in eighteenth-century German discussions by Mendelssohn, Hamann, and Herder, for instance—may serve as a suitable analogy. Perhaps the general course of history shows a development in mankind similar to that which biography discerns in the individual. If there is progress, this is certainly not due to human wisdom; for even the philosophers, Kant ironically remarks, are not wise enough to plan their lives.

Kant nevertheless sets high standards. He intends to discover the natural laws of history, just as Kepler had discovered the natural laws of the planets. When Kant talks of plans of nature in history, he does not mean that there is an actual legislator or mind called nature which has consciously made a plan to be carried out in history, but merely that if we wish to understand history as (according to him) we have to, we must resort to an Idea, such as the one that nature has a purpose in history. This Idea cannot be proved or disproved by a scientific enquiry, but without it, we cannot understand history at all. Nor must this Idea be considered to have equal status to a scientific law. Kant adopts a point of view, admittedly a subjective one, from which it is not only 'possible, but profitable, and not only profitable, but necessary'[1] to look at the facts of history. Since his main concern is with human freedom, the development of human freedom provides him with the necessary clue. He therefore assumes that a plan of nature must intend the education of mankind to a state of freedom. Or (to put it differently) since nature has endowed man with reason, and since the purpose of nature is to realise man's essence, nature has made man in order that he should become rational. Kant's view that man's essence must be realised follows an argument later developed in the *Critique of Judgement* where Kant had maintained that the teleology of nature is internal, not external. It is also a peculiarity of reason that it cannot be completely realised in the lifetime of an individual, but only in the entire species. This view represents a pivotal point in Kant's philosophy of history. His anthropological studies, to which he devoted much time and energy, had confirmed him in his conception of the unity of mankind.[2] Culture was not the result of individual effort, but was produced by mankind as a whole. Man as a rational being therefore needs to live in a historical process. History is a progress towards rationality, but it must not be thought that this process involves a con-

---

[1] R. G. Collingwood, *The Idea of History* (Oxford, 1946), p. 95.
[2] Cf. Vlachos, *La Pensée politique de Kant*, pp. 19–26.

INTRODUCTION

tinuous advance in rationality all the time. In *The Contest of Faculties*, Kant explicitly rejects the suggestion that the question of progress can be solved by appealing to experience. None of the possibilities which he can envisage supplies an answer. The first possibility is that everything is getting worse and worse. He calls it 'terrorism'. This hypothesis does not work, because after a certain stage, things would have become so bad that everything would disintegrate. The second possibility, which is called 'chiliasm',[1] implies that everything is getting better and better, but it is equally mistaken. It is false, because there is evil in any individual which cannot be diminished and because there is good which cannot be increased. To increase the good, man would need to possess more good than he has, which is untenable. The third possibility he calls 'abderitism':[2] this implies that everything gets neither better nor worse, but is simply stagnating. Good and evil seem to neutralise one another. But this is a farcical situation which must be considered unworthy of man.

We must therefore look for a principle outside experience. We can find it in the moral character of man. Outwardly, this moral character is realised in legal arrangements, i.e. by instituting a republican constitution. The French Revolution seems to him to represent this kind of event; for its aims are precisely the establishment of a republican state. To advance the spread of rationality is a moral obligation, for this advance is the only way in which our moral nature can be fully realised. It is our duty to further the establishing of a republican constitution, but it is also our duty to maintain the existing system of laws, whatever its character may be. We may, indeed we ought to improve the existing system of laws by criticism, so that it may approach the system of laws which ought to prevail in accordance with the principles of right. These aims are not chimerical; for the goal towards which history is moving is the establishment of a republican civil constitution. Since it is an ideal, it is not possible to realise it completely, but it can be approached. If it were merely to depend on man's moral decision whether a republican constitution be established, the outlook would indeed be bleak; for we must not expect too much of men. But nature is on our side. History can be interpreted only if we fully understand the conflict among men. Man is not only social, but anti-social too. The unsocial sociability, the mutual antagonism which prevails in

---

[1] Originally the belief that the millennium will be established on earth before the Day of Judgement.
[2] Abdera was a city in ancient Greece whose inhabitants were alleged to be extremely foolish. The name was popular in eighteenth-century Germany because of Christian Martin Wieland's novel *Geschichte der Abderiten* (*The Story of the Abderites*) (1774-81), in which human follies are satirised.

37

society, is thus the means which nature employs to bring about the development of all capacities implanted in men, but only in so far as the antagonism will eventually bring about an order regulated by law: 'Man wishes concord, but nature, knowing better what is good for his species, wishes discord.'[1]

Kant then certainly does not ignore the role which might and strife play in life. Like Hobbes, he sees in the antagonism among men, in the war of all against all, the mainspring for the establishment of a civil society. Logically, this view is in keeping with his assumption that, if history is the process by which man becomes rational, he cannot be rational at the beginning. Consequently, the force which serves as the mainspring of the process cannot be reason. It must be something radically different from it, such as mutual anti-rational antagonism among men.

Kant's philosophy of history is of considerable consequence for his political theory. Rebellion is condemned not only because it runs counter to the principle of law, but also because it is unnecessary in the light of historical development. Progress towards rationality, i.e. the establish-ment of a republican constitution, cannot be held up for long. To rebel against the powers that be would not hasten this process. It would even be likely to retard it; for rebellion would create a bad example. If a ruler sets men free there will usually at first be difficulties, even dangers, but 'men must be free in order to be able to use their power wisely in freedom'.[2] Sooner or later, reason will assert itself and the principles of right will be respected.

VIII

Such are the aims and principles of Kant's theory of politics. It is an impressive picture of a world that ought to be governed entirely by the principles of right. It would be easy to be sceptical and to dismiss the attempt as unrealistic. Kant anticipated this objection, and explicitly based his principles not on a high-minded view of man, but on a con-viction, doubtless inherited from the Christian dogma of original sin, of the radical evil in human nature. Kant's principles of politics are laid down neither by tradition nor by the sovereign power. They are found neither in experience nor in nature. Like Hobbes, he believes in the power of reason to judge politics. But unlike the principles of Hobbes, they are not the logical consequences of definitions derived from a detached ob-servation of life. They are independent of experience. Kant's principles

[1] *AA* VIII, 21; cf. p. 45 below.
[2] *Religion within the Limits of Reason Alone*, *AA* VI, 188.

are not part of an elaborate system of politics, but elementary principles which can help us to guide our actions. They can help us to orientate ourselves in politics if we wish to safeguard our freedom and that of others. They are analogous to the categorical imperative and require universal application. Kant, however, was not concerned with elaborating political programmes. For his conception of political freedom is not positive, but negative. It is concerned with those restraints which the individual must accept in order to avoid conflict with others so that he may enjoy the freedom of moral action.

For Kant, what is true in theory also applies in practice. By practice, he means the activities of practical life in a wide sense.[1] His theory of politics is capable of explaining political life; a theory based on heteronomous elements, i.e. a theory seeking to explain political life by reference to might, is unable to do so; for political life is only superficially concerned with political power. Power cannot be ignored, but the real problem of politics is to ensure right, i.e. law and justice. If we take the dignity of man, his freedom as a rational being, as the starting-point of our enquiry into political practice, only a theory of right based on principles of pure reason is capable of explaining political life. Other theories are false and thus mislead not only in their understanding of political practice, but also in their political repercussions.

The right theory does afford points of orientation for political practice, though it is never by itself enough. Prudence and practical skill are also needed in the conduct of political affairs. Kant was not a blinkered visionary, nor was he even an unpractical utopian dreamer. As a scientist, he had learnt to respect fact. His own philosophical polemics and his attitude to the government of the day reveal a keen awareness of the needs of the actual situation, and he did not resort to lying or to a flagrant compromise with his own principles.[2] He sought to follow the maxim accepted in *Perpetual Peace*: 'Be ye therefore wise as serpents, and harmless as doves.'[3]

Kant should be accorded a prominent place in the history of Western political thought, a place which has far too long been denied to him. He ought to be ranked among the leading political thinkers of all times. Plato, Aristotle, Hobbes are his peers. He is second to none in the acuteness of his thinking. His attempt to formulate rational principles of

[1] Dieter Henrich, Introduction to *Kant. Gentz. Rehberg. Über Theorie und Praxis*, pp. 14 ff.
[2] Hans Saner, *Kants Weg vom Krieg zum Frieden*, 1: *Widerstreit und Einheit, Wege zu Kants politischem Denken* (Munich, 1967).
[3] *AA* VIII, 370; cf. p. 116 below (Matt. x. 16).

politics on which all men can, and even ought to, agree of their own accord is as important for the modern world as Hobbes' endeavour to free political thought from the quagmire of tradition and superstition. To read Kant's political writings is to scale the heights of philosophical reflection on politics. His political thought should be of interest to all those who value the use of reason in public life.

Idea for a Universal History with a Cosmopolitan Purpose*¹

Whatever conception of the freedom of the will one may form in terms of metaphysics, the will's manifestations in the world of phenomena, i.e. human actions, are determined in accordance with natural laws, as is every other natural event. History is concerned with giving an account of these phenomena, no matter how deeply concealed their causes may be, and it allows us to hope that, if it examines the free exercise of the human will *on a large scale*, it will be able to discover a regular progression among freely willed actions. In the same way, we may hope that what strikes us in the actions of individuals as confused and fortuitous may be recognised, in the history of the entire species, as a steadily advancing but slow development of man's original capacities. Thus marriages, births, and deaths do not seem to be subject to any rule by which their numbers could be calculated in advance, since the free human will has such a great influence upon them; and yet the annual statistics for them in large countries prove that they are just as subject to constant natural laws as are the changes in the weather, which in themselves are so inconsistent that their individual occurrence cannot be determined in advance, but which nevertheless do not fail as a whole to sustain the growth of plants, the flow of rivers, and other natural functions in a uniform and uninterrupted course. Individual men and even entire nations little imagine that, while they are pursuing their own ends, each in his own way and often in opposition to others, they are unwittingly guided in their advance along a course intended by nature. They are unconsciously promoting an end which, even if they knew what it was, would scarcely arouse their interest.

Since men neither pursue their aims purely by instinct, as the animals do, nor act in accordance with any integral, prearranged plan like rational cosmopolitans, it would appear that no law-governed history of mankind

* A passage printed this year among other brief notices in the twelfth issue of the *Gothaische Gelehrte Zeitungen*, based, no doubt, on a conversation of mine with a passing scholar, calls for the present elucidation, without which the passage referred to would be unintelligible.

is possible (as it would be, for example, with bees or beavers). We can scarcely help feeling a certain distaste on observing their activities as enacted in the great world-drama, for we find that, despite the apparent wisdom of individual actions here and there, everything as a whole is made up of folly and childish vanity, and often of childish malice and destructiveness. The result is that we do not know what sort of opinion we should form of our species, which is so proud of its supposed superiority. The only way out for the philosopher, since he cannot assume that mankind follows any rational *purpose of its own* in its collective actions, is for him to attempt to discover a *purpose in nature* behind this senseless course of human events, and decide whether it is after all possible to formulate in terms of a definite plan of nature a history of creatures who act without a plan of their own.—Let us now see if we can succeed in finding a guiding principle for such a history, and then leave it to nature to produce someone capable of writing it along the lines suggested. Thus nature produced a Kepler who found an unexpected means of reducing the eccentric orbits of the planets to definite laws, and a Newton who explained these laws in terms of a universal natural cause.

First Proposition

All the natural capacities of a creature are destined sooner or later to be developed completely and in conformity with their end. This can be verified in all animals by external and internal or anatomical examination. An organ which is not meant for use or an arrangement which does not fulfil its purpose is a contradiction in the teleological theory of nature. For if we abandon this basic principle, we are faced not with a law-governed nature, but with an aimless, random process, and the dismal reign of chance replaces the guiding principle of reason.

Second Proposition

In man (as the only rational creature on earth), *those natural capacities which are directed towards the use of his reason are such that they could be fully developed only in the species, but not in the individual.* Reason, in a creature, is a faculty which enables that creature to extend far beyond the limits of natural instinct the rules and intentions it follows in using its various powers, and the range of its projects is unbounded. But reason does not itself work instinctively, for it requires trial, practice and instruction to enable it to progress gradually from one stage of insight to the next. Accordingly, every individual man would have to live for a vast length of time if he were to learn how to make complete use of all his natural capacities; or if nature has fixed only a short term for each man's life (as is in fact the case), then it will require a long, perhaps incalculable series of generations, each passing on its enlightenment to the next, before the germs implanted by nature in our species can be developed to that degree which corresponds to nature's original intention. And the point of time at which this degree of development is reached must be the goal of man's aspirations (at least as an idea in his mind), or else his natural capacities would necessarily appear by and large to be purposeless and wasted. In the latter case, all practical principles would have to be abandoned, and nature, whose wisdom we must take as axiomatic in judging all other situations, would incur the suspicion of indulging in childish play in the case of man alone.

Third Proposition

Nature has willed that man should produce entirely by his own initiative everything which goes beyond the mechanical ordering of his animal existence, and that he should not partake of any other happiness or perfection than that which he has procured for himself without instinct and by his own reason. For nature does nothing unnecessarily and is not extravagant in the means employed to reach its ends. Nature gave man reason, and freedom of will based upon reason, and this in itself was a clear indication of nature's intention as regards his endowments. For it showed that man was not meant to be guided by instinct or equipped and instructed by innate knowledge; on the contrary, he was meant to produce everything out of himself. Everything had to be entirely of his own making—the discovery of a suitable diet, of clothing, of external security and defence (for which nature gave him neither the bull's horns, the lion's claws, nor the dog's teeth, but only his hands), as well as all the pleasures that can make life agreeable, and even his insight and circumspection and the goodness of his will. Nature seems here to have taken pleasure in exercising the strictest economy and to have measured out the basic animal equipment so sparingly as to be just enough for the most pressing needs of the beginnings of existence. It seems as if nature had intended that man, once he had finally worked his way up from the uttermost barbarism to the highest degree of skill, to inner perfection in his manner of thought and thence (as far as is possible on earth) to happiness, should be able to take for himself the entire credit for doing so and have only himself to thank for it. It seems that nature has worked more with a view to man's rational *self-esteem* than to his mere well-being. For in the actual course of human

43

affairs, a whole host of hardships awaits him. Yet nature does not seem to have been concerned with seeing that man should live agreeably, but with seeing that he should work his way onwards to make himself by his own conduct worthy of life and well-being. What remains disconcerting about all this is firstly, that the earlier generations seem to perform their laborious tasks only for the sake of the later ones, so as to prepare for them a further stage from which they can raise still higher the structure intended by nature; and secondly, that only the later generations will in fact have the good fortune to inhabit the building on which a whole series of their forefathers (admittedly, without any conscious intention) had worked without themselves being able to share in the happiness they were preparing. But no matter how puzzling this may be, it will appear as necessary as it is puzzling if we simply assume that one animal species was intended to have reason, and that, as a class of rational beings who are mortal as individuals but immortal as a species, it was still meant to develop its capacities completely.

Fourth Proposition

The means which nature employs to bring about the development of innate capacities is that of antagonism within society, in so far as this antagonism becomes in the long run the cause of a law-governed social order. By antagonism, I mean in this context the *unsocial sociability* of men, that is, their tendency to come together in society, coupled, however, with a continual resistance which constantly threatens to break this society up. This propensity is obviously rooted in human nature. Man has an inclination to *live in society*, since he feels in this state more like a man, that is, he feels able to develop his natural capacities. But he also has a great tendency to *live as an individual*, to isolate himself, since he also encounters in himself the unsocial characteristic of wanting to direct everything in accordance with his own ideas. He therefore expects resistance all around, just as he knows of himself that he is in turn inclined to offer resistance to others. It is this very resistance which awakens all man's powers and induces him to overcome his tendency to laziness. Through the desire for honour, power or property, it drives him to seek status among his fellows, whom he cannot *bear* yet cannot *bear to leave*. Then the first true steps are taken from barbarism to culture, which in fact consists in the social worthiness of man. All man's talents are now gradually developed, his taste cultivated, and by a continued process of enlightenment, a beginning is made towards establishing a way of thinking which can with time transform the primitive natural capacity for moral discrimination into

44

definite practical principles; and thus a *pathologically* enforced social union is transformed into a *moral* whole. Without these asocial qualities (far from admirable in themselves) which cause the resistance inevitably encountered by each individual as he furthers his self-seeking pretensions, man would live an Arcadian, pastoral existence of perfect concord, self-sufficiency and mutual love. But all human talents would remain hidden for ever in a dormant state, and men, as good-natured as the sheep they tended, would scarcely render their existence more valuable than that of their animals. The end for which they were created, their rational nature, would be an unfilled void. Nature should thus be thanked for fostering social incompatibility, enviously competitive vanity, and insatiable desires for possession or even power. Without these desires, all man's excellent natural capacities would never be roused to develop. Man wishes concord, but nature, knowing better what is good for his species, wishes discord. Man wishes to live comfortably and pleasantly, but nature intends that he should abandon idleness and inactive self-sufficiency and plunge instead into labour and hardships, so that he may by his own adroitness find means of liberating himself from them in turn. The natural impulses which make this possible, the sources of the very unsociableness and continual resistance which cause so many evils, at the same time encourage man towards new exertions of his powers and thus towards further development of his natural capacities. They would thus seem to indicate the design of a wise creator—not, as it might seem, the hand of a malicious spirit who had meddled in the creator's glorious work or spoiled it out of envy.

Fifth Proposition

The greatest problem for the human species, the solution of which nature compels him to seek, is that of attaining a civil society which can administer justice universally.

The highest purpose of nature—i.e. the development of all natural capacities—can be fulfilled for mankind only in society, and nature intends that man should accomplish this, and indeed all his appointed ends, by his own efforts. This purpose can be fulfilled only in a society which has not only the greatest freedom, and therefore a continual antagonism among its members, but also the most precise specification and preservation of the limits of this freedom in order that it can co-exist with the freedom of others. The highest task which nature has set for mankind must therefore be that of establishing a society in which *freedom under external laws* would be combined to the greatest possible extent with irresistible force, in other words of establishing a perfectly *just civil constitution*. For only through the solution and fulfilment of this task can nature accomplish its other intentions with our species. Man, who is otherwise so enamoured with unrestrained freedom, is forced to enter this state of restriction by sheer necessity. And this is indeed the most stringent of all forms of necessity, for it is imposed by men upon themselves, in that their inclinations make it impossible for them to exist side by side for long in a state of wild freedom. But once enclosed within a precinct like that of civil union, the same inclinations have the most beneficial effect. In the same way, trees in a forest, by seeking to deprive each other of air and sunlight, compel each other to find these by upward growth, so that they grow beautiful and straight—whereas those which put out branches at will, in freedom and in isolation from others, grow stunted, bent and twisted. All the culture and art which adorn mankind and the finest social order man creates are fruits of his unsociability. For it is compelled by its own nature to discipline itself, and thus, by enforced art, to develop completely the germs which nature implanted.

Sixth Proposition

This problem is both the most difficult and the last to be solved by the human race. The difficulty (which the very idea of this problem clearly presents) is this: if he lives among others of his own species, man is *an animal who needs a master*. For he certainly abuses his freedom in relation to others of his own kind. And even although, as a rational creature, he desires a law to impose limits on the freedom of all, he is still misled by his self-seeking animal inclinations into exempting himself from the law where he can. He thus requires a *master* to break his self-will and force him to obey a universally valid will under which everyone can be free. But where is he to find such a master? Nowhere else but in the human species. But this master will also be an animal who needs a master. Thus while man may try as he will, it is hard to see how he can obtain for public justice a supreme authority which would itself be just, whether he seeks this authority in a single person or in a group of many persons selected for this purpose. For each one of them will always misuse his freedom if he does not have anyone above him to apply force to him as the laws should require it. Yet the highest authority has to be just *in itself* and yet also a *man*. This is therefore the most difficult of all tasks, and a perfect solution is impossible. Nothing straight can be constructed from such warped wood as that which man is made of. Nature only requires of us that we should

46

approximate to this idea.* A further reason why this task must be the last to be accomplished is that man needs for it a correct conception of the nature of a possible constitution, great experience tested in many affairs of the world, and above all else a good will prepared to accept the findings of this experience. But three factors such as these will not easily be found in conjunction, and if they are, it will happen only at a late stage and after many unsuccessful attempts.

Seventh Proposition

The problem of establishing a perfect civil constitution is subordinate to the problem of a law-governed external relationship with other states, and cannot be solved unless the latter is also solved. What is the use of working for a law-governed civil constitution among individual men, i.e. of planning a *commonwealth*? The same unsociability which forced men to do so gives rise in turn to a situation whereby each commonwealth, in its external relations (i.e. as a state in relation to other states), is in a position of unrestricted freedom. Each must accordingly expect from any other precisely the same evils which formerly oppressed individual men and forced them into a law-governed civil state. Nature has thus again employed the unsociableness of men, and even of the large societies and states which human beings construct, as a means of arriving at a condition of calm and security through their inevitable *antagonism.* Wars, tense and unremitting military preparations, and the resultant distress which every state must eventually feel within itself, even in the midst of peace—these are the means by which nature drives nations to make initially imperfect attempts, but finally, after many devastations, upheavals and even complete inner exhaustion of their powers, to take the step which reason could have suggested to them even without so many sad experiences—that of abandoning a lawless state of savagery and entering a federation of peoples in which every state, even the smallest, could expect to derive its security and rights not from its own power or its own legal judgement, but solely from this great federation (*Fœdus Amphictyonum*), from a united power and the law-governed decisions of a united will. However wild and fanciful this idea may appear—and it has been ridiculed as such when put forward by the Abbé St Pierre[2] and Rousseau[3] (perhaps because they

---

* Man's role is thus a highly artificial one. We do not know how it is with the inhabitants of other planets and with their nature, but if we ourselves execute this commission of nature well, we may surely flatter ourselves that we occupy no mean status among our neighbours in the cosmos. Perhaps their position is such that each individual can fulfil his destiny completely within his own lifetime. With us it is otherwise; only the species as a whole can hope for this.

47

thought that its realisation was so imminent)—it is nonetheless the inevitable outcome of the distress in which men involve one another. For this distress must force the states to make exactly the same decision (however difficult it may be for them) as that which man was forced to make, equally unwillingly, in his savage state—the decision to renounce his brutish freedom and seek calm and security within a law-governed constitution. All wars are accordingly so many attempts (not indeed by the intention of men, but by the intention of nature) to bring about new relations between states, and, by the destruction or at least the dismemberment of old entities, to create new ones. But these new bodies, either in themselves or alongside one another, will in turn be unable to survive, and will thus necessarily undergo further revolutions of a similar sort, till finally, partly by an optimal internal arrangement of the civil constitution, and partly by common external agreement and legislation, a state of affairs is created which, like a civil commonwealth, can maintain itself *automatically*.

Whether we should firstly expect that the states, by an Epicurean concourse[4] of efficient causes, should enter by random collisions (like those of small material particles) into all kinds of formations which are again destroyed by new collisions, until they arrive *by chance* at a formation which can survive in its existing form (a lucky accident which is hardly likely ever to occur); or whether we should assume as a second possibility that nature in this case follows a regular course in leading our species gradually upwards from the lower level of animality to the highest level of humanity through forcing man to employ an art which is nonetheless his own, and hence that nature develops man's original capacities by a perfectly regular process within this apparently disorderly arrangement; or whether we should rather accept the third possibility that nothing at all, or at least nothing rational, will anywhere emerge from all these actions and counter-actions among men as a whole, that things will remain as they have always been, and that it would thus be impossible to predict whether the discord which is so natural to our species is not preparing the way for a hell of evils to overtake us, however civilised our condition, in that nature, by barbaric devastation, might perhaps again destroy this civilised state and all the cultural progress hitherto achieved (a fate against which it would be impossible to guard under a rule of blind chance, with which the state of lawless freedom is in fact identical, unless we assume that the latter is secretly guided by the wisdom of nature)—these three possibilities boil down to the question of whether it is rational to assume that the order of nature is *purposive* in its parts but *purposeless* as a whole.

While the purposeless state of savagery did hold up the development of all the natural capacities of human beings, it nonetheless finally forced them, through the evils in which it involved them, to leave this state and enter into a civil constitution in which all their dormant capacities could be developed. The same applies to the barbarous freedom of established states. For while the full development of natural capacities is here likewise held up by the expenditure of each commonwealth's whole resources on armaments against the others, and by the depredations caused by war (but most of all by the necessity of constantly remaining in readiness for war), the resultant evils still have a beneficial effect. For they compel our species to discover a law of equilibrium to regulate the essentially healthy hostility which prevails among the states and is produced by their freedom. Men are compelled to reinforce this law by introducing a system of united power, hence a cosmopolitan system of general political security. This state of affairs is not completely free from *danger*, lest human energies should lapse into inactivity, but it is also not without a principle of *equality* governing the *actions and counter-actions* of these energies, lest they should destroy one another. When it is little beyond the half-way mark in its development, human nature has to endure the hardest of evils under the guise of outward prosperity before this final step (i.e. the union of states) is taken; and Rousseau's preference for the state of savagery does not appear so very mistaken if only we leave out of consideration this last stage which our species still has to surmount. We are *cultivated* to a high degree by art and science. We are *civilised* to the point of excess in all kinds of social courtesies and proprieties. But we are still a long way from the point where we could consider ourselves *morally* mature. For while the idea of morality is indeed present in culture, an application of this idea which only extends to the semblances of morality, as in love of honour and outward propriety, amounts merely to civilisation. But as long as states apply all their resources to their vain and violent schemes of expansion, thus incessantly obstructing the slow and laborious efforts of their citizens to cultivate their minds, and even deprive them of all support in these efforts, no progress in this direction can be expected. For a long internal process of careful work on the part of each commonwealth is necessary for the education of its citizens. But all good enterprises which are not grafted on to a morally good attitude of mind are nothing but illusion and outwardly glittering misery. The human race will no doubt remain in this condition until it has worked itself out of the chaotic state of its political relations in the way I have described.

Eighth Proposition

The history of the human race as a whole can be regarded as the realisation of a hidden plan of nature to bring about an internally—and for this purpose also externally—perfect political constitution as the only possible state within which all natural capacities of mankind can be developed completely. This proposition follows from the previous one. We can see that philosophy too may have its *chiliastic*⁵ expectations; but they are of such a kind that their fulfilment can be hastened, if only indirectly, by a knowledge of the idea they are based on, so that they are anything but over-fanciful. The real test is whether experience can discover anything to indicate a purposeful natural process of this kind. In my opinion, it can discover *a little*; for this cycle of events seems to take so long a time to complete, that the small part of it traversed by mankind up till now does not allow us to determine with certainty the shape of the whole cycle, and the relation of its parts to the whole. It is no easier than it is to determine, from all hitherto available astronomical observations, the path which our sun with its whole swarm of satellites is following within the vast system of the fixed stars; although from the general premise that the universe is constituted as a system and from the little which has been learnt by observation, we can conclude with sufficient certainty that a movement of this kind does exist in reality. Nevertheless, human nature is such that it cannot be indifferent even to the most remote epoch which may eventually affect our species, so long as this epoch can be expected with certainty. And in the present case, it is especially hard to be indifferent, for it appears that we might by our own rational projects accelerate the coming of this period which will be so welcome to our descendants. For this reason, even the faintest signs of its approach will be extremely important to us. The mutual relationships between states are already so sophisticated that none of them can neglect its internal culture without losing power and influence in relation to the others. Thus the purpose of nature is at least fairly well safeguarded (if not actually furthered) even by the ambitious schemes of the various states. Furthermore, civil freedom can no longer be so easily infringed without disadvantage to all trades and industries, and especially to commerce, in the event of which the state's power in its external relations will also decline. But this freedom is gradually increasing. If the citizen is deterred from seeking his personal welfare in any way he chooses which is consistent with the freedom of others, the vitality of business in general and hence also the strength of the whole are held in check. For this reason, restrictions placed upon personal activities are increasingly relaxed, and general freedom of religion is granted. And thus, although folly and caprice creep in at times, *enlightenment* gradually arises. It is a great benefit which the human race must reap even from its rulers' self-seeking schemes of expansion, if only they realise what is to their own advantage. But this enlightenment, and with it a certain sympathetic interest which the enlightened man inevitably feels for anything good which he comprehends fully, must gradually spread upwards towards the thrones and even influence their principles of government. But while, for example, the world's present rulers have no money to spare for public educational institutions or indeed for anything which concerns the world's best interests (for everything has already been calculated out in advance for the next war), they will nonetheless find that it is to their own advantage at least not to hinder their citizens' private efforts in this direction, however weak and slow they may be. But eventually, war itself gradually becomes not only a highly artificial undertaking, extremely uncertain in its outcome for both parties, but also a very dubious risk to take, since its aftermath is felt by the state in the shape of a constantly increasing national debt (a modern invention) whose repayment becomes interminable. And in addition, the effects which an upheaval in any state produces upon all the others in our continent, where all are so closely linked by trade, are so perceptible that these other states are forced by their own insecurity to offer themselves as arbiters, albeit without legal authority, so that they indirectly prepare the way for a great political body of the future, without precedent in the past. Although this political body exists for the present only in the roughest of outlines, it nonetheless seems as if a feeling is beginning to stir in all its members, each of which has an interest in maintaining the whole. And this encourages the hope that, after many revolutions, with all their transforming effects, the highest purpose of nature, a universal *cosmopolitan existence*, will at last be realised as the matrix within which all the original capacities of the human race may develop.

Ninth Proposition

A philosophical attempt to work out a universal history of the world in accordance with a plan of nature aimed at a perfect civil union of mankind, must be regarded as possible and even as capable of furthering the purpose of nature itself. It is admittedly a strange and at first sight absurd proposition to write a *history* according to an idea of how world events must develop if they are to conform to certain rational ends; it would seem that only a *novel* could result from such premises. Yet if it may be assumed that nature does not work without a plan and purposeful end, even amidst the arbitrary play of human freedom, this idea might nevertheless prove useful. And although we are too short-sighted to perceive the hidden mechanism of nature's scheme, this idea may yet serve as a guide to us in representing an otherwise planless *aggregate* of human actions as conforming, at least when considered as a whole, to a *system*. For if we start out from *Greek* history as that in which all other earlier or contemporary histories are preserved or at least authenticated,* if we next trace the influence of the Greeks upon the shaping and mis-shaping of the body politic of *Rome*, which engulfed the Greek state, and follow down to our own times the influence of Rome upon the *Barbarians* who in turn destroyed it, and if we finally add the political history of other peoples *episodically*, in so far as knowledge of them has gradually come down to us through these enlightened nations, we shall discover a regular process of improvement in the political constitutions of our continent (which will probably legislate eventually for all other continents). Furthermore, we must always concentrate our attention on civil constitutions, their laws, and the mutual relations among states, and notice how these factors, by virtue of the good they contained, served for a time to elevate and glorify nations (and with them the arts and sciences). Conversely, we should observe how their inherent defects led to their overthrow, but in such a way that a germ of enlightenment always survived, developing further with each revolution, and prepared the way for a subsequent higher level of improvement.

All this, I believe, should give us some guidance in explaining the thoroughly confused interplay of human affairs and in prophesying future political changes. Yet the same use has already been made of human history even when it was regarded as the disjointed product of unregulated freedom. But if we assume a plan of nature, we have grounds for greater hopes. For such a plan opens up the comforting prospect of a future in which we are shown from afar how the human race eventually works its way upward to a situation in which all the germs implanted by nature can be developed fully, and in which man's destiny can be fulfilled

* Only an *educated public* which has existed uninterruptedly from its origin to our times can authenticate ancient history. Beyond that, all is *terra incognita*;[6] and the history of peoples who lived outside this public can begin only from the time at which they entered it. This occurred with the *Jewish* people at the time of the Ptolemies through the Greek translation of the Bible,[7] without which their *isolated* reports would meet with little belief. From this point, once it has been properly ascertained, their narratives can be followed backwards. And it is the same with all other peoples. The first page of Thucydides, as Hume[8] puts it, is the only beginning of all true history.

here on earth. Such a *justification* of nature—or rather perhaps of *provi-dence*—is no mean motive for adopting a particular point of view in considering the world. For what is the use of lauding and holding up for contemplation the glory and wisdom of creation in the non-rational sphere of nature, if the history of mankind, the very part of this great display of supreme wisdom which contains the purpose of all the rest, is to remain a constant reproach to everything else? Such a spectacle would force us to turn away in revulsion, and, by making us despair of ever finding any completed rational aim behind it, would reduce us to hoping for it only in some other world.

It would be a misinterpretation of my intention to contend that I meant this idea of a universal history, which to some extent follows an *a priori* rule, to supersede the task of history proper, that of *empirical* composition. My idea is only a notion of what a philosophical mind, well acquainted with history, might be able to attempt from a different angle. Besides, the otherwise praiseworthy detail in which each age now composes its history must naturally cause everyone concern as to how our remote descendants will manage to cope with the burden of history which we shall bequeath to them a few centuries from now. No doubt they will value the history of the oldest times, of which the original documents would long since have vanished, only from the point of view of what interests *them*, i.e. the positive and negative achievements of nations and governments in relation to the cosmopolitan goal. We should bear this in mind, and we should likewise observe the ambitions of rulers and their servants, in order to indicate to them the only means by which they can be honourably remembered in the most distant ages. And this may provide us with another *small* motive for attempting a philosophical history of this kind.

An Answer to the Question: 'What is Enlightenment?'[1]

Enlightenment is man's emergence from his self-incurred immaturity.
Immaturity is the inability to use one's own understanding without the
guidance of another. This immaturity is *self-incurred* if its cause is not
lack of understanding, but lack of resolution and courage to use it without
the guidance of another. The motto of enlightenment is therefore: *Sapere*
aude![2] Have courage to use your *own* understanding!

Laziness and cowardice are the reasons why such a large proportion of
men, even when nature has long emancipated them from alien guidance
(*naturaliter maiorennes*),[3] nevertheless gladly remain immature for life.
For the same reasons, it is all too easy for others to set themselves up as
their guardians. It is so convenient to be immature! If I have a book to
have understanding in place of me, a spiritual adviser to have a conscience
for me, a doctor to judge my diet for me, and so on, I need not make any
efforts at all. I need not think, so long as I can pay; others will soon enough
take the tiresome job over for me. The guardians who have kindly taken
upon themselves the work of supervision will soon see to it that by far
the largest part of mankind (including the entire fair sex) should consider
the step forward to maturity not only as difficult but also as highly
dangerous. Having first infatuated their domesticated animals, and carefully prevented the docile creatures from daring to take a single step without the leading-strings to which they are tied, they next show them the
danger which threatens them if they try to walk unaided. Now this danger
is not in fact so very great, for they would certainly learn to walk eventually after a few falls. But an example of this kind is intimidating, and
usually frightens them off from further attempts.

Thus it is difficult for each separate individual to work his way out of
the immaturity which has become almost second nature to him. He has
even grown fond of it and is really incapable for the time being of using
his own understanding, because he was never allowed to make the attempt.
Dogmas and formulas, those mechanical instruments for rational use (or

rather misuse) of his natural endowments, are the ball and chain of his permanent immaturity. And if anyone did throw them off, he would still be uncertain about jumping over even the narrowest of trenches, for he would be unaccustomed to free movement of this kind. Thus only a few, by cultivating their own minds, have succeeded in freeing themselves from immaturity and in continuing boldly on their way.

There is more chance of an entire public enlightening itself. This is indeed almost inevitable, if only the public concerned is left in freedom. For there will always be a few who think for themselves, even among those appointed as guardians of the common mass. Such guardians, once they have themselves thrown off the yoke of immaturity, will disseminate the spirit of rational respect for personal value and for the duty of all men to think for themselves. The remarkable thing about this is that if the public, which was previously put under this yoke by the guardians, is suitably stirred up by some of the latter who are incapable of enlightenment, it may subsequently compel the guardians themselves to remain under the yoke. For it is very harmful to propagate prejudices, because they finally avenge themselves on the very people who first encouraged them (or whose predecessors did so). Thus a public can only achieve enlightenment slowly. A revolution may well put an end to autocratic despotism and to rapacious or power-seeking oppression, but it will never produce a true reform in ways of thinking. Instead, new prejudices, like the ones they replaced, will serve as a leash to control the great unthinking mass.

For enlightenment of this kind, all that is needed is *freedom*. And the freedom in question is the most innocuous form of all—freedom to make *public use* of one's reason in all matters. But I hear on all sides the cry: *Don't argue!* The officer says: Don't argue, get on parade! The tax-official: Don't argue, pay! The clergyman: Don't argue, believe! (Only one ruler in the world says: *Argue* as much as you like and about whatever you like, *but obey*!)⁴ All this means restrictions on freedom everywhere. But which sort of restriction prevents enlightenment, and which, instead of hindering it, can actually promote it? I reply: The *public* use of man's reason must always be free, and it alone can bring about enlightenment among men; the *private use* of reason may quite often be very narrowly restricted, however, without undue hindrance to the progress of enlightenment. But by the public use of one's own reason I mean that use which anyone may make of it *as a man of learning* addressing the entire *reading public*. What I term the private use of reason is that which a person may make of it in a particular *civil* post or office with which he is entrusted.

Now in some affairs which affect the interests of the commonwealth, we require a certain mechanism whereby some members of the commonwealth must behave purely passively, so that they may, by an artificial common agreement, be employed by the government for public ends (or at least deterred from vitiating them). It is, of course, impermissible to argue in such cases; obedience is imperative. But in so far as this or that individual who acts as part of the machine also considers himself as a member of a complete commonwealth or even of cosmopolitan society, and thence as a man of learning who may through his writings address a public in the truest sense of the word, he may indeed argue without harming the affairs in which he is employed for some of the time in a passive capacity. Thus it would be very harmful if an officer receiving an order from his superiors were to quibble openly, while on duty, about the appropriateness or usefulness of the order in question. He must simply obey. But he cannot reasonably be banned from making observations as a man of learning on the errors in the military service, and from submitting these to his public for judgement. The citizen cannot refuse to pay the taxes imposed upon him; presumptuous criticisms of such taxes, where someone is called upon to pay them, may be punished as an outrage which could lead to general insubordination. Nonetheless, the same citizen does not contravene his civil obligations if, as a learned individual, he publicly voices his thoughts on the impropriety or even injustice of such fiscal measures. In the same way, a clergyman is bound to instruct his pupils and his congregation in accordance with the doctrines of the church he serves, for he was employed by it on that condition. But as a scholar, he is completely free as well as obliged to impart to the public all his carefully considered, well-intentioned thoughts on the mistaken aspects of those doctrines, and to offer suggestions for a better arrangement of religious and ecclesiastical affairs. And there is nothing in this which need trouble the conscience. For what he teaches in pursuit of his duties as an active servant of the church is presented by him as something which he is not empowered to teach at his own discretion, but which he is employed to expound in a prescribed manner and in someone else's name. He will say: Our church teaches this or that, and these are the arguments it uses. He then extracts as much practical value as possible for his congregation from precepts to which he would not himself subscribe with full conviction, but which he can nevertheless undertake to expound, since it is not in fact wholly impossible that they may contain truth. At all events, nothing opposed to the essence of religion is present in such doctrines. For if the clergyman thought he could find anything of this sort in them, he would not be able to carry out his official duties in good conscience, and would have to resign. Thus the use which someone employed as a teacher makes of his reason in the presence of his congregation is purely *private*, since a congregation, however large it is, is never any more than a domestic gathering. In view of this, he is not and cannot be free as a priest, since he is acting on a commission imposed from outside. Conversely, as a scholar addressing the real public (i.e. the world at large) through his writings, the clergyman making *public use* of his reason enjoys unlimited freedom to use his own reason and to speak in his own person. For to maintain that the guardians of the people in spiritual matters should themselves be immature, is an absurdity which amounts to making absurdities permanent.

But should not a society of clergymen, for example an ecclesiastical synod or a venerable presbytery (as the Dutch call it), be entitled to commit itself by oath to a certain unalterable set of doctrines, in order to secure for all time a constant guardianship over each of its members, and through them over the people? I reply that this is quite impossible. A contract of this kind, concluded with a view to preventing all further enlightenment of mankind for ever, is absolutely null and void, even if it is ratified by the supreme power, by Imperial Diets and the most solemn peace treaties. One age cannot enter into an alliance on oath to put the next age in a position where it would be impossible for it to extend and correct its knowledge, particularly on such important matters, or to make any progress whatsoever in enlightenment. This would be a crime against human nature, whose original destiny lies precisely in such progress. Later generations are thus perfectly entitled to dismiss these agreements as unauthorised and criminal. To test whether any particular measure can be agreed upon as a law for a people, we need only ask whether a people could well impose such a law upon itself. This might well be possible for a specified short period as a means of introducing a certain order, pending, as it were, a better solution. This would also mean that each citizen, particularly the clergyman, would be given a free hand as a scholar to comment publicly, i.e. in his writings, on the inadequacies of current institutions. Meanwhile, the newly established order would continue to exist, until public insight into the nature of such matters had progressed and proved itself to the point where, by general consent (if not unanimously), a proposal could be submitted to the crown. This would seek to protect the congregations who had, for instance, agreed to alter their religious establishment in accordance with their own notions of what higher insight is, but it would not try to obstruct those who wanted to let things remain as before. But it is absolutely impermissible to agree, even for a single lifetime, to a permanent religious constitution which no-one might publicly question. For this would virtually nullify a phase in man's upward progress, thus making it fruitless and even detrimental to subsequent generations. A man may for his own person, and even then only for a limited period, postpone enlightening himself in matters he ought to know about. But to renounce such enlightenment completely, whether for his own person or even more so for later generations, means violating and trampling underfoot the sacred rights of mankind. But something which a people may not even impose upon itself can still less be imposed on it by a monarch; for his legislative authority depends precisely upon his uniting the collective will of the people in his own. So long as he sees to it that all true or imagined improvements are compatible with the civil order, he can otherwise leave his subjects to do whatever they find necessary for their salvation, which is none of his business. But it is his business to stop anyone forcibly hindering others from working as best they can to define and promote their salvation. It indeed detracts from his majesty if he interferes in these affairs by subjecting the writings in which his subjects attempt to clarify their religious ideas to governmental supervision. This applies if he does so acting upon his own exalted opinions—in which case he exposes himself to the reproach: *Caesar non est supra Grammaticos*[5]—but much more so if he demeans his high authority so far as to support the spiritual despotism of a few tyrants within his state against the rest of his subjects.

If it is now asked whether we at present live in an *enlightened* age, the answer is: No, but we do live in an age of *enlightenment*. As things are at present, we still have a long way to go before men as a whole can be in a position (or can even be put into a position) of using their own understanding confidently and well in religious matters, without outside guidance. But we do have distinct indications that the way is now being cleared for them to work freely in this direction, and that the obstacles to universal enlightenment, to man's emergence from his self-incurred immaturity, are gradually becoming fewer. In this respect our age is the age of enlightenment, the century of *Frederick*.[6]

A prince who does not regard it as beneath him to say that he considers it his duty, in religious matters, not to prescribe anything to his people, but to allow them complete freedom, a prince who thus even declines to accept the presumptuous title of *tolerant*, is himself enlightened. He deserves to be praised by a grateful present and posterity as the man who first liberated mankind from immaturity (as far as government is con-

cerned), and who left all men free to use their own reason in all matters
of conscience. Under his rule, ecclesiastical dignitaries, notwithstanding
their official duties, may in their capacity as scholars freely and publicly
submit to the judgement of the world their verdicts and opinions, even if
these deviate here and there from orthodox doctrine. This applies even
more to all others who are not restricted by any official duties. This spirit
of freedom is also spreading abroad, even where it has to struggle with
outward obstacles imposed by governments which misunderstand their
own function. For such governments can now witness a shining example
of how freedom may exist without in the least jeopardising public
concord and the unity of the commonwealth. Men will of their own
accord gradually work their way out of barbarism so long as artificial
measures are not deliberately adopted to keep them in it.

I have portrayed *matters of religion* as the focal point of enlightenment,
i.e. of man's emergence from his self-incurred immaturity. This is firstly
because our rulers have no interest in assuming the role of guardians over
their subjects so far as the arts and sciences are concerned, and secondly,
because religious immaturity is the most pernicious and dishonourable
variety of all. But the attitude of mind of a head of state who favours freedom in the arts and sciences extends even further, for he realises that there
is no danger even to his *legislation* if he allows his subjects to make *public*
use of their own reason and to put before the public their thoughts on
better ways of drawing up laws, even if this entails forthright criticism of
the current legislation. We have before us a brilliant example of this kind,
in which no monarch has yet surpassed the one to whom we now pay
tribute.

But only a ruler who is himself enlightened and has no fear of phantoms,
yet who likewise has at hand a well-disciplined and numerous army to
guarantee public security, may say what no republic would dare to say:
Argue as much as you like and about whatever you like, but obey! This
reveals to us a strange and unexpected pattern in human affairs (such as we
shall always find if we consider them in the widest sense, in which nearly
everything is paradoxical). A high degree of civil freedom seems advan-
tageous to a people's *intellectual* freedom, yet it also sets up insuperable
barriers to it. Conversely, a lesser degree of civil freedom gives intellectual
freedom enough room to expand to its fullest extent. Thus once the germ
on which nature has lavished most care—man's inclination and vocation
to *think freely*—has developed within this hard shell, it gradually reacts
upon the mentality of the people, who thus gradually become increasingly able to *act freely*. Eventually, it even influences the principles of

governments, which find that they can themselves profit by treating man, who is *more than a machine*,[7] in a manner appropriate to his dignity.*

Königsberg in Prussia, 30th September, 1784.

* I read today on the 30th September in Büsching's[8] *Wöchentliche Nachrichten* of 13th September a notice concerning this month's *Berlinische Monatsschrift*. The notice mentions Mendelssohn's[9] answer to the same question as that which I have answered. I have not yet seen this journal, otherwise I should have held back the above reflections. I let them stand only as a means of finding out by comparison how far the thoughts of two individuals may coincide by chance.

On the Common Saying: 'This May be True in Theory, but it does not Apply in Practice'[1]

A collection of rules, even of practical rules, is termed a *theory* if the rules concerned are envisaged as principles of a fairly general nature, and if they are abstracted from numerous conditions which, nonetheless, necessarily influence their practical application. Conversely, not all activities are called *practice*, but only those realisations of a particular purpose which are considered to comply with certain generally conceived principles of procedure.

It is obvious that no matter how complete the theory may be, a middle term is required between theory and practice, providing a link and a transition from one to the other. For a concept of the understanding, which contains the general rule, must be supplemented by an act of judgement whereby the practitioner distinguishes instances where the rule applies from those where it does not. And since rules cannot in turn be provided on every occasion to direct the judgement in subsuming each instance under the previous rule (for this would involve an infinite regress), theoreticians will be found who can never in all their lives become practical, since they lack judgement. There are, for example, doctors or lawyers who did well during their schooling but who do not know how to act when asked to give advice. But even where a natural talent for judgement is present, there may still be a lack of premises. In other words, the theory may be incomplete, and can perhaps be perfected only by future experiments and experiences from which the newly qualified doctor, agriculturalist or economist can and ought to abstract new rules for himself to complete his theory. It is therefore not the fault of the theory if it is of little practical use in such cases. The fault is that there is *not enough* theory; the person concerned ought to have learnt from experience. What he learnt from experience might well be true theory,

61

even if he were unable to impart it to others and to expound it as a teacher in systematic general propositions, and were consequently unable to claim the title of a theoretical physician, agriculturalist or the like. Thus no-one can pretend to be practically versed in a branch of knowledge and yet treat theory with scorn, without exposing the fact that he is an ignoramus in his subject. He no doubt imagines that he can get further than he could through theory if he gropes around in experiments and experiences, without collecting certain principles (which in fact amount to what we term theory) and without relating his activities to an integral whole (which, if treated methodically, is what we call a system).

Yet it is easier to excuse an ignoramus who claims that theory is unnecessary and superfluous in his supposed practice than a would-be expert who admits the value of theory for teaching purposes, for example as a mental exercise, but at the same time maintains that it is quite different in practice, and that anyone leaving his studies to go out into the world will realise he has been pursuing empty ideals and philosopher's dreams—in short, that whatever sounds good in theory has no practical validity. (This doctrine is often expressed as: 'this or that proposition is valid *in thesi*, but not *in hypothesi*'.) Now all of us would merely ridicule the empirical engineer who criticised general mechanics or the artilleryman who criticised the mathematical theory of ballistics by declaring that, while the theory is ingeniously conceived, it is not valid in practice, since experience in applying it gives results quite different from those predicted theoretically. For if mechanics were supplemented by the theory of friction and ballistics by the theory of air resistance, in other words if only more theory were added, these theoretical disciplines would harmonise very well with practice. But a theory which concerns objects of perception[2] is quite different from one in which such objects are represented only through concepts, as with objects of mathematics and of philosophy. The latter objects can perhaps quite legitimately be *thought* of by reason, yet it may be impossible for them to be *given*. They may merely exist as empty ideas which either cannot be used at all in practice or only with some practical disadvantages. This would mean that the aforesaid common saying might well be correct in such cases.

But in a theory founded on the *concept of duty*, any worries about the empty ideality of the concept completely disappear. For it would not be a duty to strive after a certain effect of our will if this effect were impossible in experience (whether we envisage the experience as complete or as progressively approximating to completion). And it is with theory of this kind that the present essay is exclusively concerned. For to the shame of philosophy, it is not uncommonly alleged of such theory that whatever may be correct in it is in fact invalid in practice. We usually hear this said in an arrogant, disdainful tone, which comes of presuming to use experience to reform reason itself in the very attributes which do it most credit. Such illusory wisdom imagines it can see further and more clearly with its mole-like gaze fixed on experience than with the eyes which were bestowed on a being designed to stand upright and to scan the heavens.

This maxim, so very common in our sententious, inactive times, does very great harm if applied to matters of morality, i.e. to moral or legal duty. For in such cases, the canon of reason is related to practice in such a way that the value of the practice depends entirely upon its appropriateness to the theory it is based on; all is lost if the empirical (hence contingent) conditions governing the execution of the law are made into conditions of the law itself, so that a practice calculated to produce a result which *previous* experience makes probable is given the right to dominate a theory which is in fact self-sufficient.

I shall divide up this essay in terms of three points of view which the worthy gentleman[3] who so boldly criticises theories and systems adopts in judging his objects. The three attitudes are those of the private individual or *man of affairs*, the *statesman*, and the *man of the world* or cosmopolitan. These three individuals are united in attacking the *academic*, who works for them all, for their own good, on matters of theory. Since they fancy that they understand this better than he does, they seek to relegate him to his classroom (*illa se iactet in aula!*)[4] as a pedant who, unfitted for practical affairs, merely stands in the way of their experienced wisdom.

We shall therefore deal with the relationship of theory to practice in three separate areas: firstly in *morality* in general, with regard to the welfare of each *individual man*, secondly in *politics*, with regard to the welfare of *states*, and thirdly in the *cosmopolitical* sphere, with regard to the welfare of the *human race* as a whole, in so far as the welfare of mankind is increasing within a series of developments extending into all future ages. The titles of the sections, for reasons arising out of the essay itself, will express the relationship of theory to practice in *morality*, in *political right* [*Staatsrecht*], and in *international right* [*Völkerrecht*].[5]

I

ON THE RELATIONSHIP OF THEORY TO PRACTICE IN MORALITY IN GENERAL

(*In Reply to some Objections by Professor Garve**)⁶*

Before I proceed to the actual controversy over what is valid in theory and practice in the application of one and the same concept, I must compare my theory, as I have myself presented it elsewhere, with the picture which Professor Garve presents of it. We may thus see in advance whether we have understood one another.

A. I had provisionally designated the study of morals as the introduction to a discipline which would teach us not how to be happy, but how we should become worthy of happiness.† Nor had I omitted to point out at the same time that man is not thereby expected to *renounce* his natural aim of attaining happiness as soon as the question of following his duty arises; for like any finite rational being, he simply cannot do so. Instead, he must completely *abstract* from such considerations as soon as the imperative of duty supervenes, and must on no account make them a *condition* of his obeying the law prescribed to him by reason. He must indeed make every possible conscious effort to ensure that no *motive* derived from the desire for happiness imperceptibly infiltrates his conceptions of duty. To do this, he should think rather of the sacrifices which obedience to duty (i.e. virtue) entails than of the benefits he might reap from it, so that he will comprehend the imperative of duty in its full authority as a self-sufficient law, independent of all other influences, which requires unconditional obedience.

a. This proposition of mine is expressed by Garve as follows: I had asserted 'that adherence to the moral law, regardless of happiness, is *the*

---

* Cf. *Versuche über verschiedne Gegenstände aus der Moral und Literatur* (*Essays on Various Topics from Morality and Literature*), by C. Garve, Pt. I, pp. 111–16. I call this estimable writer's disagreements with my propositions *objections*, for they concern matters in which (as I hope) he wishes to reach agreement with me. They are not attacks, which are disparaging statements designed to provoke defence, for which I here find neither the space nor the inclination.

† Being worthy of happiness is that quality of a person which depends upon the subject's own individual free will and in accordance with which a universal reason, legislating both to nature and to the free will, would agree with all the aims of that person. It is thus entirely different from any aptitude for attaining happiness itself. For if a person's will does not harmonise with the only form of will which is fit to legislate universally to the reason, and thus cannot be contained within the latter (in other words, if his will conflicts with morality), he is not worthy of happiness and of that gift of attaining happiness with which nature endowed him.

one and only ultimate end for man, and that it must be considered as the creator's unique intention'. (My theory is that the creator's unique inten tion is neither human morality in itself nor happiness in itself, but the highest good possible on earth, the union and harmony of them both.)

B. I had further noted that this concept of duty does not need to be based on any particular end, but rather itself *occasions* a new end for the human will, that of striving with all one's power towards the highest good possible on earth, towards the universal happiness of the whole world, combined with and in keeping with the purest morality. Since the attainment of this good lies within our power in one of its two aspects, but not in both taken together, it elicits from our reason a faith, *for practical purposes*, in a moral being who governs the world, and in a future existence. This does not mean that faith in both of these is a necessary condition lending 'support and stability' (i.e. a solid foundation and enough strength to constitute a *motive*) to the general concept of duty. It merely ensures that this concept acquires an *object* in the shape of an ideal of pure reason.* For in itself, duty is nothing more than a *limitation* of the will within a universal legislation which was made possible by an initially

* The necessity of assuming as the ultimate end of all things a *highest good* on earth, which it is possible to achieve with our collaboration, is not a necessity created by a lack of moral incentives, but by a lack of external circumstances within which an object appropriate to these incentives can alone be produced as an end in itself, as an *ultimate moral end*. For there can be no *will* without an end in view, although we must abstract from this end whenever the question of straightforward legal compulsion of our deeds arises, in which case the law alone becomes its determinant. But not every end is moral (that of personal happiness, for example, is not); the end must be an unselfish one. And the necessity of an ultimate end posited by pure reason and comprehending the totality of all ends within a single principle (i.e. a world in which the highest possible good can be realised with our collaboration) is a necessity experienced by the unselfish will as it *rises beyond* mere obedience to formal laws and creates as its own object the highest good. This idea of the totality of all ends is a peculiar kind of determinant for the will. For it basically implies that *if* we stand in a moral relationship to things in the world around us, we must everywhere obey the moral law; and to this is added the further duty of working with all our power to *ensure* that the state of affairs described (i.e. a world conforming to the highest moral ends) will actually exist. In all this, man may see himself as analogous to the divinity. For while the divinity has no subjective need of any external object, it cannot be conceived of as closed up within itself, but only as compelled by the very awareness of its own all-sufficiency to produce the highest good outside itself. In the case of the supreme being, this necessity (which corresponds to duty in man) can be envisaged *by us* only as a moral need. With man likewise, the motive provided by the idea of the highest possible earthly good, attainable through his collaboration, is therefore not that of his own intended happiness, but only that of the idea as an end in itself and of obedience to it as a duty. For it does not hold out any prospect of happiness in the absolute sense, but only of a constant ratio between happiness and the worthiness of the subject, whatever the latter may be. But a determinant of the will which imposes this restriction both on itself and on its intention of becoming part of a whole such as we have described is *not selfish*.

65

accepted maxim. The object or aim of the will can be of any kind what-soever (even including happiness). But in this case, we completely abstract from whatever particular end is adopted. Thus so far as the *principle* of morality is concerned, the doctrine of the *highest good* as the ultimate end of a will which is determined by this doctrine and which conforms to its laws can be by-passed and set aside as incidental. And it will emerge from what follows that the actual controversy is not in fact concerned with this at all, but only with morality in general.

  b. Garve expresses the above propositions as follows: 'The virtuous man cannot and may not ever lose sight of this consideration (i.e. that of his own happiness), since he would otherwise be completely without access to the invisible world and to belief in the existence of God and of immortality. Such belief, according to this theory, is absolutely neces-sary *to lend support and stability to the moral system.*' He concludes by briefly summing up as follows the statements he ascribes to me: 'The virtuous man, according to these principles, constantly strives to be worthy of happiness, but never, *in so far as* he is truly virtuous, to be actually happy.' (The words *in so far as* create an ambiguity which must be eliminated before we go any further. They can signify *in the act* of submit-ting, as a virtuous man, to one's duty—in which case the sentence is perfectly compatible with my theory—or they could imply that if he is never anything but virtuous, the virtuous man should not take happiness into consideration at all, even where the question of duty does not arise and where there is no conflict with duty—in which case the sentence is totally at variance with my statements.)

  These objections are therefore nothing but misunderstandings (for I have no wish to see them as misrepresentations). Their very possibility would astonish us, if it were not that such phenomena can be adequately explained by the human tendency to follow a habitual train of thought, even in judging the thoughts of others, and thus to carry the former over into the latter.

  Garve follows up this polemical account of the above moral principle with a dogmatic exposition of its direct opposite. By analytical methods, he comes to the following conclusion: 'In the ordering of *concepts*, the states which entitle us to give *preference* to one rather than others must first be recognised and distinguished before we choose any one of them and thus decide in advance what aim we shall pursue. But a state which a being who is aware of himself and of his own state would *prefer* to other ways of existence as soon as he saw it before him, is a *good* state; and a series of good states is the most general notion expressed by the word *happiness.*' He continues: 'A law presupposes motives, but motives presuppose that a difference has already been recognised between a worse state and a better one. This recognised difference is the element of the concept of happiness', and so on. And again: '*Happiness*, in the most general sense of the word, *is the source of the motives behind every effort*, including obedience to the moral law. I must first of all know whether something is good before I can ask whether the fulfilment of moral duties belongs to the category of good things. Man must have an *incentive* to set him in motion *before* he can be given a *goal** towards which this motion should be directed.'

This argument is nothing more than a play upon the ambiguity of the word *good*. For it can be taken to mean something absolutely good in itself, as opposed to that which is evil in itself, or something only relatively good, as opposed to something more or less good than itself. In the latter case, the preferred state may be only comparatively better, yet nonetheless evil in itself. The maxim of absolute obedience to a categorically binding law of the free will (i.e. of duty), without reference to any ulterior end, is essentially different (i.e. different *in kind*) from the maxim of pursuing, as a motive for a certain way of acting, the end which nature itself has imposed upon us and which is generally known as happiness. For the first maxim is good in itself, but the second is not. The second may, if it conflicts with duty, be thoroughly evil. But if a certain end is made basic, so that no law is absolutely binding but always relative to the end adopted, two opposing actions might both be relatively good, with one better than the other, which would then count as comparatively evil. For they would differ only in *degree*, not in *kind*. And it is the same with all actions whose motive is not the absolute law of reason (duty), but an end which we have arbitrarily taken as a basis. For this end will be a part of the total of ends whose attainment we call happiness, and one action may contribute more, and another less to my happiness, so that one will be better or worse than the other. But to *give preference* to one state rather than another as a determinant of the will is merely an act of freedom (*res merae facultatis*,[7] as the lawyers say) which takes no account of whether the particular determinant is good or evil in itself, and is thus neutral in both respects.

A state of being bound by a certain *given end* which I have preferred to all others *of the same kind*, is a comparatively better state in terms of

---

* This is exactly what I myself insist upon. The incentive which men can have before they are given a specific goal (or end) can obviously be none other than the law itself, through the esteem which it inspires (irrespective of what ends one may have and seek to attain through obedience to the law). For the law, as the formal aspect of will, is all that remains if we discount the will's particular content (i.e. the goal, as Garve calls it).

happiness (which *reason* never recognises as more than *relatively good*, according to the extent to which a person is worthy of it). But that state of consciously preferring the moral law of duty in cases where it conflicts with certain of my ends is not just a better state, but the only state which is good in itself. It is good in a completely different sense, in that it takes no account whatsoever of any ends that may present themselves (including their sum total, which is happiness). The determinant in this case is not the content of the will (i.e. a particular basic object) but the pure form of universal lawfulness embodied in its maxim.—Thus it can by no means be said that I class as happiness every state which I *prefer* to all other modes of existence. For I must first be certain that I am not acting against my duty. Only then am I entitled to look round for happiness, in so far as I can reconcile it with the state I know to be morally (not physically) good.*

The will, however, must have *motives*. But these are not objects of *physical feeling* as predetermined ends in themselves. They are none other than the absolute *law* itself, and the will's receptivity to it as an absolute compulsion is known as *moral feeling*. This feeling is therefore not the cause but the effect of the will's determinant, and we should not have the least awareness of it within ourselves if such compulsion were not already present in us. Thus the old refrain that this feeling, i.e. a desire which we take as our end, is the first cause determining the will, so that happiness (of which that desire is an element) is the basis of all objective necessity of action and thus of all moral obligations, is a piece of *trivial sophistry*. For if we go on asking even after we know the cause of a given event, we end up by making an effect the cause of itself.

I have now reached the point which really concerns us here, the task of testing and illustrating with examples the supposedly conflicting interest of theory and practice in philosophy. Garve's above-quoted essay furnishes the best possible illustration. He first says (with reference to the distinction I make between a doctrine of how to be *happy* and one of how to be *worthy* of happiness): 'For my own part, I admit that while I well understand this distinction among ideas in my *mind*, I do not find any such distinction among the desires and aspirations in my *heart*, so that I fail

* Happiness embodies everything that nature has given us and nothing else. But virtue embodies that which no-one but man can give or take away from himself. If it were replied that by deviating from the latter, man could at least incur blame and moral self-reproach, hence dissatisfaction and unhappiness, we might by all means agree. But only the virtuous man or one who is on the way to virtue is capable of this pure moral dissatisfaction, which comes not from any disadvantage resulting from his actions, but from their unlawfulness itself. His dissatisfaction is consequently not the cause but the effect of his being virtuous; and this unhappiness (if we choose to describe regrets over a crime as such) could not furnish a motive for being virtuous.

even to comprehend how anyone can be aware of having neatly set apart his actual desire for happiness and thus of having fulfilled his duty completely unselfishly.'

I shall answer the last point first. I willingly concede that no-one can have certain awareness of *having fulfilled* his duty completely unselfishly. For this is part of inward experience, and such awareness of one's psychological state would involve an absolutely clear conception of all the secondary notions and considerations which, through imagination, habit and inclination, accompany the concept of duty. And this is too much to ask for. Besides, the non-existence of something (including that of an unconsciously intended advantage) can never be an object of experience. But man is aware with the utmost clarity that he *ought to fulfil* his duty completely unselfishly, and *must* totally separate his desire for happiness from the concept of duty, in order to preserve the latter's purity. For if anyone thought he did not have this clear awareness, he could reasonably be asked to acquire it, so far as his powers might permit. And he must be able to do so, for the true value of morality consists precisely in the purity of its concept. Perhaps no recognised and respected duty has ever been carried out by anyone without some selfishness or interference from other motives; perhaps no-one will ever succeed in doing so, however hard he tries. But by careful self-examination, we can perceive a certain amount. We can be aware not so much of any accompanying motives, but rather of our own self-denial with respect to many motives which conflict with the idea of duty. In other words, we can be aware of the maxim of striving towards moral purity. And this is sufficient for us to observe our duty. On the other hand, it is the death of all morality if we make it our maxim to foster such motives, on the pretext that human nature does not permit moral purity (which no-one can say with certainty in any case).

As for Garve's above confession that he cannot find such a distinction (more correctly a separation) in his *heart*, I have no hesitation in contradicting his self-accusation outright and in championing his heart against his mind. For as an honest man, he has in fact always found this separation in his heart, i.e. in the determinants of his will. But even for the purposes of speculative thinking and of comprehending that which is incomprehensible or inexplicable (i.e. the possibility of categorical imperatives such as those of duty), he was unable in his own mind to reconcile this separation with the usual principles of psychological explanation, which are all based on the mechanism of natural necessity.*

* Garve, in his notes to Cicero's *De Officiis*, 1783 edition, p. 69, makes the following admission, which does credit to his own acuteness: 'It is my innermost conviction that

But I must loudly and resolutely disagree with Garve when he concludes by saying: 'Such subtle distinctions between ideas become *obscure* even when we *think* about particular objects; but they *vanish completely* when it comes to *action*, when they are supposed to apply to desires and intentions. The more simple, rapid and *devoid of clear ideas* the step from consideration of motives to actual action is, the less possible it is to determine exactly and unerringly the precise momentum which each motive has contributed in guiding the step in this and in no other direction.'

The concept of duty in its complete purity is incomparably simpler, clearer and more natural and easily comprehensible to everyone than any motive derived from, combined with, or influenced by happiness, for motives involving happiness always require a great deal of resourcefulness and deliberation. Besides, the concept of duty, if it is presented to the exclusive judgement of even the most ordinary human reason, and confronts the human will separately and in actual opposition to other motives, is far *more powerful*, incisive and likely to promote success than all incentives borrowed from the latter selfish principle. Let us take, for example, the case of someone who has under his trust an endowment (*depositum*), the owner of which is deceased, while the heirs are ignorant of and could never discover its existence. Let us also suppose that the trustee of this deposit, through no fault of his own, has at this very time suffered a complete collapse in his financial circumstances, and has around him a miserable family of wife and children, oppressed by want, and knows that he could at once relieve this distress if he appropriated the pledge entrusted to him. He is also benevolent and philanthropic, while the heirs are rich, uncharitable, thoroughly extravagant and luxurious, so that it would make little difference if the aforesaid addition to their property were thrown into the sea. Now if this case is explained even to a child of around eight or nine years old, and it is asked whether it might be permissible under the circumstances to devote the deposit to one's own use, the reply will undoubtedly be negative. Whoever we ask will merely answer, without further ado, that *it is wrong*, i.e. that it conflicts with duty. Nothing can be clearer than this, while it is genuinely not the case that the trustee would

freedom will always remain unresolved and will never be explained.' It is absolutely impossible to find a proof of its reality either in direct or indirect experience, and it cannot be accepted without any proof. Such a proof cannot be derived from purely theoretical considerations (for these would have to be sought in experience), nor therefore from purely practical propositions of reason, nor alternatively from practical propositions in the technical sense (for these too would have to be based on experience), but accordingly only from moral-practical ones. One must therefore wonder why Garve did not take refuge in the concept of freedom, at least in order to salvage the possibility of such imperatives.

be furthering his own *happiness* if he surrendered the deposit. For if he expected his decision to be dictated by such considerations, he might for instance reason as follows: 'If I give up unasked to the real owners the property I have here, they will presumably reward me for my honesty. Or if they do not, I will still acquire a good reputation at large, and this could prove very remunerative. But all this is most uncertain. Yet various doubts can also be raised in support of this argument. For if I were to embezzle the deposit to relieve my depressed circumstances at one stroke, I should incur suspicion, if I made quick use of it, as to how and by what means I had so soon bettered my circumstances. But if I used it slowly, my poverty would meanwhile increase so greatly that it would become impossible to alleviate it at all.' Thus a will which follows the maxim of happiness vacillates between various motives in trying to reach a decision. For it considers the possible results of its decision, and these are highly uncertain; and it takes a good head to find a way out of the host of arguments and counter-arguments without miscalculating the total effect. On the other hand, if we ask what duty requires, there is no confusion whatsoever about the answer, and we are at once certain what action to take. We even feel, if the concept of duty means anything to us, a revulsion at the very idea of calculating the advantages we might gain through violating our duty, just as if the choice were still a real one.

When Garve says that these distinctions (which, as we have shown, are not so subtle as he thinks, but are inscribed in the soul of man in the plainest and most legible characters) *vanish completely when it comes to action*, this contradicts even his own experience. Admittedly, it does not contradict the experience which the *history* of maxims derived from various principles provides. Such experience, alas, proves that most of them are based on selfishness. But it does contradict our (necessarily inward) experience that no idea can so greatly elevate the human mind and inspire it with such enthusiasm as that of a pure moral conviction, respecting duty above all else, struggling with countless evils of existence and even with their most seductive temptations, and yet overcoming them—for we may rightly assume that man can do so. The fact that man is aware that he can do this just because he ought to discloses within him an ample store of divine capabilities and inspires him, so to speak, with a holy awe at the greatness and sublimity of his true vocation. And if man were frequently enough reminded so that it became a habit for him to purge virtue of all the superfluous wealth of advantages which could be amassed through obeying his duty, and if he always conceived of virtue in its complete purity and made it a principle of private and public instruction always to use this insight (a method of inculcating duties which has almost invariably been neglected), human morality would soon be improved. Historical experience has not proved the success of our ethical doctrines. The fault lies in the erroneous assumption that a motive derived from the idea of duty in itself is far too subtle for the common understanding, whereas a cruder motive based on advantages which can be expected either in this or in a future world from obedience to duty (without consideration of the latter itself as a motive) would act more forcibly upon the mind. Another fault is that it has hitherto been a principle of education and homiletics to place more stress on the quest for happiness than on worthiness of happiness, which is the highest postulate of reason. For *precepts* on how to be happy or at least how to avoid one's own disadvantage are not the same as *commandments*. They are never absolutely binding, for having first warned us, they leave us free to choose what we think best, provided that we are prepared to face the consequences. And any evils which might result from our failure to follow the advice we were given could not justifiably be regarded as penalties. For penalties apply only to a free will which violates the law. But nature and inclination cannot give laws to the free will. It is quite different with the idea of duty, for if we violate it, even without considering the disadvantages which might result, we feel the consequences directly, and appear despicable and culpable in our own eyes.

Here, then, is a clear proof that everything in morals which is true in theory must also be valid in practice. As a human being, a being subjected by his own reason to certain duties, each of us is therefore a *man of affairs* and since, as human beings, we never grow out of the school of wisdom, we cannot arrogantly and scornfully relegate the adherent of theory to the classroom and set ourselves up as better trained by experience in all that a man is and all that can be required of him. For all this experience will not in any way help us to escape the precepts of theory, but at most to learn how to apply it in better and more universal ways after we have assimilated it into our principles. But we are here concerned only with the latter, and not with any pragmatic abilities.

II

ON THE RELATIONSHIP OF THEORY TO PRACTICE
IN POLITICAL RIGHT

(*Against Hobbes*)[8]

Among all the contracts by which a large group of men unites to form a society (*pactum sociale*), the contract establishing a *civil constitution* (*pactum unionis civilis*) is of an exceptional nature. For while, so far as its execution is concerned, it has much in common with all others that are likewise directed towards a chosen end to be pursued by joint effort, it is essentially different from all others in the principle of its constitution (*constitutionis civilis*). In all social contracts, we find a union of many individuals for some common end which they all *share*. But a union as an end in itself which they all *ought to share* and which is thus an absolute and primary duty in all external relationships whatsoever among human beings (who cannot avoid mutually influencing one another), is only found in a society in so far as it constitutes a civil state, i.e. a commonwealth. And the end which is a duty in itself in such external relationships, and which is indeed the highest formal condition (*conditio sine qua non*) of all other external duties, is the *right* of men *under coercive public laws* by which each can be given what is due to him and secured against attack from any others. But the whole concept of an external right is derived entirely from the concept of *freedom* in the mutual external relationships of human beings, and has nothing to do with the end which all men have by nature (i.e. the aim of achieving happiness) or with the recognised means of attaining this end. And thus the latter end must on no account interfere as a determinant with the laws governing external right. *Right* is the restriction of each individual's freedom so that it harmonises with the freedom of everyone else (in so far as this is possible within the terms of a general law). And *public right* is the distinctive quality of the *external laws* which make this constant harmony possible. Since every restriction of freedom through the arbitrary will of another party is termed *coercion*, it follows that a civil constitution is a relationship among *free* men who are subject to coercive laws, while they retain their freedom within the general union with their fellows. Such is the requirement of pure reason, which legislates *a priori*, regardless of all empirical ends (which can all be summed up under the general heading of happiness). Men have different views on the empirical end of happiness and what it consists of, so that as far as happiness is concerned, their will cannot be brought under any common principle nor thus under any external law harmonising with the freedom of everyone.

The civil state, regarded purely as a lawful state, is based on the following *a priori* principles:

1. The *freedom* of every member of society as a *human being*.
2. The *equality* of each with all the others as a *subject*.
3. The *independence* of each member of a commonwealth as a *citizen*.

These principles are not so much laws given by an already established state, as laws by which a state can alone be established in accordance with pure rational principles of external human right. Thus:

1. Man's *freedom* as a human being, as a principle for the constitution of a commonwealth, can be expressed in the following formula. No-one can compel me to be happy in accordance with his conception of the welfare of others, for each may seek his happiness in whatever way he sees fit, so long as he does not infringe upon the freedom of others to pursue a similar end which can be reconciled with the freedom of everyone else within a workable general law—i.e. he must accord to others the same right as he enjoys himself. A government might be established on the principle of benevolence towards the people, like that of a father towards his children. Under such a *paternal government* (*imperium paternale*), the subjects, as immature children who cannot distinguish what is truly useful or harmful to themselves, would be obliged to behave purely passively and to rely upon the judgement of the head of state as to how they *ought* to be happy, and upon his kindness in willing their happiness at all. Such a government is the greatest conceivable *despotism*, i.e. a constitution which suspends the entire freedom of its subjects, who thenceforth have no rights whatsoever. The only conceivable government for men who are capable of possessing rights, even if the ruler is benevolent, is not a *paternal* but a *patriotic* government (*imperium non paternale, sed patrioticum*). A *patriotic* attitude is one where everyone in the state, not excepting its head, regards the commonwealth as a maternal womb, or the land as the paternal ground from which he himself sprang and which he must leave to his descendants as a treasured pledge. Each regards himself as authorised to protect the rights of the commonwealth by laws of the general will, but not to submit it to his personal use at his own absolute pleasure. This right of freedom belongs to each member of the commonwealth as a human being, in so far as each is a being capable of possessing rights.

2. Man's *equality* as a subject might be formulated as follows. Each member of the commonwealth has rights of coercion in relation to all the

others, except in relation to the head of state. For he alone is not a member of the commonwealth, but its creator or preserver, and he alone is authorised to coerce others without being subject to any coercive law himself. But all who are subject to laws are the subjects of a state, and are thus subject to the right of coercion along with all other members of the commonwealth; the only exception is a single person (in either the physical or the moral sense of the word), the head of state, through whom alone the rightful coercion of all others can be exercised. For if he too could be coerced, he would not be the head of state, and the hierarchy of subordination would ascend infinitely. But if there were two persons exempt from coercion, neither would be subject to coercive laws, and neither could do to the other anything contrary to right, which is impossible.

This uniform equality of human beings as subjects of a state is, however, perfectly consistent with the utmost inequality of the mass in the degree of its possessions, whether these take the form of physical or mental superiority over others, or of fortuitous external property and of particular rights (of which there may be many) with respect to others. Thus the welfare of the one depends very much on the will of the other (the poor depending on the rich), the one must obey the other (as the child its parents or the wife her husband), the one serves (the labourer) while the other pays, etc. Nevertheless, they are all equal as subjects *before the law*, which, as the pronouncement of the general will, can only be single in form, and which concerns the form of right and not the material or object in relation to which I possess rights. For no-one can coerce anyone else other than through the public law and its executor, the head of state, while everyone else can resist the others in the same way and to the same degree. No-one, however, can lose this authority to coerce others and to have rights towards them except through committing a crime. And no-one can voluntarily renounce his rights by a contract or legal transaction to the effect that he has no rights but only duties, for such a contract would deprive him of the right to make a contract, and would thus invalidate the one he had already made.

From this idea of the equality of men as subjects in a commonwealth, there emerges this further formula: every member of the commonwealth must be entitled to reach any degree of rank which a subject can earn through his talent, his industry and his good fortune. And his fellow-subjects may not stand in his way by *hereditary* prerogatives or privileges of rank and thereby hold him and his descendants back indefinitely.

All right consists solely in the restriction of the freedom of others, with the qualification that their freedom can co-exist with my freedom within the terms of a general law; and public right in a commonwealth is simply a state of affairs regulated by a real legislation which conforms to this principle and is backed up by power, and under which a whole people live as subjects in a lawful state (*status iuridicus*). This is what we call a civil state, and it is characterised by equality in the effects and counter-effects of freely willed actions which limit one another in accordance with the general law of freedom. Thus the *birthright* of each individual in such a state (i.e. before he has performed any acts which can be judged in relation to right) is absolutely *equal* as regards his authority to coerce others to use their freedom in a way which harmonises with his freedom. Since birth is not an act on the part of the one who is born, it cannot create any inequality in his legal position and cannot make him submit to any coercive laws except in so far as he is a subject, along with all the others, of the one supreme legislative power. Thus no member of the commonwealth can have a hereditary privilege as against his fellow-subjects; and no-one can hand down to his descendants the privileges attached to the rank he occupies in the commonwealth, nor act as if he were qualified as a ruler by birth and forcibly prevent others from reaching the higher levels of the hierarchy (which are *superior* and *inferior*, but never *imperans* and *subiectus*) through their own merit. He may hand down everything else, so long as it is material and not pertaining to his person, for it may be acquired and disposed of as property and may over a series of generations create considerable inequalities in wealth among the members of the commonwealth (the employee and the employer, the landowner and the agricultural servants, etc.). But he may not prevent his subordinates from raising themselves to his own level if they are able and entitled to do so by their talent, industry and good fortune. If this were not so, he would be allowed to practise coercion without himself being subject to coercive counter-measures from others, and would thus be more than their fellow-subject. No-one who lives within the lawful state of a commonwealth can forfeit this equality other than through some crime of his own, but never by contract or through military force (*occupatio bellica*). For no legal transaction on his part or on that of anyone else can make him cease to be his own master. He cannot become like a domestic animal to be employed in any chosen capacity and retained therein without consent for any desired period, even with the reservation (which is at times sanctioned by religion, as among the Indians) that he may not be maimed or killed. He can be considered happy in any condition so long as he is aware that, if he does not reach the same level as others, the fault lies either with himself (i.e. lack of ability or serious endeavour) or with circumstances for which he cannot blame others, and not with the irresistible will of any outside party. For as far as right is concerned, his fellow-subjects have no advantage over him.*

3. The *independence* (*sibisufficientia*) of a member of the commonwealth as a *citizen*, i.e. as a co-legislator, may be defined as follows. In the question of actual legislation, all who are free and equal under existing public laws may be considered equal, but not as regards the right to make these laws. Those who are not entitled to this right are nonetheless obliged, as members of the commonwealth, to comply with these laws, and they thus likewise enjoy their protection (not as *citizens* but as co-beneficiaries of this protection). For all right depends on laws. But a public law which defines for everyone that which is permitted and prohibited by right, is the act of a public will, from which all right proceeds and which must not therefore itself be able to do an injustice to any one. And this requires no less than the will of the entire people (since all men decide for all men and each decides for himself). For only towards oneself can one never act unjustly. But on the other hand, the will of another person cannot decide anything for someone without injustice, so that the law made by this other person would require a further law to limit his legislation. Thus an individual will cannot legislate for a commonwealth. For this requires freedom, equality and *unity* of the will of *all* the members. And the prerequisite for unity, since it necessitates a general vote (if freedom and equality are both present), is independence. The basic law, which can come only from the general, united will of the people, is called the *original contract*.

Anyone who has the right to vote on this legislation is a *citizen* (*citoyen*,

---

* If we try to find a definite meaning for the word *gracious*, as distinct from kind, beneficent, protective etc., we see that it can be attributed only to a person to whom no *coercive rights* apply. Thus only the head of the *state's government*, who enacts and distributes all benefits that are possible within the public laws (for the *sovereign* who provides them is, as it were, invisible, and is not an agent but the personified law itself), can be given the title of *gracious lord*, for he is the only individual to whom coercive rights do not apply. And even in an aristocratic government, as for example in Venice, the *senate* is the only 'gracious lord'. The nobles who belong to it, even including the *Doge* (for only the *plenary council* is the sovereign), are all subjects and equal to the others so far as the exercise of rights is concerned, for each subject has coercive rights towards every one of them. Princes (i.e. persons with a hereditary right to become rulers) are themselves called gracious lords only with future reference, an account of their claims to become rulers (i.e. by courtly etiquette, *par courtoisie*). But as owners of property, they are nonetheless fellow-subjects of the others, and even the humblest of their servants must possess a right of coercion against them through the head of state. Thus there can be no more than one gracious lord in a state. And as for gracious (more correctly *distinguished*) ladies, they can be considered entitled to this appellation by their *rank* and their *sex* (thus only as opposed to the *male* sex), and this only by virtue of a refinement of manners (known as gallantry) whereby the male sex imagines that it does itself greater honour by giving the fair sex precedence over itself.

i.e. citizen of a state, not *bourgeois* or citizen of a town). The only qualification required by a citizen (apart, of course, from being an adult male)
is that he must be his *own master (sui iuris)*, and must have some *property*
(which can include any skill, trade, fine art or science) to support himself.
In cases where he must earn his living from others, he must earn it only
by *selling* that which is his,* and not by allowing others to make use of
him; for he must in the true sense of the word *serve* no-one but the
commonwealth. In this respect, artisans and large or small landowners are
all equal, and each is entitled to one vote only. As for landowners, we leave
aside the question of how anyone can have rightfully acquired more land
than he can cultivate with his own hands (for acquisition by military
seizure is not primary acquisition), and how it came about that numerous
people who might otherwise have acquired permanent property were
thereby reduced to serving someone else in order to live at all. It would
certainly conflict with the above principle of equality if a law were to
grant them a privileged status so that their descendants would always
remain feudal landowners, without their land being sold or divided by
inheritance and thus made useful to more people; it would also be unjust
if only those belonging to an arbitrarily selected class were allowed to
acquire land, should the estates in fact be divided. The owner of a large
estate keeps out as many smaller property owners (and their votes) as
could otherwise occupy his territories. He does not vote on their behalf,
and himself has only *one* vote. It should be left exclusively to the ability,
industry and good fortune of each member of the commonwealth to enable
each to acquire a part and all to acquire the whole, although this distinction cannot be observed within the general legislation itself. The number
of those entitled to vote on matters of legislation must be calculated purely
from the number of property owners, not from the size of their properties.

Those who possess this right to vote must agree *unanimously* to the law
of public justice, or else a legal contention would arise between those who

---

* He who does a piece of work (*opus*) can sell it to someone else, just as if it were his
own property. But guaranteeing one's labour (*praestatio operae*) is not the same as selling
a commodity. The domestic servant, the shop assistant, the labourer, or even the barber,
are merely labourers (*operarii*), not *artists* (*artifices*, in the wider sense) or members of the
state, and are thus unqualified to be citizens. And although the man to whom I give my
firewood to chop and the tailor to whom I give material to make into clothes both appear
to have a similar relationship towards me, the former differs from the latter in the same
way as the barber from the wig-maker (to whom I may in fact have given the requisite
hair) or the labourer from the artist or tradesman, who does a piece of work which
belongs to him until he is paid for it. For the latter, in pursuing his trade, exchanges his
property with someone else (*opus*), while the former allows someone else to make use of
him.—But I do admit that it is somewhat difficult to define the qualifications which
entitle anyone to claim the status of being his own master.

agree and those who disagree, and it would require yet another higher legal principle to resolve it. An entire people cannot, however, be expected to reach unanimity, but only to show a majority of votes (and not even of direct votes, but simply of the votes of those delegated in a large nation to represent the people). Thus the actual principle of being content with majority decisions must be accepted unanimously and embodied in a contract; and this itself must be the ultimate basis on which a civil constitution is established.

Conclusion

This, then, is an *original contract* by means of which a civil and thus completely lawful constitution and commonwealth can alone be established. But we need by no means assume that this contract (*contractus originarius* or *pactum sociale*), based on a coalition of the wills of all private individuals in a nation to form a common, public will for the purposes of rightful legislation, actually exists as a *fact*, for it cannot possibly be so. Such an assumption would mean that we would first have to prove from history that some nation, whose rights and obligations have been passed down to us, did in fact perform such an act, and handed down some authentic record or legal instrument, orally or in writing, before we could regard ourselves as bound by a pre-existing civil constitution. It is in fact merely an *idea* of reason, which nonetheless has undoubted practical reality; for it can oblige every legislator to frame his laws in such a way that they could have been produced by the united will of a whole nation, and to regard each subject, in so far as he can claim citizenship, as if he had consented within the general will. This is the test of the rightfulness of every public law. For if the law is such that a whole people could not *possibly* agree to it (for example, if it stated that a certain class of *subjects* must be privileged as a hereditary *ruling class*), it is unjust; but if it is at least *possible* that a people could agree to it, it is our duty to consider the law as just, even if the people is at present in such a position or attitude of mind that it would probably refuse its consent if it were consulted.* But this restriction obviously applies only to the judgement of the legislator,

---

* If, for example, a war tax were proportionately imposed on all subjects, they could not claim, simply because it is oppressive, that it is unjust because the war is in their opinion unnecessary. For they are not entitled to judge this issue, since it is at least *possible* that the war is inevitable and the tax indispensable, so that the tax must be deemed rightful in the judgement of the subjects. But if certain estate owners were oppressed with levies for such a war, while others of the same class were exempted, it is easily seen that a whole people could never agree to a law of this kind, and it is entitled at least to make representations against it, since an unequal distribution of burdens can never be considered just.

not to that of the subject. Thus if a people, under some existing legislation, were asked to make a judgement which in all probability would prejudice its happiness, what should it do? Should the people not oppose the measure? The only possible answer is that they can do nothing but obey. For we are not concerned here with any happiness which the subject might expect to derive from the institutions or administration of the commonwealth, but primarily with the rights which would thereby be secured for everyone. And this is the highest principle from which all maxims relating to the commonwealth must begin, and which cannot be qualified by any other principles. No generally valid principle of legislation can be based on happiness. For both the current circumstances and the highly conflicting and variable illusions as to what happiness is (and no-one can prescribe to others how they should attain it) make all fixed principles impossible, so that happiness alone can never be a suitable principle of legislation. The doctrine that *salus publica suprema civitatis lex est*⁹ retains its value and authority undiminished; but the public welfare which demands *first* consideration lies precisely in that legal constitution which guarantees everyone his freedom within the law, so that each remains free to seek his happiness in whatever way he thinks best, so long as he does not violate the lawful freedom and rights of his fellow subjects at large. If the supreme power makes laws which are primarily directed towards happiness (the affluence of the citizens, increased population etc.), this cannot be regarded as the end for which a civil constitution was established, but only as a means of *securing the rightful state*, especially against external enemies of the people. The head of state must be authorised to judge for himself whether such measures are necessary for the commonwealth's prosperity, which is required to maintain its strength and stability both internally and against external enemies. The aim is not, as it were, to make the people happy against its will, but only to ensure its continued existence as a commonwealth.* The legislator may indeed err in judging whether or not the measures he adopts are *prudent*, but not in deciding whether or not the law harmonises with the principle of right. For he has ready to hand as an infallible *a priori* standard the idea of an original contract, and he need not wait for experience to show whether the means are suitable, as would be necessary if they were based on the principle of happiness. For so long as it is not self-contra-

---

* Measures of this kind might include certain restrictions on imports, so that the means of livelihood may be developed for the benefit of the subjects themselves and not as an advantage to foreigners or an encouragement for their industry. For without the prosperity of the people, the state would not have enough strength to resist external enemies or to preserve itself as a commonwealth.

dictory to say that an entire people could agree to such a law, however painful it might seem, then the law is in harmony with right. But if a public law is beyond reproach (i.e. *irreprehensible*) with respect to right, it carries with it the authority to coerce those to whom it applies, and conversely, it forbids them to resist the will of the legislator by violent means. In other words, the power of the state to put the law into effect is also *irresistible*, and no rightfully established commonwealth can exist without a force of this kind to suppress all internal resistance. For such resistance would be dictated by a maxim which, if it became general, would destroy the whole civil constitution and put an end to the only state in which men can possess rights.

It thus follows that all resistance against the supreme legislative power, all incitement of the subjects to violent expressions of discontent, all defiance which breaks out into rebellion, is the greatest and most punishable crime in a commonwealth, for it destroys its very foundations. This prohibition is *absolute*. And even if the power of the state or its agent, the head of state, has violated the original contract by authorising the government to act tyrannically, and has thereby, in the eyes of the subject, forfeited the right to legislate, the subject is still not entitled to offer counter-resistance. The reason for this is that the people, under an existing civil constitution, has no longer any right to judge how the constitution should be administered. For if we suppose that it does have this right to judge and that it disagrees with the judgement of the actual head of state, who is to decide which side is right? Neither can act as judge of his own cause. Thus there would have to be another head above the head of state to mediate between the latter and the people, which is self-contradictory.— Nor can a right of necessity (*ius in casu necessitatis*) be invoked here as a means of removing the barriers which restrict the power of the people; for it is monstrous to suppose that we can have a right to do wrong in the direst (physical) distress.* For the head of state can just as readily claim

---

* There is no *casus necessitatis* except where duties, i.e. an *absolute* duty and another which, however pressing, is nevertheless *relative*, come into conflict. For instance, it might be necessary for someone to betray someone else, even if their relationship were that of father and son, in order to preserve the state from catastrophe. This preservation of the state from evil is an absolute duty, while the preservation of the individual is merely a relative duty (i.e. it applies only if he is not guilty of a crime against the state). The first person might denounce the second to the authorities with the utmost unwillingness, compelled only by (moral) necessity. But if a person, in order to preserve his own life, pushes a shipwrecked fellow away from the plank he grasps, it would be quite false to say that (physical) necessity gives him a right to do so. For it is only a relative duty for me to preserve my own life (i.e. it applies only if I can do so without committing a crime). But it is an absolute duty not to take the life of another person who has not offended me and does not even make me risk my own life. Yet the teachers of

that his severe treatment of his subjects is justified by their insubordination as the subjects can justify their rebellion by complaints about their unmerited suffering, and who is to decide? The decision must rest with whoever controls the ultimate enforcement of the public law, i.e. the head of state himself. Thus no-one in the commonwealth can have a right to contest his authority.

Nonetheless, estimable men have declared that the subject is justified, under certain circumstances, in using force against his superiors. I need name only Achenwall,[10] who is extremely cautious, precise and restrained in his theories of natural right.* He says: 'If the danger which threatens the commonwealth as a result of long endurance of injustices from the head of state is greater than the danger to be feared from taking up arms against him, the people may then resist him. It may use this right to abrogate its contract of subjection and to dethrone him as a tyrant.' And he concludes: 'The people, in dethroning its ruler, thus returns to the state of nature.'

I well believe that neither Achenwall nor any others of the worthy men who have speculated along the same lines as he would ever have given their advice or agreement to such hazardous projects if the case had arisen. And it can scarcely be doubted that if the revolutions whereby Switzerland, the United Netherlands or even Great Britain won their much admired constitutions had failed, the readers of their history would regard the execution of their celebrated founders as no more than the deserved punishment of great political criminals. For the result usually affects our judgement of the rightfulness of an action, although the result is uncertain, whereas the principles of right are constant. But it is clear that these peoples have done the greatest degree of wrong in seeking their rights in this way, even if we admit that such a revolution did no injustice to a ruler who had violated a specific basic agreement with the people, such as the *Joyeuse Entrée*.[11] For such procedures, if made into a maxim, make all lawful constitutions insecure and produce a state of complete lawlessness (*status naturalis*) where all rights cease at least to be effectual. In view of this tendency of so many right-thinking authors to plead on behalf of the people (and to its own detriment), I will only remark that such errors arise in part from the usual fallacy of allowing the principle of happiness

general civil law are perfectly consistent in authorising such measures in cases of distress. For the authorities cannot combine a *penalty* with this prohibition, since this penalty would have to be death. But it would be a nonsensical law which threatened anyone with death if he did not voluntarily deliver himself up to death when in dangerous circumstances.

* Ius Naturae. Editio V. Pars posterior, §§203–206.

to influence the judgement, wherever the principle of right is involved; and partly because these writers have assumed that the idea of an original contract (a basic postulate of reason) is something which must have taken place *in reality*, even where there is no document to show that any contract was actually submitted to the commonwealth, accepted by the head oı state, and sanctioned by both parties. Such writers thus believe that the people retains the right to abrogate the original contract at its own discretion, if, in the opinion of the people, the contract has been severely violated.*

It is obvious from this that the principle of happiness (which is not in fact a definite principle at all) has ill effects in political right just as in morality, however good the intentions of those who teach it. The sovereign wants to make the people happy as he thinks best, and thus becomes a despot, while the people are unwilling to give up their universal human desire to seek happiness in their own way, and thus become rebels. If they had first of all asked what is lawful (in terms of *a priori* certainty, which no empiricist can upset), the idea of a social contract would retain its authority undiminished. But it would not exist as a fact (as Danton[13] would have it, declaring that since it does not actually exist, all property and all rights under the existing civil constitution are null and void), but only as a rational principle for judging any lawful public constitution whatsoever. And it would then be seen that, until the general will is there, the people has no coercive right against its ruler, since it can apply coercion legally only through him. But if the will is there, no force can be applied to the ruler by the people, otherwise the people would be the supreme ruler. Thus the people can never possess a right of coercion against the head of state, or be entitled to oppose him in word or deed.

We can see, furthermore, that this theory is adequately confirmed in practice. In the British constitution, of which the people are so proud that they hold it up as a model for the whole world, we find no mention of what the people are entitled to do if the monarch were to violate the contract of 1688.[14] Since there is no law to cover such a case, the people

---

* Even if an actual contract of the people with the head of state has been violated, the people cannot reply immediately as a *commonwealth*, but only by forming factions. For the hitherto existing constitution has been destroyed by the people, but a new commonwealth has still to be organised. At this point, the state of anarchy supervenes, with all the terrors it may bring with it. And the wrong which is thereby done is done by each faction of the people to the others, as is clear from the case where the rebellious subjects ended up by trying to thrust upon each other a constitution which would have been far more oppressive than the one they abandoned. For they would have been devoured by ecclesiastics and aristocrats, instead of enjoying greater equality in the distribution of political burdens under a single head of state who ruled them all.[12]

tacitly reserve the right to rebel against him if he should violate the contract. And it would be an obvious contradiction if the constitution included a law for such eventualities, entitling the people to overthrow the existing constitution, from which all particular laws are derived, if the contract were violated. For there would then have to be a *publicly constituted** opposing power, hence a second head of state to protect the rights of the people against the first ruler, and then yet a third to decide which of the other two had right on his side. In fact, the leaders (or guardians—call them what you will) of the British people, fearing some such accusation if their plans did not succeed, *invented* the notion of a voluntary abdication by the monarch they forced out, rather than claim a right to depose him (which would have made the constitution self-contradictory).

While I trust that no-one will accuse me of flattering monarchs too much by declaring them inviolable, I likewise hope that I shall be spared the reproach of claiming too much for the people if I maintain that the people too have inalienable rights against the head of state, even if these cannot be rights of coercion.

Hobbes is of the opposite opinion. According to him (*De Cive*, Chap. 7, §14), the head of state has no contractual obligations towards the people; he can do no injustice to a citizen, but may act towards him as he pleases. This proposition would be perfectly correct if injustice were taken to mean any injury which gave the injured party a *coercive right* against the one who has done him injustice. But in its general form, the proposition is quite terrifying.

The non-resisting subject must be able to assume that his ruler has no *wish* to do him injustice. And everyone has his inalienable rights, which he cannot give up even if he wishes to, and about which he is entitled to make his own judgements. But if he assumes that the ruler's attitude is one of good will, any injustice which he believes he has suffered can only have resulted through error, or through ignorance of certain possible consequences of the laws which the supreme authority has made. Thus the citizen must, with the approval of the ruler, be entitled to make public his opinion on whatever of the ruler's measures seem to him to constitute an injustice against the commonwealth. For to assume that the head of state can neither make mistakes nor be ignorant of anything would be to imply that he receives divine inspiration and is more than a human being.

---

* No right in a state can be tacitly and treacherously included by a secret reservation, and least of all a right which the people claim to be part of the constitution, for all laws within it must be thought of as arising out of a public will. Thus if the constitution allowed rebellion, it would have to declare this right publicly and make clear how it might be implemented.

Thus *freedom of the pen* is the only safeguard of the rights of the people, although it must not transcend the bounds of respect and devotion towards the existing constitution, which should itself create a liberal attitude of mind among the subjects. To try to deny the citizen this freedom does not only mean, as Hobbes maintains, that the subject can claim no rights against the supreme ruler. It also means withholding from the ruler all knowledge of those matters which, if he knew about them, he would himself rectify, so that he is thereby put into a self-stultifying position. For his will issues commands to his subjects (as citizens) only in so far as he represents the general will of the people. But to encourage the head of state to fear that independent and public thought might cause political unrest is tantamount to making him distrust his own power and feel hatred towards his people.

The general principle, however, according to which a people may judge negatively whatever it believes was *not decreed* in good will by the supreme legislation, can be summed up as follows: *Whatever a people cannot impose upon itself cannot be imposed upon it by the legislator either.*

For example, if we wish to discover whether a law which declares permanently valid an ecclesiastical constitution (itself formulated at some time in the past) can be regarded as emanating from the actual will or intention of the legislator, we must first ask whether a people is *authorised* to make a law for itself whereby certain accepted doctrines and outward forms of religion are declared permanent, and whether the people may thus prevent its own descendants from making further progress in religious understanding or from correcting any past mistakes. It is clear that any original contract of the people which established such a law would in itself be null and void, for it would conflict with the appointed aim and purpose of mankind. Thus a law of this kind cannot be regarded as the actual will of the monarch, to whom counter-representations may accordingly be made. In all cases, however, where the supreme legislation did nevertheless adopt such measures, it would be permissible to pass general and public judgements upon them, but never to offer any verbal or active resistance.

In every commonwealth, there must be *obedience* to generally valid coercive laws within the mechanism of the political constitution. There must also be a *spirit of freedom*, for in all matters concerning universal human duties, each individual requires to be convinced by reason that the coercion which prevails is lawful, otherwise he would be in contradiction with himself. Obedience without the spirit of freedom is the effective cause of all *secret societies*. For it is a natural vocation of man to communicate with his fellows, especially in matters affecting mankind as a whole. Thus secret societies would disappear if freedom of this kind were encouraged. And how else can the government itself acquire the knowledge it needs to further its own basic intention, if not by allowing the spirit of freedom, so admirable in its origins and effects, to make itself heard?

Nowhere does practice so readily bypass all pure principles of reason and treat theory so presumptuously as in the question of what is needed for a good political constitution. The reason for this is that a legal constitution of long standing gradually makes the people accustomed to judging both their happiness and their rights in terms of the peaceful *status quo*. Conversely, it does not encourage them to value the existing state of affairs in the light of those concepts of happiness and right which reason provides. It rather makes them prefer this passive state to the dangerous task of looking for a better one, thus bearing out the saying which Hippocrates told physicians to remember: *iudicium anceps, experimentum periculosum.*[15] Thus all constitutions which have lasted for a sufficiently long time, whatever their inadequacies and variations, produce the same result: the people remain content with what they have. If we therefore consider the *welfare of the people*, theory is not in fact valid, for everything depends upon practice derived from experience.

But reason provides a concept which we express by the words *political right*. And this concept has binding force for human beings who coexist in a state of antagonism produced by their natural freedom, so that it has an objective, practical reality, irrespective of the good or ill it may produce (for these can only be known by experience). Thus it is based on *a priori* principles, for experience cannot provide knowledge of what is right, and there is a *theory* of political right to which practice must conform before it can be valid.

The only objection which can be raised against this is that, although men have in their minds the idea of the rights to which they are entitled, their intractability is such that they are incapable and unworthy of being treated as their rights demand, so that they can and ought to be kept under control by a supreme power acting purely from expediency. But this counsel of desperation (*salto mortale*) means that, since there is no appeal to right but only to force, the people may themselves resort to force and thus make every legal constitution insecure. If there is nothing which commands immediate respect through reason, such as the basic rights of man, no influence can prevail upon man's arbitrary will and restrain his

86

freedom. But if both benevolence and right speak out in loud tones, human nature will not prove too debased to listen to their voice with respect. *Tum pietate gravem meritisque si forte virum quem Conspexere, silent arrectisque auribus adstant* (Virgil).[16]

III

ON THE RELATIONSHIP OF THEORY TO PRACTICE IN INTERNATIONAL RIGHT

CONSIDERED FROM A UNIVERSALLY PHILANTHROPIC, I.E. COSMOPOLITAN POINT OF VIEW*

(Against Moses Mendelssohn)[17]

Is the human race as a whole likeable, or is it an object to be regarded with distaste? Must we simply wish it well (to avoid becoming misanthropists) without really expecting its efforts to succeed, and then take no further interest in it? In order to answer such questions, we must first answer the following one: Does man possess natural capacities which would indicate that the race will always progress and improve, so that the evils of the past and present will vanish in the future good? If this were the case, we could at least admire the human species for its constant advance towards the good; otherwise, we should have to hate or despise it, whatever objections might be raised by pretended philanthropists (whose feelings for mankind might at most amount to good will, but not to genuine pleasure).

For however hard we may try to awaken feelings of love in ourselves, we cannot avoid hating that which is and always will be evil, especially if it involves deliberate and general violation of the most sacred rights of man. Perhaps we may not wish to harm men, but shall not want to have any more to do with them than we can help.

Moses Mendelssohn was of the latter opinion (*Jerusalem* §II, pp. 44–47),[18] which he put forward in opposition to his friend Lessing's hypothesis of a divine education of mankind.[19] He regards it as sheer fantasy to say 'that the whole of mankind here on earth must continually progress and become more perfect through the ages'. He continues: 'We see the human race

---

* It is not immediately obvious how a universally *philanthropic* attitude can point the way to a cosmopolitan constitution, and this in turn to the establishment of *international justice* as the only state in which those capacities which make our species worthy of respect can be properly developed. But the conclusion of this essay will make this relationship clear.

as a whole moving slowly back and forth, and whenever it takes a few steps forward, it soon relapses twice as quickly into its former state.' (This is truly the stone of Sisyphus;[20] if we adopt an attitude of this kind, as the Indians do, the earth must strike us as a place of atonement for old and forgotten sins.) 'Man as an individual progresses; but mankind constantly fluctuates between fixed limits. Regarded as a whole, however, mankind maintains roughly the same level of morality, the same degree of religion and irreligion, of virtue and vice, of happiness (?) and misery.' He introduces these assertions with the words (p. 46): 'Do you presume to guess the plan of providence for mankind? Do not invent hypotheses' (he had earlier called these theories); 'just look around at what actually happens, and if you can briefly survey the history of all past ages, look at what has happened from time immemorial. All this is fact; it must have been intended and approved within the plan of higher wisdom, or at least adopted along with it.'

I beg to differ. It is a sight fit for a god to watch a virtuous man grappling with adversity and evil temptations and yet managing to hold out against them. But it is a sight quite unfit not so much for a god, but even for the most ordinary, though right-thinking man, to see the human race advancing over a period of time towards virtue, and then quickly relapsing the whole way back into vice and misery. It may perhaps be moving and instructive to watch such a drama for a while; but the curtain must eventually descend. For in the long run, it becomes a farce. And even if the actors do not tire of it—for they are fools—the spectator does, for any single act will be enough for him if he can reasonably conclude from it that the never-ending play will go on in the same way for ever. If it is only a play, the retribution at the end can make up for the unpleasant sensations the spectator has felt. But in my opinion at least, it cannot be reconciled with the morality of a wise creator and ruler of the world if countless vices, even with intermingled virtues, are in actual fact allowed to go on accumulating.

I may thus be permitted to assume that, since the human race is constantly progressing in cultural matters (in keeping with its natural purpose), it is also engaged in progressive improvement in relation to the moral end of its existence. This progress may at times be *interrupted* but never *broken off*. I do not need to prove this assumption; it is up to the adversary to prove his case. I am a member of a series of human generations, and as such, I am not as good as I ought to be or could be according to the moral requirements of my nature. I base my argument upon my inborn duty of influencing posterity in such a way that it will make constant progress (and I must thus assume that progress is possible), and that this duty may be rightfully handed down from one member of the series to the next. History may well give rise to endless doubts about my hopes, and if these doubts could be proved, they might persuade me to desist from an apparently futile task. But so long as they do not have the force of certainty, I cannot exchange my duty (as a *liquidum*)[21] for a rule of expediency which says that I ought not to attempt the impracticable (i.e. an *illiquidum*,[22] since it is purely hypothetical). And however uncertain I may be and may remain as to whether we can hope for anything better for mankind, this uncertainty cannot detract from the maxim I have adopted, or from the necessity of assuming for practical purposes that human progress is possible.

This hope for better times to come, without which an earnest desire to do something useful for the common good would never have inspired the human heart, has always influenced the activities of right-thinking men. And the worthy Mendelssohn must himself have reckoned on this, since he zealously endeavoured to promote the enlightenment and welfare of the nation to which he belonged. For he could not himself reasonably hope to do this unless others after him continued upon the same path. Confronted by the sorry spectacle not only of those evils which befall mankind from natural causes, but also of those which men inflict upon one another, our spirits can be raised by the prospect of future improvements. This, however, calls for unselfish goodwill on our part, since we shall have been long dead and buried when the fruits we helped to sow are harvested. It is quite irrelevant whether any empirical evidence suggests that these plans, which are founded only on hope, may be unsuccessful. For the idea that something which has hitherto been unsuccessful will therefore never be successful does not justify anyone in abandoning even a pragmatic or technical aim (for example, that of flights with aerostatic balloons). This applies even more to moral aims, which, so long as it is not demonstrably impossible to fulfil them, amount to duties. Besides, various evidence suggests that in our age, as compared with all previous ages, the human race has made considerable moral progress, and short-term hindrances prove nothing to the contrary. Moreover, it can be shown that the outcry about man's continually increasing decadence arises for the very reason that we can see further ahead, because we have reached a higher level of morality. We thus pass more severe judgements on what we are, comparing it with what we ought to be, so that our self-reproach increases in proportion to the number of stages of morality we have advanced through during the whole of known history.

If we now ask what means there are of maintaining and indeed accelerating this constant progress towards a better state, we soon realise that the success of this immeasurably long undertaking will depend not so much upon what *we* do (e.g. the education we impart to younger generations) and upon what methods *we* use to further it; it will rather depend upon what human *nature* may do in and through us, to *compel* us to follow a course which we would not readily adopt by choice. We must look to nature alone, or rather to *providence* (since it requires the highest wisdom to fulfil this purpose), for a successful outcome which will first affect the whole and then the individual parts. The schemes of men, on the other hand, begin with the parts, and frequently get no further than them. For the whole is too great for men to encompass; while they can reach it with their ideas, they cannot actively influence it, especially since their schemes conflict with one another to such an extent that they could hardly reach agreement of their own free volition.

On the one hand, universal violence and the distress it produces must eventually make a people decide to submit to the coercion which reason itself prescribes (i.e. the coercion of public law), and to enter into a *civil* constitution. And on the other hand, the distress produced by the constant wars in which the states try to subjugate or engulf each other must finally lead them, even against their will, to enter into a *cosmopolitan* constitution. Or if such a state of universal peace is in turn even more dangerous to freedom, for it may lead to the most fearful despotism (as has indeed occurred more than once with states which have grown too large), distress must force men to form a state which is not a cosmopolitan commonwealth under a single ruler, but a lawful *federation* under a commonly accepted *international right*.

The increasing culture of the states, along with their growing tendency to aggrandise themselves by cunning or violence at the expense of the others, must make wars more frequent. It must likewise cause increasingly high expenditure on standing armies, which must be kept in constant training and equipped with ever more numerous instruments of warfare. Meanwhile, the price of all necessities will steadily rise, while no-one can hope for any proportionate increase in the corresponding metal currencies. No peace will last long enough for the resources saved during it to meet the expenditure of the next war, while the invention of a national debt, though ingenious, is an ultimately self-defeating expedient. Thus sheer exhaustion must eventually perform what goodwill ought to have done but failed to do: each state must be organised internally in such a way that the head of state, for whom the war actually costs nothing (for he wages it at the expense of others, i.e. the people), must no longer have the deciding vote on whether war is to be declared or not, for the people who pay for it must decide. (This, of course, necessarily presupposes that the idea of an original contract has already been realised.) For the people will not readily place itself in danger of personal want (which would not affect the head of state) out of a mere desire for aggrandisement, or because of some supposed and purely verbal offence. And thus posterity will not be oppressed by any burdens which it has not brought upon itself, and it will be able to make perpetual progress towards a morally superior state. This is not produced by any love on the part of earlier ages for later ones, but only by the love of each age for itself. Each commonwealth, unable to harm the others by force, must observe the laws on its own account, and it may reasonably hope that other similarly constituted bodies will help it to do so.

But this is no more than a personal opinion and hypothesis; it is uncertain, like all judgements which profess to define the appropriate natural cause of an intended effect which is not wholly within our control. And even as such, it does not offer the subject of an existing state any principle by which he could attain the desired effect by force (as has already been demonstrated); only the head of state, who is above coercion, can do so. In the normal order of things, it cannot be expected of human nature to desist voluntarily from using force, although it is not impossible where the circumstances are sufficiently pressing. Thus it is not inappropriate to say of man's moral hopes and desires that, since he is powerless to fulfil them himself, he may look to *providence* to create the circumstances in which they can be fulfilled. The end of *man* as an entire species, i.e. that of fulfilling his ultimate appointed purpose by freely exercising his own powers, will be brought by providence to a successful issue, even although the ends of *men* as individuals run in a diametrically opposite direction. For the very conflict of individual inclinations, which is the source of all evil, gives reason a free hand to master them all; it thus gives predominance not to evil, which destroys itself, but to good, which continues to maintain itself once it has been established.

Nowhere does human nature appear less admirable than in the relationships which exist between peoples. No state is for a moment secure from the others in its independence and its possessions. The will to subjugate the others or to grow at their expense is always present, and the production of armaments for defence, which often makes peace more oppressive and more destructive of internal welfare than war itself, can never be ff1

---

relaxed. And there is no possible way of counteracting this except a state of international right, based upon enforceable public laws to which each state must submit (by analogy with a state of civil or political right among individual men). For a permanent universal peace by means of a so-called *European balance of power* is a pure illusion, like Swift's story of the house which the builder had constructed in such perfect harmony with all the laws of equilibrium that it collapsed as soon as a sparrow alighted on it.[23] But it might be objected that no states will ever submit to coercive laws of this kind, and that a proposal for a universal federation, to whose power all the individual states would voluntarily submit and whose laws they would all obey, may be all very well in the theory of the Abbé St Pierre[24] or of Rousseau, but that it does not apply in practice. For such proposals have always been ridiculed by great statesmen, and even more by heads of state, as pedantic, childish and academic ideas.

For my own part, I put my trust in the theory of what the relationships between men and states *ought to be* according to the principle of right. It recommends to us earthly gods the maxim that we should proceed in our disputes in such a way that a universal federal state may be inaugurated, so that we should therefore assume that it *is possible (in praxi)*. I likewise rely *(in subsidium)* upon the very nature of things to force men to do what they do not willingly choose *(fata volentem ducunt, nolentem trahunt)*.[25] This involves human nature, which is still animated by respect for right and duty. I therefore cannot and will not see it as so deeply immersed in evil that practical moral reason will not triumph in the end, after many unsuccessful attempts, thereby showing that it is worthy of admiration after all. On the cosmopolitan level too, it thus remains true to say that whatever reason shows to be valid in theory, is also valid in practice.

Perpetual Peace
A Philosophical Sketch [1]

'THE PERPETUAL PEACE'

A Dutch innkeeper once put this satirical inscription on his signboard, along with the picture of a graveyard. We shall not trouble to ask whether it applies to men in general, or particularly to heads of state (who can never have enough of war), or only to the philosophers who blissfully dream of perpetual peace. The author of the present essay does, however, make one reservation in advance. The practical politician tends to look down with great complacency upon the political theorist as a mere academic. The theorist's abstract ideas, the practitioner believes, cannot endanger the state, since the state must be founded upon principles of experience; it thus seems safe to let him fire off his whole broadside, and the *worldly-wise* statesman need not turn a hair. It thus follows that if the practical politician is to be consistent, he must not claim, in the event of a dispute with the theorist, to scent any danger to the state in the opinions which the theorist has randomly uttered in public. By this saving clause, the author of this essay will consider himself expressly safeguarded, in correct and proper style, against all malicious interpretation.

FIRST SECTION
Which Contains the Preliminary Articles of a Perpetual Peace Between States

1. 'No conclusion of peace shall be considered valid as such if it was made with a secret reservation of the material for a future war.'

For if this were the case, it would be a mere truce, a suspension of hostilities, not a *peace*. Peace means an end to all hostilities, and to attach the adjective 'perpetual' to it is already suspiciously close to pleonasm. A conclusion of peace nullifies all existing reasons for a future war, even if these are not yet known to the contracting parties, and no matter how acutely and carefully they may later be pieced together out of old documents. It is possible that either party may make a mental reservation with a view to reviving its old pretensions in the future. Such reservations will not be mentioned explicitly, since both parties may simply be too exhausted to continue the war, although they may nonetheless possess sufficient ill will to seize the first favourable opportunity of attaining their end. But if we consider such reservations in themselves, they soon appear as Jesuitical casuistry; they are beneath the dignity of a ruler, just as it is beneath the dignity of a minister of state to comply with any reasoning of this kind.

But if, in accordance with 'enlightened' notions of political expediency, we believe that the true glory of a state consists in the constant increase of its power by any means whatsoever, the above judgement will certainly appear academic and pedantic.

2. 'No independently existing state, whether it be large or small, may be acquired by another state by inheritance, exchange, purchase or gift.'

For a state, unlike the ground on which it is based, is not a possession (*patrimonium*). It is a society of men, which no-one other than itself can command or dispose of. Like a tree, it has its own roots, and to graft it on to another state as if it were a shoot is to terminate its existence as a moral personality and make it into a commodity. This contradicts the idea of the original contract, without which the rights of a people are unthinkable.* Everyone knows what danger the supposed right of acquiring states in this way, even in our own times, has brought upon Europe (for this practice is unknown in other continents). It has been thought that states can marry one another, and this has provided a new kind of industry by which power can be increased through family alliances, without expenditure of energy, while landed property can be extended at the same time. It is the same thing when the troops of one state are hired to another to fight an enemy who is not common to both; for the subjects are thereby used and misused as objects to be manipulated at will.

3. 'Standing armies (*miles perpetuus*) will gradually be abolished altogether.'

For they constantly threaten other states with war by the very fact that they are always prepared for it. They spur on the states to outdo one another in arming unlimited numbers of soldiers, and since the resultant costs eventually make peace more oppressive than a short war, the armies

* A hereditary kingdom is not a state which can be inherited by another state. Only the right to rule over it may be bequeathed to another physical person. In this case, the state acquires a ruler, but the ruler as such (i.e. as one who already has another kingdom) does not acquire the state.

94

are themselves the cause of wars of aggression which set out to end burdensome military expenditure. Furthermore, the hiring of men to kill or to be killed seems to mean using them as mere machines and instruments in the hands of someone else (the state), which cannot easily be reconciled with the rights of man in one's own person. It is quite a different matter if the citizens undertake voluntary military training from time to time in order to secure themselves and their fatherland against attacks from outside. But it would be just the same if wealth rather than soldiers were accumulated, for it would be seen by other states as a military threat; it might compel them to mount preventive attacks, for of the three powers within a state—the *power of the army*, the *power of alliance* and the *power of money*—the third is probably the most reliable instrument of war. It would lead more often to wars if it were not so difficult to discover the amount of wealth which another state possesses.

4. 'No national debt shall be contracted in connection with the external affairs of the state.'

There is no cause for suspicion if help for the national economy is sought inside or outside the state (e.g. for improvements to roads, new settlements, storage of foodstuffs for years of famine, etc.). But a credit system, if used by the powers as an instrument of aggression against one another, shows the power of money in its most dangerous form. For while the debts thereby incurred are always secure against present demands (because not all the creditors will demand payment at the same time), these debts go on growing indefinitely. This ingenious system, invented by a commercial people[2] in the present century, provides a military fund which may exceed the resources of all the other states put together. It can only be exhausted by an eventual tax-deficit, which may be postponed for a considerable time by the commercial stimulus which industry and trade receive through the credit system. This ease in making war, coupled with the warlike inclination of those in power (which seems to be an integral feature of human nature), is thus a great obstacle in the way of perpetual peace. Foreign debts must therefore be prohibited by a preliminary article of such a peace, otherwise national bankruptcy, inevitable in the long run, would necessarily involve various other states in the resultant loss without their having deserved it, thus inflicting upon them a public injury. Other states are therefore justified in allying themselves against such a state and its pretensions.

5. 'No state shall forcibly interfere in the constitution and government of another state.'

For what could justify such interference? Surely not any sense of scandal or offence which a state arouses in the subjects of another state. It should rather serve as a warning to others, as an example of the great evils which a people has incurred by its lawlessness. And a bad example which one free person gives to another (as a *scandalum acceptum*) is not the same as an injury to the latter. But it would be a different matter if a state, through internal discord, were to split into two parts, each of which set itself up as a separate state and claimed authority over the whole. For it could not be reckoned as interference in another state's constitution if an external state were to lend support to one of them, because their condition is one of anarchy. But as long as this internal conflict is not yet decided, the interference of external powers would be a violation of the rights of an independent people which is merely struggling with its internal ills. Such interference would be an active offence and would make the autonomy of all other states insecure.

6. 'No state at war with another shall permit such acts of hostility as would make mutual confidence impossible during a future time of peace. Such acts would include the employment of *assassins* (*percussores*) *or poisoners* (*venefici*), *breach of agreements, the instigation of treason* (*perduellio*) within the enemy state, etc.'

These are dishonourable stratagems. For it must still remain possible, even in wartime, to have some sort of trust in the attitude of the enemy, otherwise peace could not be concluded and the hostilities would turn into a war of extermination (*bellum internecinum*). After all, war is only a regrettable expedient for asserting one's rights by force within a state of nature, where no court of justice is available to judge with legal authority. In such cases, neither party can be declared an unjust enemy, for this would already presuppose a judge's decision; only the *outcome* of the conflict, as in the case of a so-called 'judgement of God', can decide who is in the right. A war of punishment (*bellum punitivum*) between states is inconceivable, since there can be no relationship of superior to inferior among them. It thus follows that a war of extermination, in which both parties and right itself might all be simultaneously annihilated, would allow perpetual peace only on the vast graveyard of the human race. A war of this kind and the employment of all means which might bring it about must thus be absolutely prohibited. But the means listed above would inevitably lead to such a war, because these diabolical arts, besides being intrinsically despicable, would not long be confined to war alone if they were brought into use. This applies, for example, to the employment of spies (*uti exploratoribus*), for it exploits only the dishonesty of others (which can never be completely eliminated). Such practices will be carried over into peacetime and will thus completely vitiate its purpose.

All of the articles listed above, when regarded objectively or in relation to the intentions of those in power, are *prohibitive laws* (*leges prohibitivae*). Yet some of them are of the *strictest* sort (*leges strictae*), being valid irrespective of differing circumstances, and they require that the abuses they prohibit should be abolished *immediately* (Nos. 1, 5, and 6). Others (Nos. 2, 3, and 4), although they are not exceptions to the rule of justice, allow some *subjective* latitude according to the circumstances in which they are applied (*leges latae*). The latter need not necessarily be executed at once, so long as their ultimate purpose (e.g. the *restoration* of freedom to certain states in accordance with the second article) is not lost sight of. But their execution may not be *put off* to a non-existent date (*ad calendas graecas*, as Augustus used to promise), for any delay is permitted only as a means of avoiding a premature implementation which might frustrate the whole purpose of the article. For in the case of the second article, the prohibition relates only to the *mode of acquisition*, which is to be forbidden hereforth, but not to the present *state of political possessions*. For although this present state is not backed up by the requisite legal authority, it was considered lawful in the public opinion of every state at the time of the putative acquisition.*

* It has hitherto been doubted, not without justification, whether there can be permissive laws (*leges permissivae*) in addition to preceptive laws (*leges praeceptivae*) and prohibitive laws (*leges prohibitivae*). For all laws embody an element of objective practical necessity as a reason for certain actions, whereas a permission depends only upon practical contingencies. Thus a *permissive law* would be a compulsion to do something which one cannot be compelled to do, and if the object of the law were the same as that of the permission, a contradiction would result. But in the permissive law contained in the second article above, the initial prohibition applies only to the mode of acquiring a right in the future (e.g. by inheritance), whereas the exemption from this prohibition (i.e. the permissive part of the law) applies to the state of political possessions in the present. For in accordance with a permissive law of natural right, this present state can be allowed to remain even although the state of nature has been abandoned for that of civil society. And even if these present possessions are unlawful, they are nevertheless *honest* (*possessio putativa*). A putative possession is prohibited, however, as soon as it has been recognised as such, both in the state of nature and after the subsequent transition to civil society (if the mode of acquisition is the same). And continued possession could not be permitted if the supposed acquisition had been made in the state of civil society, for it would then

SECOND SECTION

Which Contains the Definitive Articles of a Perpetual Peace Between States

A state of peace among men living together is not the same as the state of nature, which is rather a state of war. For even if it does not involve active hostilities, it involves a constant threat of their breaking out. Thus the state of peace must be *formally instituted*, for a suspension of hostilities is not in itself a guarantee of peace. And unless one neighbour gives a guarantee to the other at his request (which can happen only in a *lawful* state), the latter may treat him as an enemy.*

have to end immediately, as an offence against right, as soon as its unlawfulness had been discovered.

My intention here was merely to point out briefly to exponents of natural right the concept of a permissive law, which automatically presents itself within the systematic divisions of reason. It is especially noteworthy since it is frequently used in civil or statutory law, with the one difference that the prohibitive part of the law exists independently, and the permissive part is not included within the law itself as a limiting condition (as it ought to be), but added to cover exceptional cases. Such laws usually state that this or that is prohibited, *except* in cases 1, 2 or 3, and so on *ad infinitum*, for permissive clauses are only added to the law fortuitously, by a random review of particular cases, and not in accordance with any definite principle. Otherwise, the limiting conditions would have had to be included *in the actual formula of the prohibitive law*, whereby it would have become a permissive law in itself. It is therefore to be regretted that the ingenious but unsolved competition question submitted by that wise and clear-sighted gentleman, Count Windischgrätz,[3] was so soon abandoned, for it might have solved the legal difficulty we are at present discussing. For the possibility of finding a universal formula like those of mathematics is the only true test of consistent legislation, and without it, the so-called *ius certum* must remain no more than a pious hope. Otherwise, we shall only have *general* laws (i.e. laws *valid in general*), but no universal laws (i.e. laws which are *generally valid*) such as the concept of a law seems to demand.

* It is usually assumed that one cannot take hostile action against anyone unless one has already been actively *injured* by them. This is perfectly correct if both parties are living in a *legal civil state*. For the fact that the one has entered such a state gives the required guarantee to the other, since both are subject to the same authority. But man (or an individual people) in a mere state of nature robs me of any such security and injures me by virtue of this very state in which he coexists with me. He may not have injured me actively (*facto*), but he does injure me by the very lawlessness of his state (*statu iniusto*), for he is a permanent threat to me, and I can require him either to enter into a common lawful state along with me or to move away from my vicinity. Thus the postulate on which all the following articles are based is that all men who can at all influence one another must adhere to some kind of civil constitution. But any legal constitution, as far as the persons who live under it are concerned, will conform to one of the three following types:

(1) a constitution based on the *civil right* of individuals within a nation (*ius civitatis*).
(2) a constitution based on the *international right* of states in their relationships with one another (*ius gentium*).
(3) a constitution based on *cosmopolitan right*, in so far as individuals and states, coexisting in an external relationship of mutual influences, may be regarded as

First Definitive Article of a Perpetual Peace :
The Civil Constitution of Every State shall be Republican

A *republican constitution* is founded upon three principles: firstly, the principle of *freedom* for all members of a society (as men); secondly, the principle of the *dependence* of everyone upon a single common legislation (as subjects); and thirdly, the principle of legal *equality* for everyone (as citizens).* It is the only constitution which can be derived from the idea

citizens of a universal state of mankind (*ius cosmopoliticum*). This classification, with respect to the idea of a perpetual peace, is not arbitrary, but necessary. For if even one of the parties were able to influence the others physically and yet itself remained in a state of nature, there would be a risk of war, which it is precisely the aim of the above articles to prevent.

* *Rightful (i.e. external) freedom* cannot, as is usually thought, be defined as a warrant to do whatever one wishes unless it means doing injustice to others. For what is meant by a *warrant*? It means a possibility of acting in a certain way so long as this action does not do any injustice to others. Thus the definition would run as follows: freedom is the possibility of acting in ways which do no injustice to others. That is, we do no injustice to others (no matter what we may actually do) if we do no injustice to others. Thus the definition is an empty tautology. In fact, my external and rightful *freedom* should be defined as a warrant to obey no external laws except those to which I have been able to give my own consent. Similarly, external and rightful *equality* within a state is that relationship among the citizens whereby no-one can put anyone else under a legal obligation without submitting simultaneously to a law which requires that he can himself be put under the same kind of obligation by the other person. (And we do not need to define the principle of *legal* dependence, since it is always implied in the concept of a political constitution.) The validity of these innate and inalienable rights, the necessary property of mankind, is confirmed and enhanced by the principle that man may have lawful relations even with higher beings (if he believes in the latter). For he may consider himself as a citizen of a transcendental world, to which the same principles apply. And as regards my freedom, I am not under any obligation even to divine laws (which I can recognise by reason alone), except in so far as I have been able to give my own consent to them; for I can form a conception of the divine will only in terms of the law of freedom of my own reason. As for the principle of equality in relation to the most exalted being I can conceive of, apart from God (e.g. a power such as Aeon),⁴ there is no reason, if I and this higher being are both doing our duty in our own stations, why it should be my duty to obey while he should enjoy the right to command. But the reason why this principle of equality (unlike that of freedom) does not apply to a relationship towards God, is that God is the only being for whom the concept of duty ceases to be valid.

But as for the right of equality of all citizens as subjects, we may ask whether a *hereditary aristocracy* is admissible. The answer to this question will depend entirely on whether more importance is attached to the superior *rank* granted by the state to one subject over another than is attached to *merit*, or vice versa. Now it is obvious that if rank is conferred according to birth, it will be quite uncertain whether merit (skill and devotion within one's office) will accompany it; it will be tantamount to conferring a position of command upon a favoured individual without any merit on his part, and this could never be approved by the general will of the people in an original contract, which is, after all, the principle behind all rights. For it does not necessarily follow that a nobleman is also a *noble man*. And as for a nobility of office, i.e. the rank of a *higher magistracy* which can be attained by merit, the rank does not attach as a possession to the person,

99

of an original contract, upon which all rightful legislation of a people must be founded. Thus as far as right is concerned, republicanism is in itself the original basis of every kind of civil constitution, and it only remains to ask whether it is the only constitution which can lead to a perpetual peace.

The republican constitution is not only pure in its origin (since it springs from the pure concept of right); it also offers a prospect of attaining the desired result, i.e. a perpetual peace, and the reason for this is as follows.—If, as is inevitably the case under this constitution, the consent of the citizens is required to decide whether or not war is to be declared, it is very natural that they will have great hesitation in embarking on so dangerous an enterprise. For this would mean calling down on themselves all the miseries of war, such as doing the fighting themselves, supplying the costs of the war from their own resources, painfully making good the ensuing devastation, and, as the crowning evil, having to take upon themselves a burden of debt which will embitter peace itself and which can never be paid off on account of the constant threat of new wars. But under a constitution where the subject is not a citizen, and which is therefore not republican, it is the simplest thing in the world to go to war. For the head of state is not a fellow citizen, but the owner of the state, and a war will not force him to make the slightest sacrifice so far as his banquets, hunts, pleasure palaces and court festivals are concerned. He can thus decide on war, without any significant reason, as a kind of amusement, and unconcernedly leave it to the diplomatic corps (who are always ready for such purposes) to justify the war for the sake of propriety.

The following remarks are necessary to prevent the republican constitution from being confused with the democratic one, as commonly happens. The various forms of state (*civitas*) may be classified either according to the different persons who exercise supreme authority, or according to the way in which the nation is governed by its ruler, whoever he may be. The first classification goes by the form of sovereignty (*forma imperii*), and only three such forms are possible, depending on whether the ruling power is in the hands of an *individual*, of *several persons* in association, or of *all* those who together constitute civil society (i.e. *autocracy*, *aristocracy* and *democracy*—the power of a prince, the power of a nobility, and the power of the people). The second classification depends on the form of

but to the post occupied by the person, and this does not violate the principle of equality. For when a person lays down his office, he simultaneously resigns his rank and again becomes one of the people.

government (*forma regiminis*), and relates to the way in which the state, setting out from its constitution (i.e. an act of the general will whereby the mass becomes a people), makes use of its plenary power. The form of government, in this case, will be either *republican* or *despotic*. *Republicanism* is that political principle whereby the executive power (the government) is separated from the legislative power. Despotism prevails in a state if the laws are made and arbitrarily executed by one and the same power, and it reflects the will of the people only in so far as the ruler treats the will of the people as his own private will. Of the three forms of sovereignty, *democracy*, in the truest sense of the word, is necessarily a *despotism*, because it establishes an executive power through which all the citizens may make decisions about (and indeed against) the single individual without his consent, so that decisions are made by all the people and yet not by all the people; and this means that the general will is in contradiction with itself, and thus also with freedom.

For any form of government which is not *representative* is essentially an *anomaly*, because one and the same person cannot at the same time be both the legislator and the executor of his own will, just as the general proposition in logical reasoning cannot at the same time be a secondary proposition subsuming the particular within the general. And even if the other two political constitutions (i.e. autocracy and aristocracy) are always defective in as much as they leave room for a despotic form of government, it is at least possible that they will be associated with a form of government which accords with the *spirit* of a representative system. Thus Frederick II[5] at least *said* that he was merely the highest servant of the state,* while a democratic constitution makes this attitude impossible, because everyone under it wants to be a ruler. We can therefore say that the smaller the number of ruling persons in a state and the greater their powers of representation, the more the constitution will approximate to its republican potentiality, which it may hope to realise eventually by gradual reforms. For this reason, it is more difficult in an aristocracy than in a monarchy to reach this one and only perfectly lawful kind of constitution, while it is possible in a democracy only by means of violent revolution. But the

* Many have criticised the high-sounding appellations which are often bestowed on a ruler (e.g. 'the divine anointed', or 'the executor and representative of the divine will on earth') as gross and extravagant flatteries, but it seems to me without reason. Far from making the ruler of the land arrogant, they ought rather to fill his soul with humility. For if he is a man of understanding (which we must certainly assume), he will reflect that he has taken over an office which is too great for a human being, namely that of administering God's most sacred institution on earth, the rights of man; he will always live in fear of having in any way injured God's most valued possession.

people are immensely more concerned with the mode of government*
than with the form of the constitution, although a great deal also depends
on the degree to which the constitution fits the purpose of the government.
But if the mode of government is to accord with the concept of right, it
must be based on the representative system. This system alone makes
possible a republican state, and without it, despotism and violence will
result, no matter what kind of constitution is in force. None of the so-called
'republics' of antiquity employed such a system, and they thus inevitably
ended in despotism, although this is still relatively bearable under the rule
of a single individual.

*Second Definitive Article of a Perpetual Peace: The Right of Nations
shall be based on a Federation of Free States*

Peoples who have grouped themselves into nation states may be judged in
the same way as individual men living in a state of nature, independent of
external laws; for they are a standing offence to one another by the very
fact that they are neighbours. Each nation, for the sake of its own security,
can and ought to demand of the others that they should enter along with
it into a constitution, similar to the civil one, within which the rights of
each could be secured. This would mean establishing a *federation of
peoples*. But a federation of this sort would not be the same thing as an
international state. For the idea of an international state is contradictory,
since every state involves a relationship between a superior (the legislator)
and an inferior (the people obeying the laws), whereas a number of nations
forming one state would constitute a single nation. And this contradicts
our initial assumption, as we are here considering the right of nations in
relation to one another in so far as they are a group of separate states
which are not to be welded together as a unit.

We look with profound contempt upon the way in which savages cling
to their lawless freedom. They would rather engage in incessant strife

* Mallet du Pan,[6] in his flamboyant but hollow and empty style, boasts of having at last,
after many years of experience, become convinced of the truth of Pope's famous saying:
'For forms of government let fools contest; Whate'er is best administered is best.'[7] If
this means that the best administered government is the best administered, he has
cracked a nut (as Swift puts it) and been rewarded with a worm.[8] But if it means that the
best administered government is also the best kind of government (i.e. the best constitution), it is completely false, for examples of good governments prove nothing whatsoever about kinds of government. Who, indeed, governed better than a Titus[9] or a
Marcus Aurelius[10], and yet the one left a Domitian[11] as his successor, and the other a
Commodus.[12] And this could not have happened under a good constitution, since their
unsuitability for the post of ruler was known early enough, and the power of their predecessors was great enough to have excluded them from the succession.

than submit to a legal constraint which they might impose upon themselves, for they prefer the freedom of folly to the freedom of reason. We regard this as barbarism, coarseness, and brutish debasement of humanity. We might thus expect that civilised peoples, each united within itself as a state, would hasten to abandon so degrading a condition as soon as possible. But instead of doing so, each *state* sees its own majesty (for it would be absurd to speak of the majesty of a *people*) precisely in not having to submit to any external legal constraint, and the glory of its ruler consists in his power to order thousands of people to immolate themselves for a cause which does not truly concern them, while he need not himself incur any danger whatsoever.* And the main difference between the savage nations of Europe and those of America is that while some American tribes have been entirely eaten up by their enemies, the Europeans know how to make better use of those they have defeated than merely by making a meal of them. They would rather use them to increase the number of their own subjects, thereby augmenting their stock of instruments for conducting even more extensive wars.

Although it is largely concealed by governmental constraints in law-governed civil society, the depravity of human nature is displayed without disguise in the unrestricted relations which obtain between the various nations. It is therefore to be wondered at that the word *right* has not been completely banished from military politics as superfluous pedantry, and that no state has been bold enough to declare itself publicly in favour of doing so. For Hugo Grotius,[13] Pufendorf,[14] Vattel[15] and the rest (sorry comforters as they are) are still dutifully quoted in *justification* of military aggression, although their philosophically or diplomatically formulated codes do not and cannot have the slightest *legal* force, since states as such are not subject to a common external constraint. Yet there is no instance of a state ever having been moved to desist from its purpose by arguments supported by the testimonies of such notable men. This homage which every state pays (in words at least) to the concept of right proves that man possesses a greater moral capacity, still dormant at present, to overcome eventually the evil principle within him (for he cannot deny that it exists), and to hope that others will do likewise. Otherwise the word *right* would never be used by states which intend to make war on one another, unless in a derisory sense, as when a certain Gallic prince declared: 'Nature has given to the strong the prerogative of making the weak obey them.' The

---

* Thus a Bulgarian prince, replying to the Greek Emperor who had kindly offered to settle his dispute with him by a duel, declared: 'A smith who possesses tongs will not lift the glowing iron out of the coals with his own hands.'

way in which states seek their rights can only be by war, since there is no external tribunal to put their claims to trial. But rights cannot be decided by military victory, and a *peace treaty* may put an end to the current war, but not to that general warlike condition within which pretexts can always be found for a new war. And indeed, such a state of affairs cannot be pronounced completely unjust, since it allows each party to act as judge in its own cause. Yet while natural right allows us to say of men living in a lawless condition that they ought to abandon it, the right of nations does not allow us to say the same of states. For as states, they already have a lawful internal constitution, and have thus outgrown the coercive right of others to subject them to a wider legal constitution in accordance with their conception of right. On the other hand, reason, as the highest legislative moral power, absolutely condemns war as a test of rights and sets up peace as an immediate duty. But peace can neither be inaugurated nor secured without a general agreement between the nations; thus a particular kind of league, which we might call a *pacific federation* (*foedus pacificum*), is required. It would differ from a *peace treaty* (*pactum pacis*) in that the latter terminates *one* war, whereas the former would seek to end *all* wars for good. This federation does not aim to acquire any power like that of a state, but merely to preserve and secure the *freedom* of each state in itself, along with that of the other confederated states, although this does not mean that they need to submit to public laws and to a coercive power which enforces them, as do men in a state of nature. It can be shown that this idea of *federalism*, extending gradually to encompass all states and thus leading to perpetual peace, is practicable and has objective reality. For if by good fortune one powerful and enlightened nation can form a republic (which is by its nature inclined to seek perpetual peace), this will provide a focal point for federal association among other states. These will join up with the first one, thus securing the freedom of each state in accordance with the idea of international right, and the whole will gradually spread further and further by a series of alliances of this kind.

It would be understandable for a people to say: 'There shall be no war among us; for we will form ourselves into a state, appointing for ourselves a supreme legislative, executive and juridical power to resolve our conflicts by peaceful means.' But if this state says: 'There shall be no war between myself and other states, although I do not recognise any supreme legislative power which could secure my rights and whose rights I should in turn secure', it is impossible to understand what justification I can have for placing any confidence in my rights, unless I can rely on some substitute for the union of civil society, i.e. on a free federation. If the concept of international right is to retain any meaning at all, reason must necessarily couple it with a federation of this kind.

The concept of international right becomes meaningless if interpreted as a right to go to war. For this would make it a right to determine what is lawful not by means of universally valid external laws, but by means of one-sided maxims backed up by physical force. It could be taken to mean that it is perfectly just for men who adopt this attitude to destroy one another, and thus to find perpetual peace in the vast grave where all the horrors of violence and those responsible for them would be buried. There is only one rational way in which states coexisting with other states can emerge from the lawless condition of pure warfare. Just like individual men, they must renounce their savage and lawless freedom, adapt themselves to public coercive laws, and thus form an *international state (civitas gentium)*, which would necessarily continue to grow until it embraced all the peoples of the earth. But since this is not the will of the nations, according to their present conception of international right (so that they reject *in hypothesi* what is true *in thesi*), the positive idea of a *world republic* cannot be realised. If all is not to be lost, this can at best find a negative substitute in the shape of an enduring and gradually expanding *federation* likely to prevent war. The latter may check the current of man's inclination to defy the law and antagonise his fellows, although there will always be a risk of it bursting forth anew. *Furor impius intus—fremit horridus ore cruento* (Virgil).*[16]

Third Definitive Article of a Perpetual Peace: Cosmopolitan Right shall be limited to Conditions of Universal Hospitality

As in the foregoing articles, we are here concerned not with philanthropy, but with *right*. In this context, *hospitality* means the right of a stranger not to be treated with hostility when he arrives on someone else's territory. He can indeed be turned away, if this can be done without causing his

* At the end of a war, when peace is concluded, it would not be inappropriate for a people to appoint a day of atonement after the festival of thanksgiving. Heaven would be invoked in the name of the state to forgive the human race for the great sin of which it continues to be guilty, since it will not accommodate itself to a lawful constitution in international relations. Proud of its independence, each state prefers to employ the barbarous expedient of war, although war cannot produce the desired decision on the rights of particular states. The thanksgivings for individual victories during a war, the hymns which are sung (in the style of the Israelites) to the *Lord of Hosts*, contrast no less markedly with the moral conception of a father of mankind. For besides displaying indifference to the way in which nations pursue their mutual rights (deplorable though it is), they actually rejoice at having annihilated numerous human beings or their happiness.

death, but he must not be treated with hostility, so long as he behaves in a peaceable manner in the place he happens to be in. The stranger cannot claim the *right of a guest* to be entertained, for this would require a special friendly agreement whereby he might become a member of the native household for a certain time. He may only claim a *right of resort*, for all men are entitled to present themselves in the society of others by virtue of their right to communal possession of the earth's surface. Since the earth is a globe, they cannot disperse over an infinite area, but must necessarily tolerate one another's company. And no-one originally has any greater right than anyone else to occupy any particular portion of the earth. The community of man is divided by uninhabitable parts of the earth's surface such as oceans and deserts, but even then, the *ship* or the *camel* (the ship of the desert) make it possible for them to approach their fellows over these ownerless tracts, and to utilise as a means of social intercourse that *right to the earth's surface* which the human race shares in common. The inhospitable behaviour of coastal dwellers (as on the Barbary coast) in plundering ships on the adjoining seas or enslaving stranded seafarers, or that of inhabitants of the desert (as with the Arab Bedouins), who regard their proximity to nomadic tribes as a justification for plundering them, is contrary to natural right. But this natural right of hospitality, i.e. the right of strangers, does not extend beyond those conditions which make it possible for them to *attempt* to enter into relations with the native inhabitants. In this way, continents distant from each other can enter into peaceful mutual relations which may eventually be regulated by public laws, thus bringing the human race nearer and nearer to a cosmopolitan constitution.

If we compare with this ultimate end the *inhospitable* conduct of the civilised states of our continent, especially the commercial states, the injustice which they display in *visiting* foreign countries and peoples (which in their case is the same as *conquering* them) seems appallingly great. America, the negro countries, the Spice Islands, the Cape, etc. were looked upon at the time of their discovery as ownerless territories; for the native inhabitants were counted as nothing. In East India (Hindustan), foreign troops were brought in under the pretext of merely setting up trading posts. This led to oppression of the natives, incitement of the various Indian states to widespread wars, famine, insurrection, treachery and the whole litany of evils which can afflict the human race.

China* and Japan (Nippon), having had experience of such guests,

* If we wish to give this great empire the name by which it calls itself (i.e. *China*, not *Sina* or any similar form), we need only consult Georgi's[17] *Alphabetum Tibetanum*,

have wisely placed restrictions on them. China permits contact with her territories, but not entrance into them, while Japan only allows contact with a single European people, the Dutch, although they are still segregated from the native community like prisoners. The worst (or from the point of view of moral judgements, the best) thing about all this is that the commercial states do not even benefit by their violence, for all their trading companies are on the point of collapse. The Sugar Islands, that stronghold of the cruellest and most calculated slavery, do not yield any real profit; they serve only the indirect (and not entirely laudable) purpose of training sailors for warships, thereby aiding the prosecution of wars in Europe. And all this is the work of powers who make endless ado about their piety, and who wish to be considered as chosen believers while they live on the fruits of iniquity.

The peoples of the earth have thus entered in varying degrees into a universal community, and it has developed to the point where a violation

pp. 651–654, note b in particular. According to Professor Fischer[18] of Petersburg, it actually has no fixed name which it might apply to itself; the commonest one is still the word *Kin*, which means gold (the Tibetans, however, call this *Ser*), which explains why the emperor is called King of Gold (i.e. of the fairest land in the world). The word is apparently pronounced *Chin* in the land itself, but expressed as *Kin* by the Italian missionaries, who cannot pronounce the correct guttural sound. It can also be seen that what the Romans called the land of the people of *Ser* was in fact China, and silk was brought from there to Europe via Greater Tibet (probably crossing Lesser Tibet, Bukhara[19] and Persia). This led to numerous speculations on the antiquity of this extraordinary state as compared with that of Hindustan, and on its relations with Tibet as well as with Japan. But the name Sina or Tschina, which neighbouring countries allegedly use of it, leads nowhere.

Perhaps the ancient but hitherto obscure community between Europe and Tibet can be explained from what Hesychius[20] has recorded of the hierophant's[21] cry Κονξ 'Ομπαξ (*Konx Ompax*)[22] in the Eleusinian Mysteries[23] (cf. *Journey of the Younger Anacharsis*, Part V, p. 447 *et seq.*).[24] For according to Georgi's *Alphabetum Tibetanum*, the word *Concioa* means god, and it markedly resembles *Konx*, while *Pah-cio* (*ibid.* p. 520), which the Greeks might easily have pronounced *pax*, means *promulgator legis*, the divinity which pervades the whole of nature (also called *Cencresi*, p. 177). But *Om*, which La Croze[25] translates as *benedictus* (blessed), can scarcely mean anything other than *beatific* if applied to the deity (p. 507). When P. Francisco Orazio[26] asked the Tibetan lamas how they conceived of god (*Concioa*), he always received the answer: '*God is the community of all the holy ones*' (i.e. the community of blessed souls, at last reunited in the deity by being reborn as lamas after numerous migrations through all kinds of bodies, and thereby transformed into beings worthy of adoration—p. 223). Thus the mysterious name *Konx Ompax* might designate that *holy* (*Konx*), *heavenly* (*Om*) and *wise* (*Pax*) supreme being who pervades the whole world, i.e. nature personified. As used in the Greek mysteries, it may well have signified *monotheism* to the epopts,[27] as distinct from the *polytheism* of the uninitiated mass, although it savoured of atheism to P. Orazio (*loc. cit.*). Our earlier considerations should help to explain how this mysterious name reached the Greeks from Tibet; conversely, this influence makes it appear probable that Europe at an early date had contact with China by way of Tibet, perhaps even earlier than with India.[28]

of rights in *one* part of the world is felt *everywhere*. The idea of a cosmopolitan right is therefore not fantastic and overstrained; it is a necessary complement to the unwritten code of political and international right, transforming it into a universal right of humanity. Only under this condition can we flatter ourselves that we are continually advancing towards a perpetual peace.

First Supplement: On the Guarantee of a Perpetual Peace

Perpetual peace is *guaranteed* by no less an authority than the great artist *Nature* herself (*natura daedala rerum*).[29] The mechanical process of nature visibly exhibits the purposive plan of producing concord among men, even against their will and indeed by means of their very discord. This design, if we regard it as a compelling cause whose laws of operation are unknown to us, is called *fate*. But if we consider its purposive function within the world's development, whereby it appears as the underlying wisdom of a higher cause, showing the way towards the objective goal of the human race and predetermining the world's evolution, we call it *providence*.* We cannot actually observe such an agency in the artifices

* In the mechanism of nature, of which man (as a sensory being) is a part, there is evident a fundamental form on which its very existence depends. This form becomes intelligible to us only if we attribute it to the design of a universal creator who has determined it in advance. We call this predetermining influence divine *providence*, and further define it as *original providence* in so far as it is active from the earliest times onwards (*providentia conditrix*; *semel iussit, semper parent*—Augustine).[30] In as much as it sustains the course of nature in accordance with purposive universal laws, we call it *ruling providence* (*providentia gubernatrix*). If it realises particular ends which man could not have foreseen and whose existence can only be guessed at from the results, it is termed *guiding providence* (*providentia directrix*). And finally, if individual events are regarded as divinely intended, we no longer speak of providence but of a *special dispensation* (*directio extraordinaria*). But it is foolish presumption for man to claim that he can recognise this as such, since it implies that a miracle has taken place, even if the events are not specifically described as miraculous. For however pious and humble it may sound, it is absurd and self-conceited for anyone to conclude from a single event that the efficient cause is governed by a special principle, or that the event in question is an end in itself and not just the natural and mechanical consequence of another end which is completely unknown to us. Similarly, it is false and self-contradictory to classify providence in terms of worldly objects (*materialiter*), dividing it up into *general* and *particular*, as occurs in the doctrine that providence takes care to preserve the various species of creatures, but leaves chance to look after the individuals; for the whole point of saying that providence applies in general is that no single object should be excepted from it. This classification, however, was probably meant to indicate that the intentions of providence are carried out *in different ways* (*formaliter*). These might be *ordinary* (e.g. the annual death and revival of nature with the changes of seasons) or *extraordinary* (e.g. the transporting of wood by Ocean currents to Arctic coasts where it cannot grow, thus providing for the native inhabitants, who could not live without it). In the latter case, while we can well explain the physico-mechanical cause of the phenomena in question (e.g. by the fact that the riverbanks in temperate lands are of nature, nor can we even *infer* its existence from them. But as with all relations between the form of things and their ultimate purposes, we can and must *supply it mentally* in order to conceive of its possibility by analogy with human artifices. Its relationship to and conformity with the end which reason directly prescribes to us (i.e. the end of morality) can only be conceived of as an idea. Yet while this idea is indeed far-fetched in *theory*, it does possess dogmatic validity and has a very real foundation in *practice*, as with the concept of *perpetual peace*, which makes it our duty to promote it by using the natural mechanism described above. But in contexts such as this, where we are concerned purely with theory and not with religion, we should also note that it is more in keeping with the limitations of human reason to speak of *nature* and not of *providence*, for reason, in dealing with cause and effect relationships, must keep within the bounds of possible experience. *Modesty* forbids us to speak of providence as something we can recognise, for this would mean donning the wings of Icarus and presuming to approach the mystery of its inscrutable intentions.

But before we define this guarantee more precisely, we must first examine the situation in which nature has placed the actors in her great spectacle, for it is this situation which ultimately demands the guarantee of peace. We may next enquire in what manner the guarantee is provided.

Nature's provisional arrangement is as follows. Firstly, she has taken

covered in forests, so that the trees may fall into the rivers and be carried further afield by currents like the Gulf Stream), we must not on the other hand overlook teleology, which indicates the foresight of a wise agency governing nature. But the conception, current in the academic world, of a divine *participation* or *collaboration* (*concursus*) in effects experienced in the world of the senses, is superfluous. For *firstly*, it is self-contradictory to try to harness disparates together (*gryphes iungere equis*),[31] and to imply that a being who is himself the complete cause of the world's developments has to *supplement* his own predetermining providence during the course of world events (so that it must originally have been inadequate); for example, it is absurd to say that after God, the doctor acted as an assistant in curing the patient—*causa solitaria non iuvat*.[32] God is the creator of the doctor and of all his medicaments, so that the effect must be ascribed *entirely* to him if we are to ascend to that supreme original cause which is theoretically beyond our comprehension. Alternatively, it can be ascribed *entirely* to the doctor, in so far as we treat the event in question as belonging to the order of nature and as capable of explanation within the causal series of earthly occurrences. And *secondly*, if we adopt such attitudes, we are deprived of all definite principles by which we might judge effects. But the concept of a divine *concursus* is completely acceptable and indeed necessary in the moral and practical sense, which refers exclusively to the transcendental world. For example, we may say that we should never cease to strive towards goodness, for we believe that God, even by means which we cannot comprehend, will make up for our own lack of righteousness so long as our attitude is sincere. It is, however, self-evident that no-one should use such arguments to *explain* a good deed, regarded as a secular event, for this would presuppose theoretical knowledge of the transcendental, which it is absurd for us to claim.

care that human beings are able to live in all the areas where they are settled. Secondly, she has driven them in all directions by means of *war*, so that they inhabit even the most inhospitable regions. And thirdly, she has compelled them by the same means to enter into more or less legal relationships. It is in itself wonderful that moss can still grow in the cold wastes around the Arctic Ocean; the *reindeer* can scrape it out from beneath the snow, and can thus itself serve as nourishment or as a draft animal for the Ostiaks or Samoyeds. Similarly, the sandy salt deserts contain the *camel*, which seems as if it had been created for travelling over them in order that they might not be left unutilised. But evidence of design in nature emerges even more clearly when we realise that the shores of the Arctic Ocean are inhabited not only by fur-bearing animals, but also by seals, walrusses and whales, whose flesh provides food and whose fat provides warmth for the native inhabitants. Nature's care arouses most admiration, however, by carrying driftwood to these treeless regions, without anyone knowing exactly where it comes from. For if they did not have this material, the natives would not be able to construct either boats or weapons, or dwellings in which to live. And they have enough to do making war on the animals to be able to live in peace among themselves. But it was probably nothing but war which *drove* them into these regions. And the first *instrument of war* among all the animals which man learned to domesticate in the course of peopling the earth was the *horse*. For the elephant belongs to that later age of luxury which began after states had been established. The same applies to the art of cultivating certain kinds of grasses known as *cereals*, whose original nature is now unknown to us, and to the production and refinement of various *fruits* by transplanting and grafting (in Europe, perhaps only two species were involved, the crab-apple and the wild pear). Such arts could arise only within established states in which landed property was secure, after men had made the transition to an *agricultural* way of life, abandoning the lawless freedom they had enjoyed in their previous existence as hunters,* fishers and shepherds. *Salt* and *iron* were next discovered, and were perhaps the

* Of all ways of life, that of the hunter is undoubtedly most at odds with a civilised constitution. For families, having to live in separation, soon become strangers to each other, and subsequently, being scattered about in wide forests, they treat each other with hostility, since each requires a large area to provide itself with food and clothing. The command addressed to Noah forbidding the eating of blood (Genesis 9, 4–6) seems to have been originally nothing else but a prohibition of the hunter's way of life. For this must often involve eating uncooked meat, and if the latter is forbidden, the first is automatically ruled out too. This prohibition, often reiterated, was a condition later imposed by the Jewish Christians upon the newly accepted Christians of heathen origin, albeit with a different intention (Acts 15,20 and 21,25).

first articles of trade between nations to be in demand everywhere. In this way, nations first entered into *peaceful relations* with one another, and thus achieved mutual understanding, community of interests and peaceful relations, even with the most distant of their fellows.

In seeing to it that men *could* live everywhere on earth, nature has at the same time despotically willed that they *should* live everywhere, even against their own inclinations. And this obligation does not rest upon any concept of duty which might bind them to fulfil it in accordance with a moral law; on the contrary, nature has chosen war as a means of attaining this end.

We can observe nations which reveal the unity of their descent by the unity of their language. This is the case with the *Samoyeds* on the Arctic Ocean and another people with a similar language living two hundred miles away in the Altai Mountains; another people of Mongol extraction, given to horsemanship and hence to warlike pursuits, has pushed its way between them, thus driving the one part of the tribe far away from the other into the most inhospitable Arctic regions, where it would certainly not have gone by its own inclinations.* In the same way, the Finns in the northernmost region of Europe (where they are known as Lapps) are now far separated from the Hungarians, to whom they are linguistically related, by Gothic and Sarmatian peoples who have pushed their way in between them. And what else but war, nature's means of peopling the whole earth, can have driven the Eskimos so far North—for they are quite distinct from all other American races, and are perhaps descended from European adventurers of ancient times; the Pesherae have been driven South into Tierra del Fuego in the same manner. War itself, however, does not require any particular kind of motivation, for it seems to be ingrained in human nature, and even to be regarded as something noble to which man is inspired by his love of honour, without selfish motives. Thus warlike courage, with the American savages as with their European counterparts in medieval times, is held to be of great and immediate value—and not just *in times of* war (as might be expected), but also *in order that* there may be war. Thus wars are often started merely to display this quality, so

* The following question might be raised. If nature intended that these frozen shores should not remain uninhabited, what will happen to their inhabitants if nature, as indeed may well happen, ceases to provide them with driftwood? For we may well believe that the natives of temperate zones, as their culture progresses, will make better use of the wood which grows on the banks of their rivers, and will not allow it to fall into them and be swept out to sea. I should reply that those who live on the Ob, the Yenisei, the Lena etc. will supply them with it commercially, bartering it for the animal products in which the Arctic coasts are so plentiful—but only after nature has compelled them to live in peace with one another.

III

that war itself is invested with an inherent *dignity*; for even philosophers have eulogised it as a kind of ennobling influence on man, forgetting the Greek saying that 'war is bad in that it produces more evil people than it destroys'. So much, then, for what nature does to further *her own end* with respect to the human race as an animal species.

We now come to the essential question regarding the prospect of perpetual peace. What does nature do in relation to the end which man's own reason prescribes to him as a duty, i.e. how does nature help to promote his *moral purpose*? And how does nature guarantee that what man *ought* to do by the laws of his freedom (but does not do) will in fact be done through nature's compulsion, without prejudice to the free agency of man? This question arises, moreover, in all three areas of public right—in *political, international* and *cosmopolitan right*. For if I say that nature *wills* that this or that should happen, this does not mean that nature imposes on us a *duty* to do it, for duties can only be imposed by practical reason, acting without any external constraint. On the contrary, nature does it herself, whether we are willing or not: *fata volentem ducunt, nolentem trahunt*.[33]

I. Even if people were not compelled by internal dissent to submit to the coercion of public laws, war would produce the same effect from outside. For in accordance with the natural arrangement described above, each people would find itself confronted by another neighbouring people pressing in upon it, thus forcing it to form itself internally into a *state* in order to encounter the other as an armed *power*. Now the *republican* constitution is the only one which does complete justice to the rights of man. But it is also the most difficult to establish, and even more so to preserve, so that many maintain that it would only be possible within a state of *angels*, since men, with their self-seeking inclinations, would be incapable of adhering to a constitution of so sublime a nature. But in fact, nature comes to the aid of the universal and rational human will, so admirable in itself but so impotent in practice, and makes use of precisely those self-seeking inclinations in order to do so. It only remains for men to create a good organisation for the state, a task which is well within their capability, and to arrange it in such a way that their self-seeking energies are opposed to one another, each thereby neutralising or eliminating the destructive effects of the rest. And as far as reason is concerned, the result is the same as if man's selfish tendencies were non-existent, so that man, even if he is not morally good in himself, is nevertheless compelled to be a good citizen. As hard as it may sound, the problem of setting up a state can be solved even by a nation of devils (so long as they possess understanding). It may be stated as follows: 'In order to organise a group of rational beings who together require universal laws for their survival, but of whom each separate individual is secretly inclined to exempt himself from them, the constitution must be so designed that, although the citizens are opposed to one another in their private attitudes, these opposing views may inhibit one another in such a way that the public conduct of the citizens will be the same as if they did not have such evil attitudes.' A problem of this kind must be soluble. For such a task does not involve the moral improvement of man; it only means finding out how the mechanism of nature can be applied to men in such a manner that the antagonism of their hostile attitudes will make them compel one another to submit to coercive laws, thereby producing a condition of peace within which the laws can be enforced. We can even see this principle at work among the actually existing (although as yet very imperfectly organised) states. For in their external relations, they have already approached what the idea of right prescribes, although the reason for this is certainly not their internal moral attitudes. In the same way, we cannot expect their moral attitudes to produce a good political constitution; on the contrary, it is only through the latter that the people can be expected to attain a good level of moral culture. Thus that mechanism of nature by which selfish inclinations are naturally opposed to one another in their external relations can be used by reason to facilitate the attainment of its own end, the reign of established right. Internal and external peace are thereby furthered and assured, so far as it lies within the power of the state itself to do so. We may therefore say that nature *irresistibly wills* that right should eventually gain the upper hand. What men have neglected to do will ultimately happen of its own accord, albeit with much inconvenience. As Bouterwek[34] puts it: 'If the reed is bent too far, it breaks; and he who wants too much gets nothing.'

2. The idea of international right presupposes the separate existence of many independent adjoining states. And such a state of affairs is essentially a state of war, unless there is a federal union to prevent hostilities breaking out. But in the light of the idea of reason, this state is still to be preferred to an amalgamation of the separate nations under a single power which has overruled the rest and created a universal monarchy. For the laws progressively lose their impact as the government increases its range, and a soulless despotism, after crushing the germs of goodness, will finally lapse into anarchy. It is nonetheless the desire of every state (or its ruler) to achieve lasting peace by thus dominating the whole world, if at all possible. But *nature* wills it otherwise, and uses two means to separate the nations and prevent them from intermingling—*linguistic* and

*religious** differences. These may certainly occasion mutual hatred and provide pretexts for wars, but as culture grows and men gradually move towards greater agreement over their principles, they lead to mutual understanding and peace. And unlike that universal despotism which saps all man's energies and ends in the graveyard of freedom, this peace is created and guaranteed by an equilibrium of forces and a most vigorous rivalry.

3. Thus nature wisely separates the nations, although the will of each individual state, even basing its arguments on international right, would gladly unite them under its own sway by force or by cunning. On the other hand, nature also unites nations which the concept of cosmopolitan right would not have protected from violence and war, and does so by means of their mutual self-interest. For the *spirit of commerce* sooner or later takes hold of every people, and it cannot exist side by side with war. And of all the powers (or means) at the disposal of the power of the state, *financial power* can probably be relied on most. Thus states find themselves compelled to promote the noble cause of peace, though not exactly from motives of morality. And wherever in the world there is a threat of war breaking out, they will try to prevent it by mediation, just as if they had entered into a permanent league for this purpose; for by the very nature of things, large military alliances can only rarely be formed, and will even more rarely be successful.

In this way, nature guarantees perpetual peace by the actual mechanism of human inclinations. And while the likelihood of its being attained is not sufficient to enable us to *prophesy* the future theoretically, it is enough for practical purposes. It makes it our duty to work our way towards this goal, which is more than an empty chimera.

Second Supplement: Secret Article of a Perpetual Peace

In transactions involving public right, a secret article (regarded objectively or in terms of its content) is a contradiction. But in subjective terms, i.e. in relation to the sort of person who dictates it, an article may well contain a secret element, for the person concerned may consider it prejudicial to his own dignity to name himself publicly as its originator.

The only article of this kind is embodied in the following sentence:

* *Religious differences*—an odd expression! As if we were to speak of different *moralities*. There may certainly be different historical *confessions*, although these have nothing to do with religion itself but only with changes in the means used to further religion, and are thus the province of historical research. And there may be just as many different religious *books* (the Zend-Avesta, the Vedas, the Koran, etc.). But there can only be *one religion* which is valid for all men and at all times. Thus the different confessions can scarcely be more than the vehicles of religion; these are fortuitous, and may vary with differences in time or place.

'The maxims of the philosophers on the conditions under which public peace is possible shall be consulted by states which are armed for war.'

Although it may seem humiliating for the legislative authority of a state, to which we must naturally attribute the highest degree of wisdom, to seek instruction from *subjects* (the philosophers) regarding the principles on which it should act in its relations with other states, it is nevertheless extremely advisable that it should do so. The state will therefore invite their help *silently*, making a secret of it. In other words, it will *allow them to speak* freely and publicly on the universal maxims of warfare and peace-making, and they will indeed do so of their own accord if no-one forbids their discussions. And no special formal arrangement among the states is necessary to enable them to agree on this issue, for the agreement already lies in the obligations imposed by universal human reason in its capacity as a moral legislator. This does not, however, imply that the state must give the principles of the philosopher precedence over the pronouncements of the jurist (who represents the power of the state), but only that the philosopher should be given a *hearing*. The jurist, who has taken as his symbol the scales of right and the sword of justice, usually uses the latter not merely to keep any extraneous influences away from the former, but will throw the *sword* into one of the *scales* if it refuses to sink (*vae victis!*).[35] Unless the jurist is at the same time a philosopher, at any rate in moral matters, he is under the greatest temptation to do this, for his business is merely to apply existing laws, and not to enquire whether they are in need of improvement. He acts as if this truly low rank of his faculty were in fact one of the higher ones, for the simple reason that it is accompanied by power (as is also the case with two of the other faculties). But the philosophical faculty occupies a very low position in face of the combined power of the others. Thus we are told, for instance, that philosophy is the *handmaid* of theology, and something similar in relation to the others. But it is far from clear whether this handmaid bears the torch before her gracious lady, or carries the train behind.

It is not to be expected that kings will philosophise or that philosophers will become kings; nor is it to be desired, however, since the possession of power inevitably corrupts the free judgement of reason. Kings or sovereign peoples (i.e. those governing themselves by egalitarian laws) should not, however, force the class of philosophers to disappear or to remain silent, but should allow them to speak publicly. This is essential to both in order that light may be thrown on their affairs. And since the class of philosophers is by nature incapable of forming seditious factions or clubs, they cannot incur suspicion of disseminating propaganda.

Appendix

I

ON THE DISAGREEMENT BETWEEN MORALS AND POLITICS IN RELATION TO PERPETUAL PEACE

Morality, as a collection of absolutely binding laws by which our actions *ought* to be governed, belongs essentially, in an objective sense, to the practical sphere. And if we have once acknowledged the authority of this concept of duty, it is patently absurd to say that we *cannot* act as the moral laws require. For if this were the case, the concept of duty would automatically be dropped from morals (*ultra posse nemo obligatur*).[36] Hence there can be no conflict between politics, as an applied branch of right, and morality, as a theoretical branch of right (i.e. between theory and practice); for such a conflict could occur only if morality were taken to mean a general doctrine of expediency, i.e. a theory of the maxims by which one might select the most useful means of furthering one's own advantage—and this would be tantamount to denying that morality exists.

If politics were to say: '*Be ye therefore wise as serpents*', morality might add, by way of qualification: '*and harmless as doves*'.[37] If these two precepts cannot exist together within a single commandment, then there is indeed a disagreement between politics and morality. But if the two are to be united, it is absurd to suppose that they are in opposition, and the question of how such a conflict could be resolved cannot even be posed as a mental exercise. It is true, alas, that the saying '*Honesty is the best policy*' embodies a theory which is frequently contradicted by practice. Yet the equally theoretical proposition '*Honesty is better than any policy*' infinitely transcends all objections, and it is indeed an indispensable condition of any policy whatsoever. The god of morality does not yield to Jupiter, the custodian of violence, for even Jupiter is still subject to fate. In short, reason is not sufficiently enlightened to discover the whole series of predetermining causes which would allow it to predict accurately the happy or unhappy consequences of human activities as dictated by the mechanism of nature; it can only hope that the result will meet with its wishes. But reason at all times shows us clearly enough what we have to do in order to remain in the paths of duty, as the rules of wisdom require, and thus shows us the way towards our ultimate goal.

But the man of practice, to whom morality is pure theory, coldly repudiates our well-intentioned hopes, even if he does concede that we *can* do what we *ought* to do. He bases his argument on the claim that we can tell in advance from human nature that man will never *want* to do what is necessary in order to attain the goal of eternal peace. It is perfectly true that the will of all *individual* men to live in accordance with principles of freedom within a lawful constitution (i.e. the *distributive* unity of the will of all) is not sufficient for this purpose. Before so difficult a problem can be solved, all men *together* (i.e. the *collective* unity of the combined will) must desire to attain this goal; only then can civil society exist as a single whole. Since an additional unifying cause must therefore overrule the differences in the particular wishes of all individuals before a common will can arise, and since no single individual can create it, the only conceivable way of executing the original idea *in practice*, and hence of inaugurating a state of right, is by *force*. On its coercive authority, public right will subsequently be based.

We can certainly expect in advance that there will be considerable deviations in actual experience from the original theoretical idea. For we cannot assume that the moral attitude of the legislator will be such that, after the disorderly mass has been united into a people, he will leave them to create a lawful constitution by their own common will.

It might thus be said that, once a person has the power in his own hands, he will not let the people prescribe laws for him. Similarly, a state which is self-governing and free from all external laws will not let itself become dependent on the judgement of other states in seeking to uphold its rights against them. And even a whole continent, if it feels itself in a superior position to another one, will not hesitate to plunder it or actually to extend its rule over it, irrespective of whether the other is in its way or not. In this way, all the plans which theory lays for political, international or cosmopolitan right dissolve into empty and impracticable ideals; but a practice which is based on empirical principles of human nature, and which does not consider it beneath its dignity to shape its maxims according to the way of the world, can alone hope to find a solid foundation for its system of political opportunism.

If, of course, there is neither freedom nor any moral law based on freedom, but only a state in which everything that happens or can happen simply obeys the mechanical workings of nature, politics would mean the art of utilising nature for the government of men, and this would constitute the whole of practical wisdom; the concept of right would then be only an empty idea. But if we consider it absolutely necessary to couple the concept of right with politics, or even to make it a limiting condition of politics, it must be conceded that the two are compatible. And I can indeed imagine a *moral politician*, i.e. someone who conceives of the principles of political expediency in such a way that they can co-exist with morality, but I cannot imagine a *political moralist*, i.e. one who fashions his morality to suit his own advantage as a statesman.

The moral politician will make it a principle that, if any faults which could not have been prevented are discovered in the political constitution or in the relations between states, it is a duty, especially for heads of state, to see to it that they are corrected as soon as possible; it should be ensured that these political institutions are made to conform to natural right, which stands before us as a model in the idea of practical reason, and this should be done even if selfish interests have to be sacrificed. It would be contrary to all political expediency, which in this case agrees with morality, to destroy any of the existing bonds of political or cosmopolitan union before a better constitution has been prepared to take their place. And while it would be absurd to demand that their faults be repaired at once and by violent measures, it can still be required of the individual in power that he should be intimately aware of the maxim that changes for the better are necessary, in order that the constitution may constantly approach the optimum end prescribed by laws of right. A state may well *govern* itself in a republican way, even if its existing constitution provides for a despotic *ruling power*; and it will gradually come to the stage where the people can be influenced by the mere idea of the law's authority, just as if it were backed up by physical force, so that they will be able to create for themselves a legislation ultimately founded on right. If, however, a more lawful constitution were attained by unlawful means, i.e. by a violent *revolution* resulting from a previous bad constitution, it would then no longer be permissible to lead the people back to the original one, even although everyone who had interfered with the old constitution by violence or conspiracy would rightly have been subject to the penalties of rebellion during the revolution itself. But as for the external relationship between states, no state can be required to relinquish its constitution, even if the latter is despotic (and hence stronger in relation to external enemies), so long as this state is in danger of being engulfed at any moment by other states; hence while plans must be made for political improvement, it must be permissible to delay their execution until a better opportunity arises.*

* These are permissive laws of reason, which allow a state of public right to continue, even if it is affected by injustice, until all is ripe for a complete revolution or has been prepared for it by peaceful means. For any *legal* constitution, even if it is only in small measure *lawful*, is better than none at all, and the fate of a premature reform would be anarchy. Thus political prudence, with things as they are at present, will make it a duty

It may well be the case that despotic moralists, i.e. those who err in practice, frequently act contrary to political prudence by adopting or recommending premature measures, yet experience must gradually bring them out of their opposition to nature and make them adopt better ways. But moralising politicians, for what they are worth, try to cover up political principles which are contrary to right, under the pretext that human nature is *incapable* of attaining the good which reason prescribes as an idea. They thereby make progress *impossible*, and eternalise the violation of right.

Instead of applying the correct practice they boast of, these worldly-wise politicians resort to despicable tricks, for they are only out to exploit the people (and if possible the whole world) by influencing the current ruling power in such a way as to ensure their own private advantage. They are just like lawyers (i.e. those for whom law is a profession, not a matter of legislation) who have found their way into politics. For since it is not their business to argue over legislation itself, but to fulfil the present instructions of the law of the land, they will always regard the existing legal constitution (or if this is altered by a higher authority, the subsequent one) as the best, because everything in it will follow a proper mechanical order. But this skill in being all things to all men may give them the illusion that they can also pass judgement, in accordance with concepts of right (i.e. *a priori*, not empirically), on the principles of any *political constitution* whatsoever. And they may boast that they know *men* (which is certainly to be expected, since they have to do with so many of them), although they do not know *man* and his potentialities, for this requires a higher anthropological vantage-point.

Armed with concepts such as these, they proceed to take up political and international law as prescribed by reason. But they cannot take this step except in a spirit of chicanery, for they will follow their usual procedure of applying despotically formulated coercive laws in a mechanical manner, even in a sphere where the concepts of reason only allow for lawful coercion, in keeping with the principles of freedom, which alone makes possible a rightfully established political constitution. The supposed practitioner believes he can solve this problem empirically, ignoring the idea of reason and drawing on experience of how the (largely unlawful) constitutions which have hitherto survived best were organised. And the

to carry out reforms appropriate to the ideal of public right. But where revolutions are brought about by nature alone, it will not use them as a good excuse for even greater oppression, but will treat them as a call of nature to create a lawful constitution based on the principles of freedom, for a thorough reform of this kind is the only one which will last.

maxims which he employs for this purpose, although he does not make them public, can roughly be expressed in the following sophistries:

1. *Fac et excusa.*[38] Seize any favourable opportunity of arbitrarily expropriating a right which the state enjoys over its own or over a neighbouring people; the justification can be presented far more easily and elegantly and the use of violence can be glossed over far more readily *after the fact* than if one were to think out convincing reasons in advance and then wait for counter-arguments to be offered. This is particularly true of the first case, where the highest power in the state is also the legislative authority which must be obeyed without argument. Such audacity itself gives a certain appearance of inner conviction that the deed is right and just, and the god of success (*bonus eventus*) will then be the best of advocates.

2. *Si fecisti, nega.*[39] If you have committed a crime, for instance, in order to lead your people to desperation and thence to rebellion, deny that the guilt is yours. Maintain instead that it arose from the intransigence of the subjects; or if you have seized control of a neighbouring people, say that the very nature of man is responsible, for if he does not anticipate others in resorting to violence, he may count on it that they will anticipate and overpower him.

3. *Divide et impera.*[40] That is, if there are certain privileged persons among the people who have chosen you for their ruler merely as *primus inter pares*,[41] make sure to disunite them among themselves and set them at odds with the people. And if you back up the people with false promises of greater freedom, everything will be dependent on your absolute will. Or if you are dealing with foreign states, to stir up discord among them is a fairly certain method of subjugating them one by one while merely appearing to lend support to the weaker.

No-one, it must be confessed, will be taken in by these political maxims, for they are all generally known. And it is not the case that men are ashamed of them, as if their injustice were all too obviously visible. For great powers are never embarrassed about how the common mass might judge them, but only about one another's opinions. And as for the principles listed above, the powers will feel no shame if they become publicly known, but only if they *fail to succeed*, for they are all agreed on the moral status of the maxims. They are left with *political honour*, on which they can always rely if they *enlarge their power* by whatever means they care to use.*

* It might be doubted whether any inherent wickedness rooted in human nature influences *men* who live together within a single state, for one might instead (with some plausibility) adduce the deficiencies of their as yet underdeveloped culture (i.e. their

From all these twists and turns of an immoral and opportunistic doctrine of how to create peace among men out of the warlike state of nature, this much at least is clear: men can as little escape the concept of right in their private relations as in their public ones, and they will not openly dare to base their politics on opportunistic machinations alone and thus to refuse altogether to obey any concept of public right (which is particularly remarkable in the case of international right). Instead, they pay such concepts all the honour they deserve, even although they may also devise a hundred excuses and subterfuges to get out of observing them in practice and to pretend that brute force and cunning can possess that authority which is the source and unifying bond of all right.

In order to end this sophistry (if not the actual injustice which it covers over) and to make the false representatives of those who wield power on earth confess that they are advocating might instead of right (adopting as they do the tone of persons entitled to give orders), it will be well to discover the ultimate principle from which the end of perpetual peace is derived, and thus to destroy the illusions with which men deceive themselves and others. It must likewise be demonstrated that all the evil which stands in the way of perpetual peace results from the fact that the political moralist starts out from the very point at which the moral politician rightly stops; he thus makes his principles subordinate to his end (i.e. puts the cart before the horse), thereby defeating his own purpose of reconciling politics with morality.

To ensure that practical philosophy is at one with itself, it is first necessary to resolve the question of whether, in problems of practical

barbarism) as the cause of the unlawful elements in their thinking. But in the external relationships between *states*, this wickedness is quite undisguisedly and irrefutably apparent. Within each individual state, it is concealed by the coercion embodied in the civil laws, for the citizens' inclination to do violence to one another is counteracted by a more powerful force—that of the government. This not only gives the whole a veneer of morality (*causae non causae*),[42] but by putting an end to outbreaks of lawless proclivities, it genuinely makes it much easier for the moral capacities of men to develop into an immediate respect for right. For each individual believes of himself that he would by all means maintain the sanctity of the concept of right and obey it faithfully, if only he could be certain that all the others would do likewise, and the government in part guarantees this for him; thus a great step is taken *towards* morality (although this is still not the same as a moral step), towards a state where the concept of duty is recognised for its own sake, irrespective of any possible gain in return. But since each individual, despite his good opinion of himself, assumes bad faith in everyone else, men thereby pass judgement on one another to the effect that they are all in point of *fact* of little worth— although it is a moot point why this should be so, since we cannot blame it on the *nature* of man as a free being. Since, however, that respect for the concept of right which man is absolutely incapable of renouncing gives the most solemn sanction to the theory that man is also capable of conforming to this concept, everyone can see that he must himself act in accordance with it, no matter how others may behave.

reason, we should begin with its *material* principle, i.e. its *end*, as an object of the will, or with its *formal* principle, i.e. the principle which rests on man's freedom in his external relations and which states: 'Act in such a way that you can wish your maxim to become a universal law (irrespective of what the end in view may be).'

The latter principle must undoubtedly take precedence. For as a principle of right, it has absolute necessity, whereas the former is necessary only if the empirical conditions which permit the proposed end to be realised can be assumed to exist. And if this end were also a duty, as with the end of perpetual peace, it would itself have to be deduced from the formal principle of the maxims governing external action. Now the former (i.e. material) principle is that of the *political moralist*, and it treats the problems of political, international and cosmopolitan right as mere *technical tasks*; but the latter (i.e. formal) principle is that of the *moral politician*, for whom it is a *moral task*, totally different in its execution from technical problems, to bring about perpetual peace, which is desirable not just as a physical good, but also as a state of affairs which must arise out of recognising one's duty.

For the solution of the first problem (that of political expediency), much knowledge of nature is required, so that one can use its mechanism to promote the intended end. Nevertheless, all this is uncertain so far as its repercussions on perpetual peace are concerned, no matter which of the three departments of public right one considers. For it is uncertain whether the obedience and prosperity of the people can be better maintained over a long period by strict discipline or by appeals to their vanity, by conferring supreme power upon a single individual or upon several united leaders, or perhaps merely by means of an aristocracy of office or by popular internal government. History offers examples of the opposite effect being produced by all forms of government, with the single exception of genuine republicanism, which, however, could be the object only of a moral politician. And it is even more uncertain in the case of an *international right* supposedly based on statutes worked out by ministers, for it is in fact a mere word with nothing behind it, since it depends upon treaties which contain in the very act of their conclusion the secret reservation that they may be violated. On the other hand, the solution of the second problem, that of *political wisdom*, presents itself as it were automatically; it is obvious to everyone, it defeats all artifices, and leads straight to its goal, so long as we prudently remember that it cannot be realised by violent and precipitate means, but must be steadily approached as favourable opportunities present themselves.

We may therefore offer the following advice: 'Seek ye first the kingdom of pure practical reason and its *righteousness*, and your object (the blessing of perpetual peace) will be added unto you.' For morality, with regard to its principles of public right (hence in relation to a political code which can be known *a priori*), has the peculiar feature that the less it makes its conduct depend upon the end it envisages (whether this be a physical or moral advantage), the more it will in general harmonise with this end. And the reason for this is that it is precisely the general will as it is given *a priori*, within a single people or in the mutual relationships of various peoples, which alone determines what is right among men. But this union of the will of all, if only it is put into practice in a consistent way, can also, within the mechanism of nature, be the cause which leads to the intended result and gives effect to the concept of right. For example, it is a principle of moral politics that a people should combine to form a state in accordance with freedom and equality as its sole concepts of right, and this principle is based not on expediency, but on duty. Political moralists, on the other hand, do not deserve a hearing, however much they argue about the natural mechanism of a mass of people who enter into society, or claim that this mechanism would invalidate the above principles and frustrate their fulfilment, or try to prove their assertions by citing examples of badly organised constitutions of ancient and modern times (e.g. of democracies without a system of representation). Such theories are particularly damaging, because they may themselves produce the very evil they predict. For they put man into the same class as other living machines, which only need to realise consciously that they are not free beings for them to become in their own eyes the most wretched of all earthly creatures.

The proverbial saying *fiat iustitia, pereat mundus*[43] (i.e. let justice reign, even if all the rogues in the world must perish) may sound somewhat inflated, but it is nonetheless true. It is a sound principle of right, which blocks up all the devious paths followed by cunning or violence. But it must not be misunderstood, or taken, for example, as a permit to apply one's own rights with the utmost rigour (which would conflict with ethical duty), but should be seen as an obligation of those in power not to deny or detract from the rights of anyone out of disfavour or sympathy for others. And this requires above all that the state should have an internal constitution organised in accordance with pure principles of right, and also that it unite with other neighbouring or even distant states to arrive at a lawful settlement of their differences by forming something analogous to a universal state. This proposition simply means that whatever the physical consequences may be, the political maxims adopted must not be influenced by the prospect of any benefit or happiness which might accrue to the state if it followed them, i.e. by the end which each state takes as the object of its will (as the highest *empirical* principle of political wisdom); they should be influenced only by the pure concept of rightful duty, i.e. by an obligation whose principle is given *a priori* by pure reason. The world will certainly not come to an end if there are fewer bad men. Moral evil has by nature the inherent quality of being self-destructive and self-contradictory in its aims (especially in relations between persons of a like mind), so that it makes way for the moral principle of goodness, even if such progress is slow.

Thus in *objective* or theoretical terms, there is no conflict whatsoever between morality and politics. In a *subjective* sense, however (i.e. in relation to the selfish disposition of man, which, since it is not based on maxims of reason, cannot however be called practice), this conflict will and ought to remain active, since it serves as a whetstone of virtue. The true courage of virtue, according to the principle *tu ne cede malis, sed contra audentior ito*,[44] does not so much consist, in the present case, in resolutely standing up to the evils and sacrifices which must be encountered, as in facing the evil principle within ourselves and overcoming its wiles. For this principle is far more dangerous, since it is deceitful, treacherous, and liable to exploit the weakness of human nature in order to justify any violation of justice.

The political moralist may indeed say that the ruler and people, or one people and another people, do no injustice to *each other* if they enter into mutual conflict through violence or cunning, although they act completely unjustly in refusing to respect the concept of right, which would alone be capable of establishing perpetual peace. For if one party violates his duty towards another who is just as lawlessly disposed towards him, that which actually *happens* to them in wearing each other out is perfectly just, and enough of their kind will always survive to keep this process going without interruption into the most distant future, so that later generations may take them as a warning example. Providence is justified in disposing the course of world events in this way; for the moral principle in man is never extinguished, and reason, which is pragmatically capable of applying the ideas of right according to this principle, constantly increases with the continuous progress of culture, while the guilt attending violations of right increases proportionately. If we suppose that mankind never can and will be in a better condition, it seems impossible to justify by any kind of theodicy the mere fact that such a race of corrupt beings could have been created on earth at all. But this kind of judgement is far too exalted for us; we cannot theoretically attribute our conception of wisdom to the supreme power whose nature is beyond our understanding.

Such are the desperate conclusions to which we are inevitably driven if we do not assume that the pure principles of right have an objective reality, i.e. that they can be applied in practice. And whatever empirical politics may say to the contrary, the people within the state, as well as the states in their relations with one another, must act accordingly. A true system of politics cannot therefore take a single step without first paying tribute to morality. And although politics in itself is a difficult art, no art is required to combine it with morality. For as soon as the two come into conflict, morality can cut through the knot which politics cannot untie.

The rights of man must be held sacred, however great a sacrifice the ruling power may have to make. There can be no half measures here; it is no use devising hybrid solutions such as a pragmatically conditioned right halfway between right and utility. For all politics must bend the knee before right, although politics may hope in return to arrive, however slowly, at a stage of lasting brilliance.

II

ON THE AGREEMENT BETWEEN POLITICS AND MORALITŸ ACCORDING TO THE TRANSCENDENTAL CONCEPT OF PUBLIC RIGHT

If, in considering public right as the jurists usually conceive of it, I abstract from all its *material* aspects (as determined by the various empirically given relationships of men within a state, or of states with one another), I am left with the *formal attribute of publicness*. For every claim upon right potentially possesses this attribute, and without it, there can be no justice (which can only be conceived of as *publicly knowable*) and therefore no right, since right can only come from justice.

Every claim upon right must have this public quality, and since it is very easy to judge whether or not it is present in a particular instance, i.e. whether or not it can be combined with the principles of the agent concerned, it provides us with a readily applicable criterion which can be discovered *a priori* within reason itself. If it cannot be reconciled with the agent's principles, it enables us to recognise at once the falseness (i.e. unrightfulness) of the claim (*praetensio iuris*) in question, as if by an experiment of pure reason.

After we have abstracted in this way from all the empirical elements contained within the concept of political and international right (including that evil aspect of human nature which makes coercion necessary), we may specify the following proposition as the *transcendental formula* of public right: 'All actions affecting the rights of other human beings are wrong if their maxim is not compatible with their being made public.'

This principle should be regarded not only as *ethical* (i.e. pertaining to the theory of virtue) but also as *juridical* (i.e. affecting the rights of man). For a maxim which I may not *declare openly* without thereby frustrating my own intention, or which must at all costs be *kept secret* if it is to succeed, or which I cannot *publicly acknowledge* without thereby inevitably arousing the resistance of everyone to my plans, can only have stirred up this necessary and general (hence *a priori* foreseeable) opposition against me because it is itself unjust and thus constitutes a threat to everyone. Besides, this is a purely *negative* test, i.e. it serves only as a means of detecting what is *not* right in relation to others. Like any axiom, it is valid without demonstration, and besides, it is easy to apply, as can be seen from the following examples of public right.

1. In the *internal right of a state* (*ius civitatis*), a question may arise which many people consider difficult to answer, although it can be resolved quite easily by means of the transcendental principle of publicness. It runs as follows: 'Is rebellion a rightful means for a people to use in order to overthrow the oppressive power of a so-called tyrant (*non titulo, sed exercitio talis*)?' The rights of the people have been violated, and there can be no doubt that the tyrant would not be receiving unjust treatment if he were dethroned. Nevertheless, it is in the highest degree wrong if the subjects pursue their rights in this way, and they cannot in the least complain of injustice if they are defeated in the ensuing conflict and subsequently have to endure the most severe penalties.

Much can be said in arguments both for and against such a course of action if we try to settle the matter by dogmatic deduction of the principles of right. But the transcendental principle of publicness in questions of right can get round such long-winded discussion. According to this principle, the people, before establishing the civil contract, asks itself whether it dares to make public the maxim of its intention to rebel on certain occasions. It is easily seen that if one were to make it a condition of founding a political constitution that force might in certain eventualities be used against the head of state, the people would have to claim rightful authority over its ruler. But if this were so, the ruler would not be the head of state; or if *both* parties were given authority as a prior condition of establishing the state, the existence of the state itself, which it was the people's intention to establish, would become impossible. The injustice of rebellion is thus apparent from the fact that if the maxim upon which it would act *were publicly acknowledged*, it would defeat its own purpose. This maxim would therefore have to be kept secret.

But it would not be necessary for the head of state to conceal his intentions. He may say quite openly that he will punish any rebellion by putting the ringleaders to death, even if they believed that he was himself the first to infringe the fundamental law. For if he is aware that he possesses *irresistible* supreme power (and this must be assumed in any civil constitution, for a ruler who does not have sufficient power to protect each individual among the people against the others cannot have the right to give the people orders either), he does not have to worry that his own aims might be frustrated if his maxim became generally known. And it is perfectly consistent with this argument that if the people were to rebel successfully, the head of state would revert to the position of a subject; but he would not be justified in starting a new rebellion to restore his former position, nor should he have to fear being called to account for his previous administration.

2. We now come to *international right*.—We can speak of international right only on the assumption that some kind of lawful condition exists, i.e. that external circumstances are such that a man can genuinely be accorded his rights. For as a form of public right, it implies by definition that there is a general will which publicly assigns to each individual that which is his due. And this *status iuridicus* must be derived from some sort of contract, which, unlike that from which a state originates, must not be based on coercive laws, but may at most be a state of *permanent and free association* like the above-mentioned federation of different states. For without some kind of *lawful condition* which actively links together the various physical or moral persons (as is the case in the state of nature), the only possible form of right is a private one. This again involves a conflict between politics and morality (the latter in the shape of a theory of right). The criterion of publicness in the relevant maxims can, however, once again be easily applied, but only on condition that the contract binds the states for the single purpose of preserving peace amongst themselves and in relation to other states, and on no account with a view to military conquest. We can thus envisage the following instances of an antinomy between politics and morality, along with the appropriate solution in each case.

(*a*) 'If one of these states has promised something to another, whether it be assistance, cession of certain territories, subsidies, or the like, it may be asked whether this state, on occasions when its own welfare is at stake, may free itself from the obligation to keep its word, maintaining that it[45] ought to be regarded as a dual person—on the one hand, as a *sovereign* who is not responsible to anyone within the state, and on the other, merely as the highest political *official* who is responsible to the state; and the conclusion to be drawn from this is that the state (or its ruler) can be exempted in the latter capacity from obligations it incurred in the first.' But if the ruler of a state were to let it be known that this was his maxim, everyone else would naturally flee from him, or unite with others in order to resist his pretensions; which proves that such a system of politics, for all its cunning, would defeat its own purpose if it operated on a public footing, so that the above maxim must be wrong.

(*b*) 'If a neighbouring power which has grown to a formidable size (*potentia tremenda*) gives cause for anxiety, can one assume that it will *wish* to oppress other states because is *is able* to do so, and does this give the less powerful party a right to mount a concerted attack upon it, even if no offence has been offered?' If a state were to *let it be known* that it affirmed this maxim, it would merely bring about more surely and more quickly the very evil it feared. For the greater power would anticipate the lesser ones, and the possibility that they might unite would be but a feeble reed against one who knew how to use the tactics of *divide et impera*. Thus this maxim of political expediency, if acknowledged publicly, necessarily defeats its own purpose and is consequently unjust.

(*c*) 'If a smaller state, by its geographical situation, constitutes a gap in the territory of a larger state, and this larger state requires the intrusive territory for its own preservation, is not the larger state justified in sub-jugating the smaller one and in annexing its territory?' One can easily see that the larger state must on no account let it be known that it has adopted such a maxim. For the smaller states would either unite in good time, or other powerful states would quarrel over the proposed prey, so that the plan would be rendered impracticable if it were made public. This is a sign that it is unjust, and it would in fact be an injustice of very great magnitude; for the fact that the object of an injustice is small does not mean that the injustice done to it may not be very great.

3. As for *cosmopolitan right*, I pass over it here in silence, for its maxims are easy to formulate and assess on account of its analogy with international right.

In the principle that the maxims of international right may be incom-patible with publicity, we thus have a good indication that politics and morality (in the sense of a theory of right) are *not in agreement*. But it is also necessary that we should know what the condition is under which its maxims will agree with international right. For we cannot simply conclude by a reverse process that all maxims which can be made public are therefore also just, because the person who has decisive supremacy has no need to conceal his maxims. The condition which must be fulfilled before any kind of international right is possible is that a *lawful state* must already be in existence. For without this, there can be no public right, and any right which can be conceived of outside it, i.e. in a state of nature, will be merely a private right. Now we have already seen above that a federative association of states whose sole intention is to eliminate war is the only *lawful* arrangement which can be reconciled with their *freedom*. Thus politics and morality can only be in agreement within a federal union, which is therefore necessary and given *a priori* through the principles of right. And the rightful basis of all political prudence is the founding of such a union in the most comprehensive form possible; for without this aim, all its reasonings are unwisdom and veiled injustice. This kind of false politics has its own *casuistry* to match that of the best Jesuit scholars. For it includes the *reservatio mentalis* whereby public contracts are formulated in terms which one can interpret to one's own advantage as required (for example, the distinction between the *status quo* of fact and the *status quo* of right); it also includes the *probabilismus*, i.e. it tries to think out evil intentions which it might attribute to others, or uses the likelihood of their gaining predominance as a legal justification for undermining other peaceful states; and finally, it has the principle of the philosophical sin (*peccatum philosophicum*, *peccatillum*, or *bagatelle*), whereby it can be regarded as a readily pardonable trifle to seize a *small* state if a much *larger* state gains in the process, to the supposed advantage of the world in general.*

All this is occasioned by the duplicity of politics in relation to morality, for it makes use of whatever branch of morality suits its purposes. But *both* aspects, philanthropy and respect for the *rights* of man, are obligatory. And while the former is only a *conditional* duty, the latter is an *unconditional* and absolutely imperative one; anyone must first be completely sure that he has not infringed it if he wishes to enjoy the sweet sense of

---

* One can find examples of such maxims in Garve's[46] treatise *Über die Verbindung der Moral mit der Politik*[47] (*On Combining Morality with Politics*), 1788. This estimable scholar admits from the very outset that he is unable to offer a satisfactory answer to this question. But to condone such procedures while admitting that one cannot fully answer the objections which can be raised against them seems to constitute a greater concession to those who are most inclined to misuse it than it is advisable for anyone to make.

having acted justly. Politics can easily be reconciled with morality in the former sense (i.e. as ethics), for both demand that men should give up their rights to their rulers. But when it comes to morality in its second sense (i.e. as the theory of right), which requires that politics should actively defer to it, politics finds it advisable not to enter into any contract at all, preferring to deny that the theory of right has any reality and to reduce all duties to mere acts of goodwill. This subterfuge of a secretive system of politics could, however, easily be defeated if philosophy were to make its maxims public, would it but dare to allow the philosopher to publicise his own maxims.

With this in mind, I now put forward another transcendental and affirmative principle of public right. It might be formulated as follows: 'All maxims which *require* publicity if they are not to fail in their purpose can be reconciled both with right and with politics.'

For if they can only attain their end by being publicised, they must conform to the universal aim of the public (which is happiness), and it is the particular task of politics to remain in harmony with the aim of the public through making it satisfied with its condition. But if this end is to be attained *only* through publicity (i.e. by dispelling all distrust of the maxims employed), the maxims in question must also be in harmony with public right; for only within this right is it possible to unite the ends of everyone. I must, however, postpone the further elaboration and discussion of this principle until another occasion, although it can already be seen that it is a transcendental formula if one removes all the empirical conditions relating to happiness, i.e. the substance of the law, and looks exclusively to the form of universal lawfulness.

If it is a duty to bring about in reality a state of public right (albeit by an infinite process of gradual approximation), and if there are also good grounds for hoping that we shall succeed, then it is not just an empty idea that *perpetual peace* will eventually replace what have hitherto been wrongly called peace treaties (which are actually only truces). On the contrary, it is a task which, as solutions are gradually found, constantly draws nearer fulfilment, for we may hope that the periods within which equal amounts of progress are made will become progressively shorter.

The Metaphysics of Morals [1]

This work begins with a preface and a general introduction. Its main body falls
into two parts—*The Metaphysical Elements of the Theory of Right* and *The
Metaphysical Elements of the Theory of Virtue*. The extracts included in the
present edition are taken only from *The Metaphysical Elements of the Theory of
Right*. They include the most important paragraphs from the introduction to
this part of the work, and its second main section, which deals with *The Theory
of Public Right*. In order to place the relevant passages in their proper context,
I have provided a brief summary of the other sections preceding *The Theory of
Public Right*.

In the preface to *The Metaphysics of Morals*, Kant points out that a complete
metaphysics of right is impossible because completeness in an account of empirical matters is impossible. He refers only to *The Metaphysical Elements of the
Theory of Right* because the second part, *The Metaphysical Elements of the Theory
of Virtue*, was published at a later date. Kant also states that, in his treatise, he
has put into the body of the text those arguments relating to the system of right
which were arrived at by *a priori* reasoning and has relegated those relating to
specific empirical cases to the notes. Kant then defends the apparent obscurity
of his style by saying that it is impossible to aim at popularity in a work involving
a system of criticism of the faculty of reason.

In his general introduction to the *Metaphysics of Morals*, Kant discusses the
fundamental terms and presuppositions of this work, pointing out that science
can make progress without explicit reference to *a priori* laws, but that the case
of morality is different. Moral laws are laws only in so far as they have an
a priori basis and are necessary. He explains why he distinguishes between legal
and moral laws: the former admit of no incentive except that of duty, the latter
do not.

A full account of this introduction would be too long to justify inclusion here.
Kant proceeds to provide definitions for many of the terms which he uses, thus
supplying a brief account of the principles underlying his moral philosophy
(cf. my introduction pp. 17–21 for a brief discussion of his moral philosophy). In
the course of the argument Kant also states that a collision of duties is impossible, because two opposing rules involving the objective-practical necessity
of an action cannot exist side by side. If there are conflicting obligations, the
stronger obligation always prevails.

This introduction is followed by *The Metaphysical Elements of the Theory of
Right*.

INTRODUCTION TO THE THEORY OF RIGHT[2]

§ A

Definition of the Theory of Right

The sum total of those laws which can be incorporated in external legislation is termed the *theory of right* (*Ius*). If legislation of this kind actually exists, the theory is one of *positive right*. If a person who is conversant with it or has studied it (*Iuriconsultus*) is acquainted with the external laws in their external function, i.e. in their application to instances encountered in experience, he is said to be *experienced in matters of right* (*Iurisperitus*). This body of theory may amount to the same as *jurisprudence* (*Iurisprudentia*), but it will remain only the *science of right* (*Iuriscientia*) unless both its elements are present. The latter designation applies to a *systematic* knowledge of the theory of natural right (*Ius naturae*), although it is the student of natural right who has to supply the immutable principles on which all positive legislation must rest.

§ B

What is Right?

The *jurist*, if he does not wish to lapse into tautology or to base his answer on the laws of a particular country at a particular time instead of offering a comprehensive solution, may well be just as perplexed on being asked this as the logician is by the notorious question: '*What is truth?*' He will certainly be able to tell us what is legally right (*quid sit iuris*) within a given context, i.e. what the laws say or have said in a particular place and at a particular time: but whether their provisions are also in keeping with right, and whether they constitute a universal criterion by which we may recognise in general what is right and what is unjust (*iustum et iniustum*), are questions whose answers will remain concealed from him unless he abandons such empirical principles for a time and looks for the sources of these judgements in the realm of pure reason. This will enable him to lay the foundations of all possible positive legislations. And while empirical laws may give him valuable guidance, a purely empirical theory of right, like the wooden head in Phaedrus'[3] fable, may have a fine appearance, but will unfortunately contain no brain.

The concept of right, in so far as it is connected with a corresponding obligation (i.e. the moral concept of right), applies within the following conditions. *Firstly*, it applies only to those relationships between one person and another which are both external and practical, that is, in so far as their actions can in fact influence each other either directly or indirectly. But *secondly*, it does not concern the relationship between the will[4] of one person and the *desires* of another (and hence only the latter's needs, as in acts of benevolence or hardheartedness); it concerns only the relationship between the will of the first and the *will* of the second. And *thirdly*, the will's *material* aspect, i.e. the end which each party intends to accomplish by means of the object of his will, is completely irrelevant in this mutual relationship; for example, we need not ask whether someone who buys goods from me for his own commercial use will gain anything in the process. For we are interested only in the *form* of the relationship between the two wills, in so far as they are regarded as *free*, and in whether the action of one of the two parties can be reconciled with the freedom of the other in accordance with a universal law.

Right is therefore the sum total of those conditions within which the will of one person can be reconciled with the will of another in accordance with a universal law of freedom.

§ C

The Universal Principle of Right

'Every action which by itself or by its maxim enables the freedom of each individual's will to co-exist with the freedom of everyone else in accordance with a universal law is *right*.'

Thus if my action or my situation in general can co-exist with the freedom of everyone in accordance with a universal law, anyone who hinders me in either does me an injustice; for this hindrance or resistance cannot co-exist with freedom in accordance with universal laws.

It also follows from this that I cannot be required to make this principle of all maxims my own maxim, i.e. *to make it the maxim of my own actions*; for each individual can be free so long as I do not interfere with his freedom by my *external actions*, even although his freedom may be a matter of total indifference to me or although I may wish in my heart to deprive him of it. That I should make it my maxim to *act* in accordance with right is a requirement laid down for me by ethics.

Thus the universal law of right is as follows: let your external actions be such that the free application of your will can co-exist with the freedom of everyone in accordance with a universal law. And although this law imposes an obligation on me, it does not mean that I am in any way expected, far less required, to restrict my freedom *myself* to these conditions purely for the sake of this obligation. On the contrary, reason merely says that individual freedom *is* restricted in this way by virtue of the idea behind it, and that it may also be actively restricted by others; and it states this as a postulate which does not admit of any further proof.

If it is not our intention to teach virtue, but only to state what is *right*, we may not and should not ourselves represent this law of right as a possible motive for actions.

§ D

Right entails the Authority to use Coercion

Any resistance which counteracts the hindrance of an effect helps to promote this effect and is consonant with it. Now everything that is contrary to right is a hindrance to freedom based on universal laws, while coercion is a hindrance or resistance to freedom. Consequently, if a certain use to which freedom is put is itself a hindrance to freedom in accordance with universal laws (i.e. if it is contrary to right), any coercion which is used against it will be a *hindrance* to a *hindrance of freedom*, and will thus be consonant with freedom in accordance with universal laws—that is, it will be right. It thus follows by the law of contradiction that right entails the authority to apply coercion to anyone who infringes it.

§ E

In its 'strict' Sense, Right can also be envisaged as the Possibility of a general and reciprocal Coercion consonant with the Freedom of Everyone in accordance with Universal Laws

This proposition implies that we should not conceive of right as being composed of two elements, namely the obligation imposed by a law, and the authority which someone who obligates another party through his will possesses to coerce the latter into carrying out the obligation in question. Instead, the concept of right should be seen as consisting immediately of the possibility of universal reciprocal coercion being combined with the freedom of everyone. For just as the only object of right in general is the external aspect of actions, right in its strict sense, i.e. right unmixed with any ethical considerations, requires no determinants of the will apart from purely external ones; for it will then be pure and will not be confounded with any precepts of virtue. Thus only a completely external right can be called right in the *strict* (or narrow) sense. This right is certainly based on each individual's awareness of his obligations within the law; but if it is to remain pure, it may not and cannot appeal to this awareness as a motive which might determine the will to act in accordance with it, and it therefore depends rather on the principle of the possibility of an external coercion which can coexist with the freedom of everyone in accordance with universal laws.

Thus when it is said that a creditor has a right to require the debtor to pay his debt, it does not mean that he can make the latter feel that his reason itself obliges him to act in this way. It means instead that the use of coercion to compel everyone to do this can very well be reconciled with everyone's freedom, hence also with the debtor's freedom, in accordance with a universal external law: thus right and the authority to apply coercion mean one and the same thing.

The law of reciprocal coercion, which is necessarily consonant with the freedom of everyone within the principle of universal freedom, is in a sense the *construction* of the concept of right: that is, it represents this concept in pure *a priori* intuition by analogy with the possibility of free movement of bodies within the law of the *equality of action and reaction*. Just as the qualities of an object of pure mathematics cannot be directly deduced from the concept but can only be discovered from its construction, it is not so much the *concept* of right but rather a general, reciprocal and uniform coercion, subject to universal laws and harmonising with the concept itself, which makes any representation of the concept possible. But while this concept of dynamics (i.e. that of the equality of action and reaction) is based upon a purely formal concept of pure mathematics (e.g. of geometry), reason has taken care that the understanding is likewise as fully equipped as possible with *a priori* intuitions for the construction of the concept of right.

In geometry, the term 'right' (*rectum*), in the sense of '*straight*', can be used either as the opposite of '*curved*' or of '*oblique*'. In the first sense, it applies to a line whose *intrinsic nature* is such that there can be only *one* of its kind between two given *points*. But in the second sense, it applies to an *angle* between two intersecting or coincident *lines* whose nature is such that there can be only *one* of its kind (a right angle) between the given lines. The perpendicular line which forms a right angle will not incline more to one side than to the other, and will divide the area on either side of it into two equal parts. By this analogy, the theory of right will also seek an assurance that each individual receives (with mathematical precision) *what is his due*. This cannot be expected of *ethics*, however, for it cannot refuse to allow some room for exceptions (*latitudinem*).[5]

Kant then adds some remarks on 'equivocal right'. He does not mean right in the strict sense, but in the wider sense of the word. Only two aspects of right arise here: equity and the right of necessity. Kant remarks of equity that it concerns only such cases as are outside strict right, i.e. where there is no case in law at all. The right of necessity applies to cases where one acts against someone else (for instance, by taking someone else's life because one's own life is in danger). A man cannot be punished with any greater punishment than the loss of life itself. There can be therefore no law punishing a man who acts out of necessity.

Kant explains the division of the theory of right into private and public right. He also distinguishes between innate and acquired rights. In his view, freedom (i.e. independence from the coercive will of another), in so far as it can coexist with the freedom of everyone else in accordance with a universal law, is the sole original right. It belongs to every man by virtue of his humanity. Equality, honesty and the right to act towards others in such a way that their rights are not infringed all derive from this right of freedom. Kant also provides a general division of the metaphysics of morals, distinguishing between those duties which are duties of right and those which are duties of virtue.

In the first section of *The Metaphysical Elements of Right*, Kant deals with private right which is concerned with property. There are two kinds of property: property which one possesses directly through physical possession and property which one only possesses indirectly. Kant examines the philosophical foundations of the law of property, deducing it from the idea of original communal possession of the soil. He also argues that external possession of things of which we are not in physical possession is possible only because we are noumenal beings, not necessarily bound by the limits of mere empirical (phenomenal) possessions. Kant goes on to argue that external possessions are possible only in a state of civil society, whereas in a state of nature, such possession can have only a provisional character.

Subsequently, Kant deals with the right of acquiring things and with various other rights, such as the rights of persons, marriage, parentage, landlords, contract, money, books, inheritance, etc. His discussion of the theory of private right is followed by a discussion of the theory of public right, which is printed below.

THE THEORY OF RIGHT, PART II: PUBLIC RIGHT[6]

SECTION I: POLITICAL RIGHT

§ 43

Public right is the sum total of those laws which require to be made universally public in order to produce a state of right. It is therefore a system of laws for a people, i.e. an aggregate of human beings, or for an aggregate of peoples. Since these individuals or peoples must influence one another, they need to live in a state of right under a unifying will: that is, they require a *constitution* in order to enjoy their rights.

A condition in which the individual members of a people are related to each other in this way is said to be a *civil* one (*status civilis*), and when considered as a whole in relation to its own members, it is called a *state* (*civitas*). Since the state takes the form of a union created by the common interest of everyone in living in a state of right, it is called a *commonwealth* (*res publica latius sic dicta*). In relation to other peoples, however, it is simply called a *power* (*potentia*—hence the word 'potentate'); and if it claims to be united by heredity, it may also call itself a *congeneric nation* (*gens*). Within the general concept of public right, we must therefore include not only *political right* but also *international right* (*ius gentium*). And since the earth's surface is not infinite but limited by its own configuration, these two concepts taken together necessarily lead to the idea of an *international political right* (*ius gentium*) or a *cosmopolitan right* (*ius cosmopoliticum*). Consequently, if even only one of these three possible forms of rightful state lacks a principle which limits external freedom by means of laws, the structure of all the rest must inevitably be undermined, and finally collapse.

§ 44

Experience teaches us the maxim that human beings act in a violent and malevolent manner, and that they tend to fight among themselves until an external coercive legislation supervenes. But it is not experience or any kind of factual knowledge which makes public legal coercion necessary. On the contrary, even if we imagine men to be as benevolent and law-abiding as we please, the *a priori* rational idea of a non-lawful state will still tell us that before a public and legal state is established, individual men, peoples and states can never be secure against acts of violence from one another, since each will have his own right to do *what seems right and good to him*, independently of the opinion of others. Thus the first decision the individual is obliged to make, if he does not wish to renounce all concepts of right, will be to adopt the principle that one must abandon the state of nature in which everyone follows his own desires, and unite with everyone else (with whom he cannot avoid having intercourse) in order to submit to external, public and lawful coercion. He must accordingly enter into a state wherein that which is to be recognised as belonging to each person is allotted to him *by law* and guaranteed to him by an adequate power (which is not his own, but external to him). In other words, he should at all costs enter into a state of civil society.

The state of nature need not necessarily be a *state of injustice* (*iniustus*) merely because those who live in it treat one another solely in terms of the amount of power they possess. But it is a *state devoid of justice* (*status iustitia vacuus*), for if a *dispute* over rights (*ius controversum*) occurs in it, there is no competent judge to pronounce legally valid decisions. Anyone may thus use force to impel the others to abandon this state for a state of right. For although each individual's *concepts of right* may imply that an external object can be acquired by occupation or by contract, this acquisition is only *provisional* until it has been sanctioned by a public law, since it is not determined by any public (distributive) form of justice and is not guaranteed by any institution empowered to exercise this right.

If no-one were willing to recognise any acquisition as rightful, not even provisionally so, before a civil state had been established, the civil state would itself be impossible. For in relation to their form, the laws relating to property contain exactly the same things in a state of nature as they would prescribe in a civil state, in so far as we conceive of this state only in terms of concepts of pure reason. The only difference is that in the second case, the conditions under which the laws are applied (in accordance with distributive justice) are given. Thus if there were not even a *provisional* system of external property in the state of nature, there would not be any rightful duties in it either, so that there could not be any commandment to abandon it.

§ 45

A state (*civitas*) is a union of an aggregate of men under rightful laws. In so far as these laws are necessary *a priori* and follow automatically from concepts of external right in general (and are not just set up by statute), the form of the state will be that of a state in the absolute sense, i.e. as the idea of what a state ought to be according to pure principles of right. This idea can serve as an internal guide (*norma*) for every actual case where men unite to form a commonwealth.

Every state contains three powers, i.e. the universally united will is made up of three separate persons (*trias politica*). These are the *ruling power* (or sovereignty) in the person of the legislator, the *executive power* in the person of the individual who governs in accordance with the law, and the *judicial power* (which allots to everyone what is his by law) in the person of the judge (*potestas legislatoria, rectoria et iudiciaria*). They can be likened to the three propositions in a practical operation of reason: the major premise, which contains the *law* of the sovereign will, the minor premise, which contains the *command* to act in accordance with the law (i.e. the principle of subsumption under the general will), and the conclusion, which contains the *legal decision* (the sentence) as to the rights and wrongs of each particular case.

§ 46

The legislative power can belong only to the united will of the people. For since all right is supposed to emanate from this power, the laws it gives must be absolutely *incapable* of doing anyone an injustice. Now if someone makes dispositions for *another* person, it is always possible that he may thereby do him an injustice, although this is never possible in the case of decisions he makes for himself (for *volenti non fit iniuria*).[7] Thus only the unanimous and combined will of everyone whereby each decides the same for all and all decide the same for each—in other words, the general united will of the people—can legislate.

The members of such a society (*societas civilis*) or state who unite for the purpose of legislating are known as *citizens* (*cives*), and the three rightful attributes which are inseparable from the nature of a citizen as such are as follows: firstly, lawful *freedom* to obey no law other than that to which he has given his consent; secondly, civil *equality* in recognising no-one among the people as superior to himself, unless it be someone whom he is just as morally entitled to bind by law as the other is to bind him; and thirdly, the attribute of civil *independence* which allows him to owe his existence and sustenance not to the arbitrary will of anyone else among the people, but purely to his own rights and powers as a member of the commonwealth (so that he may not, as a civil personality, be represented by anyone else in matters of right).

Fitness to vote is the necessary qualification which every citizen must possess. To be fit to vote, a person must have an independent position among the people. He must therefore be not just a part of the commonwealth, but a member of it, i.e. he must by his own free will actively participate in a community of other people. But this latter quality makes it necessary to distinguish between the *active* and the *passive* citizen, although the latter concept seems to contradict the definition of the concept of a citizen altogether. The following examples may serve to overcome this difficulty. Apprentices to merchants or tradesmen, servants who are not employed by the state, minors (*naturaliter vel civiliter*),[8] women in general and all those who are obliged to depend for their living (i.e. for food and protection) on the offices of others (excluding the state)—all of these people have no civil personality, and their existence is, so to speak, purely inherent. The woodcutter whom I employ on my premises; the blacksmith in India who goes from house to house with his hammer, anvil and bellows to do work with iron, as opposed to the European carpenter or smith who can put the products of his work up for public sale; the domestic tutor as opposed to the academic, the tithe-holder as opposed to the farmer; and so on—they are all mere auxiliaries to the commonwealth, for they have to receive orders or protection from other individuals, so that they do not possess civil independence.

This dependence upon the will of others and consequent inequality does not, however, in any way conflict with the freedom and equality of all men as *human beings* who together constitute a people. On the contrary, it is only by accepting these conditions that such a people can become a state and enter into a civil constitution. But all are not equally qualified within this constitution to possess the right to vote, i.e. to be citizens and not just subjects among other subjects. For from the fact that as passive members of the state, they can demand to be treated by all others in accordance with laws of natural freedom and equality, it does not follow that they also have a right to influence or organise the state itself as *active* members, or to co-operate in introducing particular laws. Instead, it only means that the positive laws to which the voters agree, of whatever sort they may be, must not be at variance with the natural laws of freedom and with the corresponding equality of all members of the people whereby they are allowed to work their way up from their passive condition to an active one.

§ 47

All of the three powers within the state are dignities, and since they necessarily follow from the general idea of a state as elements essential for its establishment (constitution), they are *political dignities*. They involve a relationship between a universal *sovereign* (who, if considered in the light of laws of freedom, can be none other than the united people itself) and the scattered mass of the people as subjects, i.e. a relationship of *commander* (*imperans*) to him who *obeys* (*subditus*). The act by which the people constitutes a state for itself, or more precisely, the mere idea of such an act (which alone enables us to consider it valid in terms of right), is the *original contract*. By this contract, all members of the people (*omnes et singuli*)⁹ give up their external freedom in order to receive it back at once as members of a commonwealth, i.e. of the people regarded as a state (*universi*). And we cannot say that men within a state have sacrificed a *part* of their inborn external freedom for a specific purpose; they have in fact completely abandoned their wild and lawless freedom, in order to find again their entire and undiminished freedom in a state of lawful dependence (i.e. in a state of right), for this dependence is created by their own legislative will.

§ 48

The three powers in the state are related to one another in the following ways. Firstly, as moral persons, they are co-ordinate (*potestates coordinatae*), i.e. each is complementary to the others in forming the complete constitution of the state (*complementum ad sufficientiam*). But secondly, they are also *subordinate* (*subordinatae*) to one another, so that the one cannot usurp any function of the others to which it ministers; for each has its own principle, so that although it issues orders in the quality of a distinct person, it does so under the condition of a superior person's will. Thirdly, the combination of both relationships described above assures every subject of his rights.

It can be said of these powers, considered in their appropriate dignity, that the will of the *legislator* (*legislatoris*) in relation to external property cannot be reproached (i.e. it is irreprehensible), that the executive power of the supreme *ruler* (*summi rectoris*) cannot be opposed (i.e. it is irresistible), and that the verdict of the supreme *judge* (*supremi iudicis*) cannot be altered (i.e. it is without appeal).

§ 49

The *ruler* of the state (*rex, princeps*) is that moral or physical person who wields the executive power (*potestas executoria*). He is the *agent* of the state who appoints the magistrates, and who prescribes rules for the people so that each may acquire something or retain what is his by law (i.e. by subsuming individual cases under the law). If the ruler is taken to be a moral person, he is called the *directory* or government. His *commands* to the people, the magistrates, and their superiors (ministers) who are responsible for *administering the state* (*gubernatio*), are not laws but ordinances or decrees; for they depend upon decisions in particular cases and are issued subject to revision. A *government* which were also to make *laws* would be called a *despotic* as opposed to a *patriotic* government. This is not to be confused with a *paternal* government (*regimen paternale*); the latter is the most despotic kind of all, for it treats the citizens like children. A patriotic government (*regimen civitatis et patriae*) means that although the state itself (*civitas*) treats its subjects as if they were members of one family, it also treats them as citizens of the state, i.e. in accordance with laws guaranteeing their own independence. Thus each is responsible for himself and does not depend upon the absolute will of anyone equal or superior to him.

The sovereign of the people (the legislator) cannot therefore also be the *ruler*, for the ruler is subject to the law, through which he is consequently beholden to *another* party, i.e. the sovereign. The sovereign may divest the ruler of his power, depose him, or reform his administration, but he cannot *punish* him. (And that is the real meaning of the common English saying that the king—i.e. the supreme executive authority—can do no wrong.) For to punish the ruler would in turn be an act of the executive power, which alone possesses the supreme authority to apply *coercion* in accordance with the law, and such a punishment would mean subjecting the executive power itself to coercion, which is self-contradictory.

Finally, neither the sovereign nor the ruler may *pass judgement*; they can only appoint judges as magistrates. The people judge themselves, through those fellow-citizens whom they have nominated as their representatives, by free election, for each particular juridical act. For a legal decision or sentence is a particular act of public justice (*iustitiae distributivae*) by an administrator of the state (a judge or court of law) upon a subject, i.e. one who belongs to the people, and it does not carry the necessary authority to grant or assign to the subject that which is his. Now since each member of the people is purely passive in his relationship to the supreme authority, it would be possible for either the legislative or the executive power to do him an injustice in any decision it might make in a controversial case involving that which belongs to the subject; for it would not be an action of the people themselves in pronouncing a fellow citizen *guilty* or *not guilty*. After the facts of a legal suit have thus been established, the court of law has the judicial authority to put the law into practice and to ensure, by means of the executive authority, that each person receives his due. Thus only the *people*, albeit through the indirect means of the representatives they have themselves appointed (i.e. the jury), can pass judgement upon anyone of their own number. Besides, it would be beneath the dignity of the head of state to act the part of a judge, i.e. to put himself in a position where he could do some injustice, and thus give cause for an appeal to some higher authority (*a rege male informato ad regem melius informandum*).[10]

There are thus three distinct powers (*potestas legislatoria, executoria, iudiciaria*) which give the state (*civitas*) its autonomy, that is, which enable the state to establish and maintain itself in accordance with laws of freedom. The *welfare* of the state consists in the union of these powers (*salus reipublicae suprema lex est*).[11] But this welfare must not be understood as synonymous with the *well-being* and *happiness* of the citizens, for it may well be possible to attain these in a more convenient and desirable way within a state of nature (as Rousseau declares), or even under a despotic regime. On the contrary, the welfare of the state should be seen as that condition in which the constitution most closely approximates to the principles of right; and reason, *by a categorical imperative*, obliges us to strive for its realisation.

General Remarks On the Legal Consequences of the Nature of the Civil Union

A

The origin of the supreme power, for all practical purposes, is *not discoverable* by the people who are subject to it. In other words, the subject *ought not* to indulge in *speculations* about its origin with a view to acting upon them, as if its right to be obeyed were open to doubt (*ius controversum*). For since the people must already be considered as united under a general legislative will before they can pass rightful judgement upon the highest power within the state (*summum imperium*), they cannot and may not pass any judgement other than that which is willed by the current head of state (*summus imperans*). Whether in fact an actual contract originally preceded their submission to the state's authority (*pactum subiectionis civilis*), whether the power came first and the law only appeared after it, or whether they ought to have followed this order—these are completely futile arguments for a people which is already subject to civil law, and they constitute a menace to the state. For if the subject, having delved out the ultimate origin, were then to offer resistance to the authority currently in power, he might by the laws of this authority (i.e. with complete justice) be punished, eliminated or banished as an outlaw (*exlex*). A law which is so sacred (i.e. inviolable) that it is practically a crime even to cast doubt upon it and thus to suspend its effectiveness for even an instant, cannot be thought of as coming from human beings, but from some infallible supreme legislator. That is what is meant by the saying that 'all authority comes from God', which is not a *historical derivation* of the civil constitution, but an idea expressed as a practical principle of reason, requiring men to obey the legislative authority now in power, irrespective of its origin.

From this there follows the proposition that the sovereign of a state has only rights in relation to the subject, and no (coercive) duties. Furthermore, if the organ of the sovereign, the ruler, does anything against the laws (e.g. if he infringes the law of equal distribution of political burdens in taxation, recruiting, or the like), the subject may lodge *complaints* (*gravamina*) about this injustice, but he may not offer resistance.

Indeed, even the actual constitution cannot contain any article which might make it possible for some power within the state to resist or hold in check the supreme executive in cases where he violates the constitutional laws. For a person who is supposed to hold the power of the state in check must have more power than (or at least as much power as) the one who is held in check; and if, as a rightful commander, he ordered the subjects to offer resistance, he would also have to be able to *protect* them and to pass legally valid judgements in each particular case which arose, so that he would have to be able to order resistance publicly. But if this were so, the latter instead of the former would be the supreme executive, which is self-contradictory. In such a case, the sovereign would simultaneously be acting through his minister as a ruler, i.e. despotically, and any attempt to pretend that the people (whose power is purely legislative) can hold the executive in check through their deputies cannot conceal the underlying despotism successfully enough to prevent it becoming apparent in the means which the minister employs. The people, who are represented in parliament by their deputies, have in these men guarantors of their freedom and their rights. These deputies, however, will also be actively interested in themselves and their own families, and they will depend upon the minister to supply them with positions in the army, navy or civil service. And even disregarding the fact that there would have to be a pre-arranged agreement among the people before any resistance could be publicly proclaimed (although such agreements are impermissible in times of peace), we can thus see that the deputies, instead of offering resistance to the pretensions of the government, will always be ready to play into its hands. A so-called 'moderate' political constitution, as a constitution regulating the internal rights of the state, is therefore an absurdity. Far from harmonising with right, it is merely a clever expedient, designed to make it as easy as possible for the powerful transgressor of popular rights to exercise his arbitrary influence upon the government, disguising this influence as a right of opposition to which the people are entitled.

There can thus be no rightful resistance on the part of the people to the legislative head of state.[12] For a state of right becomes possible only through submission to his universal legislative will. Thus there can be no right of *sedition (seditio)*, and still less a right of *rebellion (rebellio)*, least of all a right to *lay hands on* the person of the monarch as an individual, or to take his life on the pretext that he has misused his power (*monarcho-machismus sub specie tyrannicidii*). The least attempt to do so is *high treason (proditio eminens)*, and a traitor of this kind, as one who has tried to *destroy his fatherland (parricida)*, may be punished with nothing less than death.

The reason why it is the duty of the people to tolerate even what is apparently the most intolerable misuse of supreme power is that it is impossible ever to conceive of their resistance to the supreme legislation as being anything other than unlawful and liable to nullify the entire legal constitution. For before such resistance could be authorised, there would have to be a public law which permitted the people to offer resistance: in other words, the supreme legislation would have to contain a provision to the effect that it is not supreme, so that in one and the same judgement, the people as subjects would be made sovereign over the individual to whom they are subject. This is self-contradictory, and the contradiction is at once obvious if we ask who would act as judge in this dispute between the people and the sovereign (for in terms of right, they are still two distinct moral persons). It then becomes clear that the people would set themselves up as judges of their own cause.*

* It is possible to conceive of a monarch's *dethronement* as a *voluntary* abdication of the crown and a renunciation of his power by giving it back to the people, or as a forfeiture of power, without violation of the monarch's person, whereby he is simply relegated to the rank of a private citizen. And while one might at least appeal to a supposed *right of necessity* (*casus necessitatis*) as an excuse for the people's action in forcibly dethroning the head of state, they can never have the slightest right to punish him for his previous administration. For everything which he previously did in his capacity as head of state must be considered to have been outwardly in keeping with right, and he himself, regarded as the source of all laws, is incapable of any unjust action. But of all the outrages attending a revolution through rebellion, even the *murder* of the monarch is not the worst; for it is still possible to imagine that the people did it because they *feared* that if he were allowed to survive, he might recover his power and mete out to the people the punishment they deserved, in which case their behaviour would not be an act of penal justice but simply an act of self-preservation. It is the formal *execution* of a monarch which must arouse dread in any soul imbued with ideas of human right, and this feeling will recur whenever one thinks of events like the fate of Charles I or Louis XVI. But how are we to explain this feeling? It is not aesthetic (like that sympathy which comes from imagining oneself placed in the sufferer's situation), but rather moral, being our reaction to the complete reversal of all concepts of right. It is seen as a crime which must always remain as such and which can never be effaced (*crimen immortale, inexpiabile*), and it might be likened to that sin which the theologians maintain can never be forgiven either in this world or the next. The explanation of this phenomenon of the human psyche would seem to lie in the following reflections concerning our own nature, reflections which also cast some light on the principles of political right.

Every transgression of the law can and must be explained only as the result of a maxim of the criminal whereby he makes a rule out of misdeeds like the one in question. For if we were to explain such transgressions in terms of a motive of the senses, the deed could not have been committed by the criminal as a free being, and he could not consequently be held responsible for it. But it is absolutely impossible to explain how the subject is able to formulate a maxim contrary to the clear prohibition of legislative reason, for only those events which follow the mechanism of nature are capable of explanation. Now the criminal can commit his misdeed either by adopting a maxim based on an assumed objective rule (as if it were universally valid), or merely as an exception to the rule (by exempting himself from it as the occasion requires). In the *latter* case, he merely

Furthermore, if a revolution has succeeded and a new constitution has been established, the unlawfulness of its origin and success cannot free the subjects from the obligation to accommodate themselves as good citizens to the new order of things, and they cannot refuse to obey in an honest way the authority now in power. The dethroned monarch, if he survives such a revolution, cannot be taken to task for his earlier management of the state, far less punished for it. This applies so long as he has retired to the status of a citizen, preferring his own peace and that of the state to the hazards of abandoning his position and embarking as a pretender on the enterprise of restoration, whether through secretly instigated counter-revolution or the support of other powers. But if he prefers the latter course, his right to his property remains intact, since the rebellion which deprived him of it was unjust. It must, however, be left to international right to decide whether other powers have the right to join in an association for the benefit of this fallen monarch simply in order that the people's crime should not go unpunished or remain as a scandal in the eyes of other states, and whether they are entitled or called upon to overthrow a constitution established in any other state by revolution, and to restore the old one by forcible means.

B

Can the sovereign be regarded as the supreme proprietor of the land, or must he be regarded only as one who exercises supreme command over the people by means of laws? Since the land is the ultimate condition under which it is alone possible to possess external objects as one's own, while the possession and use of such objects in turn constitutes the primary hereditary right, all such rights must be derived from the sovereign as *lord of the land*, or rather as the supreme proprietor (*dominus territorii*). The people, as a mass of subjects, also belong to him (i.e. they are his people), although they do not belong to him as an owner by the right of property, but as a supreme commander by the right of persons.

But this supreme ownership is only an idea of the civil union, designed to represent through concepts of right the need to unite the private property of all members of the people under a universal public owner; for this makes it possible to define particular ownership by means of the necessary formal principle of *distribution* (division of the land), rather than by principles of *aggregation* (which proceeds empirically from the parts to the whole). The principles of right require that the supreme proprietor should not possess any land as private property (otherwise he would become a private person), for all land belongs exclusively to the people (not collectively, but distributively). Nomadic peoples, however, would be an exception to this rule, for they do not have any private property in the shape of land. Thus the supreme commander cannot own any *domains*, i.e. land reserved for his private use or for the maintenance of his court. For since the extent of his lands would then depend on his own discretion, the state would run the risk of finding all landed property in the hands of the government, and all the subjects would be treated as serfs bound to the soil (*glebae adscripti*) or holders of what always remained the property of someone else; they would consequently appear devoid of all freedom (*servi*). One can thus say of a lord of the land that he *possesses nothing* of his own (except his own person). For if he owned something on equal terms with anyone else in the state, he could conceivably come into conflict with this other person without there being any judge to settle it. But it can also be said that he *possesses everything*, because he has the right to exercise command over the people, to whom all external objects (*divisim*) belong, and to give each person whatever is his due.

It follows from this that there can be no corporation, class or order within the state which may as an owner hand down land indefinitely, by appropriate statutes, for the exclusive use of subsequent generations. The state can at all times repeal such statutes, with the one condition that it must compensate those still alive. The *order of knights* (either as a corporation or simply as a class of eminently distinguished individual persons) and the *order of the clergy* (i.e. the church) can never acquire ownership of land to pass on to their successors by virtue of the privileges with which they have been favoured; they may acquire only the temporary use of it. Either the land tenure of the military orders or the estates of the church can be suspended without hesitation, so long as the above-named condition is fulfilled. This could happen to the military orders if public opinion no longer wished to use *military honour* as a means of protecting the state against indifference in matters of defence, or alternatively to the church if the public no longer wished to use masses for the dead, prayers and a host of men employed as spiritual advisers as means of urging on the citizens to preserve them from eternal fire. Those who are affected by such a reform cannot complain of being expropriated, for *public opinion* was the only ground on which their previous possessions were based, and they remained legitimate so long as this opinion remained constant. But as soon as public opinion changes (above all in the judgement of those who, by virtue of their merit, have the strongest claim to lead it), the pretended ownership must cease as if by public appeal to the state (*a rege male informato ad regem melius informandum*).[13]

From this basic right of ownership as it was originally acquired, the supreme commander (as the supreme proprietor or lord of the land) derives his right to *tax* the private landowners, i.e. to impose levies in the shape of land taxes, excises and customs duties, or to require work such as military service. But it must be done in such a way that the people tax themselves, for this alone would be in keeping with laws of right. It is therefore done through the corps of deputies of the people, although it may be permissible to impose an enforced loan (i.e. a loan not provided for in the law as it has hitherto stood) by the right of majesty in cases where the state is threatened with dissolution.

From the same source, the rights of economic and financial administration and of the police force are derived. The police look after public *security*, *convenience* and also *propriety*; for it makes it much easier for the government to perform its business of governing the people by laws if the public sense of propriety (*sensus decori*—a negative taste) is not dulled by affronts to the moral sense such as begging, uproar in the streets, offensive smells and public prostitution (*venus volgivaga*).

A third kind of right is necessary for the preservation of the state—the right of *inspection* (*ius inspectionis*). This requires that no association which could influence the *public* welfare of society (*publicum*), such as an association of political or religious *illuminati*, may be kept secret; at the request of the police, it must not refuse to disclose its constitution. But only in cases of emergency may the police search anyone's private residence, and in each case, they must be authorised to do so by a higher authority.

C

Indirectly, i.e. in so far as he takes the duty of the people upon himself, the supreme commander has the right to impose taxes upon the people for their own preservation, e.g. for the *care of the poor*, for *foundling hospitals* and *church activities*, or for what are otherwise known as charitable or pious institutions.

For the general will of the people has united to form a society which must constantly maintain itself, and to this end, it has subjected itself to the internal power of the state so as to preserve those members of the society who cannot do so themselves. The nature of the state thus justifies the government in compelling prosperous citizens to provide the means of preserving those who are unable to provide themselves with even the most rudimentary necessities of nature. For since their existence itself is an act of submission to the protection of the commonwealth and to the care it must give them to enable them to live, they have committed themselves in such a way that the state has a right to make them contribute their share to maintaining their fellow citizens. This may be done by taxing the citizens' property or their commercial transactions, or by instituting funds and using the interest from them—not for the needs of the state (for it is rich), but for the needs of the people. The contributions should not be purely *voluntary* (for we are here concerned only with the *rights* of the state as against the subjects), they must in fact be compulsory political impositions. Some voluntary contributions such as lotteries, which are made from profit-seeking motives, should not be permitted, since they create greater than usual numbers of poor who become a danger to public property.

It might at this point be asked whether the poor ought to be provided for by *current contributions* so that each generation would support its own members, or by gradually accumulated *capital funds* and *pious foundations* at large (such as widows' homes, hospitals, etc.). Funds must certainly not be raised by begging, which has close affinities with robbery, but by lawful taxation. The first arrangement (that of current contributions) must be considered the only one appropriate to the rights of the state, for noone who wishes to be sure of his livelihood can be exempt from it. These contributions increase with the numbers of poor, and they do not make poverty a means of support for the indolent (as is to be feared in the case of pious foundations), so that the government need not impose an *unjust* burden on the people.

As for the support of children abandoned through need or through shame (and who may even be murdered for such reasons), the state has a right to make it a duty for the people not to let them perish knowingly, even although they are an unwelcome increase to the state's population. But whether this can justly be done by taxing bachelors of both sexes (i.e. single persons of *means*) as a class which is partly responsible for the situation, using the proceeds to set up foundling hospitals, or whether any other method is preferable (although it is scarcely likely that any means of preventing the evil can be found)—this is a problem which has not yet been successfully solved without prejudice to right or to morality.

The *church*, as an institution for public *divine service* among the people whose opinions or convictions created it, must be carefully distinguished from religion, which is an inward attitude of mind quite outside the sphere of influence of the civil power. As such, the church fulfils a genuine political necessity, for it enables the people to regard themselves as subjects of an *invisible* supreme power to which they must pay homage and which may often come into very unequal conflict with the civil power. The state certainly has no right to legislate on the internal constitution of the church, to arrange church affairs to suit its own advantage, or to issue directions and commands to the people in matters of faith and liturgical forms (*ritus*); for all this must be left entirely to the teachers and supervisors whom the people have themselves elected. It has only a *negative* right to prevent the public teachers of religion from exercising any influence on the *visible* political commonwealth such as might threaten the public peace, and to ensure that internal conflicts within the church or conflicts between different churches do not endanger civil concord. That is, it has a right like that of the police. It would be *beneath the dignity* of the ruling authority to interfere in church affairs by requiring that a church should have a certain belief and by laying down which belief it should have, or by demanding that it should preserve this belief without alteration and never attempt to reform itself. For by becoming involved in a scholastic quarrel, the supreme power would be placing itself on an equal footing with the subjects and the monarch setting himself up as a priest. The subjects may tell him outright that he does not understand the affairs in question, especially if he attempts to prohibit internal reforms, for anything which the entire people cannot decide for itself cannot be decided for the people by the legislator either. But no people can decide never to make further progress in opinions relating to its faith (i.e. in enlightenment), nor can it decide never to undertake reforms in affairs of the church, for this would be contrary to humanity as represented in the person of the people, hence also to the people's highest rights. Thus no ruling authority may make such a decision for the people. But for precisely the same reason, the onus of paying the costs of maintaining the church cannot fall upon the state; they must be met by that portion of the people which follows one or other particular creed, i.e. by the congregation.

D

The rights of the supreme commander in the state also include (1) the distribution of *offices* as jobs involving remuneration; (2) the distribution of *dignities*, i.e. distinctions of rank without remuneration, based purely on honour, giving rise to a division between the superior or commanding class and the inferior class which, although free and bound only by public law, is predetermined to obey the former; (3) *penal right* (over and above the more or less benevolent rights already described).

If we consider civil offices, we are faced with the question of whether the sovereign has a right to take away an office at his discretion without any misdemeanour on the part of the person to whom he had given it. I reply in the negative. For a decision which the united will of the people would never make about a civil official cannot be made by the head of state either. Now the people (who will have to bear the costs incurred in appointing an official) will undoubtedly wish this official to be fully qualified to perform the work he is given. But he cannot be fully qualified unless he has been able to devote a sufficient period to extended preparation and training, during which period he will have sacrificed the time he could have spent learning some other profession as a means of supporting himself. Thus if people were dismissed without reason, the office would as a rule be filled with individuals who had not acquired the necessary skill or achieved through practice a mature faculty of judgement. But this is contrary to the intention of the state; and besides, the state also requires that every individual should be able to rise from a lower office to higher ones (which would otherwise fall into the hands of utterly unsuitable persons), and hence to count on receiving a livelihood throughout his life.

As for civil *dignities*, the *nobility* includes not only those positions to which an office is attached, but also those which make the holder a member of a higher class, even if he performs no particular services. The nobility is distinct from the civil status occupied by the people, for it is inherited by the male descendants. Through the latter, it can also be conferred upon female relatives of ignoble birth, although a woman of noble birth cannot in turn confer noble status upon a husband who was not born a nobleman, but must herself revert to the purely civil status of the people. The question which now arises is whether the sovereign is entitled to create a nobility as a *hereditary* class between himself and the rest of the citizens. The answer will not, however, depend upon whether it suits the sovereign's policies for furthering his own or the people's advantage, but simply upon whether it is in keeping with right that anyone should have above him a class of persons who, although themselves subjects, will in relation to the people be commanders by birth, or at least possess greater privileges than they do.

As before, the answer to this question will be found in the principle that anything which the people (i.e. the entire mass of subjects) cannot decide for themselves and their fellows cannot be decided for the people by the sovereign either. Now a *hereditary* nobility is a distinction bestowed before it is earned, and since it gives no grounds for hoping that it will be earned, it is wholly unreal and fanciful. For if an ancestor has earned his position through merit, he still cannot pass on his merit to his descendants. On the contrary, the latter must always earn it themselves, for nature is not such that the talent and will which enable a person to serve the state meritoriously can be *inherited*. Now since it cannot be assumed of anyone that he will throw his freedom away, it is impossible for the universal will of the people to agree to so groundless a prerogative; thus the sovereign cannot make it valid either.

It may be, however, that an anomaly of this sort has crept into the mechanism of government in past ages (as with the feudal system, which was almost entirely geared to making war), so that some subjects claim that they are more than citizens and are entitled by birth to official posts (a hereditary professorship, let us say). In this case, the state can make good its mistake of unrightfully bestowing hereditary privileges only by a gradual process, by allowing the posts to fall vacant and omitting to fill them again. The state thus has a provisional right to allow such dignities to persist as titles until public opinion itself realises that the hierarchy of sovereign, nobility and people should give way to the more natural division of sovereign and people.

No human being in the state can be totally without a position of dignity, for each at least has that of a citizen, unless he has forfeited it through some *crime* of his own doing. If the latter is the case, he may indeed be kept alive, but he will be made a mere instrument of another person (either the state or another citizen). Anyone in this position is a *bondsman or slave* (*servus in sensu stricto*) and is part of the *property* (*dominium*) of someone else, who is therefore not just his *master* (*herus*), but also his *owner* (*dominus*); the latter may accordingly make him over to anyone else as a chattel or use him as he wishes (except for infamous purposes), and he may *dispose of* his powers, although not of his life and limbs, at his own discretion. No-one can enter by contract into such a state of dependence and thus cease to be a person; for only as a person is he able to make a contract. Now it may seem that in return for payment, food or protection, a man can bind himself to another person by a contract of hire (*locatio conductio*) whereby he must perform certain services of a permissible nature but of an *indeterminate amount*, and that this will merely make him a *servant* (*subiectus*) but not a *slave* (*servus*). But this is an illusion. For if the master is authorised to use the powers of his servant as he pleases, he may (as happens with the negroes in the West Indies) exhaust him to the point of death or despair, and the servant will really have made himself over to his master as property, which is impossible. The servant can thus hire himself out only for work which is determinate both in nature and in quantity, either as a day labourer or a resident servant. In the latter case, he will not receive a wage, but will be allowed to use his master's land; and he will fulfil his side of the contract of tenure partly by serving on this land and partly by paying definite sums (i.e. a rent) for his own use of it. He can do this without making himself a *serf of the soil* (*glebae adscriptus*) and thereby forfeiting his personality, and he may enter into a temporary or hereditary leasehold. He may, however, have become a *personal* subject through some misdemeanour he has committed, but he cannot *inherit* any such position of servitude, for he can acquire this status only through his own guilt. And it is in no way more permissible for anyone to claim ownership of a bondsman's offspring on account of the costs incurred in educating him, for education is an absolute natural duty of parents, and if the parents' status is servile, it is in turn the duty of the masters, since the latter cannot take possession of their bondsmen without also taking over their duties.

E

The Right of Punishment and the Right of Pardon

I

The *right of punishment* is the right of the commander as against the subject to inflict pain on him for some crime he has committed. Thus the supreme authority in the state cannot be punished; a subject may at most withdraw from his rule. An infringement of the public law which renders the guilty person incapable of citizenship is known as a *crime* (*crimen*) in the absolute sense, or alternatively, as a public crime (*crimen publicum*). The former (a private crime) will be dealt with by a court of civil justice, the latter (a public crime) by a court of criminal justice. *Embezzlement* (i.e. misappropriation of money or goods entrusted to someone for commercial purposes) and fraudulent dealings in buying and selling under the eyes of another party are private crimes. On the other hand, counterfeiting money or bills of exchange, theft, robbery, and the like are public crimes, because they endanger the commonwealth and not merely an individual person. Such crimes might in turn be divided into those of *base* motivation (*indolis abiectae*) and those of *violent* motivation (*indolis violentae*).

Judicial punishment (*poena forensis*) should be distinguished from *natural punishment* (*poena naturalis*); the latter is found where vice punishes itself, and is thus no concern of the legislator. Judicial punishment can never be merely a means of furthering some extraneous good for the criminal himself or for civil society, but must always be imposed on the criminal simply *because he has committed a crime*. For a human being can never be manipulated just as a means of realising someone else's intentions, and is not to be confused with the objects of the law of kind. He is protected against this by his inherent personality, although he may well be sentenced to forfeit his civil personality. He must first be found worthy of punishment before any thought is given to the possible utility which he or his fellow citizens might derive from his punishment. The penal law is a categorical imperative, and woe betide anyone who winds his way through the labyrinth of the theory of happiness in search of some possible advantage to be gained by releasing the criminal from his punishment or from any part of it, or who acts in the spirit of the pharisaical saying: 'It is better that one man should die than that the whole people should go to ruin.' For if justice perishes, there is no further point in men living on earth. What then are we to think of the proposal that the life of a condemned criminal should be spared if he agrees to let dangerous experiments be carried out on him in order that the doctors may gain new information of value to the commonwealth, and is fortunate enough to survive? A court of justice would dismiss with contempt any medical institution which made such a proposal; for justice ceases to be justice if it can be bought at a price.

But what kind and what degree of punishment does public justice take as its principle and norm? None other than the principle of equality in the movement of the pointer on the scales of justice, the principle of not inclining to one side more than to the other. Thus any undeserved evil which you do to someone else among the people is an evil done to yourself. If you slander him, you slander yourself; if you rob him, you rob yourself; if you strike him, you strike yourself; and if you kill him, you kill yourself. But it should be understood that only the *law of retribution* (*ius talionis*) can determine exactly what quality and quantity of punishment is required, and it must do so in court, not within your private judgement. All other criteria are inconstant; they cannot be reconciled with the findings of pure and strict justice, because they introduce other outside considerations.

Now it may well appear that class differences do not allow for the principle of retribution whereby like is exchanged for like. But although it is impossible according to the letter, it may still remain valid in terms of effect if we consider the sensibilities of the more distinguished classes. Thus a monetary fine on account of a verbal injury, for example, bears no relation to the actual offence, for anyone who has plenty of money could allow himself such an offence whenever he pleased. But the injured honour of one individual might well be closely matched by the wounded pride of the other, as would happen if the latter were compelled by judgement and right not only to apologise publicly, but also, let us say, to kiss the hand of the former, even though he were of lower station. The same would apply if a high-ranking individual convicted of violence were sentenced, in return for the blows he had dealt an inferior but guiltless citizen, not only to make an apology but also to undergo a period of painful solitary confinement; for apart from the resultant discomfort, the perpetrator's vanity would also be painfully affected, and this humiliation would provide an appropriate repayment of like with like.

But what does it mean to say: 'If you rob him, you rob yourself'? Anyone who steals makes the property of everyone else insecure; by the right of retribution, he thus robs himself of the security of all possible ownership. He has nothing and he cannot acquire anything, but he still wishes to live, and this is possible only if others provide him with sustenance. But since the state will not do this for nothing, he must place his powers at the state's disposal for whatever tasks it chooses (i.e. hard labour), and he is relegated to the status of a slave for a certain period or even permanently, according to circumstances. But if he has committed murder, he must *die*. In this case, no possible substitute can satisfy justice. For there is no *parallel* between death and even the most miserable life, so that there is no equality of crime and retribution unless the perpetrator is judicially put to death (at all events without any maltreatment which might make humanity an object of horror in the person of the sufferer). Even if civil society were to dissolve itself with the consent of all its members (for example, if a people who inhabited an island decided to separate and to disperse to other parts of the world), the last murderer in prison would first have to be executed in order that each should receive his deserts and that the people should not bear the guilt of a capital crime through failing to insist on its punishment; for if they do not do so, they can be regarded as accomplices in the public violation of justice.

This equality of punishments is therefore possible only if the judge passes the death sentence in accordance with the strict law of retribution. It will be a sign of such equality if the death sentence is pronounced on all criminals in proportion to their inner *malice* (even if the crime in question is not murder, but some other crime against the state which can only be effaced by death). Let us take the case of the last Scottish rebellion, in which various participants (such as Balmerino[14] and others) considered that they were only fulfilling a duty they owed to the house of Stuart, while others were furthering their personal aims. If the supreme court had passed judgement to the effect that each should be free to choose between death and penal servitude, I say that the honourable man would choose death and the scoundrel penal servitude; for such is the nature of man. The former knows something which he values more highly than life itself, namely *honour*; but the latter considers even a life of disgrace better than no life at all (*animam praeferre pudori*—Juvenal).[15] Now the first is unquestionably less culpable than the second, so that if they are both condemned to death, they each receive punishment proportionate to their deserts; for the first will be punished mildly in relation to his own sensibility, and the second severely in relation to his. On the other hand, if both were sentenced to penal servitude, the first would be punished too severely, and the second too mildly for the degree of his baseness. Thus in sentencing a number of criminals who have joined in a conspiracy, the most balanced solution in terms of public justice is once again the *death penalty*. Besides, no-one has ever heard of a criminal condemned to death for murder complaining that the punishment was excessive and therefore unjust; everyone would laugh in his face if he said so. Otherwise, it would have to be assumed that although no injustice is done to the criminal according to the law, the legislative power in the state is not authorised to impose this sort of penalty, and that if it does so, it is in contradiction with itself.

All murderers, whether they have themselves done the deed, ordered it to be done, or acted as accomplices, must suffer the death penalty. This is what justice, as the idea of judicial power, wills in accordance with universal laws of *a priori* origin. But the number of accomplices (*correi*) in such a deed might be so great that the state, in order to rid itself of such criminals, would soon reach the stage of having no more subjects, and yet it would not wish to dissolve itself and revert to the state of nature, for the latter, devoid of all external justice, is much worse still. And above all, the state will not wish to blunt the people's feelings by a spectacle of mass slaughter. The sovereign must therefore have the power to act as judge himself in such an emergency (*casus necessitatis*), and to pass a sentence which imposes a penalty other than death on the criminals so that the community of people may be preserved (e.g. a sentence of deportation). This procedure, however, may not be adopted in consequence of any public law, but only as a peremptory order, i.e. an act based on the right of majesty; and this, as a right of mercy, may only be exercised in isolated cases.

But the Marchese Beccaria,[16] from motives of compassionate sentimentality and affected humanity (*compassibilitas*), has set up in opposition to this view his claim that capital punishment is always *contrary to right*. For he maintains that it could not have been contained in the original civil contract, since this would have compelled each individual to agree to forfeit his life if he were to murder anyone else (among his own people), and such an agreement is impossible because no-one can dispose of his own life.

This is pure sophistry and distortion of the principles of right. For a person does not suffer punishment because he wished to have *the punishment itself*, but because he wished to commit a *punishable deed*. After all, it is not a punishment if a person is subjected to something which he wishes, and it is impossible to *wish* to be punished. To say: 'I wish to be punished if I murder anyone' means nothing more than 'I submit along with the rest of the people to the laws, which, if there are criminals among the people, will naturally include penal laws.' As a co-legislator who dictates the *penal law*, I cannot possibly be the same person who, as a subject, is punished in accordance with the law. For in the latter capacity, i.e. as a criminal, I cannot possibly have a say in the legislation, since the legislator is holy. Thus if I promulgate a penal law against myself as a criminal, it is the pure rightful and legislative reason within me (*homo noumenon*) which subjects me as a person capable of crime, hence as one person (*homo phaenomenon*) along with all the others within the civil union, to the penal law. In other words, it is not the people (i.e. all individuals) who dictate the death penalty, but the court of public justice, i.e. someone other than the criminal; and the social contract does not contain a promise by anyone to let himself be punished and hence to dispose of himself and his own life. For if the authority to impose punishments had to depend upon a *promise* on the part of the malefactor to *will* his own punishment, it would also have to be left to him to declare himself culpable, and the criminal would thus be his own judge. The cardinal error (πρῶτον φεῦδος) in this sophistry consists in regarding the criminal's own judgement that he must forfeit his life (a judgement which one must necessarily attribute to his *reason*) as a decision on the part of his *will* to take his own life: this amounts to representing the execution of right and the adjudication of right as united in one and the same person.

There are, however, two further crimes worthy of the death penalty, but it remains doubtful whether the *legislature* has the authority to impose this penalty upon them. Both of them are actuated by a sense of honour, but the first involves *sexual honour* whereas the second involves *military honour*. Both are true forms of honour, and it is a duty of the two classes of people involved (women and soldiers respectively) to uphold them.

The first crime is *infanticide* by the mother (*infanticidium maternale*), and the second is *murder of a comrade in arms* (*commilitonicidium*) in a duel. No legislation can remove the disgrace of an illegitimate birth; nor can it efface the stain which is left when suspicions of cowardice fall upon a subordinate officer who does not react to a humiliating encounter with a vigour surpassing the fear of death. It therefore appears that in cases of this kind, men find themselves in a state of nature. And while their *killing* of each other (*homicidium*) should not then be called *murder* (*homicidium dolosum*), it still remains punishable, although the supreme power cannot punish it with death. The child born outside marriage is outside the law (for marriage is a lawful institution), and it is therefore also outside the protection of the law. It has found its way into the commonwealth by stealth, so to speak, like contraband goods, so that the commonwealth can ignore its existence and hence also its destruction, for it ought not to have come into existence at all in this way; and no decree can remove the mother's disgrace if the illegitimate birth becomes known. In the same way, if a military man with the rank of a junior officer is offered an affront, he finds himself compelled by the universal opinion of his equals to seek satisfaction and to punish the offender, although not through the workings of the law in a court of justice, but by means of a duel as in the state of nature. He thereby risks losing his own life in order to prove his martial courage, on which the honour of his profession is essentially based; and even if it involves *killing* his opponent, the deed may not actually be called *murder* (*homicidium dolosum*), because it occurred in a public conflict to which both parties (however unwillingly) consented.

What, then, are the rights and wrongs of these two cases in so far as they are subject to criminal justice? Penal justice is here faced with a very difficult problem, for it must either declare that the concept of honour, which in the present case is no mere illusion, is null and void before the law and ought to be punished by death, or it must exempt the crimes in question from the death penalty. And while the first course would be cruel, the second would be over-indulgent. The solution to this dilemma is that the categorical imperative of penal justice (whereby the unlawful killing of another person must be punished by death) remains in force, although the legislation itself (hence also the civil constitution), so long as it remains barbarous and undeveloped, is to blame for the fact that the motives of honour obeyed by the people are subjectively incompatible with those measures which are objectively suited to their realisation, so that public justice as dispensed by the state is *injustice* in the eyes of the people.

II

The *right of pardon* (*ius aggratiandi*), whereby the criminal's punishment is either mitigated or completely remitted, is certainly the most equivocal of all the rights exercised by the sovereign; for while it may confirm the aura of his majesty, it can at the same time do a great deal of injustice. In cases involving crimes of the subjects against one another, the sovereign should on no account exercise this right, for exemption from punishment (*impunitas criminis*) in such cases means doing the greatest injustice to the subjects. Thus he can only make use of it when *he himself* has been done an injury (*crimen laesae maiestatis*), and he may not do so even then if a remittance of punishment might endanger the security of the people. This right is the only one which deserves to be called a right of majesty.

On the Relationship of the Citizen to his own and other Countries with Regard to Right

§ 50

A country (*territorium*) whose inhabitants are fellow citizens of one and the same commonwealth by the very nature of the constitution (i.e. without having to exercise any particular right, so that they are already citizens by birth) is called the *fatherland* of these citizens. Lands in which this condition of citizenship does not apply to them are *foreign countries*. And a country which is part of a wider system of government is called a *province* (in the sense in which the Romans used this word); since it is not, however, an integrated part of an empire (*imperii*) whose inhabitants are all fellow-citizens, but is only a *possession* and *subordinate realm* of the empire, it must respect the territory of the ruling state as its *motherland* (*regio domina*).

   1. The *subject* (considered also as a citizen) has the right of emigration, for the state could not hold him back as it might a piece of property. But he can take only his mobile belongings with him; he cannot take his fixed possessions, as would indeed be the case if he were authorised to sell the land he had hitherto possessed and to take the money he received for it with him.

   2. The *lord of the land* has the right to encourage the immigration and settlement of foreigners (colonists), even though the native subjects should look askance at it. But he must see to it that private ownership of the land by the native subjects is not diminished.

   3. If a subject should commit a crime which makes it a danger to the state for him to associate with his fellow citizens, the lord of the land has

the right to *banish* him to a foreign province where he will not share any of the rights of a citizen, i.e. he has a right to *deport* him.

4. The lord indeed has the right to exile him completely (*ius exilii*), to send him out into the world at large, i.e. to foreign countries (for which the old German word was 'Elend', the same word as that denoting misery). And since the lord of the land thereby withdraws his protection from him, it is tantamount to making him an outlaw within his own frontiers.

§51

The three powers within the state, which emerge from the general concept of a *commonwealth* (*res publica latius dicta*), are simply so many relationships within the united will of the people (which is derived *a priori* from reason itself), and are likewise a pure idea of the supreme head of state, which also has objective and practical reality. But this head of state (the sovereign) is only an abstraction (representing the entire people) so long as there is no physical person to represent the highest power in the state and to make this idea influence the will of the people. Now the relationship between the head of state and the people can be envisaged in three different ways. Either *one* person within the state will rule over everyone, or *several* persons of equal rank will unite to rule over all others, or *all* will rule collectively over each (hence also over themselves). That is, the *form of the state* will either be *autocratic*, *aristocratic*, or *democratic*. (The expression 'monarchic' instead of 'autocratic' does not properly cover the concept here intended, for a *monarch* is one who has the *highest* power, while an *autocrat* or absolute ruler is one who has *all* the power; the latter is the sovereign, whereas the former merely represents him.)

It can readily be seen that the autocratic form is the *simplest* form of state, for it involves only a relationship between one individual (the king) and the people, and the legislator is a single person. An aristocratic state is *composite*, involving two kinds of relationship: that of the aristocrats (as legislators) towards one another, thereby constituting the sovereign, and then the relationship between this sovereign and the people. But the democratic form is the most composite of all. For it must first unite the will of all in order to make a people; it must then unite the will of the citizens to make a commonwealth; and finally, it must unite their will to place at the head of the commonwealth a sovereign, who is simply this united will itself.* As far as the actual *manipulation* of right within the

* I make no mention here of perversions of these forms by the interference of unauthorised rulers (as in *oligarchy* and *ochlocracy*), nor of so-called *mixed* constitutions, since this would go beyond the scope of the present work.

state is concerned, the simplest form is of course also the best, but in relation to *right* itself, it is the most dangerous from the point of view of the people, for it is extremely conducive to despotism. Simplification is certainly the most rational maxim for the mechanical process of uniting the people by means of coercive laws, so long as all the people are passive and obedient to a single individual above them—but this would mean that no subjects could be *citizens*. Perhaps, however, the people are supposed to content themselves with the consolation that monarchy (in this case, autocracy) is the best political constitution *if the monarch is a good one* (i.e. if he has not only the will but also the necessary insight to be one). But this saying is a tautology, for it merely means that the best constitution is that *by which* the administrator of the state is made into the best ruler, i.e. that the best constitution is that which is best.

§ 52

It is futile to hunt for *historical documentation* of the origins of this mechanism. That is, we cannot reach back to the time at which civil society first emerged (for savages do not set up any formal instruments in submitting themselves to the law, and it can easily be gathered from the nature of uncivilised man that they must have initially used violent means). But it would be quite culpable to undertake such researches with a view to forcibly changing the constitution at present in existence. For this sort of change could only be effected by the people by means of revolutionary conspiracy, and not by the legislature. But revolution under an already existing constitution means the destruction of all relationships governed by civil right, and thus of right altogether. And this is not a change but a dissolution of the civil constitution; and the transition to a better one would not then be a metamorphosis but a palingenesis, for it would require a new social contract on which the previous one (which is now dissolved) could have no influence. But it must still be possible for the sovereign to alter the existing constitution if it cannot readily be reconciled with the idea of the original contract, and yet in so doing to leave untouched that basic form which is essential if the people are to constitute a state. This alteration cannot be such that the state abandons one of the three fundamental forms and reconstitutes itself in accordance with one of the two remaining ones, as would happen, for example, if the aristocrats agreed to submit to an autocracy or to disband and create a democracy or vice versa. This would imply that it depended on the sovereign's own free choice and discretion to subject the people to whatever constitution he wished. For even if the sovereign decided to go over to democracy, he might still be doing the people an injustice; for they might themselves detest this form of constitution and find one of the two others more congenial.

The three forms of state are merely the *letter* (*littera*) of the original legislation within civil society, and they may therefore remain as part of the mechanism of the constitution for as long as they are considered necessary by old and long established custom (i.e. purely subjectively). But the *spirit* of the original contract (*anima pacti originarii*) contains an obligation on the part of the constitutive power to make the *mode of government* conform to the original idea, and thus to alter the mode of government by a gradual and continuous process (if it cannot be done at once) until it accords *in its effects* with the only rightful constitution, that of a pure republic. The old empirical (and statutory) forms, which serve only to effect the *subjection* of the people, should accordingly resolve themselves into the original (rational) form which alone makes *freedom* the principle and indeed the condition of all *coercion*. For coercion is required for a just political constitution in the truest sense, and this will eventually be realised in letter as well as in spirit.

This, then, is the only lasting political constitution in which the *law* is the sole ruler, independent of all particular persons; it is the ultimate end of all public right, and the only condition in which each individual can be given his due *peremptorily*. But as long as the various forms of the state are supposed to be represented literally by an equivalent number of distinct moral persons invested with supreme power, only a *provisional* internal right instead of an absolute condition of right can obtain within civil society.

Any true republic, however, is and cannot be anything other than a *representative system* of the people whereby the people's rights are looked after on their behalf by deputies who represent the united will of the citizens. But as soon as a head of state in person (whether this head of state be a king, a nobility, or the whole populace as a democratic association) also allows himself to be represented, the united people then does not merely represent the sovereign, but actually *is* the sovereign itself. For the supreme power originally rests with the people, and all the rights of individuals as mere subjects (and particularly as state officials) must be derived from this supreme power. Once it has been established, the republic will therefore no longer need to release the reins of government from its own hands and to give them back to those who previously held them, for they might then destroy all the new institutions again by their absolute and arbitrary will.

It was thus a great error of judgement on the part of a certain powerful ruler in our own times when he tried to relieve himself of the embarrassment of large national debts by leaving it to the people to assume and distribute this burden at their own discretion.[17] It was thus natural that the people should acquire legislative powers not only in matters of taxation but also in matters of government, for they had to ensure that the government would incur no new debts by extravagance or by war. The monarch's ruling authority thus disappeared completely; for it was not merely suspended but actually passed over to the people, to whose legislative will the property of every subject was now submitted. Nor is it possible to say that we must postulate a tacit yet contractual promise on the part of the national assembly not to take over the sovereignty, but only to administer the sovereign's business and to hand back the reins of government to the monarch after the business had been completed. For a contract of this kind would in itself be null and void. The right of the supreme legislation in the commonwealth is not alienable; on the contrary, it is the most personal right of all. Whoever possesses it can only exercise control over the people through the people's collective will, but not over the collective will itself, the original foundation of all public contracts. A contract which obliged the people to give back their authority would not be in accord with the people's function as a legislative power. And this, according to the proposition that no man can serve two masters, is self-contradictory.

SECTION II: INTERNATIONAL RIGHT

§ 53

The human beings who make up a nation can, as natives of the country, be represented as analogous to descendants from a common ancestry (*congeniti*) even if this is not in fact the case. But in an intellectual sense or for the purposes of right, they can be thought of as the offspring of a common mother (the republic), constituting, as it were, a single family (*gens, natio*) whose members (the citizens) are all equal by birth. These citizens will not intermix with any neighbouring people who live in a state of nature, but will consider them ignoble, even though such savages for their own part may regard themselves as superior on account of the lawless freedom they have chosen. The latter likewise constitute national groups, but they do not constitute states.

What we are now about to consider under the name of international right or the right of nations is the right of *states* in relation to one another (although it is not strictly correct to speak, as we usually do, of the *right of nations*; it should rather be called the *right of states—ius publicum civitatum*). The situation in question is that in which one state, as a moral person, is considered as existing in a state of nature in relation to another state, hence in a condition of constant war. International right is thus concerned partly with the right to make war, partly with the right of war itself, and partly with questions of right after a war, i.e. with the right of states to compel each other to abandon their warlike condition and to create a constitution which will establish an enduring peace. A state of nature among individuals or families (in their relations with one another) is different from a state of nature among entire nations, because international right involves not only the relationship between one state and another within a larger whole, but also the relationship between individual persons in one state and individuals in the other or between such individuals and the other state as a whole. But this difference between international right and the right of individuals in a mere state of nature is easily deducible from the latter concept without need of any further definitions.

§ 54

The elements of international right are as follows. Firstly, in their external relationships with one another, states, like lawless savages, exist in a condition devoid of right. Secondly, this *condition* is one of war (the right of the stronger), even if there is no actual war or continuous active fighting (i.e. hostilities). But even although neither of two states is done any injustice by the other in this condition, it is nevertheless in the highest degree unjust in itself, for it implies that neither wishes to experience anything better. Adjacent states are thus bound to abandon such a condition. Thirdly, it is necessary to establish a federation of peoples in accordance with the idea of an original social contract, so that states will protect one another against external aggression while refraining from interference in one another's internal disagreements. And fourthly, this association must not embody a sovereign power as in a civil constitution, but only a partnership or *confederation*. It must therefore be an alliance which can be terminated at any time, so that it has to be renewed periodically. This right is derived *in subsidium* from another original right, that of preventing oneself from lapsing into a state of actual war with one's partners in the confederation (*foedus Amphictyonum*).

§ 55

If we consider the original right of free states in the state of nature to make war upon one another (for example, in order to bring about a condition closer to that governed by right), we must first ask what right the state has *as against its own subjects* to employ them in a war on othe states, and to expend or hazard their possessions or even their lives in the process. Does it not then depend upon their own judgement whether they wish to go to war or not? May they simply be sent thither at the sovereign's supreme command?

This right might seem an obvious consequence of the right to do what one wishes with one's own property. Whatever someone has himself substantially *made* is his own undisputed property. These are the premises from which a mere jurist would deduce the right in question.

A country may yield various *natural products*, some of which, because of their very *abundance*, must also be regarded as *artefacts* of the state. For the country would not yield them in such quantities if there were no state or proper government in control and if the inhabitants still lived in a state of nature. For example, domestic poultry (the most useful kind of fowl), sheep, pigs, cattle, etc. would be completely unknown in the country I live in (or would only rarely be encountered) if there were no government to guarantee the inhabitants their acquisitions and possessions. The same applies to the number of human beings, for there can only be few of them in a state of nature, as in the wilds of America, even if we credit them with great industry (which they do not have). The inhabitants would be very sparsely scattered, for no-one could spread very far afield with his household in a land constantly threatened with devastation by other human beings, wild animals, or beasts of prey. There would thus be no adequate support for so large a population as now inhabits a country.

Now one can say that vegetables (e.g. potatoes) and domestic animals, in quantity at least, are *made* by human beings, and that they may therefore be used, expended or consumed (i.e. killed) at will. One might therefore appear justified in saying that the supreme power in the state, the sovereign, has the right to lead his subjects to war as if on a hunt, or into battle as if on an excursion, simply because they are for the most part produced by the sovereign himself.

But while this legal argument (of which monarchs are no doubt dimly aware) is certainly valid in the case of animals, which can be the *property* of human beings, it is absolutely impermissible to apply it to human beings themselves, particularly in their capacity as citizens. For a citizen

Any alteration to a defective political constitution, which may certainly be necessary at times, can thus be carried out only by the sovereign himself through *reform*, but not through revolution by the people. And if any such alteration takes place, it can only affect the *executive power*, not the legislature.

A constitution may be arranged in such a way that the people, through their representatives in parliament, are lawfully able to *resist* the executive power and its representative (the minister). This is known as a limited constitution. But even a constitution of this kind cannot permit any active resistance (i.e. an arbitrary association of the people designed to force the government to adopt a certain mode of action, and hence an attempt by the people themselves to act as the executive power). The people may offer only a *negative* form of resistance, in that they may *refuse* in parliament to comply on all occasions with those demands which the executive says must necessarily be met for administrative purposes. In fact, if the people were to comply on all occasions, it would be a sure indication that they were decadent, their representatives venal, the head of the government a despot through his minister, and the minister himself a traitor to the people.

deviates (albeit deliberately) from the law, for he may at the same time deplore his own transgression and simply wish to get round the law without formally terminating his obedience to it. But in the *former* case, he rejects the authority of the law itself (although he cannot deny its validity in the light of his own reason), and makes it his rule to act in opposition to it; his maxim is thus at variance with the law not simply through *deficiency* (*negative*); it is actually *contrary* to the law (*contrarie*), or, so to speak, diametrically opposed to it as a contradiction (i.e. virtually hostile to it). So far as can be seen, it is impossible for men to commit a crime of such formal and completely futile malice, although no system of morality should omit to consider it, if only as a pure idea representing ultimate evil.

Thus the reason why the thought of the formal execution of a monarch *by his people* inspires us with dread is that, while his *murder* must be regarded merely as an exception to the rule which the people have taken as their maxim, his *execution* must be seen as a complete *reversal* of the principles which govern the relationship between the sovereign and the people. For it amounts to making the people, who owe their existence purely to the legislation of the sovereign, into rulers over the sovereign, thereby brazenly adopting violence as a deliberate principle and exalting it above the most sacred canons of right. And this, like an abyss which engulfs everything beyond hope of return, is an act of suicide by the state, and it would seem to be a crime for which there can be no atonement. There are therefore grounds for assuming that agreements to perform such executions do not really proceed from any supposed principle of right, but from the people's fear of revenge from the state if it should ever recover, and that such formalities are introduced only in order to give the deed an air of penal justice and of *rightful procedure* (with which murder, on the other hand, could not be reconciled). But this disguise is futile, since any such presumption on the part of the people is more atrocious than murder itself, for it in fact embodies a principle which must make it impossible for an overthrown state to be reconstituted.

must always be regarded as a co-legislative member of the state (i.e. not just as a means, but also as an end in himself), and he must therefore give his free consent through his representatives not only to the waging of war in general, but also to every particular declaration of war. Only under this limiting condition may the state put him to service in dangerous enterprises.

We shall therefore have to derive the right under discussion from the *duty* of the sovereign towards the people, not vice versa. The people must be seen to have given their consent to military action, and although they remain passive in this capacity (for they allow themselves to be directed), they are still acting spontaneously and they represent the sovereign himself.

§ 56

In the state of nature, the *right to make war* (i.e. to enter into hostilities) is the permitted means by which one state prosecutes its rights against another. Thus if a state believes that it has been injured by another state, it is entitled to resort to violence, for it cannot in the state of nature gain satisfaction through *legal proceedings*, the only means of settling disputes in a state governed by right. Apart from an actively inflicted injury (the first aggression, as distinct from the first hostilities), a state may be subjected to *threats*. Such threats may arise either if another state is the first to make *military preparations*, on which the right of *anticipatory attack* (*ius praeventionis*) is based, or simply if there is an alarming increase of power (*potentia tremenda*) in another state which has acquired new territories. This is an injury to the less powerful state by the mere fact that the other state, even without offering any active offence, is *more powerful*; and any attack upon it is legitimate in the state of nature. On this is based the right to maintain a balance of power among all states which have active contact with one another.

Those *active injuries* which give a state the *right to make war* on another state include any unilateral attempt to gain satisfaction for an affront which the people of one state have offered to the people of the other. Such an act of *retribution* (*retorsio*) without any attempt to obtain compensation from the other state by peaceful means is similar in form to starting war without prior declaration. For if one wishes to find any rights in wartime, one must assume the existence of something analogous to a contract; in other words, one must assume that the other party has *accepted* the declaration of war and that both parties therefore wish to prosecute their rights in this manner.

§ 57

The most problematic task in international right is that of determining rights in wartime. For it is very difficult to form any conception at all of such rights and to imagine any law whatsoever in this lawless state without involving oneself in contradictions (*inter arma silent leges*).[18] The only possible solution would be to conduct the war in accordance with principles which would still leave the states with the possibility of abandoning the state of nature in their external relations and of entering a state of right.

No war between independent states can be a *punitive* one (*bellum punitivum*). For a punishment can only occur in a relationship between a superior (*imperantis*) and a subject (*subditum*), and this is not the relationship which exists between states. Nor can there be a *war of extermination* (*bellum internecinum*) or a *war of subjugation* (*bellum subiugatorium*); for these would involve the moral annihilation of a state, and its people would either merge with those of the victorious state or be reduced to bondage. Not that this expedient, to which a state might resort in order to obtain peace, would in itself contradict the rights of a state. But the fact remains that the only concept of antagonism which the idea of international right includes is that of an antagonism regulated by principles of external freedom. This requires that violence be used only to preserve one's existing property, but not as a method of further acquisition; for the latter procedure would create a threat to one state by augmenting the power of another.

The attacked state is allowed to use any means of defence except those whose use would render its subjects unfit to be citizens. For if it did not observe this condition, it would render itself unfit in the eyes of international right to function as a person in relation to other states and to share equal rights with them. It must accordingly be prohibited for a state to use its own subjects as spies, and to use them, or indeed foreigners, as poisoners or assassins (to which class the so-called sharpshooters who wait in ambush on individual victims also belong), or even just to spread false reports. In short, a state must not use such treacherous methods as would destroy that confidence which is required for the future establishment of a lasting peace.

It is permissible in war to impose levies and contributions on the conquered enemy, but not to plunder the people, i.e. to force individual persons to part with their belongings (for this would be robbery, since it was not the conquered people who waged the war, but the state of which they were subjects which waged it *through them*). Bills of receipt should be issued for any contributions that are exacted, so that the burden imposed on the country or province can be distributed proportionately when peace is concluded.

§ 58

The right which applies *after* a war, i.e. with regard to the peace treaty at the time of its conclusion and also to its later consequences, consists of the following elements. The victor sets out the conditions, and these are drawn up in a *treaty* on which agreement is reached with the defeated party in order that peace may be concluded. A treaty of this kind is not determined by any pretended right which the victor possesses over his opponent because of an alleged injury the latter has done him; the victor should not concern himself with such questions, but should rely only on his own power for support. Thus he cannot claim compensation for the costs of the war, for he would then have to pronounce his opponent unjust in waging it. And even if this argument should occur to him, he could not make use of it, or else he would have to maintain that the war was a punitive one, which would in turn mean that he had committed an offence in waging it himself. A peace treaty should also provide for the exchange of prisoners without ransom, whether the numbers on both sides are equal or not.

The vanquished state and its subjects cannot forfeit their civil freedom through the conquest of the country. Consequently, the former cannot be degraded to the rank of a colony or the latter to the rank of bondsmen. Otherwise, the war would have been a punitive one, which is self-contradictory.

A *colony* or province is a nation which has its own constitution, legislation and territory, and all members of any other state are no more than foreigners on its soil, even if the state to which they belong has supreme *executive* power over the colonial nation. The state with executive power is called the *mother state*. The daughter state is *ruled* by it, although it *governs* itself through its own parliament, which in turn functions under the presidency of a viceroy (*civitas hybrida*). The relationship of Athens to various islands was of this kind, as is that of Great Britain towards Ireland at the present moment.

It is even less possible to infer the rightful existence of *slavery* from the military conquest of a people, for one would then have to assume that the war had been a punitive one. Least of all would this justify hereditary slavery, which is completely absurd, for the guilt of a person's crime cannot be inherited.

It is implicit in the very concept of a peace treaty that it includes an *amnesty*.

§ 59

The *rights of peace* are as follows: firstly, the right to remain at peace when nearby states are at war (i.e. the right of *neutrality*); secondly, the right to secure the continued maintenance of peace once it has been concluded (i.e. the right of *guarantee*); and thirdly, the right to form *alliances* or confederate leagues of several states for the purpose of communal defence against any possible attacks from internal or external sources—although these must never become leagues for promoting aggression and internal expansion.

§ 60

The rights of a state against an *unjust enemy* are unlimited in quantity or degree, although they do have limits in relation to quality. In other words, while the threatened state may not employ *every* means to assert its own rights, it may employ any intrinsically permissible means to whatever degree its own strength allows. But what can the expression 'an unjust enemy' mean in relation to the concepts of international right, which requires that every state should act as judge of its own cause just as it would do in a state of nature? It must mean someone whose publicly expressed will, whether expressed in word or in deed, displays a maxim which would make peace among nations impossible and would lead to a perpetual state of nature if it were made into a general rule. Under this heading would come violations of public contracts, which can be assumed to affect the interests of all nations. For they are a threat to their freedom, and a challenge to them to unite against such misconduct and to deprive the culprit of the power to act in a similar way again. But this does *not* entitle them *to divide up the offending state among themselves* and to make it disappear, as it were, from the face of the earth. For this would be an injustice against the people, who cannot lose their original right to unite into a commonwealth. They can only be made to accept a new constitution of a nature that is unlikely to encourage their warlike inclinations.

Besides, the expression 'an unjust enemy' is a *pleonasm* if applied to any situation in a state of nature, for this state is itself one of injustice. A just enemy would be one whom I could not resist without injustice. But if this were so, he would not be my enemy in any case.

§61

Since the state of nature among nations (as among individual human beings) is a state which one ought to abandon in order to enter a state governed by law, all international rights, as well as all the external property of states such as can be acquired or preserved by war, are purely *provisional* until the state of nature has been abandoned. Only within a universal *union of states* (analogous to the union through which a nation becomes a state) can such rights and property acquire *peremptory* validity and a true *state of peace* be attained. But if an international state of this kind extends over too wide an area of land, it will eventually become impossible to govern it and thence to protect each of its members, and the multitude of corporations this would require must again lead to a state of war. It naturally follows that *perpetual peace*, the ultimate end of all international right, is an idea incapable of realisation. But the political principles which have this aim, i.e. those principles which encourage the formation of international alliances designed to *approach* the idea itself by a continual process, are not impracticable. For this is a project based upon duty, hence also upon the rights of man and of states, and it can indeed be put into execution.

Such a *union of several states* designed to preserve peace may be called a *permanent congress of states*, and all neighbouring states are free to join it. A congress of this very kind (at least as far as the formalities of international right in relation to the preservation of peace are concerned) found expression in the assembly of the States General at The Hague in the first half of this century.[19] To this assembly, the ministers of most European courts and even of the smallest republics brought their complaints about any aggression suffered by one of their number at the hands of another. They thus thought of all Europe as a single federated state, which they accepted as an arbiter in all their public disputes. Since then, however, international right has disappeared from cabinets, surviving only in books, or it has been consigned to the obscurity of the archives as a form of empty deduction after violent measures have already been employed.

In the present context, however, a *congress* merely signifies a voluntary gathering of various states which can be *dissolved* at any time, not an association which, like that of the American states, is based on a political constitution and is therefore indissoluble. For this is the only means of realising the idea of public international right as it ought to be instituted, thereby enabling the nations to settle their disputes in a civilised manner by legal proceedings, not in a barbaric manner (like that of the savages) by acts of war.

SECTION III: COSMOPOLITAN RIGHT

§ 62

The rational idea, as discussed above, of a *peaceful* (if not exactly amicable) international community of all those of the earth's peoples who can enter into active relations with one another, is not a philanthropic principle of ethics, but a principle of *right*. Through the spherical shape of the planet they inhabit (*globus terraqueus*), nature has confined them all within an area of definite limits. Accordingly, the only conceivable way in which anyone can possess habitable land on earth is by possessing a part within a determinate whole in which everyone has an original right to share. Thus all nations are *originally* members of a community of the land. But this is not a *legal community* of possession (*communio*) and utilisation of the land, nor a community of ownership. It is a community of reciprocal action (*commercium*), which is physically possible, and each member of it accordingly has constant relations with all the others. Each may *offer* to have commerce with the rest, and they all have a right to make such overtures without being treated by foreigners as enemies. This right, in so far as it affords the prospect that all nations may unite for the purpose of creating certain universal laws to regulate the intercourse they may have with one another, may be termed *cosmopolitan* (*ius cosmopoliticum*).

The oceans may appear to cut nations off from the community of their fellows. But with the art of navigation, they constitute the greatest natural incentive to international commerce, and the greater the number of neighbouring coastlines there are (as in the Mediterranean), the livelier this commerce will be. Yet these visits to foreign shores, and even more so, attempts to settle on them with a view to linking them with the motherland, can also occasion evil and violence in one part of the globe with ensuing repercussions which are felt everywhere else. But although such abuses are possible, they do not deprive the world's citizens of the right to *attempt* to enter into a community with everyone else and to *visit* all regions of the earth with this intention. This does not, however, amount to a right to *settle* on another nation's territory (*ius incolatus*), for the latter would require a special contract.

But one might ask whether a nation may establish a *settlement alongside another nation* (*accolatus*) in newly discovered regions, or whether it may take possession of land in the vicinity of a nation which has already settled in the same area, even without the latter's consent. The answer is that the right to do so is incontestable, so long as such settlements are established sufficiently far away from the territory of the original nation for neither party to interfere with the other in their use of the land. But if the nations involved are pastoral or hunting peoples (like the Hottentots, the Tunguses, and most native American nations) who rely upon large tracts of wasteland for their sustenance, settlements should not be established by violence, but only by treaty; and even then, there must be no attempt to exploit the ignorance of the natives in persuading them to give up their territories. Nevertheless, there are plausible enough arguments for the use of violence on the grounds that it is in the best interests of the world as a whole. For on the one hand, it may bring culture to uncivilised peoples (this is the excuse with which even Büsching[20] tries to extenuate the bloodshed which accompanied the introduction of Christianity into Germany); and on the other, it may help us to purge our country of depraved characters, at the same time affording the hope that they or their offspring will become reformed in another continent (as in New Holland). But all these supposedly good intentions cannot wash away the stain of injustice from the means which are used to implement them. Yet one might object that the whole world would perhaps still be in a lawless condition if men had had any such compunction about using violence when they first created a law-governed state. But this can as little annul the above condition of right as can the plea of political revolutionaries that the people are entitled to reform constitutions by force if they have become corrupt, and to act completely unjustly for once and for all, in order to put justice on a more secure basis and ensure that it flourishes in the future.

Conclusion

If a person cannot prove that a thing exists, he may attempt to prove that it does not exist. If neither approach succeeds (as often happens), he may still ask whether it is *in his interest to assume* one or other possibility as a hypothesis, either from theoretical or from practical considerations. In other words, he may wish on the one hand simply to explain a certain phenomenon (as the astronomer, for example, may wish to explain the sporadic movements of the planets), or on the other, to achieve a certain end which may itself be either *pragmatic* (purely technical) or *moral* (i.e. an end which it is our duty to take as a maxim). It is, of course, self-evident that no-one is duty-bound to make an *assumption* (*suppositio*) that the end in question can be realised, since this would involve a purely theoretical and indeed problematic judgement; for no-one can be obliged to accept a given belief. But we can have a duty to act in accordance with the idea of such an end, even if there is not the slightest theoretical probability of its realisation, provided that there is no means of demonstrating that it cannot be realised either.

Now, moral-practical reason within us pronounces the following irresistible veto: *There shall be no war*, either between individual human beings in the state of nature, or between separate states, which, although internally law-governed, still live in a lawless condition in their external relationships with one another. For war is not the way in which anyone should pursue his rights. Thus it is no longer a question of whether perpetual peace is really possible or not, or whether we are not perhaps mistaken in our theoretical judgement if we assume that it is. On the contrary, we must simply act as if it could really come about (which is perhaps impossible), and turn our efforts towards realising it and towards establishing that constitution which seems most suitable for this purpose (perhaps that of republicanism in all states, individually and collectively). By working towards this end, we may hope to terminate the disastrous practice of war, which up till now has been the main object to which all states, without exception, have accommodated their internal institutions. And even if the fulfilment of this pacific intention were forever to remain a pious hope, we should still not be deceiving ourselves if we made it our maxim to work unceasingly towards it, for it is our duty to do so. To assume, on the other hand, that the moral law within us might be misleading, would give rise to the execrable wish to dispense with all reason and to regard ourselves, along with our principles, as subject to the same mechanism of nature as the other animal species.

It can indeed be said that this task of establishing a universal and lasting peace is not just a part of the theory of right within the limits of pure reason, but its entire ultimate purpose. For the condition of peace is the only state in which the property of a large number of people living together as neighbours under a single constitution can be guaranteed by *laws*. The rule on which this constitution is based must not simply be derived from the experience of those who have hitherto fared best under it, and then set up as a norm for others. On the contrary, it should be derived *a priori* by reason from the absolute ideal of a rightful association of men under public laws. For all particular examples are deceptive (an example can only illustrate a point, but does not prove anything), so that one must have recourse to metaphysics. And even those who scorn metaphysics admit its necessity involuntarily when they say, for example (as they often do): 'The best constitution is that in which the power rests with laws instead of with men.' For what can be more metaphysically sublime than this idea, although by the admission of those who express it, it also has a well-authenticated objective reality which can easily be demonstrated from particular instances as they arise. But no attempt should be made to put it into practice overnight by revolution, i.e. by forcibly overthrowing a defective constitution which has existed in the past; for there would then be an interval of time during which the condition of right would be nullified. If we try instead to give it reality by means of gradual reforms carried out in accordance with definite principles, we shall see that it is the only means of continually approaching the supreme political good—perpetual peace.

A brief appendix follows in which Kant, in a reply to an anonymous review,[21] comments mainly on the theory of private right, but also repeats his views on the sacredness and inviolability of civil constitutions and again denies absolutely any right to rebellion.

The Contest of Faculties [1]

In the introductory part of the work, Kant explains how the division into the three 'higher faculties' (Theology, Law and Medicine) on the one hand, and the 'lower faculty' (Philosophy) on the other, arose. He explains that governments must take an interest in the so-called 'higher faculties', because their work has an influence on the people, whereas the philosophical faculty is free to pursue scholarship and judge the teaching of the other faculties without interference from the government. Its only concern is to speak the truth freely, thus merely following the commands of man, who is free by nature.

Kant further points out that there must be statutes issued by the government regulating the teaching of the 'higher faculties'. The Bible, the law of the land and the medical regulations of the state form the basis of the teaching of the 'higher faculties', but if they violate these boundaries and seek to enter the field in which reason rules, they come into conflict with the philosophical faculty.

Kant subsequently points out that it is legitimate for the philosophical faculty to question the findings of the higher faculties. To do so does not imply criticism of the government; it involves merely a contest between the faculties (though not a war) about what is true. The government never protects the higher faculties because their public doctrines, opinions and statements are true. It protects them only because advantages may accrue to the government if it does so.

In the next section, Kant examines the contest between the philosophical and the theological faculties, which arises from the divergence between ecclesiastical doctrine and religious faith, between laws given by the arbitrary will of another person and the laws arrived at by inner reason. The next section (printed below) deals with the contest between the faculty of philosophy and the faculty of law. In the final section of the work, he discusses the contest between the faculties of philosophy and medicine. Kant writes rather amusingly, though somewhat bizarrely, about various kinds of psychological therapy, about the power of the mind to conquer sensations of disease merely by strength of will. He further discourses on diet, hypochondria, sleep, eating, drinking, and the alleviation and prevention of disease by correct breathing. This section concludes this interesting, though strange, work. It was the last large work to be published by Kant in his lifetime.

A RENEWED ATTEMPT TO ANSWER THE QUESTION: 'IS THE HUMAN RACE CONTINUALLY IMPROVING?'[2]

1

WHAT SORT OF KNOWLEDGE ARE WE LOOKING FOR?

What we are seeking to know is a portion of human history. It is not a history of the past, however, but a history of future times, i.e. a *predictive* history. But if it is not discoverable from known laws of nature (as with eclipses of the sun and moon, which can be foretold by natural means) and can only be learnt through additional insight into the future supplied by supernatural revelation, it must be termed *prognosticative* or *prophetic*.* Besides, we are here concerned not with the natural history of mankind (as we should be if we asked, for example, whether new races of man might emerge in future times), but with the *history of civilisation*. And we are not dealing with any *specific* conception of mankind (*singulorum*), but with the *whole* of humanity (*universorum*), united in earthly society and distributed in national groups. All this is implied if we ask whether the human *race* (as a whole) is continually improving.

2

HOW CAN WE ATTAIN SUCH KNOWLEDGE?

We can obtain a prophetic historical narrative of things to come by depicting those events whose *a priori* possibility suggests that they will in fact happen. But how is it possible to have history *a priori*? The answer is that it is possible if the prophet himself occasions and *produces* the events he predicts.

It was all very well for the Jewish prophets to foretell that the state to which they belonged would sooner or later suffer not only decline, but also complete dissolution; for they were themselves the architects of their fate. As leaders of the people, they had loaded their constitution with so many ecclesiastical (and thence also civil) burdens that their state became completely unfit to exist in its own right, particularly in its relations with neighbouring nations. Thus the jeremiads of the priests naturally went unheeded, because these same priests stubbornly stuck to their belief in the untenable constitution they had themselves created, so that they were themselves able to foresee the consequences with infallible certainty.

---

* Those, from pythonesses[3] to gypsies, who dabble in prophecy with neither knowledge nor honesty, are known as *false prophets*.

Our politicians, so far as their influence extends, behave in exactly the same way, and they are just as successful in their prophecies. One must take men as they are, they tell us, and not as the world's uninformed pedants or good-natured dreamers fancy that they ought to be. But 'as they are' ought to read 'as we have *made them* by unjust coercion, by treacherous designs which the government is in a good position to carry out'. For that is why they are intransigent and inclined to rebellion, and why regrettable consequences ensue if discipline is relaxed in the slightest. In this way, the prophecy of the supposedly clever statesmen is fulfilled.

Various divines also at times prophesy the complete decline of religion and the imminent appearance of the Antichrist, all the while doing the very things that are best calculated to create the state of affairs they describe. For they are not taking care to impress on the hearts of their congregation moral principles which would directly lead to an improvement. Instead, they see observances and historical beliefs as the essential duties, supposing that these will indirectly produce the same results; but although they may lead to mechanical conformity (as within a civil constitution), they cannot produce conformity in moral attitudes. Nevertheless, these divines complain at the irreligion which they have themselves created, and which they could accordingly have foretold without any special gift of prophecy.

3

SUBDIVISIONS WITHIN THE CONCEPT OF WHAT WE
WISH TO KNOW OF THE FUTURE

There are three possible forms which our prophecy might take. The human race is either continually *regressing* and deteriorating, continually *progressing* and improving, or at a permanent *standstill*, in relation to other created beings, at its present level of moral attainment (which is the same as continually revolving in a circle around a fixed point).

The first statement might be designated *moral terrorism*, the second *eudaemonism*[4] (which, if the goal of human progress were already visible from afar, might also be termed *chiliasm*),[5] while the third could be called *abderitism*.[6] For in the latter case, since a genuine standstill is impossible in moral affairs, rises and falls of equal magnitude constantly alternate, in endless fluctuation, and produce no more effect than if the subject of them had remained stationary in one place.

a
The terroristic conception of human history

A process of deterioration in the human race cannot go on indefinitely, for mankind would wear itself out after a certain point had been reached. Consequently, when enormities go on piling up and up and the evils they produce continue to increase, we say: 'It can't get much worse now.' It seems that the day of judgement is at hand, and the pious zealot already dreams of the rebirth of everything and of a world created anew after the present world has been destroyed by fire.

b
The eudaemonistic conception of human history

We may readily agree that the sum total of good and evil of which our nature is capable always remains unchanged, and can neither be augmented nor reduced within any one individual. And how could the quantity of good of which a person is capable possibly be increased? For it would have to be done by his own free agency as a subject, and before he could do it, he would in turn require a greater store of goodness than he already possessed int he first place. After all, no effects can exceed the capacity of their effective cause; and the quantity of goodness in man must therefore remain below a certain level in proportion to the amount of evil with which it is intermixed, so that man cannot work his way beyond a given limit and go on improving further. Thus eudaemonism, with its sanguine hopes, appears to be untenable. Its ideas of constant human progress and improvement would seem of little use to a prophetic history of mankind.

c
The hypothesis of abderitism in the human race as a definition of its future history

This point of view probably has the majority of subscribers on its side. To start off swiftly along the way of goodness without persevering on it, and instead, to reverse the plan of progress in order at all costs to avoid being tied to a single aim (even if only from a desire for variety); to construct in order to demolish; to take upon ourselves the hopeless task of rolling the stone of Sisyphus uphill, only to let it roll back down again: such is the industrious folly which characterises our race. In view of all this, it does not so much seem that the principle of evil within the natural character of mankind is amalgamated or fused with that of goodness, but rather that the one is neutralised by the other, with inactivity as the result (or a standstill, as in the case under discussion). This empty activity of backward and forward motion, with good and evil continually alternating, would mean that all the interplay of members of our species on earth ought merely to be regarded as a farce. And in the eyes of reason, this cannot give any higher a value to mankind than to the other animal species, whose interaction takes place at less cost and without any conscious understanding.

4

THE PROBLEM OF PROGRESS CANNOT BE SOLVED
DIRECTLY FROM EXPERIENCE

Even if it were found that the human race as a whole had been moving forward and progressing for an indefinitely long time, no-one could guarantee that its era of decline was not beginning at that very moment, by virtue of the physical character of our race. And conversely, if it is regressing and deteriorating at an accelerating pace, there are no grounds for giving up hope that we are just about to reach the turning point (*punctum flexus contrarii*) at which our affairs will take a turn for the better, by virtue of the moral character of our race. For we are dealing with freely acting beings to whom one can *dictate* in advance what they *ought* to do, but of whom one cannot *predict* what they actually *will* do, and who are capable, if things go really badly and they experience evils incurred through their own actions, of regarding these evils as a greater incentive to do better than they did in the past. But as the Abbé Coyer[7] says: 'Poor mortals! Nothing is constant among you but inconstancy.'

Perhaps it is because we have chosen the wrong point of view from which to contemplate the course of human affairs that the latter seems so absurd to us. The planets, as seen from the earth, sometimes move backward, sometimes forward, and at other times remain motionless. But seen from the sun—the point of view of reason—they continually follow their regular paths as in the Copernican hypothesis. Yet some thinkers, otherwise not deficient in wisdom, prefer to stick firmly to their own interpretation of phenomena and to the point of view they originally adopted, even at the price of involving themselves to an absurd degree in Tychonic[8] cycles and epicycles. It is our misfortune, however, that we are unable to adopt an absolute point of view when trying to predict free actions. For this, exalted above all human wisdom, would be the point of view of *providence*, which extends even to *free* human actions. And although man may *see* the latter, he cannot *foresee* them with certainty (a distinction which does not exist in the eyes of the divinity); for while he needs to perceive a connection governed by natural laws before he can foresee anything, he must do without such hints or guidance when dealing with *free* actions in the future.

If it were possible to credit human beings with even a limited will of innate and unvarying goodness, we could certainly predict a general improvement of mankind, for this would involve events which man could himself control. But if man's natural endowments consist of a mixture of evil and goodness in unknown proportions, no-one can tell what effects he should expect from his own actions.

5

A PROPHETIC HISTORY OF THE HUMAN RACE MUST NEVERTHELESS START FROM SOME SORT OF EXPERIENCE

In human affairs, there must be some experience or other which, as an event which has actually occurred, might suggest that man has the quality or power of being the *cause* and (since his actions are supposed to be those of a being endowed with freedom) the *author* of his own improvement. But an event can be predicted as the effect of a given cause only when the circumstances which help to shape it actually arise. And while it can well be predicted in general that these circumstances must arise at some time or another (as in calculating probabilities in games of chance), it is impossible to determine whether this will happen during my lifetime, and whether I shall myself experience it and thus be able to confirm the original prediction.

We must therefore search for an event which would indicate that such a cause exists and that it is causally active within the human race, irrespective of the time at which it might actually operate; and it would have to be a cause which allowed us to conclude, as an inevitable consequence of its operation, that mankind is improving. This inference could then be extended to cover the history of former times so as to show that mankind has always been progressing, yet in such a way that the event originally chosen as an example would not in itself be regarded as the cause of progress in the past, but only as a rough indication or *historical sign (signum rememorativum, demonstrativum, prognostikon)*. It might then serve to prove the existence of a *tendency* within the human race as a *whole*, considered not as a series of individuals (for this would result in interminable enumerations and calculations) but as a body distributed over the earth in states and national groups.

6

AN OCCURRENCE IN OUR OWN TIMES WHICH PROVES
THIS MORAL TENDENCY OF THE HUMAN RACE

The occurrence in question does not involve any of those momentous deeds or misdeeds of men which make small in their eyes what was formerly great or make great what was formerly small, and which cause ancient and illustrious states to vanish as if by magic, and others to arise in their place as if from the bowels of the earth. No, it has nothing to do with all this. We are here concerned only with the attitude of the onlookers as it reveals itself *in public* while the drama of great political changes is taking place: for they openly express universal yet disinterested sympathy for one set of protagonists against their adversaries, even at the risk that their partiality could be of great disadvantage to themselves. Their reaction (because of its universality) proves that mankind as a whole shares a certain character in common, and it also proves (because of its disinterestedness) that man has a moral character, or at least the makings of one. And this does not merely allow us to hope for human improvement; it is already a form of improvement in itself, in so far as its influence is strong enough for the present.

The revolution which we have seen taking place in our own times in a nation of gifted people[9] may succeed, or it may fail. It may be so filled with misery and atrocities that no right-thinking man would ever decide to make the same experiment again at such a price, even if he could hope to carry it out successfully at the second attempt. But I maintain that this revolution has aroused in the hearts and desires of all spectators who are not themselves caught up in it a *sympathy* which borders almost on enthusiasm, although the very utterance of this sympathy was fraught with danger. It cannot therefore have been caused by anything other than a moral disposition within the human race.

The moral cause which is at work here is composed of two elements. Firstly, there is the *right* of every people to give itself a civil constitution of the kind that it sees fit, without interference from other powers. And secondly, once it is accepted that the only intrinsically *rightful* and morally good constitution which a people can have is by its very nature disposed to avoid wars of aggression (i.e. that the only possible constitution is a republican one, at least in its conception),* there is the *aim*, which is also

* This does not mean, however, that a people which has a monarchic constitution can thereby claim the right to alter it, or even nurse a secret desire to do so. For a people which occupies extended territories in Europe may feel that monarchy is the only kind

a duty, of submitting to those conditions by which war, the source of all evils and moral corruption, can be prevented. If this aim is recognised, the human race, for all its frailty, has a negative guarantee that it will progressively improve or at least that it will not be disturbed in its progress.

All this, along with the *passion* or *enthusiasm* with which men embrace the cause of goodness (although the former cannot be entirely applauded, since all passion as such is blameworthy), gives historical support for the following assertion, which is of considerable anthropological significance: true enthusiasm is always directed exclusively towards the *ideal*, particularly towards that which is purely moral (such as the concept of right), and it cannot be coupled with selfish interests. No pecuniary rewards could inspire the opponents of the revolutionaries with that zeal and greatness of soul which the concept of right could alone produce in them, and even the old military aristocracy's concept of honour (which is analogous to enthusiasm) vanished before the arms[10] of those who had fixed their gaze on the *rights* of the people to which they belonged,* and who regarded themselves as its protectors. And then the external public of onlookers sympathised with their exaltation, without the slightest intention of actively participating in their affairs.

of constitution which can enable it to preserve its own existence between powerful neighbours. And if the subjects should complain, not because of their internal government but because of their government's behaviour towards the citizens of foreign states (for example, if it were to discourage republicanism abroad), this does not prove that the people are dissatisfied with their own constitution, but rather that they are profoundly attached to it; for it becomes progressively more secure from danger as more of the other nations become republics. Nevertheless, slanderous sycophants, bent on increasing their own importance, have tried to portray this innocuous political gossip as innovationism, Jacobinism and conspiracy, constituting a menace to the state. But there was never the slightest reason for such allegations, particularly in a country more than a hundred miles removed from the scene of the revolution.

* It may be said of such enthusiasm for asserting the rights of man: *postquam ad arma Vulcania ventum est,—mortalis mucro glacies ceu futilis ictu dissiluit.*[11]—Why has no ruler ever dared to say openly that he does not recognise any *rights* of the people against himself? Or that the people owe their happiness only to the *beneficence* of a government which confers it upon them, and that any pretensions on the part of the subject that he has rights against the government are absurd or even punishable, since they imply that resistance to authority is permissible? The reason is that any such public declaration would rouse up all the subjects against the ruler, even although they had been like docile sheep, well fed, powerfully protected and led by a kind and understanding master, and had no lack of welfare to complain of. For beings endowed with freedom cannot be content merely to enjoy the comforts of existence, which may well be provided by others (in this case, by the government); it all depends on the *principle* which governs the provision of such comforts. But welfare does not have any ruling principle, either for the recipient or for the one who provides it, for each individual will define it differently. It depends, in fact, upon the will's *material* aspect, which is empirical and thus incapable

183

7

THE PROPHETIC HISTORY OF MANKIND

In these principles, there must be something *moral* which reason recognises not only as pure, but also (because of its great and epoch-making influence) as something to which the human soul manifestly acknowledges a duty. Moreover, it concerns the human race as a complete association of men (*non singulorum, sed universorum*),[12] for they rejoice with universal and disinterested sympathy at its anticipated success and at all attempts to make it succeed.

The occurrence in question is not, however, a phenomenon of revolution, but (as Erhard[13] puts it) of the *evolution* of a constitution governed by *natural right*. Such a constitution cannot itself be achieved by furious struggles—for civil and foreign wars will destroy whatever *statutory* order has hitherto prevailed—but it does lead us to strive for a constitution which would be incapable of bellicosity, i.e. a republican one. The actual *form* of the desired state might be republican, or alternatively, it might only be republican in its *mode of government*, in that the state would be administered by a single ruler (the monarch) acting by analogy with the laws which a people would give itself in conformity with universal principles of right.

Even without the mind of a seer, I now maintain that I can predict from the aspects and signs of our times that the human race will achieve this end, and that it will henceforth progressively improve without any more total reversals. For a phenomenon of this kind which has taken place in human history *can never be forgotten*, since it has revealed in human nature an aptitude and power for improvement of a kind which no politician could have thought up by examining the course of events in the past. Only nature and freedom, combined within mankind in accordance

of becoming a universal rule. A being endowed with freedom, aware of the advantage he possesses over non-rational animals, can and must therefore follow the *formal* principle of his will and demand for the people to which he belongs nothing short of a government in which the people are co-legislators. In other words, the rights of men who are expected to obey must necessarily come before all considerations of their actual wellbeing, for they are a sacred institution, exalted above all utilitarian values; and no matter how benevolent a government is, it may not tamper with them. These rights, however, always remain an idea which can be fulfilled only on condition that the *means* employed to do so are compatible with morality. This limiting condition must not be overstepped by the people, who may not therefore pursue their rights by revolution, which is at all times unjust. The best way of making a nation content with its constitution is to *rule* autocratically and at the same time to *govern* in a republican manner, i.e. to govern in the spirit of republicanism and by analogy with it.

with principles of right, have enabled us to forecast it; but the precise time at which it will occur must remain indefinite and dependent upon chance.

But even if the intended object behind the occurrence we have described were not to be achieved for the present, or if a people's revolution or constitutional reform were ultimately to fail, or if, after the latter had lasted for a certain time, everything were to be brought back onto its original course (as politicians now claim to prophesy), our own philosophical prediction still loses none of its force. For the occurrence in question is too momentous, too intimately interwoven with the interests of humanity and too widespread in its influence upon all parts of the world for nations not to be reminded of it when favourable circumstances present themselves, and to rise up and make renewed attempts of the same kind as before. After all, since it is such an important concern of the human race, the intended constitution must at some time or another finally reach that degree of stability which the lessons of repeated experience will not fail to instil into the hearts of everyone.

Thus the proposition that the human race has always been progressively improving and will continue to develop in the same way is not just a well-meant saying to be recommended for practical purposes. Whatever unbelievers may say, it is tenable within the most strictly theoretical context. And if one considers not only the events which may happen within a particular nation, but also their repercussions upon all the nations of the earth which might gradually begin to participate in them, a view opens up into the unbounded future. This would not be true, of course, if the first epoch of natural convulsions, which (according to Camper[14] and Blumenbach[15]) engulfed the animal and vegetable kingdoms before the era of man, were to be followed by a second in which the human race were given the same treatment so that other creatures might take the stage instead, etc. For man in turn is a mere trifle in relation to the omnipotence of nature, or rather to its inaccessible highest cause. But if the rulers of man's own species regard him as such and treat him accordingly, either by burdening him like a beast and using him as a mere instrument of their ends, or by setting him up to fight in their disputes and slaughter his fellows, it is not just a trifle but a reversal of the *ultimate purpose* of creation.

8

THE DIFFICULTY OF MAXIMS DIRECTED TOWARDS THE WORLD'S PROGRESSIVE IMPROVEMENT AS REGARDS THEIR PUBLICITY

Popular enlightenment is the public instruction of the people upon their duties and rights towards the state to which they belong. Since this concerns only natural rights and rights which can be derived from ordinary common sense, their obvious exponents and interpreters among the people will not be officials appointed by the state, but free teachers of right, i.e. the philosophers. The latter, on account of the very freedom which they allow themselves, are a stumbling-block to the state, whose only wish is to rule; they are accordingly given the appellation of 'enlighteners', and decried as a menace to the state. And yet they do not address themselves in familiar tones to the *people* (who themselves take little or no notice of them and their writings), but in *respectful* tones to the state, which is thereby implored to take the rightful needs of the people to heart. And if a whole people wishes to present its grievance (*gravamen*), the only way in which this can be done is by publicity. A *ban* on publicity will therefore hinder a nation's progress, even with regard to the least of its claims, the claim for natural rights.

Another thing which is concealed (transparently enough) by legal measures from a certain people is the true nature of its constitution. It would be an affront to the majesty of the people of Great Britain to say that they lived under an *absolute monarchy*. Instead, it is said that their constitution is one which *limits* the will of the monarch through the two houses of parliament, acting as representatives of the people. Yet everyone knows very well that the influence of the monarch upon these representatives is so great and so infallible that the aforesaid houses make no decisions except those which His Majesty wishes and recommends through his minister. Now and again, the latter will certainly recommend decisions wherein he[16] knows and indeed *ensures* that he will meet with contradiction (as with the abolition of the slave trade), simply in order to furnish ostensible proof of parliamentary freedom. But this sort of approach has the insidious effect of discouraging people from looking for the true and rightfully established constitution, for they imagine they have discovered it in an instance which is already before them. Thus a mendacious form of publicity deceives the people with the illusion that the monarchy is *limited**

---

* A cause whose nature is not directly perceptible can be discovered through the effect which invariably accompanies it. What is an *absolute* monarch? He is one at whose comby a law which emanates from them, while their representatives, won over by bribery, secretly subject them to an *absolute monarch*.

All forms of state are based on the idea of a constitution which is compatible with the natural rights of man, so that those who obey the law should also act as a unified body of legislators. And if we accordingly think of the commonwealth in terms of concepts of pure reason, it may be called a Platonic *ideal* (*respublica noumenon*), which is not an empty figment of the imagination, but the eternal norm for all civil constitutions whatsoever, and a means of ending all wars. A civil society organised in conformity with it and governed by laws of freedom is an example representing it in the world of experience (*respublica phaenomenon*), and it can only be achieved by a laborious process, after innumerable wars and conflicts. But its constitution, once it has been attained as a whole, is the best qualified of all to keep out war, the destroyer of everything good. Thus it is our duty to enter into a constitution of this kind; and in the meantime, since it will be a considerable time before this takes place, it is the duty of monarchs to govern in a *republican* (not a democratic) manner, even although they may *rule autocratically*. In other words, they should treat the people in accordance with principles akin in spirit to the laws of freedom which a people of mature rational powers would prescribe for itself, even if the people is not literally asked for its consent.

9

WHAT PROFIT WILL THE HUMAN RACE DERIVE FROM PROGRESSIVE IMPROVEMENT?

The profit which will accrue to the human race as it works its way forward will not be an ever increasing quantity of *morality* in its attitudes. Instead, the *legality* of its attitudes will produce an increasing number of actions governed by duty, whatever the particular motive behind these actions

mand war at once begins when he says it shall do so. And conversely, what is a *limited* monarch? He is one who must first ask the people whether or not there is to be a war, and if the people say that there shall be no war, then there will be none. For war is a condition in which *all* the powers of the state must be at the head of state's disposal.

Now the monarch of Great Britain has waged numerous wars without asking the people's consent. This king is therefore an absolute monarch, although he should not be so according to the constitution. But he can always bypass the latter, since he can always be assured, by controlling the various powers of the state, that the people's representatives will agree with him; for he has the authority to award all offices and dignities. This corrupt system, however, must naturally be given no publicity if it is to succeed. It therefore remains under a very transparent veil of secrecy.

may be. In other words, the profit will result from man's good *deeds* as they grow ever more numerous and successful, i.e. from the external phenomena of man's moral nature. For we have only *empirical* data (our experiences) on which to base this prediction—that is, we base it on the physical cause of our actions in so far as they actually take place as phenomena, not on the moral cause which contains the concept of duty as applied to what ought to happen, and which can be determined by processes of pure *a priori* thinking.

Violence will gradually become less on the part of those in power, and obedience towards the laws will increase. There will no doubt be more charity, less quarrels in legal actions, more reliability in keeping one's word, and so on in the commonwealth, partly from a love of honour, and partly from a lively awareness of where one's own advantage lies; and this will ultimately extend to the external relations between the various peoples, until a cosmopolitan society is created. Such developments do not mean, however, that the basic moral capacity of mankind will increase in the slightest, for this would require a kind of new creation or supernatural influence. For we must not expect too much of human beings in their progressive improvements, or else we shall merit the scorn of those politicians who would gladly treat man's hopes of progress as the fantasies of an overheated mind.*

10

WHAT SEQUENCE CAN PROGRESS BE EXPECTED TO FOLLOW?

The answer is: not the usual sequence *from the bottom upwards*, but *from the top downwards*.

To expect that the education of young people in intellectual and moral culture, reinforced by the doctrines of religion, firstly through domestic instruction and then through a series of schools from the lowest to the

* It is certainly *agreeable* to think up political constitutions which meet the requirements of reason (particularly in matters of right). But it is *foolhardy* to put them forward seriously, and *punishable* to incite the people to do away with the existing constitution.

Plato's *Atlantis*,[17] More's *Utopia*,[18] Harrington's *Oceana*[19] and Allais' *Severambia*[20] have successively made their appearance, but they have never (with the exception of Cromwell's abortive attempt to establish a despotic republic) been tried out in practice. It is the same with these political creations as with the creation of the world: no-one was present at it, nor could anyone have been present, or else he would have been his own creator. It is a pleasant dream to hope that a political product of the sort we here have in mind will one day be brought to perfection, at however remote a date. But it is not merely *conceivable* that we can continually approach such a state; so long as it can be reconciled with the moral law, it is also the *duty* of the head of state (not of the citizens) to do so.

highest grade, will eventually not only make them good citizens, but will also bring them up to practise a kind of goodness which can continually progress and maintain itself, is a plan which is scarcely likely to achieve the desired success. For on the one hand, the people believe that the expense of educating their children should be met not by them but by the state; and on the other, the state itself (as Büsching[21] laments) has no money left over to pay qualified teachers who will carry out their duties with enthusiasm, since it needs it all for war. But apart from this, the whole mechanism of education as described above will be completely disjointed unless it is designed on the considered plan and intention of the highest authority in the state, then set in motion and constantly maintained in uniform operation thereafter. And this will mean that the state too will reform itself from time to time, pursuing evolution instead of revolution, and will thus make continuous progress. But those responsible for the desired education are also *human beings* who will therefore have to have had a suitable education themselves. And in view of the frailty of human nature and the fortuitous circumstances which can intensify its effects, we can expect man's hopes of progress to be fulfilled only under the positive condition of a higher wisdom (which, if it is invisible to us, is known as providence); and in so far as *human beings* can themselves accomplish anything or anything can be expected of them, it can only be through their negative wisdom in furthering their own ends. In the latter event, they will find themselves compelled to ensure that *war*, the greatest obstacle to morality and the invariable enemy of progress, first becomes gradually more humane, then more infrequent, and finally disappears completely as a mode of aggression. They will thereby enter into a constitution based on genuine principles of right, which is by its very nature capable of constant progress and improvement without forfeiting its strength.

Conclusion

A doctor who used to console his patients from day to day with hopes of imminent recovery, telling one that his pulse was better, and others that their faeces or perspiration heralded an improvement, etc., received a visit from one of his friends. 'How are you, my friend, and how is your illness?' was the first question. 'How do you think,' was the reply. '*I am dying of sheer recovery!*'

I do not blame anyone if political evils make him begin to despair of the welfare and progress of mankind. But I have confidence in the heroic medicine to which Hume refers, for it ought to produce a speedy cure.

'When I now see the nations engaged in war', he says, 'it is as if I witnessed two drunken wretches bludgeoning each other in a china-shop. For it is not just that the injuries they inflict on each other will be long in healing; they will also have to pay for all the damage they have caused.'[22] *Sero sapiunt Phryges.*[23] But the after-pains of the present war[24] will force the political prophet to admit that the human race must soon take a turn for the better, and this turn is now already in sight.

Appendix from 'The Critique of Pure Reason'[1]

TRANSCENDENTAL LOGIC II, DIALECTIC, I, 1:
OF IDEAS IN GENERAL

A constitution allowing the *greatest possible human freedom* in accordance with laws which ensure *that the freedom of each can co-exist with the freedom of all the others* (not one designed to provide the greatest possible happiness, as this will in any case follow automatically), is at all events a necessary idea which must be made the basis not only of the first outline of a political constitution but of all laws as well. It requires that we should abstract at the outset from present hindrances, which perhaps do not arise inevitably out of human nature, but are rather occasioned by neglect of genuine ideas in the process of legislation. For there is nothing more harmful, or more unworthy of a philosopher, than the vulgar appeal to an allegedly contrary experience, which would not have existed at all if the above measures had been taken at the right time in accordance with ideas, and if crude concepts, for the very reason that they were derived from experience, had not instead vitiated every good intention. The more closely the legislation and government were made to harmonise with this idea, the rarer punishments would become, and it is thus quite rational to maintain (as Plato does) that none would be necessary at all in a perfect state. Even if the latter should never come about, the idea which sets up this maximum as an archetype, in order to bring the legal constitution of mankind nearer and nearer to its greatest possible perfection, still remains correct. For no-one can or ought to decide what the highest degree may be at which mankind may have to stop progressing, and hence how wide a gap may still of necessity remain between the idea and its execution. For this will depend on freedom, which can transcend any limit we care to impose.

Reviews of Herder's Ideas on the Philosophy of the History of Mankind
AND
Conjectures on the Beginning of Human History

Kant's reviews (1785) of the first instalments of Johann Gottfried Herder's *Ideas on the Philosophy of the History of Mankind* (1784–91) and his *Conjectures on the Beginning of Human History* (1786) (which is virtually another reply to Herder's *Ideas* and also to his *Oldest Document of Mankind*[1] are not specifically concerned with political questions—they do not deal with the theory of right which for Kant sets the framework within which politics ought to be conducted—but they deal with, and amplify, his conception of history, which is an integral part of his political thought. They also strikingly bring out the manner of his reasoning when interpreting history philosophically, thus revealing the boundaries between those interpretations and theories which can, in his view, be justified in relation to empirical or rational enquiries and those which must be dismissed as untenable speculations.

To appreciate these writings properly it is necessary to set them in the context of Kant's attitude to Herder (1744–1803), one of the seminal thinkers of eighteenth-century Germany. Herder's influence has been immense. His impact on literature, above all through his friendship with Goethe, whose mentor he was in his youth (they met in Strasbourg in 1770 where Goethe was a student of law and Herder had just undergone an eye operation) can hardly be overestimated. His contributions to aesthetics and poetics are also important. He proclaimed the inner coherence and historical uniqueness of works of literature which should not, in his view, be judged by an appeal to universal aesthetic criteria. He thus furthered, perhaps more than anyone else, the historical and genetic approach to the study of literature and history. He

---

[1] *Älteste Urkunde des Menschengeschlechts*, Part I–III, Riga, 1774; *SW* VI, 193–511; Part IV, Riga, 1776; *SW* VII, 1–171.

also put folk poetry on the map of literary taste. His writings engendered the belief in the nation as a cultural entity and promoted cultural and eventually political nationalism, although he himself never abandoned his eighteenth-century cosmopolitanism; that step was taken only by the German Romantics.[1]

Herder was born in Morungen in East Prussia on 25 August 1744, the son of an impecunious school-teacher. By a stroke of good fortune he was able in 1762 to go to Königsberg (now Kaliningrad) to study at the university, earning his living as a tutor at the local grammar school, the Fridericianum. He attended Kant's lectures, which he found impressive. Later in life he gave a memorable account of this experience:

I enjoyed the good fortune to know a philosopher who was my teacher. In the prime of his life, he had the joyful cheerfulness of a young man which, I believe, remains with him in his most advanced years. His broad brow, built for thought, was the seat of an indestructible serenity and joy. Words, full of ideas, flowed from his lips, jocularity, wit and humour were at his disposal, and his didactic discourse was like the most entertaining conversation. With the same intelligence with which he analysed *Leibniz, Wolff, Baumgarten, Crusius* and *Hume* and followed up *Kepler's*, *Newton's* and the *physicists'* laws of nature, he took cognisance of *Rousseau's* writings, his *Émile* and *Héloise* (which were just appearing at that time), as well as of any discovery in the realm of nature which had come to his attention. He appreciated them and dwelt repeatedly on the unbiassed *knowledge of nature* and the *moral worth of man*. The history of man, nations and nature, natural science, mathematics and experience were the sources from which he enlivened his discourse and his conversation. Nothing worth knowing was indifferent to him; no intrigue, no fashion, no advantage, no ambition to enhance his reputation at any time distracted him in the least from the furtherance and clarification of truth. He encouraged and agreeably compelled one to think for oneself. Despotism was foreign to his mind. This man, whom I mention with the greatest gratitude and respect, is Immanuel Kant. I recall his image with pleasure.[2]

Herder was probably not exaggerating in the glow of recollection. To cite only one instance concerning Kant's appeal as a lecturer: it is recorded that Russian officers, while Russian troops occupied Königsberg during the Seven Years War, attended Kant's lectures for the sake of intellectual enjoyment. Kant himself took an interest in Herder as a gifted and lively young student, and although he was himself an unpaid lecturer (*Privatdozent*) who had to eke out his living from lecture fees paid by his students, he remitted Herder's fees and

---

[1] Cf. Reiss, *The Political Thought of the German Romantics*, particularly pp. 40–43.
[2] Herder, *Briefe zu Beförderung der Humanität*, No. 79; *SW* XVII, 404.

helped him in other ways. He hoped that Herder might write a didactic poem illustrating Kant's own (pre-critical) philosophy. But Herder, already as a student, went his own way. Having entered the Church as a Lutheran clergyman he obtained an important appointment as pastor at the principal German Lutheran church in Riga, the capital of Latvia, which, though under Russian sovereignty, enjoyed a large measure of political autonomy and as a former Hanseatic city contained a substantial German Lutheran population. His sermons attracted much attention, as did his literary writings. But being endowed with a restless temperament he resigned his post after a few years and became tutor to the Prince of Holstein–Gottorp, the son of a minor German ruler; later he took up an appointment as a pastor and consistorial councillor in Bückeburg in the employment of another petty German prince, the Count of Schaumburg–Lippe. In 1776, Goethe, who valued Herder's conversation and literary advice, persuaded the Duke Karl August of Saxe–Weimar–Eisenach (on whose privy council he was serving at the time) to offer Herder the post of General Superintendent of the Lutheran church of his duchy. Herder accepted the offer and stayed in that post until his death in 1803. He was thus part of that group of great German writers of the day, including Wieland, Goethe and Schiller, which set about establishing a classical German culture.

Kant was by nature a man who, as he himself said, wanted to live at peace with the world, but he thought it necessary to defend his own philosophy against those who attacked it and who, in his view, had fallen victim to intellectual error. Thus, in order to live at peace he had to engage in polemics (which was in any case a characteristic eighteenth-century pursuit). By the use of polemical argument, Kant sought to clarify the underlying principles of reason and to refute unsound arguments. After all, it was necessary to separate the wheat from the chaff.

After leaving Königsberg, Herder became one of the most productive and well-known writers in Germany. Kant was disappointed that the gifted younger man abandoned sound philosophical discussion and preferred to write essays whose style was not at all characterised by sobriety and carefulness of argument. The publication of the first part of Herder's *Ideas* coincided with Kant's own attempt to construct a philosophy of history in his *Idea for a Universal History with a Cosmopolitan Purpose*. At that stage, in 1784, the *Critique of Pure Reason* had not yet been widely hailed as the masterpiece which it is. The more reason therefore for Kant to combat an interpretation of history which, despite its brilliance, fell short of the philosophical rigour which he thought essential, especially if it came from the pen of so influential a writer (who was, moreover, his own former pupil).

Kant's criticism of Herder in his first review, published in January 1785 in the *Allgemeine Literaturzeitung* of Jena, was trenchant, though he did pay tribute to Herder's wide reading and imagination. Although the tone of Kant's review was friendly, Herder was deeply disappointed. He thought Kant's criticism mistaken and, always quick to take offence, he attacked him sharply in the next instalment of the *Ideas*, though without mentioning him by name. He criticised Kant's view that man needs a master, calling it an evil principle.[1] In so doing he thought he was defending the independence of the individual, which was threatened, in his view, by Kant's assumption that human progress is possible only for the species but not for the individual, an assumption which entails the existence of the state and of external coercion. Moreover, he understandably thought that his own method of reasoning was entirely legitimate.

Carl Leonhard Reinhold (1758–1823), who later, as professor of philosophy in Jena, did much to spread Kant's fame but who at this time had not yet been converted to Kant's thought, rallied to Herder's defence. In an anonymous review, entitled *The Letter of a Pastor* and published in the February 1785 issue of the *Teutsche Merkur*,[2] a widely read literary journal edited by his father-in-law, Christoph Martin Wieland, he berated Kant for viewing the *Ideas* from the point of view of the narrow metaphysics of the schools. Kant, in a brief but magisterial reply in the March issue of the *Allgemeine Literaturzeitung*, trounced Reinhold's not very incisive argument without any difficulty. He also defended his position in his review of the second instalment of the *Ideas* in the November issue of the *Allgemeine Literaturzeitung*, where he ironically pointed out the logical defects of Herder's approach and insisted that some measure of coercion in public life cannot be avoided; for there can be no freedom without law, and law implies coercion.

After the publication of this second review, Kant, in a brief essay

---

[1] Herder, *Ideen zur Philosophie der Geschichte der Menschheit* (further abbreviated as *Ideen*), II, 260; *SW* XIII, 383. Cf. also F. M. Barnard, *Herder's Social and Political Thought. From Enlightenment to Nationalism* (Oxford, 1965), for a perceptive discussion of Herder's attitude to politics.

[2] 'Schreiben des Pfarrers zu *** an den H[erausgeber] des T[eutschen] M[erkurs]. *Ueber eine Recension* von Herders Ideen zur Philosophie der Geschichte der Menschheit', *Teutscher Merkur* (February 1785), 148–74.

entitled *Conjectures on the Beginning of Human History*, once again rebutted Herder, without mentioning his name. He showed, in an ironic manner, that by interpreting the origins of mankind as a narration along biblical lines, it is possible to arrive at the opposite conclusion from that drawn by Herder in the tenth book of the *Ideas*. Herder had argued that mankind had been given language and reason by a transcendental power. Kant rejected that view and maintained that man had to take the first steps himself. He had to leave nature in order to achieve freedom under the law and to lead a moral life. After this rebuttal he remained silent and refused to review the next instalment of the *Ideas*, although Herder gave full vent to his disappointment and anger in two works, the *Metacritique of Pure Reason* (1799) in which he attacked Kant's epistemology and *Kalligone* (1800) in which he sought to refute Kant's aesthetics. They are anything but impressive and did not cut much ice with the public.

Nonetheless, there are also affinities between the two thinkers.[1] For both Kant and Herder, the individual's independence and maturity were a major concern, and both saw these in a social context. Both believed it necessary and possible for human beings to develop all the faculties with which nature had endowed them. Both believed that progress was ensured by the natural antagonism between human beings, and neither of them claimed to have provided a definitive picture of history.

Yet the differences between them, both in the method and the content of their thought, are substantial and striking. For Herder, who did not entirely agree even with Kant's so-called pre-critical writings, was decidedly out of sympathy with the *Critique of Pure Reason* and Kant's subsequent works. His concern was with experience and feeling, on which he wished to base his philosophy, and he felt that critical reason was incapable of doing justice to these spheres of his life, and indeed to life as a whole. He was also unable to accept Kant's distinction between phenomenon and noumenon, for he believed that experience is able to tell us something about the essence of the world.

In the *Ideas* Herder made the attempt, not unusual at that time, to

[1] Cf. H. D. Irmscher, 'Die geschichtsphilosophische Kontroverse zwischen Kant und Herder', in *Hamann–Kant–Herder* (Acta des vierten Internationalen Hamann–Kolloquiums), ed. Bernhard Gajek (Frankfurt/Main, 1987), pp. 111–92, for a penetrating and full analysis of the affinities and differences between Kant's and Herder's approach to history, an analysis to which my following argument is greatly indebted. Cf. also Rudolf Haym, *Herder* (2nd ed.), (Berlin, 1954), II, pp. 274–92 for a detailed discussion of the relationship between Kant and Herder.

present a theodicy, to justify the ways of God to man. Although Kant's philosophy of history contains the implications of a theodicy, it is mainly concerned with emphasising the overriding importance of political freedom which can be achieved only within the framework of a just legal order.

For Herder, man's appearance, his *Gestalt*, presents a microcosm of life. Nature has endowed man with the ability to find in himself the guide which leads him through 'the great labyrinth of living creation'.[1] From his own nature he derives his human character, his *Humanität*, which reflects his creation in the image of God who was his first teacher and who intervened to allow him to emerge from immaturity. Kant, in *Conjectures on the Beginning of Human History*, expressly refutes this view. Man cannot derive his destiny from his nature. He was able to overcome his natural inclinations only by taking an independent step forward in the light of *a priori* principles established by reason. In doing so he lost his innocence and abandoned the happiness of a purely natural and instinctual life. Kant also takes a sombre view of the dangers, of the 'radical evil'[2] lurking in human nature which may lead man to act immorally when swayed by his impulses. Consequently, in the sphere of public life, there will always be a need for the state to coerce its citizens to obey the law so that they may carry out their legal duties. Herder rejects this view. For him, man is essentially good. Evil is only the absence of what is good, but not a fundamental stain on our species. Man is indeed capable of that perfection which he will eventually reach and coercion is therefore in principle unnecessary.

Kant and Herder differ even more radically in their conception of progress. Kant maintains that, in order to interpret history philosophically, we must assume a goal in history; for him, this is to be found in an approximation to a condition of perpetual peace enjoyed by free citizens living in a federation of republican states. Earlier stages can, so to speak, at most be only steps in the progress towards that goal. For Herder, too, there can be progress in history, but he did not postulate a political goal. Moreover, his conception of individuality convinced him that every period must be valued for its own sake; it cannot be seen simply as a precursor or prelude to later periods. God is present in every period, and each nation has a character and culture of its own. Herder thus paves the way for the conception formulated by the great German historian Leopold von Ranke that every period of history is

---

[1] Herder, *Ideen*, I, 92; *SW* XIII, 69.
[2] Cf. *Religion within the Limits of Reason Alone*, I; *AA* VI, 17–53.

'immediately related to God'. Yet Herder also believes that all periods of history coalesce into a whole, that each one of them is part of a chain of development, of *Bildung* (the process of cultivation). Reason, too, is a historical phenomenon; it is an aggregate of spiritual experience, a sign of the education of the human race. It is also closely connected with language, and language itself is in turn linked to tradition, a view which Kant rejected.

Kant's view of history makes him assume that it is not the achievement, let alone the happiness, of any particular individual that matters, but man's moral achievement. This can be gauged only by reference to the existence of a state, or states, with a republican constitution in which individuals have the right to pursue their own happiness freely, equally and independently. Herder rejects this criterion as incapable of recognising individual achievement. He is therefore opposed to the notion of progress in so far as it fails to do justice to individuality.

Herder, like Kant, was opposed to dynastic absolutism, and indeed, to any kind of authoritarian rule, but unlike Kant, he never accepted the need for coercion by the state to safeguard individual freedom. Any political arrangements which implicitly or explicitly entail coercion would, in his view, impair or suppress individual development. He believed that natural conditions, the individual nature of a nation as expressed in its citizens' language, inclinations, and character, are capable of bringing men together into a coherent community where there is no need for a master. He appears not to have understood Kant's view of a republican constitution properly. He thought it an evil principle to maintain that men need a master;[1] for he mistakenly believed that Kant's view was inimical to human freedom and independence— the very ideas which Kant sought to safeguard by his political philosophy.

Kant's criticism of Herder's methodology is even more important. While Kant seeks to discover the basic principle which allows us to attribute a purpose to history, Herder, who does not mistrust the senses, believes that truth—which for him is God—is revealed in history. In other words, God is present in history, and it is our task to grasp what has been revealed. For Kant, this conception is epistemologically naive. Reason is the criterion of truth, and there is no way in which God's existence or actions—or, for that matter human immortality— can be discerned by means of experience alone.

[1] Cf. p. 195 above n. 1.

The use of analogy is central to Herder's approach.[1] Since each event in history is singular, the method of analogy alone allows us to discern similarities. For in his view, history does reveal analogical structures. Analogy is a tool of imaginative discovery. Only poetry, myth or story can do justice to this world. Herder thus belongs to a tradition, Neo-Platonic in character, which also goes back as far as Plato himself and beyond him to pre-philosophical thought. Indeed, Herder thought that the use of analogy had been sanctioned by Kant's early treatise *General History of Nature and Theory of the Heavens* (1755). For Kant, too, historical analogies are by no means unfruitful. He used that mode of reasoning himself, but he did so with great care. What he held to be entirely illegitimate was Herder's attempt to write about things-in-themselves, to argue from knowledge of the world of phenomena to that of noumena. For Kant, Herder had abandoned scholarship (*Wissenschaft*) for *belles-lettres*, producing stimulating but basically unsound writing.

Such fundamental methodological differences could not be bridged. In attacking Herder, Kant clarified his own position, and, in his reviews of Herder's *Ideas* and in *Conjectures on the Beginning of Human History*, he further delimited his own approach to history and politics. But it would be wrong to dismiss Herder as a thinker because of Kant's (justified) methodological criticism. He was a man of wide-ranging interests, a polymath, a most fertile mind, unfortunately not always sufficiently critical of his own ideas. Nevertheless, he was not a political thinker of the first rank. Politics was peripheral rather than central to his thought. His main concern was with culture. In the field of politics, he advocated a pluralism which verged on anarchism. In his view, the state ought to express the spirit of nature and the nation was a body politic representing a common culture. He believed, quite unrealistically, that there is no need for government since everyone should be able in principle to participate in politics on an equal and independent footing. From this stance his espousal of republicanism and democracy and his hostility to authoritarian government of any kind are derived. But although his belief in the spirit of the nation makes him a harbinger of nationalist thought, he himself was not a nationalist in politics; he remained true to the cosmopolitanism of the Enlightenment and did

[1] Cf. H. D. Irmscher, 'Beobachtungen zur Funktion der Analogie im Denken Herders'. *Deutsche Vierteljahrsschrift für Literaturwissenschaft und Geistesgeschichte*, LV (1981), 64–97, for a perceptive analysis of Herder's use of analogy. Cf. also H. B. Nisbet, *Herder and the Philosophy and History of Science* (Cambridge, 1970), pp. 20–109 for an authoritative analysis of Herder's methodology (cf. particularly pp. 32–6 for a discussion of his use of analogy).

not believe in the superiority of any one race or people. His conviction of the historical nature of all events, whether past, present or future, prevented him from promoting this dangerous intellectual aberration. In this respect, like Kant, he belongs squarely to the Enlightenment. His writings and Kant's response to them help us to assess the impact of that great intellectual current which Kant so perceptively defined and robustly defended in his argument with Herder.

Reviews of Herder's Ideas on the Philosophy of the History of Mankind[1]

I

Ideas on the Philosophy of the History of Mankind by Johann Gottfried Herder. *Quem te Deus esse iussit et humana qua parte locatus es in re disce.*[2] Part One. 318 pp. Quarto. Hartknoch: Riga and Leipzig. 1784.

In this work, our ingenious and eloquent author displays those distinctive qualities of mind for which he has already gained recognition. For this reason, the work is perhaps as little subject to ordinary standards of judgement as are some of the other products of his pen. It is as if his genius did not simply bring together ideas from the broad sphere of the arts and sciences in order to supplement them with other ideas which might be communicated to others, but as if he adapted them, by a certain law of *assimilation* (to borrow his own expression) and in a way peculiar to himself, to his own specific mode of thinking. They thus become markedly different from those by which other minds are furthered and sustained (p.292),[3] and are accordingly less capable of being communicated to others. Consequently, what he understands by the philosophy of the history of mankind may well be something quite different from what is usually understood by that term. His approach does not entail, for example, a logical precision in the definition of concepts or careful distinctions and consistency in the use of principles, but rather a cursory and comprehensive vision and a ready facility for discovering analogies, together with a bold imagination in putting these analogies to use. This is combined with an aptitude for arousing sympathy for his subject—which is always kept at an obscure distance—by means of feelings and sentiments; and these in turn, as the product of weighty thoughts or as highly significant pointers, lead us to expect more of them than cool assessment would ever be likely to discover. Nevertheless, since freedom of thought (which is present here in ample measure), as exercised by a fertile mind, always affords food for thought, we shall attempt as far as possible to extract the most important and characteristic of the author's ideas and to present them in his own words, adding in conclusion a few remarks concerning the whole.

Our author begins by broadening his viewpoint to define the place of man among the other inhabitants of the planets of our solar system. From the middle position of the planet which man inhabits—a position which is not without advantages—he deduces a merely 'mediocre earthly understanding and an even more equivocal human virtue on which man must here depend. But since our thoughts and faculties are manifestly only the product of our earthly organism, striving to change and adapt until they attain as much purity and refinement as this creation of ours will permit, and since—if analogy may be our guide— it cannot be any different on other celestial bodies, we may conjecture that man must have the same goal as the inhabitants of the latter—i.e. not only to embark eventually on a voyage to more than one such body, but perhaps even to join the company of all those creatures from our many and varied sister-worlds who have also reached maturity.'[4] He then goes on to reflect on the revolutions which preceded the creation of man. 'Before our air, our water, and our earth could be produced, there had to be numerous constituents which dissolved and pre- cipitated one another. And how many dissolutions and transformations of the one into the other were not presupposed before the manifold species of the earth—minerals, crystals, not to mention the organic realm of shells, plants, animals, and finally man—could arise? Man, the son of all elements and forms of being, their ultimate quintessence and, so to speak, the flower of earthly creation, could be none other than the last and favourite child of nature, whose formation and reception were necessarily preceded by numerous earlier developments and revolutions.'[5]

In the spherical shape of the earth, the author finds another cause for wonder at the unity to which it gives rise in spite of all conceivable diversity. 'How could anyone who has ever reflected on this figure ever proceed to convert others to a philosophy and religion based solely on words, or to commit murder for its sake with obtuse but holy zeal?'[6] Similarly, the angle of the ecliptic [to the earth's axis] gives him cause to reflect on the destiny of man: 'Under our sun's oblique path, all human activity follows an annual rhythm.'[7] A more precise knowledge of the atmosphere, and even the influence of the heavenly bodies upon it, once this is better understood, seem to him to indicate a major influence on human history. In the section concerning the distribution of land and the oceans, the structure of the earth is adduced as an explanation for differences in the histories of nations. 'Asia is no less consistent in its manners and customs than it is united as a single land-mass; the narrow Red Sea, on the other hand, already marks a boundary in the realm of manners, and the narrow Persian Gulf even more so. But it was not without reason that the many lakes, mountains, and rivers of America and the land itself filled so large a part of the temperate zone, and it was by nature's intention that the structure of the old continent, as the first abode of man, was of a different design from that of the new world.'[8] The second book deals with the organised forms on earth, and begins with granite, on which light, heat, and a primitive air and water acted; perhaps they transformed silica into lime, in which the first living creatures of the sea, the shellfish, were formed. Vegetation makes its appearance next.—Comparison of man's development with that of the plants, and of man's sexual love with the efflorescence of flowers. Uses of the plant kingdom in relation to man. The animal kingdom. Changes of animals and plants in response to different climates. Those of the primeval world are imperfect. 'The classes of creatures grow more numerous the more distant they are from man, and less numerous the closer they are to him.—They all have a single basic form, a similar bone structure.—These transitions make it seem not unlikely that one and the same organisational plan prevails in marine creatures, plants, and perhaps even in *supposedly inanimate* entities, if only in an infinitely cruder and more confused form. From the point of view of the eternal being who perceives the connections between all things, the shape of the ice crystal as it comes into being and of the snowflake to which it gives rise may still retain an analogy to the formation of the embryo in the womb.—Man is an intermediate creature among the animals—that is, the most comprehensive form, in which *all the characteristics of all the species* around him come together as in their quintessential embodiment.—From air and water, from the heights and the depths, I see the animals converge on man, as it were, and gradually approximate to his form.'[9] This book concludes with the words 'Rejoice in your station, o man, and study yourself, noble centre of creation, in all that lives around you!'[10]

The third book compares the structure of plants and animals with the organisation of man. We cannot follow the author here as he employs the reflections of natural historians for his own purposes; we shall merely cite some of the results. 'By means of this or that organ, the animal generates a living stimulus out of dead vegetable life, and from the product of this, filtered through subtle channels, it generates the medium of sensation. The result of these stimuli is *instinct*, and the result of sensation is *thought*, in an eternal process of organic creation *which was implanted in every living creature*.'" The author bases his argument not on germs but on an organic force, in plants as well as in animals. He says 'Just as the plant is itself organic life, so also is the polyp. There are therefore many organic forces, those of vegetation, muscular irritability, and sensation. The finer and more numerous the nerves and the larger the brain, the more intelligent the species will be. The *animal soul* is the sum of all the forces at work in an organism',[12] and instinct is not a particular natural force, but the direction given by nature to all of these forces by virtue of their overall combination. The more that single organic principle of nature which we now describe as *formative* (in rocks), now as *generative* (in plants), now as *sensitive*, now as *constructive*, and which is basically only one and the same organic force, is distributed among various organs and separate limbs, and the more it forms a world of its own in each of them, the more does instinct disappear and a free and independent use of senses and limbs begin (for example, in man). Finally, the author comes to that essential natural attribute which distinguishes man. 'The erect gait of man is *alone* natural to him; indeed, it is the organisation appropriate to the entire vocation of his species, and his distinguishing characteristic.'[13]

It was not because he was destined to be rational that man was endowed with the erect posture which allows him to make rational use of his limbs; on the contrary, he acquired reason as a result of his erect posture, as the natural effect of that same constitution which he required in order to walk upright. 'Let us pause for a moment to contemplate with gratitude this sacred work of art, this blessing which enabled our race to become human, and to wonder at it as we perceive the new organisation of forces which arose out of man's erect stature, and as we see that it was through this alone that man became man!'[14]

In the fourth book, the author develops this point further: 'What does this man-like creature (the ape) lack that it did not become human?'[15]—And how did man become human? He became human because his head is adapted *to an erect posture*, and because he is organised internally and externally on a perpendicular centre of gravity.— The ape has all the parts of the brain which man possesses; but in keeping with the shape of its skull, they are in a retroverted position, and this in turn derives from the fact that its head was set at a different angle because it was not made to walk erect. The immediate consequence was that all of its organic powers functioned differently. 'Raise your eyes to the heavens, o man, and rejoice and tremble at the immeasurable advantage which the creator of the world attached to so simple a principle as your erect posture.—Elevated above the earth and the plants, it is no longer the sense of smell which predominates, but the eye.—With his upright gait, man acquired free and inventive hands and became a creator of artifacts. Only in conjunction with his erect gait does true human language appear.—Both in theory and in practice, reason is merely something *acquired*[16] and learned, a proportion and direction of man's ideas and faculties to which he was predetermined by his organisation and way of life.'[17] And then freedom: 'Man is the first emancipated being in creation; he stands upright.'[18] As for modesty, 'it soon developed as a necessary consequence of the erect posture'.[19] Man's nature is not subject to any particular variation. 'Why is this so? Because of his erect posture and for no other reason.—He is predisposed to humanity; peaceableness, sexual love, sympathy, maternal love—all are offshoots of that humanity which comes from his upright stance. The rule of justice and truth is based on that same erect posture of man which also inclines him to decency; religion is the supreme expression of humanity. The stooping animal has only obscure sensations; God raised man up so that, even without knowing or willing it, he might investigate the causes of things and discover thee, thou great conjunction of all things. But religion gives rise to hope and to belief in immortality.'[20] The latter is discussed in the fifth book. 'From rocks to crystals, from crystals to metals, from metals to the world of plants, from plants to animals and finally to man, we saw the form of organisation ascend and the powers and instincts of creatures simultaneously become more diverse and finally come together in the human figure (in so far as this could encompass them).—'[21]

'Throughout this series of beings, we observed a similar basic form which came ever closer to the figure of man; we likewise saw the powers and instincts converge on him.—The lifespan of every creature was adapted to the end of nature which it had to serve.—The more advanced the organism, the more its structure is compounded of the lower realms. Man is a compendium of the world: lime, earth, salts, acids, oil, and water, powers of vegetation, irritability, and sensation are organically united in him.—This impels us to postulate in turn an *invisible realm of forces* with precisely the same links and transitions as those in the visible realm of creation, and an ascending series of invisible powers like those in the visible world.—This is *all-important* not only for the immortality of the soul, but also for the continued existence of all active living forces in the created world. No force can perish, although its organ may be destroyed. All that is called to life by the giver of all life will live; whatever acts will act for ever in its eternal context.'[22] These principles are not analysed, 'for this is not the place in which to do so'.[23] Nevertheless, 'we see in matter so many spirit-like forces that a complete opposition and contradiction between these two (admittedly very different) forms of being—i.e. spirit and matter— seems at least wholly unconfirmed, if not itself contradictory.'[24]—'No eye has seen preformed germs. And if we speak of epigenesis, we are speaking figuratively, as if the limbs [of an embryo] were accretions *from without*. What is involved is formation (*genesis*), the effect of *inner forces* for which nature has prepared a mass to which they might *give their own form* and in which they might make themselves visible. It is not our rational soul which formed our body, but the finger of the deity, i.e. organic force.'[25] We are then told: '1. Force and organ are indeed most intimately linked, but they are not one and the same thing. 2. Every force works in harmony with its organ, for it has formed the latter and assimilated it to itself solely in order to manifest its own essence. 3. When the vessel falls away, the force which was already present, if only in a lower (though equally organic) state but before the vessel itself existed, still remains.'[26] The author then says to the materialists: 'Even if we accept that our soul is originally identical with all the forces of matter, irritability, movement, and life, and that it simply functions on a higher plane and within a finer and more fully developed organis- ation, has anyone ever seen even a single force of movement or irrita- bility cease to exist, and are these lower forces one and the same thing as their organs?'[27] Of the context to which this relates, we are told that it can only be one of progressive development. 'The human race can be regarded as the great gathering-point of lower organic forces which were destined to germinate within it in order that humanity might develop.'[28]

That the organisation of man comes into being in a realm of spiritual forces is demonstrated as follows: '1. Thought is something quite dis- tinct from what sense conveys to it; all the information we have on its origin suggests that it is the effect of an essence which, though organic in character, is nevertheless autonomous and acts in accordance with laws of spiritual association. 2. Just as the body grows larger through the intake of food, so also is the mind enlarged by ideas; indeed, we can observe in it precisely the same laws of assimilation, growth, and repro- duction. In short, there is formed within us an inner, spiritual man whose nature is distinct and for whom the body is merely an instrument.—The human soul first acquired this great asset of a more lucid consciousness in a spiritual manner, as a result of its humanity', etc.[29] In a word—if we understand this correctly—the soul first arose out of spiritual forces which it accumulated by a gradual process.—'Our humanity is only a preparation, the bud of a future flower. Step by step, nature discards what is base and promotes the spiritual instead, refining what is already fine even further. We may consequently hope that, through her creative agency, our budding humanity will likewise appear in the life hereafter in its true, distinctive, and divine human form.'[30]

The conclusion is as follows: 'The present condition of man is probably the connecting link between two separate worlds.—If man forms the end of the chain of earthly organisms as its last and highest link, he is also by the same token the first and lowest in the chain of a higher order of creatures; hence he is probably the intermediate link between two interlocking systems of creation.—He confronts us with two worlds simultaneously, and this explains the apparent duality of his nature.—Life is a struggle, and the flower of pure and immortal humanity is a crown which is difficult to attain.—Thus, our brothers in the higher realm doubtless love us more than we can reach out to and love them; for they see our condition more clearly—and perhaps they will educate us to share in their happiness.—It is scarcely conceivable that the future state is so utterly unintelligible to our present condition as the animal in man would like to believe; for instance, language and man's earliest knowledge seem impossible to explain in the absence of higher instruction.—Even in later times, the greatest effects on earth have come about as a result of inexplicable circumstances, and even illnesses have often been the occasion for such events when the organ has ceased to be of use in the normal round of earthly life; it then appears natural that the restless inner power may be open to impressions which the unimpaired organism was incapable of registering.— But man is not meant to see his way into his future state; he should simply believe in it.'[31] (But if he happens to believe that he can see his way into it, how can he be prevented from trying to make use of this ability from time to time?)—'This much is certain, that an infinity is present in each of man's powers; the forces of the universe also seem to lie hidden within the soul, which merely requires an organism, or a series of organisms, to give these forces an active function.—Thus, just as the flower stood out *in its erect form*, marking the end of the realm of subterranean and as yet inanimate creation, so does man in turn stand *erect* above all those (i.e. the animals) who stoop towards the earth. With exalted gaze and uplifted hands he stands there, as a son of the house awaiting the call of his father.'[32]

Supplement

The idea and ultimate aim of this first part (of a work which is apparently designed to fill many volumes) are as follows. The spiritual nature of the human soul, its enduring quality and increasing perfection, are to be demonstrated by analogy with the natural forms of matter, particularly in their organisation, without the help of any metaphysical investigations. To this end, spiritual forces are assumed to exist, a certain invisible realm of creation which uses matter simply as its raw material. It contains the animating force which organises everything in such a way that the perfect model for this organisation is man. All earthly creatures, from the lowest level upwards, draw progressively closer to him until man himself at last emerged, solely as a result of this perfected organisation whose chief precondition is that the animal should walk upright. His death cannot possibly terminate that progress and enhancement of organic forms which was previously described in detail with reference to creatures of all kinds; on the contrary, it leads us to expect a natural transition to even more refined operations whereby man will be raised and advanced to even higher grades of life in the future, and so on *ad infinitum*. The reviewer must confess that he does not comprehend this line of reasoning from the analogy of nature, even if he were prepared to accept that continuous gradation of natural creatures and its rule of a gradual approximation to man. For the various stages of ever more perfect organisation are occupied by *different* beings. Consequently, it could only be concluded from such an analogy that *somewhere else*, perhaps on another planet, there might in turn be creatures representing the next higher stage of organisation above man, but not that *the same individual* will progress to it. In the case of flying insects which develop from grubs or caterpillars, a quite unique arrangement is involved which is different from the usual procedure of nature; yet even here, palingenesis is the sequel not of *death* but merely of the *pupal phase*. To counter this objection, it would have to be shown that nature raised up animals in a specifically more perfect kind of organisation, even after they had decomposed or been reduced to ashes, before one could deduce from this analogy that the same is true of man, who is turned to ashes in his present existence. There is accordingly not the slightest resemblance between the elevation of one and the same human being to a more perfect level of organisation in another life, and that scale of being which can be envisaged among completely different species and individuals within a single realm of nature. Here, all that nature reveals to us is that it abandons individuals to total destruction and preserves only the species. There, on the other hand, the question is asked whether human individuality will also survive its destruction here on earth, a consequence which can perhaps be deduced from moral or, if one prefers, metaphysical premises, but never from any analogy with visible creation. But as far as that invisible realm of active and autonomous forces is concerned, it is difficult to see why the author, given his belief that he could reliably deduce the existence of such a realm from organic creation, did not transfer the thinking principle in man, which is of a purely spiritual nature, to this realm directly, without first raising it up out of chaos through the structure of organisation. Unless, that is, he regarded these spiritual forces as something altogether different from the human soul, and the latter not as a particular substance, but merely as the effect of an invisible universal nature which acts on matter and gives it life; yet we should in fairness hesitate to ascribe this opinion to him. But what are we to think of the whole hypothesis of invisible forces which give rise to organisation, and hence of the author's attempt to explain *what is not understood* in terms of *what is understood even less?* In the former case, we can at least discover its laws through experience, although the causes underlying them will of course remain unknown; but in the latter case, we are denied even the possibility of experiencing it, and what can the philosopher then adduce in support of his assertion except despair of ever finding the answer in any knowledge of nature, and an enforced decision to look for this answer in the fertile field of the poetic imagination? And this will still be metaphysics, indeed highly dogmatic metaphysics, however much our author, in keeping with the current fashion, rejects this implication.

But as far as the ladder of organisation is concerned, the author should not be reproached too harshly if it has proved inadequate for his purpose, which extends far beyond the present world; for its application to the natural kingdoms here on earth likewise leads nowhere. Given the great diversity of genera, the fact that the differences between them appear small when they are arranged in order of *similarity* is a necessary consequence of this very diversity. A *relationship* between them, on the other hand, whereby one genus arose out of the other and all of them out of a single original genus, or alternatively, whereby all of them emerged from a single procreative womb, would lead to *ideas* so monstrous that reason recoils from them; but we cannot attribute such ideas to our author without doing him an injustice. As for his contribution to comparative anatomy through all the animal genera down to the level of the plants, those whose business is natural history may judge for themselves how far they can profit from the suggestions he offers here with regard to new observations, and whether these suggestions are at all firmly based. But the unity of organic force (p. 141)[33] which, as an autonomous formative principle in relation to the diversity of all organic creatures and subsequently as the producer of various kinds of effect appropriate to the variety of these organisms, supposedly constitutes the entire difference between the various genera and species, is an idea which lies wholly outside the field of scientific observation. It belongs to purely speculative philosophy; but even in the latter, if it were once to gain admission, it would cause much havoc among previously accepted concepts. To try to determine what arrangement of the head, both in its external shape and in the internal configuration of the brain within it, is necessarily associated with the propensity to walk upright—let alone to try to determine how an organisation directed solely to this end can contain the basis of that rational faculty which the animal thereby acquires—is obviously beyond the scope of human reason, whether the latter gropes its way with the aid of physiology or attempts to fly with the aid of metaphysics.

But these objections do not seek to deny all merit to so thoughtful a work as this. One of its outstanding qualities—not to mention here those many reflections which are as aptly formulated as the thoughts they express are noble and true—is the courage with which the author has succeeded in overcoming those doubts which his profession entertains with regard to the ability of reason to make significant progress by its own unaided efforts—doubts which so often exercise a constricting influence on all philosophy; in this respect, we hope that many others will follow his example. Futhermore, the mysterious obscurity in which nature itself has concealed its organic functions and the classes into which its creatures are divided bears some responsiblity for the obscurity and uncertainty which affect the first part of this philosophical history of man. The aim of this first section was to establish a link, if possible, between the outer limits of the subject—the point from which it began, and the point at which it loses itself in the infinite realm above and beyond earthly history. This attempt is a bold one, yet it is natural that the enquiring spirit of human reason should make it, and it is not discreditable for it to do so, even if it does not entirely succeed in practice. But it is all the more essential that, in the next instalment of his work, in which he will have firm ground beneath his feet, our resourceful author should curb his lively genius somewhat, and that philosophy, which is more concerned with pruning luxuriant growths than with propagating them, should guide him towards the completion of his enterprise. It should do so not through hints but through precise concepts, not through laws based on conjecture but through laws derived from observation, and not by means of an imagination inspired by metaphysics or emotions, but by means of a reason which, while committed to broad objectives, exercises caution in pursuing them.

II

Comments by the reviewer of Herder's *Ideas on the Philosophy of the History of Mankind* (No. 4 and supplement, *Allgemeine Literaturzeitung*) on a refutation of this review published in the February issue of the *Teutsche Merkur*.

In the February issue of the *Teutsche Merkur*, page 148,[34] a self-styled clergyman seeks to defend Herr Herder's book against the supposed attack in our *Allgemeine Literaturzeitung*. It would be unfair to drag the name of a respected author into a dispute between a reviewer and his adversary; we therefore propose merely to justify the procedure we adopted in publicising and evaluating the work in question as being consonant with those maxims of conscientiousness, impartiality, and moderation which this journal has taken as its guide. In his article, the clergyman quarrels at length with a metaphysician as he imagines him—a metaphysician who, in his view, is utterly resistant to all instruction by empirical means (or, if this proves inadequate, to all conclusions based on the analogy of nature) and who seeks to force everything into his mould of sterile scholastic abstractions. The reviewer has no objections whatsoever to this quarrel, for he is in this respect completely at one with the clergyman—indeed, the review itself is the best proof of this. But since he believes he is tolerably familiar with the basic materials of anthropology, and also to some extent with the method of using them in any attempt to write a history of man's destiny as a whole, he is convinced that these materials are to be found neither in metaphysics nor in a museum of natural history in which the skeleton of man can be compared with that of other kinds of animal (and such comparisons do not in the least suggest that man's destiny lies in another world). On the contrary, these materials are to be found only in human *actions*, in which the human character is revealed. The reviewer is also convinced that Herr Herder did not even intend to supply the proper materials for a history of man in the first part of his work (which simply portrays man as an animal in the universal system of nature and thus serves as a preamble to ideas which are still to come). His intention was rather to put forward thoughts which might persuade the physiologists to extend their research, which is normally focused exclusively on the mechanical functions of animal structure, to further areas if possible, and to consider what organisation is appropriate to the use of reason by this particular creature. In this context, he has admittedly credited such research with greater importance than it can ever in fact attain. Besides, it is not incumbent on anyone who shares the latter opinion to prove (as the clergyman demands on page 161) that it would actually be *possible* for human reason to exist in *another form* of organisation, for this can no more be demonstrated than can the proposition that reason is possible *only* in its present form. The rational use of experience also has its limits. For although experience can teach us that something is constituted in such and such a way, it can never prove that it *could not possibly be otherwise*; nor can any analogy fill this immeasurable gap between the contingent and the necessary. It was stated in the review: 'Given the great diversity of genera, the fact that the differences between them appear small when they are arranged in order of *similarity* is a necessary consequence of this diversity itself. A *relationship* between them, on the other hand, whereby one genus arose out of the other or all of them arose out of a single original genus and perhaps emerged from a single procreative womb,[35] would lead to *ideas* so monstrous that *reason recoils* from them; but we cannot attribute such ideas to our author without doing him an injustice.' These words have misled the clergyman into believing that the review of the work displays *metaphysical orthodoxy* and hence intolerance, and he adds: '*Healthy reason, if allowed to operate freely, does not recoil from any idea.*'[36] But there is no need to fear anything of the kind which he imagines. It is merely the *horror vacui* of human reason in general which leads it *to recoil* when it comes across an idea about which *no thought is possible*, and in this respect, the ontological code might well serve as a model for the theological code, particularly in the matter of tolerance. The clergyman also finds the merit of *freedom of thought* which we ascribed to the book much too commonplace for so famous an author. He doubtless imagines that we were referring to that *external* freedom which, since it depends on time and place, is not in fact a merit at all. But the review had in mind that *inner* freedom from the fetters of customary concepts and modes of thought reinforced by public opinion, a freedom which is *not at all* commonplace—so little so that even those who profess loyalty only to philosophy have rarely been able to aspire to it. What he finds fault with in the review, namely '*that it cites only passages which express the conclusions, but not those which prepare the way for them*',[37] is probably a necessary evil of authorship in general, an evil which, in spite of everything, is still more acceptable than general praise or condemnation which cites only this or that particular passage. We accordingly stick to our judgement on the work in question, which was passed with all due respect, and even sympathy, for the author's *fame*, and even more for his *future reputation*. This judgement is consequently quite different from the one which the clergyman rather inaccurately imputes to the reviewer on page 161, namely *that the book has not delivered what its title promised*. For the title did not in fact promise to deliver in the first volume, which contains only general physiological preliminaries, what we expect to find in the subsequent volumes (which, as far as can be judged, will deal with anthropology proper); and it was not superfluous to remind the reader that the first imposes restrictions on that freedom which might well merit consideration in the later volumes. Besides, it now depends entirely on the author himself to accomplish what the title promised, and his talents and learning give us reason to hope that he will do so.

III

Hartknoch: Riga and Leipzig. *Ideas on the Philosophy of the History of Mankind* by Johann Gottfried Herder. Part Two. 344 pp. Octavo. 1785.

This part, which continues as far as the tenth book, first describes in six sections of Book VI the organisation of the peoples in the vicinity of the North Pole and around the Asiatic massif, in the zones inhabited by the physically beautiful races and the African nations, and on the tropical islands and in America. The author concludes his description by calling for a collection of new ethnographical illustrations, the basis of which has already been laid by Niebuhr,[38] Parkinson,[39] Cook,[40] Höst,[41] Georgi,[42] and others. 'It would be of great service if someone with the means to do so would gather together the faithful portraits which are scattered here and there of the different branches of our race, and would thereby lay the foundations of an *explicit natural science and physiognomy of the human race*. Art could scarcely be applied in a more philosophical way, and an anthropological chart similar to the zoological chart which *Zimmermann*[43] tried to construct, and on which only information concerning the diversity of mankind should be recorded—but in all its aspects and manifestations—would be the crowning achievement of this philanthropic work.'[44]

The seventh book first considers the propositions that, despite such variations of form, the human race is nevertheless one and the same species everywhere, and that this single race has acclimatised itself to every part of the world. Next, the effects of climate on man's physical and spiritual development are considered. The author acutely observes that much preliminary work remains to be done before we can arrive at a physiological and pathological climatology, let alone a climatology of all the intellectual and sensory powers of man. He notes that it is impossible to transform that chaos of causes and effects which the height and depth of a given terrain, its nature and that of its products, the varieties of food and drink, the way of life, kinds of work, dress, and even customary attitudes, entertainments, and arts, together with other circumstances, cumulatively constitute, into an orderly world in which each thing and each separate region is given its due and none receives too much or too little. With commendable modesty, he duly describes (p. 92)[45] the general remarks which follow (p. 99)[46] simply as problems. These are grouped under the following headings. 1. All kinds of causes combine to produce a climatic community on earth which is conducive to the existence of living creatures. 2. The habitable land on our planet is concentrated in areas where the greatest number of living creatures can function in the form most suited to them; this distribution of the continents has an influence on the climate of them all. 3. The fact that the earth was built around mountain ranges means not only that its climate was modified in endless ways appropriate to the enormous variety of living creatures, but also that the dispersal of the human race was as far as possible averted. In the fourth section of this book, the author maintains that the genetic force is the mother of all earthly forms, and that climate merely acts upon it in a favourable or hostile manner; he concludes with observations on the *conflict between genetics and climate,* and *calls,* among other things, *for a physico-geographical history of the descent and variation of our race in different climates and eras.*

In the *eighth book,* Herr Herder examines the use of the human senses, the human imagination, man's practical understanding, his instincts, and his happiness, and illustrates the influence of tradition, opinions, practice, and custom by means of examples from various nations.

The *ninth* book deals with man's dependence on others in the development of his abilities, with language as a means of human education, with the invention of the arts and sciences through imitation, reason, and language, and with governments as systems of human organisation based for the most part on inherited traditions. The book concludes with remarks on religion and the most ancient tradition.

The *tenth* book consists chiefly of consequences drawn from thoughts which the author has already expounded elsewhere; for in addition to reflections on man's earliest habitat and on Asiatic traditions concerning the creation of the earth and of man, it reiterates in essentials the author's hypothesis concerning the Mosaic account of creation as expressed in his book *The Oldest Document of the Human Race.*[47]

Here again, this bald outline seeks only to describe the content of the relevant part of the work, not to convey its spirit. It is intended as an encouragement to others to read the work, not as a substitute which might render such reading unnecessary.

The sixth and seventh books consist almost entirely of extracts from ethnographical reports. These are undoubtedly selected with skill and discrimination, arranged in a masterly fashion, and accompanied throughout by the author's shrewd assessments; but for this very reason, it is all the more difficult to compile detailed extracts from them. Besides, it is not our intention here to single out or analyse some of those fine passages full of poetic eloquence which will commend themselves to every reader of sensibility. But we do not intend either to consider whether that poetic spirit which enlivens the author's expression has not also at times done violence to his philosophy; whether synonyms do not on occasion act as substitutes for explanations, and allegories for truths; whether, instead of neighbourly excursions from the region of philosophic language into that of poetic language, the limits and provinces of both are not at times completely disregarded; and whether the fabric of bold metaphors, poetic images, and mythological allusions does not serve in some instances to conceal the body of thought as under a *farthingale*, instead of making it agreeably visible as if through a transparent garment. We leave it to critics of the elegant style in philosophy, or to the author's own ultimate revision of his work, to consider whether it would not, for example, be better to say *'not only day and night and the changes of season alter the climate'*[48] than (as on page 99) 'not only day and night and the *roundelay* of the changing seasons alter the climate'; whether the following image—no doubt admirably suited to a dithyrambic ode—can appropriately be used in conjunction with a description of such changes in terms of natural history (p. 100): 'Round Jupiter's throne its (i.e. the earth's) *Horae* dance a roundelay, and although what takes shape beneath their feet is only an imperfect perfection (for everything is based on the union of disparates), the child of nature—physical regularity and beauty—is everywhere born of an inner love and marital union';[49] or whether the following turn of phrase at the beginning of the eighth book is not too *epic* in character for the transition from travellers' remarks on climate and on the organisation of various peoples to a series of general conclusions based on these: 'I feel like one about to ascend from the waves of the sea on a voyage into the air as I turn now from the forms and natural powers of man to his spirit, and as I venture to explore the latter's changing qualities on the earth's broad sphere with the help of the defective and somewhat uncertain reports of others.'[50] We shall likewise refrain from asking whether the flow of his eloquence does not involve him here and there in contradictions. For instance, when it is pointed out on page 248[51] that inventors have often had to leave it to posterity to reap greater benefits from their discoveries than they themselves enjoyed, does not this example further confirm the proposition that man's natural aptitudes, as far as the use of his reason is concerned, were meant to develop fully only within the species, but not in the individual? Yet the author is inclined (p. 206)[52] to censure this proposition, along with others which follow from it—although he does not grasp the latter entirely accurately—almost as an *offence against the majesty of nature* (which others more prosaically describe as blasphemy). All of this we must pass over here, mindful of the limits of length to which this review is subject.

There is one precondition which the reviewer would have liked to see realised, both for our author and for any other philosopher who should embark on a general natural history of mankind—namely that a historical and critical mind had done all the preparatory work for them, selecting from the boundless mass of ethnographical descriptions or travelogues, and from all the reports in these which can be presumed to shed light on human nature, those in particular which are mutually contradictory, placing them side by side and supplementing them with comments on the credibility of their respective authors; for if this had been done, no one would so boldly rely on one-sided accounts without first having carefully assessed the reports of others. But as it is, one may prove, if one wishes, from numerous descriptions of various countries, that Americans, Tibetans, and other genuine Mongolian peoples are beardless—but also, if one prefers, that they are all naturally bearded and merely pluck their hair out. Or one may prove that Americans and Negroes are races which have sunk below the level of other members of the species in terms of intellectual abilities—or alternatively, on the evidence of no less plausible accounts, that they should be regarded as equal in natural ability to all the other inhabitants of the world. Thus, the philosopher is at liberty to choose whether he wishes to assume natural differences or to judge everything by the principle *tout comme chez nous*, with the result that all the systems he constructs on such unstable foundations must take on the appearance of ramshackle hypotheses. Our author disapproves of the division of mankind into *races*, especially on the basis of inherited colour, presumably because he believes that the concept of race is not yet clearly defined. In the third numbered section of Book VII, he calls the cause of the climatic differences between human beings a *genetic* force. As the reviewer understands it, the sense in which the author uses this expression is as follows. He wishes to reject the system of evolution on the one hand, but also the purely mechanical influence of external causes on the other, as worthless explanations. He assumes that the cause of such differences is a vital principle which modifies *itself* from within in accordance with variations in external circumstances, and in a manner appropriate to these. The reviewer is fully in agreement with him here, but with this reservation: if the cause which organises *from within* were limited by its nature to only a certain number and degree of differences in the development of the creature which it organises (so that, once these differences were exhausted, it would no longer be free to work from another archetype under altered circumstances), one could well describe this natural determinant of formative nature in terms of germs or predispositions, without thereby regarding the differences in question as originally implanted and only occasionally activated mechanisms or buds (as in the system of evolution); on the contrary, such differences should be regarded simply as limitations imposed on a self-determining power, limitations which are as inexplicable as the power itself is incapable of being explained or rendered comprehensible.

A new train of thought begins with the *eighth book* and continues to the end of this portion of the work. It deals with the origin of man's education as a rational and moral creature, and hence with the beginning of all culture. This, in the author's opinion, is to be sought not in an inherent capacity of the human species, but completely outside it in the instruction and guidance provided by other natures. From this beginning, as he sees it, all cultural advances are simply the further transmission and casual exploitation of an original tradition; and it is this, rather than his own efforts, that man has to thank for all his progress towards wisdom. Since the reviewer becomes completely lost as soon as he strays from the path of nature and rational knowledge— for he is not conversant with learned philology nor familiar with ancient documents and able to assess them, and therefore has no idea how to make philosophic use of the facts they relate and attest—he readily accepts that he cannot pass judgement on such matters. Nevertheless, the author's wide reading and his particular aptitude for bringing scattered data into focus probably allow us to expect that we shall at least read many valuable observations on the course of human affairs, in so far as this can afford greater insight into the character of the species, and even perhaps into certain classical differences within it—observations which could be instructive even for someone who held different views on the ulimate origin of all human culture. The author briefly defines the basis of his own view as follows (pp. 338–9, including the footnote). 'This didactic (Mosaic) history tells us that the first human beings to be created were in contact with, and instructed by, the Elohim, under whose guidance, through familiarity with the animals, they acquired language and dominant reason; and when man illicitly aspired to become like the Elohim in knowledge of evil, he attained this knowledge to his own detriment and henceforth occupied a new status, adopting a new and more artificial way of life. Thus, if the deity wished man to exercise reason and foresight, it was necessary that the deity should itself look after him in a rational and far-sighted manner.—But how did the *Elohim* look after human beings—i.e. teach, warn, and instruct them? If it is not equally audacious to ask this question as to answer it, tradition itself will provide the solution in another context.'[53]

In a trackless desert, a thinker, like a traveller, must be free to choose his path at his discretion. We must wait to discover how he succeeds and whether, after reaching his goal, he will find his way home again— i.e. to the seat of reason—safe and sound and at the appointed time, so that he may expect that others will also follow in his footsteps. For this reason, the reviewer has no comment to make on the direction of thought which the author has followed; he does, however, consider himself justified in defending some of the propositions which the author has attacked on the way, for the reviewer must also be free to map out his own route. More precisely, we read on page 260: 'It would be an *easy* principle, but an *evil* one, to maintain in the philosophy of human history that man is an animal who needs a master, and who expects from this master, or from his association with him, the happiness of his ultimate destiny.'[54] It may well be an easy principle—because it is confirmed by the experience of all ages and peoples—but is it also an evil one? We are told on page 205: 'It was a benevolent thought of providence to give the more easily attained happiness of individual human beings priority over the artificial ends of large societies, and to save those expensive machines of state as far as possible for a later age.'[55] Quite so; but first comes the happiness of the animal, then that of the child, then that of the youth, and finally that of the man. In all the epochs of mankind, as in all sections of society at any given time, we find a happiness which is precisely commensurate with the concepts and habits of the creature in question with regard to the circumstances in which it was born and grew up; indeed, it is not even possible in this connection to draw a comparison between the respective degrees of happiness or to define the advantage of one class of people or generation over another. But what if the true end of providence were not this shadowy image of happiness which each individual creates for himself, but the ever continuing and growing activity and culture which are thereby set in motion, and whose highest possible expression can only be the product of a political constitution based on concepts of human right, and consequently an achievement of human beings themselves? Thus, we read on page 206 that 'each human individual has the measure of his happiness within him',[56] and that he does not yield in the enjoyment of this happiness to any of those who come after him; but as far as the value of their existence itself is concerned—i.e. the reason why they are there in the first place, as distinct from the conditions in which they exist—it is in this alone that a wise intention might be discernible within the whole. Does the author really mean that, if the happy inhabitants of Tahiti, never visited by more civilised nations, were destined to live in their peaceful indolence for thousands of centuries, it would be possible to give a satisfactory answer to the question of why they should exist at all, and of whether it would not have been just as good if this island had been occupied by happy sheep and cattle as by happy human beings who merely enjoy themselves? The above principle is therefore not as *evil* as the author believes— although it may well have been stated by an *evil man*.[57]—A second proposition which ought to be defended is as follows. We read on page 212: 'If someone said that it is not the individual human being but the human race which receives an education, I would find his words incomprehensible; for race and species are only general concepts except in so far as they exist in individual beings.—I might just as well speak of animality, stonality, or metality in general and deck them out with the most splendid attributes which are mutually incompatible in individual instances!—Our philosophy of history will not take this path of Averroistic[58] philosophy.'[59] Certainly, anyone who said that no single horse has horns although the horse as a species is horned would be uttering a gross absurdity. For in this instance, 'species' signifies nothing more than that precise quality in which all individuals must be identical. But if the human species signifies the *totality* of a series of generations which runs on into infinity (i.e. the indeterminable)—and the term is commonly used in this sense—and if it is assumed that this series constantly approximates to the line of its destiny which runs alongside it, it is not a contradiction to say that the series in all its parts is asymptotic to this line yet coincides with it as a whole. In other words, no single member of all the generations of the human race, but only the species, attains its destiny completely. The mathematician can provide eludication here; the philosopher would say that the destiny of the human race as a whole is *incessant progress*, and that its fulfilment is merely an idea—but in every respect a very useful idea—of the goal to which, in keeping with the intention of providence, we have to direct our endeavours. But this misconception in the polemical passage quoted above is only a trifle. More important is its conclusion. 'Our philosophy of history (as the author puts it) will not take this path of Averroistic philosophy.'[60] We may conclude from this that our author, who has so often deprecated all that has hitherto claimed to be philosophy, will now provide the world with a model of the true mode of philosophising—not in sterile verbal explanations, but by deed and example in this comprehensive work.

Conjectures on the Beginning of Human History[1]

To *introduce* conjectures at various points in the *course* of a historical account in order to fill gaps in the record is surely permissible; for what comes before and after these gaps—i.e. the remote cause and the effect respectively—can enable us to discover the intermediate causes with reasonable certainty, thereby rendering the intervening process intelligible. But to *base* a historical account solely on conjectures would seem little better than drawing up a plan for a novel. Indeed, such an account could not be described as a *conjectural history* at all, but merely as a *work of fiction*.—Nevertheless, what it may be presumptuous to introduce in the course of a history of human actions may well be permissible with reference to the *first beginning* of that history, for if the beginning is a product of *nature*, it may be discoverable by conjectural means. In other words, it does not have to be invented but can be deduced from experience, assuming that what was experienced at the beginning of history was no better or worse than what is experienced now—an assumption which accords with the analogy of nature and which has nothing presumptuous about it. Thus, a history of the first development of freedom from its origins as a predisposition in human nature is something quite different from a history of its subsequent course, which must be based exclusively on historical records.

Nevertheless, conjectures should not make undue claims on our assent. On the contrary, they should not present themselves as a serious activity but merely as an exercise in which the imagination, supported by reason, may be allowed to indulge as a healthy mental recreation. Consequently, they cannot stand comparison with a historical account which is put forward and accepted as a genuine record of the same event, a record which is tested by criteria quite different from those derived merely from the philosophy of nature. For this very reason, and because the journey on which I am about to venture is no more than a pleasure trip, I may perhaps hope to be granted permission to employ a sacred document as my map, and at the same time to speculate that the journey which I shall make on the wings of imagination—although not without the guidance of experience as mediated by reason—will follow precisely the same course as that which the sacred text records as history. The reader will have the document in question before him (Genesis, Chapters II–VI), and may consult it at every step to see whether the route which philosophy follows with the help of concepts accords with that which the Bible story describes.

If we are not to indulge in wild conjectures, we must begin with something which human reason cannot deduce from prior natural causes—that is, with the *existence of human beings*. These human beings must also be *fully developed*, for they have no mother to support them, and they must be a *pair* in order that they may reproduce their kind. Besides, there must be only *one* couple if war is not to break out at once—as would happen if the people in question were close to one another yet strangers—and if nature is not to be accused of having failed, by permitting descent from different ancestors, to take the most appropriate measures to promote sociability as the principal end of human destiny; for the common descent of all human beings from a single family unit was undoubtedly the best means of attaining this end. I then place this couple in a setting secure from the attacks of wild beasts and amply provided by nature with every means of sustenance— a *garden*, so to speak, in a climate of constant mildness. What is more, I imagine them not in their wholly primitive natural state, but only after they have made significant advances in the skilful use of their powers. For the reader might well find too many conjectures and too few probabilities if I were to try to fill this gap, which presumably occupied a considerable interval of time. The first human being could therefore *stand* and *walk*; he could *speak* (cf. Genesis II.20)* and indeed *talk*—i.e. speak with the help of coherent concepts (II.23)—and consequently *think*. These are all skills which he had to acquire for himself (for if they were innate, they would also be inherited, which does not tally with experience); I assume, however, that he is already in possession of

* The *urge to communicate* must have been the original motive for human beings who were still alone to announce their existence to living creatures outside themselves, especially to those which emit sounds which can be imitated and which can subsequently serve as a name. A similar effect of this urge can still be seen in children and thoughtless people who disturb the thinking section of the community by banging, shouting, whistling, singing and other noisy pastimes (and often even by noisy religious devotions). For I can see no motive for such behaviour other than a desire on the part of those concerned to proclaim their existence to the world at large.

them, for I wish merely to consider the development of human behaviour from the ethical point of view, and this necessarily presupposes that the skills in question are already present.

Initially, the newcomer must have been guided solely by instinct, that *voice of God* which all animals obey. It permitted him to use some things as food and forbade him to use others (III.2–3).—It is unnecessary, however, to assume for this purpose a particular instinct which has now been lost. It could simply have been the sense of smell and its affinity with the organ of taste, along with that sympathy which is known to exist between the latter and the digestive organs—in other words an ability, which is still in evidence today, to sense in advance whether a given food is suitable for consumption or not. We need not even assume that this sense was more acute in the first couple than it is now; for it is common knowledge that the perceptive powers of those who employ only their senses differ greatly from those of people who are also engaged in thought, and who accordingly pay less attention to their sensations.

So long as inexperienced man obeyed this call of nature, his lot was a happy one. But *reason* soon made its presence felt and sought to extend his knowledge of foodstuffs beyond the bounds of instinct; it did so by comparing his usual diet with anything which a sense other than that to which his instinct was tied—for example, the sense of sight—represented as similar in character (III. 6). Even if instinct did not recommend it, this experiment had a chance of succeeding so long as instinct did not contradict it. But it is a peculiarity of reason that it is able, with the help of the imagination, to invent desires which not only *lack* any corresponding natural impulse, but which are even *at variance* with the latter. Such desires, which are known primarily as *lasciviousness*, gradually engender a whole host of superfluous or even unnatural inclinations to which the term *luxuriousness* applies. The initial incentive to abandon natural impulses may have been quite trivial. But the outcome of that first experiment whereby man became conscious of his reason as a faculty which can extend beyond the limits to which all animals are confined was of great importance, and it influenced his way of life decisively. Thus, it may have been only a fruit which, because it looked similar to other agreeable fruits which he had previously tasted, encouraged him to make the experiment. There may also have been the example of an animal to which such food was naturally congenial, although it had an opposite and harmful effect on human beings, whose natural instinct was consequently opposed to it.

Nevertheless, this was enough to give reason the initial inducement to quibble with the voice of nature (III. 1), and despite the latter's objections, to make the first experiment in free choice—an experiment which, since it was the first, probably did not turn out as expected. No matter how trivial the harm it did may have been, it was nevertheless enough to open man's eyes (III. 7). He discovered in himself an ability to choose his own way of life without being tied to any single one like the other animals. But the momentary gratification which this realisation of his superiority may have afforded him was inevitably followed at once by anxiety and fear as to how he should employ his newly discovered ability, given that he did not yet know the hidden properties or remote effects of anything. He stood, as it were, on the edge of an abyss. For whereas instinct had hitherto directed him towards individual objects of his desire, an infinite range of objects now opened up, and he did not yet know how to choose between them. Yet now that he had tasted this state of freedom, it was impossible for him to return to a state of servitude under the rule of instinct.

Next to the instinct for food by which nature preserves each individual, the *sexual instinct*, by which nature ensures the survival of each species, is the most prominent. Once reason had awakened, it was not slow to make its influence felt in this area either. Man soon discovered that the sexual stimulus, which in the case of animals is based merely on a transient and largely periodic urge, could in his case be prolonged and even increased by means of the imagination. For although the imagination performs its function with greater moderation the further its object is *withdrawn from the senses*, it also functions more constantly and uniformly, thereby avoiding that satiety which follows the satisfaction of a purely animal desire. The fig-leaf was accordingly the product of a much stronger assertion of reason than had been evident in the first phase of its development. For to render an inclination more intense and lasting by withdrawing its object from the senses already displays a consciousness of some rational control over the impulses, and not just an ability, as in the first stage of rationality, to obey the impulses to a greater or lesser extent. *Refusal* was the device which invested purely sensuous stimuli with an ideal quality, and which gradually showed the way from purely animal desire to love, and so also from a feeling for the merely agreeable to a taste for beauty (initially only in human form, but subsequently also in nature). Furthermore, the first incentive for man's development as a moral being came from his *sense of decency*, his inclination to inspire respect in others by good manners (i.e. by concealing all that might invite contempt) as the proper foundation of all true sociability.—A small beginning such as this, which nevertheless has epoch-making effects in imparting a wholly new direction to thought, is more important than the whole endless series of subsequent cultural developments.

The third step which reason took after its intervention in man's basic and immediately felt needs was to reflect in *anticipation of the future*. This ability not just to enjoy the present moment of life but also to visualise what is yet to come, often in the distant future, is the most decisive proof of man's advantage, in that he is able to prepare for remote objectives in keeping with his destiny. But this same ability is also the most inexhaustible source of cares and worries which an uncertain future evokes, and from which all animals are exempt (III. 13–19). The man who had to provide for himself, his wife, and his future children foresaw the increasing laboriousness of his work; the woman foresaw the hardships to which nature had subjected her sex, as well as those which the more powerful man would inflict upon her. Both foresaw with apprehension, at the end of a life of toil and as yet in the background of the picture, the fate which must befall all animals but which causes them no concern, namely death; and they seemed to reproach themselves for, and regard as a crime, that use of reason which had brought all these ills upon them. Perhaps the only comfort and reassurance they had was the prospect of living through their offspring, whose lot might be better than theirs or who might even, as members of one family, alleviate their parents' troubles (III. 16–20).

The fourth and last step which reason took, thereby raising man completely above animal society, was his (albeit obscure) realisation that he is the true *end of nature*, and that nothing which lives on earth can compete with him in this respect. When he first said to the sheep '*the fleece which you wear was given to you by nature not for your own use, but for mine*' and took it from the sheep to wear it himself (III. 21), he became aware of a prerogative which, by his nature, he enjoyed over all the animals; and he now no longer regarded them as fellow creatures, but as means and instruments to be used at will for the attainment of whatever ends he pleased. This notion implies (if only obscurely) an awareness of the following distinction: man should not address other *human beings* in the same way as animals, but should regard them as having an equal share in the gifts of nature. This was a distant preparation for those restrictions which reason would in future impose on man's will in relation to his fellows, a preparation which is much more essential for the establishment of society than is inclination or love.

Thus, man had attained a position of *equality with all rational beings*, whatever their rank (III. 22), because he could claim *to be an end in himself*, to be accepted as such by all others, and not to be used by anyone else simply as a means to other ends. This, rather than reason considered merely as an instrument for the satisfaction of various inclinations, is the basis of man's unconditional equality even with higher beings; for even if the latter are incomparably superior to him in natural gifts, they do not have a right to use him as they please. Consequently, this fourth step of reason is also associated with man's *release* from the womb of nature, a change of status which undoubtedly does him honour, but is at the same time fraught with danger; for it expelled him from the harmless and secure condition of a protected childhood—from a garden, as it were, which provided for him without any effort on his part (III. 23)—and thrust him out into the world at large, where so many cares, labours, and unknown evils awaited him. In the future, the hardships of life would often arouse in him the wish for a paradise created by his imagination, a paradise where he could dream or idle away his existence in quiet inactivity and everlasting peace. But restless reason, irresistibly driving him on to develop his innate capacities, stands between him and that imagined seat of bliss, and does not allow him to return to the state of rude simplicity from which it had originally extracted him (III. 24). It urges him to submit patiently to the labours he detests, to pursue the trivialities he despises, and to forget even his terror of death in favour of all those trifles whose loss he fears even more.

Note

From this account of the earliest history of man, the following conclusion can be drawn. Man's emergence from that paradise which reason represents to him as the first abode of his species was nothing other than his transition from a rude and purely animal existence to a state of humanity, from the leading-strings of instinct to the guidance of reason—in a word, from the guardianship of nature to the state of freedom. Whether he gained or lost through this change is no longer a question when we consider the destiny of his species, which consists quite simply in *progress* towards perfection, however flawed his first attempts to attain this end—even if they are followed by a long series of further attempts—may prove to be.—But while this course represents a *progression* from worse to better for the species as a whole, this is not so in the case of the individual. Before reason awoke, there were no commandments or prohibitions, so that violations of these were also impossible. But when reason began to function and, in all its weakness, came into conflict with animality in all its strength, evils necessarily ensued; and even worse, as reason grew more cultivated, vices emerged which were quite foreign to the state of ignorance and hence of innocence. From the moral point of view, therefore, the first step beyond this state was a *fall*; and from the physical point of view, this fall was a punishment, for it led to a host of hitherto unknown evils. Thus, the history of ˙nature begins with goodness, for it is the *work of God*; but the history of *freedom* begins with evil, for it is the *work of man*. For the individual, who looks only to himself in the exercise of his freedom, a change of this kind represented a loss; for nature, whose end in relation to man concerns the species, it represented a gain. The individual therefore has cause to blame himself for all the ills which he endures and for all the evil which he perpetrates; but at the same time, as the member of a whole (of a species), he has cause to admire and praise the wisdom and purposiveness of the overall arrangement.—In this way, it is possible to reconcile with each other and with reason the often misunderstood and apparently contradictory pronouncements of the celebrated *J.J. Rousseau*.[2] In his esays *On the Influence of the Sciences*[3] and *On the Inequality of Man*,[4] he shows quite correctly that there is an inevitable conflict between culture and the nature of the human race as a *physical* species each of whose individual members is meant to fulfil his destiny completely. But in his *Émile*,[5] his *Social Contract*,[6] and other writings, he attempts in turn to solve the more difficult problem of what course culture should take in order to ensure the proper development, in keeping with their destiny, of man's capacities as a *moral* species, so that this [moral] destiny will no longer conflict with his character as a natural species. Since culture has perhaps not yet really begun—let alone completed—its development in accordance with the true principles of man's *education* as a human being and citizen, the above conflict is the source of all the genuine evils which oppress human life, and of all the vices which dishonour it.* At the same time, the very impulses which are blamed as the causes of vice are good in themselves, fulfilling their function as abilities implanted by nature. But since these abilities are adapted to the state of nature, they are undermined by the advance of culture and themselves undermine the latter in turn, until art, when it reaches perfection, once more becomes nature—and this is the ultimate goal of man's moral destiny.

* The following may be cited as only a few examples of this conflict between man's aspiration towards his moral destiny on the one hand, and his unchanging obedience to laws inherent in his nature and appropriate to a crude and animal condition on the other.
  Nature has fixed the time at which human beings reach maturity—in terms of their urge and ability to reproduce their kind—at the age of approximately sixteen or seventeen. This is the age at which, in the raw state of nature, a youth literally becomes a man; for he then has the capacity to look after himself, to reproduce his kind, and to look after his children as well as his wife. The simplicity of his needs makes this an easy task. But in a civilised state, he requires numerous means of support, in terms both of skill and of favourable external circumstances, in order to perform these functions. In the context of civil society, the corresponding stage is therefore postponed—at least on average—by a further ten years. Nevertheless, nature has not altered the age of puberty to match the progressive refinement of society, but sticks stubbornly to the law which it has imposed on the survival of the human race as an animal species. As a result, the effect of social customs on the end of nature—and vice versa—is inevitably prejudicial. For in the state of nature, a human being is already a man at an age when civilised man (who nevertheless still retains his character as natural man) is merely a youth, or even only a child; for we may well describe as a child someone who, in the civil state, is unable because of his age to support even himself, let alone others of his kind, despite having the urge and capacity to produce offspring as called upon by nature. For nature has certainly not endowed living creatures with instincts and capacities in order that they should resist and suppress them. Such abilities were consequently not designed for a state of civilisation, but merely for the survival of the human race as an animal species; and the civilised state thus inevitably comes into conflict with the latter, a conflict which only a perfect civil constitution—the ultimate goal of culture—can resolve. Meanwhile, the intervening period [between the state of nature and the state of perfection] is filled as a rule with vices and their consequences, i.e. with human misery in its various forms.
  A further example may confirm the truth of the proposition that nature has endowed us with two distinct abilities for two distinct purposes, namely that of man as an animal species and that of man as a moral species. The example in question is the saying of Hippocrates 'ars longa, vita brevis'. The arts and sciences could be advanced much further by one individual with the appropriate talents, once he had attained the necessary maturity of judgement through long practice and the acquisition of knowledge, than by whole generations of scholars in succession, provided that this individual could live and retain his youthful mental capacities for the total lifetimes of the generations in question. Now it is evident that nature has fixed the length of human life with a view to ends other than that of the advancement of the sciences. For just when the most fortunate of thinkers is on the verge of the greatest discoveries which his skill and experience entitle him to expect, old age intervenes; he loses his acuteness and must leave it to the next generation (which starts once more from the ABC and must again traverse the entire distance which had already been covered) to take a further step in the progress of culture. Thus, the course which the human race follows on the way to fulfilling its destiny appears subject to incessant interruptions, with a constant risk of reverting to the original barbarism; and the Greek philosopher had

The End of History

The following period began with man's transition from the age of leisure and peace to the age of *labour and discord* as the prelude to social union. Here, we must make another major leap and suddenly put him in possession of domestic animals and of crops which he can propagate himself for his own consumption by sowing and planting (IV. 2). In fact, the transition from the savage life of the hunter to the former [pastoral] state, and from sporadic digging for roots or gathering of fruit to the second [agricultural] state, may have taken place very gradually. It was at this point that strife inevitably arose between those who had hitherto lived together in peace, with the result that those whose ways of life were different became separated and dispersed throughout the world. *Pastoral life* is not only leisurely, but also the most reliable means of support, for there is no lack of fodder for animals in a largely uninhabited country. *Agriculture* or the planting of crops, on the other hand, is extremely laborious, subject to the vagaries of climate, and consequently insecure; it also requires permanent settlements, ownership of land, and sufficient strength to defend the latter. The herdsman, however, abhors such property because it limits his freedom of pasture. As far as agriculture is concerned, the farmer may have seemed to envy the herdsman as someone more favoured by heaven (IV. 4); but in fact, the herdsman caused him great inconvenience so long as he remained in the neighbourhood, for grazing animals do not spare the farmer's crops. It is also easy for the herdsman to move further afield with his animals, thus avoiding the need to make any restitution for the damage he has done, for he leaves nothing behind which he could not just as easily find elsewhere. Thus, the farmer no doubt had to use force to prevent these incursions, which were not considered unlawful by his

some justification when he complained that *it is a pity that we have to die just when we have begun to realise how we ought to have lived.*

As a third example, we may cite the *inequality* of men—not their inequality in terms of natural gifts or goods bestowed on them by fortune, but in terms of universal *human rights*, about which *Rousseau* complains with a great deal of truth. Yet this inequality is inseparable from culture, so long as the latter proceeds, as it were, without a plan (and this is inevitably the case for a considerable period of time). But it was surely not imposed on man by nature, for nature gave him both freedom and reason, and reason decreed that this freedom is subject to no other limits than those of its own universal and external legality, which is known as *civil right*. Man was meant to rise, by his own efforts, above the barbarism of his natural abilities, but to take care not to contravene them even as he rises above them. He can expect to attain this skill only at a late stage and after many unsuccessful attempts; and in the meantime, the human race groans under the evils which it inflicts on itself as a result of its own inexperience.

adversary; and since the cause of such incursions could never be entirely eliminated, he was no doubt eventually compelled to *distance* himself as far as possible from those who lived a pastoral existence, unless he wished to lose the fruits of his long and diligent efforts (IV. 16). This separation marks the beginning of the third epoch.

Where people depend for their livelihood on the cultivation of the soil (and on the planting of trees in particular), they require permanent accommodation; and the defence of such property against all encroachment requires a large number of people who are prepared to assist one another. Hence those who adopted this way of life could no longer live in scattered family units, but had to stick together and set up village communities (incorrectly described as *towns*) in order to protect their property against savage hunters or tribes of pastoral nomads. The first essentials of life which a *changed mode of living* makes necessary (IV. 20) could now be acquired by mutual *exchange*. This inevitably gave rise to *culture* and the beginnings of *art*, both as a pastime and as an occupation (IV. 21f); but first and foremost, it also meant that certain steps were taken to establish a civil constitution and the public administration of justice. Initially, the latter was no doubt concerned only with major acts of violence, the avenging of which was now no longer left to individuals as in the savage state, but assigned to a lawful authority which served to unite the whole—i.e. to a kind of government which was not itself subject to the rule of force (IV. 23f.).—From these first crude beginnings, all human aptitudes could now gradually develop, the most beneficial of these being *sociability and civil security*. The human race could multiply and, like a beehive, send out colonists in all directions from the centre—colonists who were already civilised. This epoch also saw the beginning of human *inequality*, that abundant source of so much evil but also of everything good; this inequality continued to increase thereafter.

So long as the nations of nomadic herdsmen, who recognise only God as their master, continued to swarm around the town-dwellers and farmers, who are governed by a human master or civil authority (VI. 4),* and, as declared enemies of all land ownership, treated the latter with hostility and were hated by them in turn, the two sides were continually at war, or at least at constant risk of war. But as a consequence, both

* The *Bedouins* of Arabia still describe themselves as children of a former *sheikh*, the founder of their tribe (such as *Beni Haled* and others). But the sheikh is by no means their *master*, and he cannot force his will upon them as he chooses. For in a nation of herdsmen, no one has fixed property which he cannot take with him, so that any family which is discontented with its tribe can easily leave it and join forces with another.

nations could at least enjoy the priceless asset of internal freedom. (For even now, the risk of war is the only thing which keeps despotism in check, because a state must now have wealth before it can be powerful, and there can be no wealth-producing activity without *freedom*. In a poor nation, this lack of wealth must be compensated for by widespread efforts to preserve the commonwealth, and this is again impossible unless the nation feels that such efforts can be freely made.)—In the course of time, however, the growing luxury of the town-dwellers, and in particular the seductive arts in which the women of the towns surpassed the unkempt wenches of the wilderness, must have been a powerful temptation to the herdsmen to enter into relations with them and to let themselves be drawn into the glittering misery of the towns (VI. 2). The consequent amalgamation of two formerly hostile populations put an end to the danger of war, but it also put an end to freedom. This led on the one hand to a despotism of powerful tyrants, and—since culture had only just begun—to soulless extravagance and the most abject slavery, combined with all the vices of the uncivilised state. On the other hand, the human race was irresistibly deflected from the course marked out for it by nature, namely the progressive cultivation of its capacities for goodness. It thus became unworthy of its very existence as a species whose destiny was to rule over the earth rather than to live in brutish indulgence and grovelling servitude (VI. 17).

Concluding Note

Thinking people are subject to a malaise which may even turn into moral corruption, a malaise of which the unthinking are ignorant— namely discontent with that providence by which the course of the world as a whole is governed. They feel this sentiment when they contemplate the evils which so greatly oppress the human race, with no hope (as it seems) of any improvement. Yet it is of the utmost importance *that we should be content with providence*, even if the path it has laid out for us on earth is an arduous one. We should be content with it partly in order that we may take courage even in the midst of hardships, and partly in order that we should not blame all such evils on fate and fail to notice that we may ourselves be entirely responsible for them, thereby losing the chance to remedy them by improving ourselves.

We have to admit that the greatest evils which oppress civilised nations are the result of *war*—not so much of actual wars in the past or present as of the unremitting, indeed ever-increasing *preparation* for war in the future. All the resources of the state, and all the fruits of its culture which might be used to enhance that culture even further, are devoted to this purpose. Freedom suffers greatly in numerous areas, and the state's maternal care for its individual members is replaced by demands of implacable harshness (even if this harshness is justified by fear of external threats). But if the constant fear of war did not compel even heads of state to show this *respect for humanity*, would we still encounter the same culture, or that close association of social classes within the commonwealth which promotes the wellbeing of all? Would we still encounter the same population, or even that degree of freedom which is still present in spite of highly restrictive laws? We need only look at *China*, whose position may expose it to occasional unforeseen incursions but not to attack by a powerful enemy, and we shall find that, for this very reason, it has been stripped of every vestige of freedom.— So long as human culture remains at its present stage, war is therefore an indispensable means of advancing it further; and only when culture has reached its full development—and only God knows when that will be—will perpetual peace become possible and of benefit to us. In this connection, therefore, we surely have only ourselves to blame for the evils which we so bitterly lament; and the Holy Scripture is quite justified in regarding the amalgamation of nations into one society, and their complete liberation from external danger at a time when their culture had scarcely emerged, as an obstacle to all further cultural progress and a descent into irremediable corruption.

The *second source of man's dissatisfaction* with the order of nature is the *shortness of life*. It is true that anyone who continues to wish that life might last longer than it actually does must have little appreciation of its value, for to prolong it would merely add to the length of a drama made up of endless struggles with adversity. Nevertheless, we may excuse those of childish judgement who fear death but have no love of life, and who find it hard to complete each day of their existence with some degree of contentment, yet can never have days enough in which to repeat this painful experience. But if we stop to think of all the care that afflicts us in our search for ways of passing a life as short as this, and of all the injustice that is done in the hope of a future enjoyment which will last for so short a time, it is reasonable to conclude that a life-expectancy of 800 years or more would not be to our advantage. Fathers would live in mortal fear of their sons, brothers of brothers, and friends of friends, and the vices of a human race of such longevity would necessarily reach such a pitch that it would deserve no better a fate than to be wiped from the face of the earth by a universal flood (VI. 12f.).

The *third* wish (which is in fact an empty yearning, for it knows that its object can never be attained) is a reflection of that *golden age* which poets have praised so highly. In it, we are supposedly relieved of all those imaginary needs with which luxury encumbers us, we are content with the bare necessities of nature, and there is complete equality and perpetual peace among men—in a word, there is pure enjoyment of a carefree life, frittered away in idle dreams or childish play. It is yearnings such as these which make tales of Robinson Crusoe and voyages to the South Sea islands so attractive; but in a wider sense, they are symptoms of that weariness of civilised life which thinking people feel when they seek its value in *pleasure* alone, and when they resort to idleness as an antidote as soon as reason reminds them that they ought to give value to their life through their *actions*. The vacuity of this wish for a return to the past age of simplicity and innocence is adequately demonstrated by the foregoing account of man's original state. For as we have seen, man cannot remain in this state because it does not satisfy him, and he is even less inclined to go back to it once he has left it. Consequently, he must continue to ascribe his present condition and all its hardships to himself and his own choice.

An account of human history will be of benefit to man and will serve to instruct and improve him if it contains the following lessons. It must show him that he should not blame providence for the evils which oppress him, and that he is not entitled to ascribe his own mis- demeanours to an original crime committed by his earliest ancestors, by alleging, for example, that a disposition to commit similar offences has been passed down to their descendants; for there can be nothing in- herited about arbitrary actions. It should show him instead that he has every justification for acknowledging the action of his first ancestors as his own, and that he should hold himself wholly responsible for all the evils which spring from the misuse of his reason; for he is quite capable of realising that, in the same circumstances, he would have behaved in exactly the same way, in that his first act in using reason would have been to misuse it (even if nature advised him otherwise). Once this point concerning moral evils has been correctly understood, the strictly physical evils will scarcely tip the balance in our favour when merits and faults are weighed against each other.

The conclusion to be drawn from this attempt to describe the earliest history of mankind with the help of philosophy is therefore as follows.

We should be content with providence and with the course of human affairs as a whole, which does not begin with good and then proceed to evil, but develops gradually from the worse to the better; and each individual is for his own part called upon by nature itself to contribute towards this progress to the best of his ability.

INTRODUCTION TO

What is Orientation in Thinking?

Kant's essay was occasioned by a dispute between Moses Mendelssohn (1729–86), a Jewish philosopher of Berlin with whom Kant corresponded and whom he esteemed greatly, and Friedrich Heinrich Jacobi (1743–1819), a writer and friend of Goethe's who had attacked Mendelssohn's interpretation of Spinoza.[1] It was a bitter dispute because Jacobi had, in Mendelssohn's view, maligned the reputation of their late common friend, the writer and dramatist Gotthold Ephraim Lessing (1729–81) when he claimed that Lessing had been a follower of Spinoza and hence a pantheist who did not believe in a personal God. Mendelssohn rebutted this charge and maintained that Jacobi had misunderstood Lessing. Their argument is of historical interest only.[2]

Kant's essay, however, provides an introduction to his critical philosophy and shows how his discussion of the theoretical use of reason, as argued in detail in the *Critique of Pure Reason* and in the *Prolegomena to Any Future Metaphysics That Can Claim the Status of a Science (Prolegomena zu einer jeden künftigen Metaphysik die als Wissenschaft wird auftreten können)* (1783), necessarily leads on to the practical use of reason as defined in his writings on ethics (for instance, in the *Critique of Practical Reason* (1788) and the *Groundwork of the Metaphysics of Morals*

[1] The relevant works by Mendelssohn are *Morgenstunden oder Vorlesungen über das Daseyn Gottes* (Berlin, 1785) and *An die Freunde Lessings. Ein Anhang zu Herrn Jacobis Briefwechsel über die Lehre des Spinoza* (Berlin, 1786). Both works are reprinted in his *Gesammelte Schriften*. Jubiläumsausgabe, III, 2 (Stuttgart and Bad Cannstatt, 1974) (abbreviated as *GS*), 1–218. The relevant works by Jacobi are *Über die Lehre des Spinoza in Briefen an den Herrn Moses Mendelssohn* (Breslau, 1785) and *Wider Mendelssohns Beschuldigungen betreffend die Briefe über die Lehre des Spinoza* (Leipzig, 1786). Both works are reprinted in Jacobi's *Werke*, IV, 1 and 2 (Leipzig, 1819), 1–276.
[2] Cf. Heinrich Scholz (ed. with an introduction), *Die Hauptschriften zum Pantheismusstreit zwischen Jacobi und Mendelssohn*. Neudrucke seltener philosophischer Werke (ed. Kantgesellschaft, 6), (Berlin, 1916), who discusses this dispute (pp. XI–CXXVIII) and reprints the major parts of the polemical writings in question.

(*Grundlegung zur Metaphysik der Sitten*) (1785)), which in turn provide the foundation of his political writing. Kant did not openly attack either of the two writings in question, but thought it necessary to defend his late friend Mendelssohn while at the same time pointing out some shortcomings in Mendelssohn's argument (Mendelssohn had put forward proofs for the existence of God which Kant held to be illegitimate). He proceeds to show that the belief in reason is a 'signpost or compass'[1] which enables us to orientate our thinking. The use of reason is necessary in order to limit our enquiries to what can, in principle, be discovered and to prevent us from seeking to discover what is beyond the boundaries of knowledge. But the right use of reason also makes it possible for us to act morally. We have to avoid falling victim to zealotry or superstition—that would even be politically dangerous, for it would sooner or later lead to political repression by the authorities who would not be willing to tolerate the spreading of foolish and subversive opinions.

We must therefore act responsibly so that we can enjoy the freedom to use reason without hindrance. Consequently, reason must not be subjected to any laws except 'those *which it imposes on itself*'.[2] Political freedom is imperative for the free use of reason, because we need to communicate our arguments and findings to others and have them criticised by them. Without the public use of reason we cannot orientate our thinking properly. The essay thus shows how, in Kant's view, epistemology and ethics are closely interlinked with politics as well as how, in his opinion, rational enquiry and moral conduct can be practised properly only in a society governed according to principles of politics based on the Idea of freedom. In other words, Kant's theory of politics, as this essay shows, is not an unimportant appendix to his critical philosophy, but a necessary consequence of it.

[1] Cf. p. 245 below.   [2] Cf. p. 247 below.

What is Orientation in Thinking?[1]

However exalted we may wish our concepts to be, and however abstract we may make them in relation to the realm of the senses, they will continue to be associated with *figurative* notions. The proper function of these is to make such concepts, which are not in other respects derived from experience, suitable for *use in the experiential world*. For how else could we endow our concepts with sense and significance if we did not attach them to some intuition[2] (which must ultimately always be an example derived from some possible experience)? If we then subtract the figurative associations from this concrete act of the understanding—first those of fortuitous sense-perception, and then the pure sensuous intuition itself—we are left with the pure concept of the understanding, but with its scope now enlarged so as to constitute a complete rule of thought. This is the way in which even universal logic came into being; and in the application of our understanding and reason to experience, there may still lie hidden certain *heuristic* methods of thought which, if we could carefully extract them from experience, might well enrich philosophy with useful maxims, even in abstract thought.

To this category belongs that principle to which the late Moses *Mendelssohn*[3] expressly declared his allegiance—but only, so far as I know, in his last writings (see his *Morgenstunden* (*Morning Hours*), pp. 164 f.[4] and his letter *An die Freunde Lessings*[5] (*To Lessing's Friends*), pp. 33 and 67):[6] namely the maxim that it is necessary to **orientate** oneself in the speculative use of reason (which Mendelssohn, on other occasions, credited with considerable powers in the cognition of supra-sensory objects, and even with the power of conclusive proof) by means of a certain guideline which he sometimes described as *common sense* (in his *Morgenstunden*), sometimes as *healthy reason*, and sometimes as *plain understanding* (in *An die Freunde Lessings*). Who would have thought that this admission would not only have such disastrous effects on his favourable opinion of the power of *speculative* reasoning in theological matters (which was in fact inevitable), but also that even ordinary healthy reason, given the ambiguous position to which he relegated the use of this faculty in contrast to speculation, would risk becoming the basic principle of zealotry[7] and of the complete subversion of reason? And yet this is what happened in the controversy between *Mendelssohn* and *Jacobi*,[8] particularly as a result of the important conclusions reached by the perceptive author of the *Resultate*.*[9] Nevertheless, I do not wish to imply that either of the contestants intended to give currency to so pernicious an attitude; on the contrary, I prefer to regard the latter's [i.e. Jacobi's] enterprise as an *argumentum ad hominem*[10] which one is entitled to use purely in self-defence in order to turn one's opponent's weaknesses to his disadvantage. On the other hand, I shall also show that it was in fact reason *alone* which Mendelssohn recommended as a necessary means of orientation—not a supposed sense of truth of a mysterious kind or an effusive intuition in the name of faith to which tradition or revelation can be grafted on without the consent of reason, but as he staunchly affirmed with righteous fervour, human reason pure and simple. But if this is so, the latter can no longer make lofty claims for its speculative powers, or claim in particular that they possess exclusive authority as a means of demonstration; and in so far as it is speculative in character, it will be left with the sole function of purging the ordinary concept of reason of contradictions, and of defending the maxims of healthy reason against the sophistical attacks of speculative reason *itself*.—If the concept of *orientation* is extended and defined more precisely, it may help us to cast light on the various ways in which the maxim of healthy reason is applied to the cognition of supra-sensory objects.

To *orientate* oneself, in the proper sense of the word, means to use a given direction—and we divide the horizon into four of these—in order to find the others, and in particular that of *sunrise*. If I see the sun in the sky and know that it is now midday, I know how to find south, west, north, and east. For this purpose, however, I must necessarily be able to feel a difference within my own *subject*, namely that between my right and left hands. I call this a *feeling*, because these two sides display no perceptible difference as far as external intuition is concerned. If I were not able, in describing a circle, to distinguish between movement

---

* Jacobi, *Briefe über die Lehre des Spinoza (Letters Concerning the Doctrine of Spinoza)*, Breslau, 1785.—Jacobi, *Wider Mendelssohns Beschuldigung betreffend die Briefe über die Lehre des Spinoza (Against Mendelssohn's Accusation with Regard to the Letters Concerning the Doctrine of Spinoza)*, Leipzig, 1786.—*Die Resultate der Jacobischen und Mendelssohnschen Philosophie, kritisch untersucht von einem Freiwilligen (The Results of Jacobi's and Mendelssohn's Philosophy, Critically Examined by a Voluntary Contributor)*, ibidem.

from left to right and movement from right to left without reference to any differences between objects within the circle, and hence to define the different positions of such objects by *a priori* means, I would not know whether to locate west to the right or to the left of the southernmost point of the horizon in order to complete the circle through north and east and so back to south. Thus, in spite of all the objective data in the sky, I orientate myself *geographically* purely by means of a *subjective* distinction; and if all the constellations, while in other respects retaining the same shape and the same position in relation to each other, were one day miraculously transposed so that their former easterly direction now became west, no human eye would notice the slightest change on the next clear night, and even the astronomer, if he heeded only what he saw and not at the same time what he felt, would inevitably become *disorientated*. But in fact, the ability to make distinctions by means of the feeling of right and left comes quite naturally to his aid—an ability which, though implanted by nature, has become a habit as a result of frequent practice; and if he simply directs his eyes to the Pole Star, he will not only notice the change which has occurred, but will still be able to *orientate* himself in spite of it.

I can now extend this geographical concept of the process of orientation to signify any kind of orientation within a given space, i.e. orientation in a purely *mathematical* sense. In the darkness, I can orientate myself in a familiar room so long as I can touch any one object whose position I remember. But it is obvious that the only thing which assists me here is an ability to define the position of the objects by means of a *subjective* distinction: for I cannot see the objects whose position I am supposed to find; and if, for a joke, someone had shifted all the objects round in such a way that their relative positions remained the same but what was previously on the right was now on the left, I would be quite unable to find my way about a room whose walls were in other respects identical. But in fact, I can soon orientate myself simply by the feeling of difference between my two sides, my right and my left. This is what happens if I have to walk and take the correct turnings at night on streets with which I am otherwise familiar, but in which I cannot at present distinguish any of the houses.

Finally, I can extend this concept even further if I equate it with the ability to orientate oneself not just in space, i.e. mathematically, but also in *thought*, i.e. *logically*. It is easy to guess by analogy that this will be the means whereby pure reason regulates its use when, taking leave of known objects (of experience), it seeks to extend its sphere beyond the

239

frontiers of experience and no longer encounters any objects of intuition whatsoever, but merely a space for the latter to operate in. It will then no longer be in a position, in determining its own faculty of judgement, to subsume its judgements under a specific maxim with the help of objective criteria of knowledge, but only with the help of a subjective distinction.* This subjective means which still remains available to it is simply the feeling of a **need** which is inherent in reason itself. It is possible to remain secure against all error if one does not venture to pass judgement in cases where one's knowledge is insufficient for the judgement in question. Consequently, while ignorance is in itself the cause of the limits of our knowledge, it is not the cause of the errors within it. But if it is not just a matter of indifference whether one wishes to make a definite judgement on something or not, if this judgement is made necessary by a real *need* (in fact by a need which reason imposes on itself), and if we are at the same time limited by lack of knowledge in respect of factors essential to the judgement, we require a maxim in the light of which this judgement can be passed; for reason must sooner or later be satisfied. But if it has been established in advance that no intuition of the object is possible here, and that it is not even possible to find something of a similar kind which might enable us to provide our extended concepts [of the object in question] with a representation appropriate to them and hence also with a guarantee of their own real possibility, only two further steps remain to be taken. Firstly, we must carefully examine whether the concept with which we wish to venture beyond all possible experience is itself free from contradiction; and secondly, we must reduce at least the *relationship* between the object in question and the objects of experience to pure concepts of the understanding. In so doing, we certainly do not turn the object into an object of the senses; but we do at least think of something which is itself supra-sensory as capable of being applied by our reason to the world of experience. Without these precautions, we would be unable to make any use whatsoever of such a concept, and would indulge in fantasy instead of thinking.

But this—i.e. the concept in itself—tells us nothing as far as the existence of this object and its real connection with the world (as the embodiment of all objects of possible experience) are concerned. It is at this point, however, that *the right of the need* of reason supervenes as a subjective ground for presupposing and accepting something which

* Thus, to *orientate* oneself in thought means to be guided, in one's conviction of truth, by a subjective principle of reason where objective principles of reason are inadequate.

reason cannot presume to know on objective grounds, and hence for *orientating* ourselves in thought—i.e. in the immeasurable space of the supra-sensory realm which we see as full of utter darkness—purely by means of the need of reason itself.

Since objects of the senses do not exhaust the entire field of possibility, it is possible to think of various things in the supra-sensory world, even if reason feels no need to extend its scope to include them, let alone to assume that they exist. Reason finds enough to do with those causes within the world which reveal themselves to the senses (or which are at least similar in kind to those which are so revealed) without needing to concern itself with the influence of beings of a purely spiritual nature; on the contrary, to assume such an influence would hinder it in its operations. For since we know nothing of the laws by which such beings may operate, whereas we know—or can at least hope to discover—a great deal about the former (i.e. the objects of the senses), a presupposition of this kind would in fact undermine the use of reason. To search for such influences, or to play with such imaginings, is therefore not a need at all, but merely a kind of inquisitiveness which leads only to empty dreaming. But it is quite a different matter with the concept of an original *archetypal being*, both as the supreme intelligence and as the highest good. For not only does our reason itself feel a need to make the *concept* of the unlimited the basis of the concept of everything limited—and hence of all other things;* this need in fact also extends to the assumption that the unlimited *exists*, for without this assumption, our reason can find no satisfactory basis for the contingent existence of worldly things, let alone for the purposiveness and order which are evident to such a remarkable degree in everything (in the small even more than in the large, since the former is closer to us).

---

* Since reason needs to assume reality as given before it can conceive the possibility of anything, and since it regards those differences between things which result from the negations inherent in them simply as limits, it finds itself compelled to take a single possibility—namely that of an unlimited being—as basic and original, and conversely, to regard all other possibilities as derivative. Since even the general possibility of each particular thing must necessarily be present within the totality of existence as a whole—or at least since this is the only way in which the principle of universal determination allows our reason to distinguish between the possible and the actual—we find a subjective ground for this necessity, i.e. a need on the part of our reason itself to base all possibility on the existence of an utterly real (supreme) being. This is the source of the *Cartesian*[n] proof of God's existence, inasmuch as subjective grounds for presupposing something for the use of reason (whose use always remains basically confined to experience) are treated as objective: in other words, *a need is regarded as an insight*. This proof is like all the other proofs of the worthy *Mendelssohn* in his *Morgenstunden* (*Morning Hours*): they accomplish nothing in the way of demonstration. But they are not for this reason by any means useless.

Without the assumption of an intelligent creator, no explanation can be given for this circumstance—or at least no *intelligible* explanation— without falling into complete absurdities; and even if we cannot *prove* that this purposiveness is impossible without an *intelligent first cause*— for we would in that case have sufficient objective grounds for this assertion and would have no need to appeal to subjective ones—we are still, despite our lack of insight, subjectively justified in *assuming* that this is so because reason *needs* to make this assumption. That is, in order to explain the phenomenon in question, reason needs to presuppose something which it can understand; for nothing else to which it can attach a concept is able to remedy this need.

But the need of reason can be regarded as twofold in character: *firstly*, it has a *theoretical* use, and *secondly*, a *practical* use. The first of these has just been mentioned, but it is quite plain that it is merely conditional—that is, we must assume that God exists if we *wish to pass judgement* on the first causes of all contingent things, especially in the ordering of those purposes which are actually present within the world. Much more important, however, is the need of reason in its practical use, because this is unconditional, and because we are compelled to assume that God exists not only if we *wish* to pass judgement, but because we *must pass judgement*. For the purely practical use of reason consists in the formulation of moral laws. All of these lead, however, to the idea of the *highest good* that is possible in the world, in so far as it is attainable by means of *freedom* alone—i.e. to *morality* [*Sittlichkeit*]; and on the other hand, they also lead to something which depends not just on human freedom, but also on *nature*—namely the greatest *happiness*, in so far as its distribution is proportionate to that of morality. Now

For on the one hand, such highly perceptive accounts of the subjective conditions under which our reason operates give us an excellent incentive to perfect our knowledge of this faculty (and in this respect they remain exemplary); and on the other hand, when we are compelled to pass judgement but lack objective grounds for doing so, a conviction of truth based on subjective aspects of the use of reason continues to be of great importance. We must simply refrain from claiming that what is only a necessary *presupposition* is in fact a *free insight*, so as not to show our adversary in *dogmatism* needless weaknesses which he can exploit to our disadvantage. It probably did not occur to Mendelssohn that *dogmatising* in the supra-sensory sphere with the help of pure reason leads straight to philosophical zealotry, and that only a critique of this same faculty of reason can thoroughly cure this evil. It is true that the discipline of the scholastic method (e.g. the Wolffian[12] method which Mendelssohn recommended for this very reason), whereby all concepts must be furnished with definitions and all inferences justified by means of principles, really can put a stop to this mischief for a time; but it can never entirely prevent it. For what right has anyone who himself admits that reason has enjoyed great success in the area in question to prohibit it from going further in the same direction? And where is the boundary at which it must stop?

reason *needs* to assume [the existence of] a *dependent* highest good of this kind, and for this purpose, it must also assume [the existence of] a supreme intelligence as the highest *independent* good. It does so not in order to derive from it the binding authority of the moral laws or the motive for observing them (for they would have no moral value if the motive for obeying them were derived from anything other than the law alone, which is apodictically certain in itself), but only in order to give objective reality to the concept of the highest good—i.e. to prevent the latter, along with morality [*Sittlichkeit*] as a whole, from being regarded merely as an ideal, as would be the case if that [being] whose idea is an inseparable accompaniment to morality [*Moralität*] did not itself exist.

Thus, it was not by *knowledge* but by a felt* *need* of reason that *Mendelssohn* (unwittingly) orientated himself in speculative thought. Such guidance is provided not by an objective principle of reason—i.e. a principle based on insight—but by a purely subjective principle (or maxim) of the only use of reason which the limits of reason itself allow—i.e. a principle based on need. It is this principle which, *alone* and *in itself*, constitutes the sole determinant of our judgement concerning the existence of the supreme being, and its use as a means of orientation in attempts to speculate on this same subject is purely contingent. Thus, Mendelssohn was certainly mistaken in believing that such speculation was nevertheless capable, alone and in itself, of settling all these questions by means of demonstration. The necessity of the former means [of orientation] could be established only after the inadequacy of the latter [means of demonstration] had been fully admitted; and Mendelssohn's perspicacity would eventually have led him to make this admission if he had lived longer and been able to retain that mental agility, more commonly associated with youth, which readily allows us to alter old and accustomed ways of thinking in the light of changes in the state of knowledge. Nevertheless, he still deserves credit for having insisted that the ultimate touchstone of the reliability of a judgement, in this case as in all other cases, is to be found *in reason alone*, whether the latter is guided by insight in its choice of propositions or merely by need and by the maxim of its own advantage. He described the latter use of reason as 'ordinary human reason'; for this always looks primarily to its own interest, whereas we

* Reason does not feel. It perceives its own deficiency and produces a feeling of need through the *cognitive impulse*. The same applies in this case as in the case of moral feeling, which is not the source of moral law, for this is entirely the product of reason; on the contrary, moral feeling is itself produced or occasioned by moral laws and hence by reason, because the active yet free will needs specific grounds [on which to act].

must already have abandoned the path of nature before we can forget this interest and examine concepts in a leisurely and objective manner simply in order to extend our knowledge and irrespective of any need to do so.

But the expression '*a pronouncement of healthy reason*' still remains ambiguous in the present context, for it can be taken to mean either a judgement based on *rational insight* (as in Mendelssohn's own misunderstanding) or a judgement based on *rational inspiration* (as the author of the *Resultate* appears to think). It will therefore be necessary to give this source of judgement another name, and none is more appropriate than '**rational belief**'. Every belief, even of a historical kind, must of course be *rational* (for reason is always the ultimate touchstone of truth); but a rational belief is one which is based on no other data than those which are inherent in *pure* reason. Now all *belief* is a conviction of truth which is subjectively adequate but *consciously* regarded as objectively inadequate; it is therefore treated as the opposite of *knowledge*. On the other hand, if something is considered true on objective grounds which are nevertheless consciously regarded as inadequate, and is therefore no more than an *opinion*, this *opinion* can nevertheless eventually become *knowledge* if it is gradually corroborated by further grounds of the same kind. If, on the other hand, the grounds for considering something to be true are by nature devoid of all objective validity, the belief can never become knowledge by any exercise of reason. The historical belief that a certain event has taken place (for example, the death of a great man, as reported in various letters) *can become knowledge* if the event in question (the funeral, will, etc.) is reported by the local authorities. It is therefore perfectly consistent that something should be considered historically true purely on the strength of testimonies, as in the belief that there is a city called Rome and the fact that someone who has never been there should nevertheless be able to say '*I know*' and not just '*I believe* that Rome exists'. On the other hand, a purely *rational belief* can never be transformed into *knowledge* by any natural data of reason and experience, for in this case, the grounds on which it is held to be true are (and always will be, so long as we are human beings) purely subjective; in other words, reason has an essential need simply *to presuppose*, rather than to demonstrate, the existence of a supreme being. This need of reason to be used in a *theoretical* way which it itself finds satisfactory would be nothing other than a purely *rational hypothesis*, i.e. an opinion which is adequate on subjective grounds as a basis for considering something to be true, simply because one cannot ever expect to find grounds other than these on which *to explain the effects* in question, although reason needs to have a means of explaining them. On the other hand, a *rational belief* which is based on the need to use reason for *practical* purposes could be described as a *postulate* of reason; for although it is not an insight capable of fulfilling all the logical requirements for certainty, this conviction of truth is not inferior in degree to knowledge* (provided that the person who holds it is of sound moral character), even if it is totally different from it in kind.

Thus, a purely rational belief is the signpost or compass by means of which the speculative thinker can orientate himself on his rational wanderings in the field of supra-sensory objects, while the man of ordinary but (morally) healthy reason can use it to plan his course, for both theoretical and practical purposes, in complete conformity with the whole end of his destiny; and this same rational belief must also be made the basis of every other belief, and indeed of every revelation.

The *concept* of God and even the conviction of his *existence* is to be found only in reason as its exclusive source, and it cannot first enter our minds either through inspiration or through any external communication, however great the authority from which the latter may come. If I experience an immediate intuition of such a kind as cannot originate in nature (in so far as the latter is known to me), a concept of God must furnish guidance as to whether the phenomenon in question is also compatible with all the essential attributes of a deity. Although I quite fail to see how it is possible for any phenomenon to represent, even in terms of quality, what can always only be thought but never intuited, this much at least is clear: before I can judge whether the phenomenon which acts internally or externally upon my feelings is God, I must measure it against my rational concept of God in order to decide not whether it corresponds to the latter, but merely whether it does not contradict it. In the same way, even if nothing is found to contradict that concept in the whole manner in which the phenomenon in question made itself immediately apparent to me, this phenomenon, intuition, or immediate revelation—or whatever else one wishes to call a representation of this kind—would never prove the existence of a being

* *Firmness* of belief requires a consciousness that the belief is *unalterable*. Now I can be wholly certain that no one will be able to refute the proposition 'There is a God'; for where could anyone attain such an insight? Rational belief is therefore not the same as historical belief, for in the latter case, it is always possible that opposite evidence may be found, and one must always reserve the right to change one's opinion in the light of increased knowledge of the matters in question.

whose concept (unless it is imprecisely defined and hence liable to be associated with every possible illusion) requires that it be of *infinite* magnitude to distinguish it from all created things; but no experience or intuition whatsoever can be adequate to this concept, or ever prove the existence of such a being in an unambiguous manner. Thus, no intuition can ever convince anyone *initially* of the existence of the supreme being; the rational belief must come first, and it is possible that certain phenomena or revelations may then give us cause to enquire whether we are justified in ascribing divine status to whatever speaks or manifests itself to us, and that these phenomena may be found to confirm the belief in question.

Consequently, if we deny reason its due right to make the *initial* pronouncement in matters relating to supra-sensory objects such as the existence of God and the world hereafter, the way is wide open for every kind of zealotry, superstition, and even atheism. And yet in the controversy between Jacobi and Mendelssohn, everything seems calculated to overthrow the authority of reason in this way. I am not sure whether this affects only *rational insight* and knowledge (in view of the supposed strength of speculation), or whether even *rational belief* is also rejected in favour of an alternative belief which anyone can fashion as he pleases. One is almost inclined to draw the latter inference on discovering that *Spinoza's* concept of God is said to be alone consistent* with all the principles of reason but nevertheless worthy of

---

* It is almost impossible to understand how the above-mentioned scholars were able to find support for Spinozism in the *Critique of Pure Reason*. The *Critique* clips the wings of dogmatism completely as far as knowledge of supra-sensory objects is concerned, and Spinozism is so dogmatic in this respect that it rivals even mathematics in the rigour of its demonstrations. The *Critique* demonstrates that the table of pure concepts of the understanding must contain all the materials of pure thought; yet Spinozism speaks of thoughts which themselves think, and hence of an accidental property which nevertheless exists simultaneously in its own right as a subject—a concept which has no place in the human understanding and which is also incompatible with it. The *Critique* shows that, in order to assert the possibility of a being which is itself an object of thought, it is not nearly enough that its concept should be free from contradiction (although it remains permissible to assume this possibility at a later stage if the need arises). Spinozism,[13] however, claims to have perceived the impossibility of a being the idea of which consists solely of pure concepts of the understanding which have simply been detached from all conditions of sense-experience, and in which it is therefore impossible ever to discover a contradiction; yet it is unable to adduce any evidence whatsoever in support of this extravagant assumption. This is precisely why Spinozism leads directly to zealotry. Conversely, the only sure means of rooting zealotry out completely is by delimiting the faculty of pure reason in the manner described above.—Similarly, another scholar detects *scepticism* in the *Critique of Pure Reason*, although the whole intention of this work is to reach firm and definite conclusions on the scope of our *a priori* knowledge. He likewise discovers a *dialectic* in these critical investigations, although their whole aim is to resolve and eliminate for good that

rejection. For although it is perfectly in keeping with rational belief to concede that speculative reason itself is unable to comprehend even the *possibility* of a being such as we must imagine God to be, to argue that reason might even be able to comprehend the *impossibility* of a given object, but that it might also be able to recognise this object's reality from other sources, is quite incompatible with any belief whatsoever and certainly with the conviction that such an object truly exists.

Men of intellectual ability and breadth of mind! I venerate your talents and cherish your human feelings. But have you also fully considered what you are doing, and what your attacks on reason are likely to lead to? You doubtless wish that *freedom of thought* should remain inviolate; for without it, even the free flights of your genius would soon come to an end. Let us consider what must naturally become of this freedom of thought if a procedure such as you have initiated should become generally accepted.

Opposition to freedom of thought comes firstly from *civil coercion*. We do admittedly say that, whereas a higher authority may deprive us of freedom of *speech* or of *writing*, it cannot deprive us of freedom of *thought*. But how much and how accurately would we *think* if we did not think, so to speak, in community with others to whom we *communicate* our thoughts and who communicate their thoughts to us! We may therefore conclude that the same external constraint which deprives people of the freedom to *communicate* their thoughts in public also removes their freedom of *thought*, the one treasure which remains to us amidst all the burdens of civil life, and which alone offers us a means of overcoming all the evils of this condition.

Secondly, freedom of thought is also used to denote the opposite of that *moral constraint* whereby some citizens, without the use of external force, set themselves up as the guardians of others in religious matters, and succeed in outlawing all rational enquiry—not by argument, but by prescribing articles of faith backed up by a nervous fear of the *dangers of independent investigation*, impressing these articles from an early stage on the minds of those concerned.

Thirdly, freedom of thought also signifies the subjection of reason to no laws other than those *which it imposes on itself*; and its opposite is the maxim of the **lawless use** of reason (in order that it may, as the

dialectic in which pure reason inevitably becomes trapped and entangled when everyone uses it in a dogmatic manner. The Neo-Platonists, who called themselves Eclectics because they managed to discover their own conceits throughout the works of earlier authors after they had themselves imported them into these, proceeded in exactly the same way; so in this respect, there is nothing new under the sun.

genius imagines, see further than it does when restricted by laws). Naturally enough, the result of this is that, if reason does not wish to be subject to the law which it imposes on itself, it must bow beneath the yoke of laws which someone else imposes upon it; for nothing—not even the greatest absurdity—can continue to operate for long without some kind of law. Thus, the inevitable result of *self-confessed* lawlessness in thinking (i.e. of emancipation from the restrictions of reason) is this: freedom of thought is thereby ultimately forfeited and, since the fault lies not with misfortune, for example, but with genuine presumption, this freedom is in the true sense of the word *thrown away*.

The sequence of events is roughly as follows. The *genius* is at first delighted with its daring flights, having cast aside the thread by which reason formerly guided it. It soon captivates others in turn with its authoritative pronouncements and great expectations, and now appears to have set itself up on a throne on which slow and ponderous reason looked so out of place; nevertheless, it still continues to use the language of reason. It then adopts the maxim that the supreme legislation of reason is invalid, a maxim which we ordinary mortals describe as **zealotry**, but which those favourites of benevolent nature describe as *illumination*. Meanwhile, a confusion of tongues must soon arise among them, for while reason alone can issue instructions which are valid for everyone, each individual now follows his own inspiration. The ultimate consequence of all this is that inner inspirations are inevitably transformed into facts confirmed by external evidence, and traditions which were originally freely chosen eventually become *binding* documents; in a word, the complete subjugation of reason to facts—i.e. **superstition**—must ensue, for this at least can be reduced to a *legal form* so that peace can then be restored.

But since human reason nevertheless continues to strive for freedom, the first use which it makes of its long unaccustomed liberty, once it has broken its bonds, must degenerate into misuse, into a presumptuous confidence in the independence of its own powers from every restriction, and into a conviction of the sole authority of speculative reason which accepts only what can be justified on *objective* grounds and by dogmatic conviction, but brashly dismisses everything else. Now the maxim of the independence of reason from its *own need* (i.e. the renunciation of rational belief) is called **unbelief**. But this is not the same thing as unbelief in the historical sense, for it is impossible to think of the latter as intentional and hence to imagine that those who espouse it are responsible for their action (for everyone must believe a fact, so long as it is sufficiently well attested, just as much as a mathematical demonstration, whether they wish to or not). On the contrary, it is a **rational unbelief**, an undesirable state of mind which first deprives the moral laws of all their power to motivate the heart, and eventually even deprives them of all authority, so giving rise to the attitude known as **libertinism** (i.e. the principle of no longer acknowledging any duty). At this point, the authorities intervene to ensure that civil affairs are not themselves plunged into complete disorder; and since they regard the most expeditious and forceful measures as the most appropriate, they may even abolish freedom of thought altogether and make thought itself, like other professions, subject to the laws of the land. Hence freedom of thought, if it tries to act independently even of the laws of reason, eventually destroys itself.

Friends of the human race and of all that it holds most sacred! Accept whatever seems most credible to you after careful and honest examination, whether it is a matter of facts or of rational arguments; but do not deny reason that prerogative which makes it the greatest good on earth, namely its right to be the ultimate touchstone of truth.* If you fail in this respect, you will be unworthy of this freedom and will surely forfeit it; and you will bring the same misfortune down upon those other guiltless souls who would otherwise have been inclined to employ their freedom *lawfully* and hence in a manner conducive to the world's best interests!

---

* *To think for oneself* means to look within oneself (i.e. in one's own reason) for the supreme touchstone of truth; and the maxim of thinking for oneself at all times is **enlightenment**. Now this requires less effort than is imagined by those who equate enlightenment with *knowledge*, for enlightenment consists rather in a negative principle in the use of one's cognitive powers, and those who are exceedingly rich in knowledge are often least enlightened in their use of it. To employ one's own reason means simply to ask oneself, whenever one is urged to accept something, whether one finds it possible to transform the reason for accepting it, or the rule which follows from what is accepted, into a universal principle governing the use of one's reason. Everyone can apply this test to himself; and when it is carried out, superstition and zealotry will be seen to vanish immediately, even if the individual in question does not have nearly enough knowledge to refute them on objective grounds. For he is merely employing the maxim of the *self-preservation* of reason. It is consequently very easy to lay the basis of enlightenment in *individual subjects* by means of education; one must merely begin at an early stage to accustom young minds to this reflection. To enlighten an *era*, however, is a very protracted process; for there are numerous external obstacles which either preclude that mode of education or make it more difficult to implement.

Postscript

Kant's standing as a political thinker has been substantially enhanced in the English-speaking world since this volume went to the printers just over two decades ago. More and more scholars are willing to rank him among the leading figures in the history of political thought. John Rawls's important and much discussed treatise *A Theory of Justice* is indebted to him,[1] and that has certainly made an impact. (Even legal historians and jurists have taken note of his writings, but to discuss their findings would go beyond the scope of this edition.)[2] The secondary literature on his political thought has grown appreciably, and not only in Germany where research on Kant flourishes as always. Yet much of this writing, perhaps inevitably, covers well-tilled ground; there has been no revolution in the interpretation of Kant's political thought. Nevertheless, in view of this growing interest, it is perhaps justifiable not only to raise some new issues but also to elaborate some of the features which were mentioned only briefly, or merely alluded to, in my original introduction. Some of the following remarks are of a general nature, and others refer to specific issues. For ease of reference, they are grouped under the following headings: 'the nature of rational discourse in politics'; 'the nature of mature political judgement'; 'property as the basis of the legal order'; 'morality and politics'; 'the republican constitution: representation and the separation of powers'; 'Kant and the French Revolution'; 'Kant's rejection of the right of rebellion'; 'the rejection of the right of rebellion and twentieth-century totalitarianism'; 'the limits of obedience to goverment'; 'the Prussian context'; and 'Kant's argument against world government'.

---

[1] (Cambridge, Mass., 1971), *passim.*, but cf. particularly pp. 251–7, 'The Kantian Interpretation of Justice as Fairness'.
[2] Cf. for instance the essays by various scholars in *Columbia Law Review*, LXXXVII, 1987, 421–591; cf. also Charles Taylor, 'Kant's Theory of Freedom', *Philosophy and the Human Sciences. Philosophical Papers*, II (Cambridge, 1985), p. 337 who emphasises Kant's impact on Rawls and on Ronald Dworkin, *Taking Rights Seriously* (London, 1977).

I

THE NATURE OF RATIONAL DISCOURSE IN POLITICS

To tackle the more general issues first: Hans Saner, in his challenging, and, on the whole, well-received study *Kants Weg vom Krieg zum Frieden. Widerstreit und Einheit. Wege zu Kants politischem Denken*[1] (which has been translated into English with the somewhat misleading title *Kant's Political Thought. Its Origins and Development*),[2] has argued that Kant's metaphors indicate a profound interest in politics from the very beginnings of his academic career; he points out that, from 1755 onwards, Kant continuously uses images of war and peace in his writings. Saner overstates a good case; for metaphors have to be interpreted with much care. To draw valid inferences from them, other evidence is usually needed. There is, as stated in my introduction, no overt reference to politics in Kant's unpublished writings before 1763, and none in his published writings until later. Nor did he lecture on Public Law before that date. But even if there were allusions or references to politics in his (published) pre-critical writings from their earliest stage, they would be of little weight in comparison with what he has to say about politics in the *Critique of Pure Reason*, where he produced the most incisive formulation[3] of what I have called 'the universal [Kantian] principle of politics'.[4] However, there is in the first Critique a further passage, to which I have not previously referred, which throws much light on his attitude to politics. For here, political metaphors are used to illustrate the very manner in which politics ought, in Kant's view, to be tackled, namely by an appeal to the principles established by reason. Here he points to a mature approach to politics which does not conflict with morality and yet is also practical. It concerns the fundamental problem of what role reason can play in politics. The passage in question occurs in the final part of the second edition of the *Critique of Pure Reason*, in the section entitled 'The Discipline of Pure Reason with Respect to its Polemical Use'.[5] At the very outset of this section,

---

[1] (Munich, 1967).
[2] (Chicago and London, 1973). It deals mainly with Kant's strategy as a polemicist, as Patrick Riley, *Kant's Political Philosophy* (Totowa, N.J., 1983), p. 158 points out.
[3] Cf. *AA* III, 247f.; *AA* IV, 201; cf. p. 191 above.   [4] Cf. p. 23 above.
[5] Cf. *AA* III, 491–5. My attention was drawn to this passage, which appears in the second edition (1787) only, by Onora O'Neill in the first of her penetrating Tucker–Read lectures in the University of Bristol in 1986. Cf. also her stimulating essay

Kant states that, in all its enterprises, reason must subject itself to criticism. Critical investigation is open to all, and reason's status can impose no restrictions on it. For the very existence of reason is based on freedom and therefore rules out any kind of despotism. The Idea of freedom itself, although a transcendental Idea belonging to the realm of noumena, is indeed the only one for whose existence we can find evidence in the phenomenal world, namely in our ability to act morally. Consequently, any discussion of conflicting views must take place in an arena where freedom prevails. Since reason must always be open to argument, it must not seek to subject itself needlessly to censorship—that would be folly. Nor ought it be subjected to it—that would be unjust. Reason must be able to carry out its task of seeking to refute all statements incapable of being justified at the bar of the rightful principles of politics.

The court before which disputes ought to be argued and settled is that of reason itself. It is not, however, a court of justice where a judge can hand down a verdict from above, but rather one where arguments are examined and a conclusion is reached by the exercise of thought. Reason must seek to establish the first principles on which the criteria for settling political disputes are to be based. To that end, argument and counter-argument are necessary until, in the end, the better argument, based on the rightful principles of politics and arrived at by the use of reason, will prevail. Only by way of discussion before the court of reason can we avoid 'war' (Kant expressly uses this term, emphasised in print by italics). By turning away from reason, particularly by the use of force, at best a temporary truce can be achieved; for any peace which results from the victory (Kant specifically uses this term, which here denotes the use of force) of one of the contending sides is no real peace at all, but an armistice leading to further endless wars. Only too often, both sides will claim victory or a peace will be imposed by one side which later turns out to have been a Pyrrhic victory.

By the right use of reason, disputes are settled in a different way. They are resolved by argument in a manner practised in a court of law which, as the German term *Prozeß* (which may mean either a process or a law-suit) indicates, is a continuous and consistent mode of arguing

---

'Kantian Politics. I: The Public Use of Reason', *PTh*, XIV (1986), 523–35; cf. also Friedrich Kaulbach, *Studien zur späten Rechtsphilosophie Kants und ihrer transzendentalen Methode* (Würzburg, 1982), p. 130, who points out that, in Kant's view, the criticism of pure reason is the only genuine court of justice capable of judging problems discerned by itself.

and seeks to go to the root of the disputes by unearthing their under-lying principles. It is 'an open-ended commitment to reasoned debate'.[1] It is, indeed, our moral duty to discover the better argument and, once we are convinced by it, to concede its rightness. Thus, reason is able to establish perpetual peace which, as Kant emphasised, is not a definitive condition ever likely to be attained on this earth, but a goal to be striven after and approximated to ever more closely.

Kant's metaphorical use of the terms 'war' and 'peace' in the *Critique of Pure Reason* foreshadows the thrust of his political thought which he develops more fully in the political writings printed in this volume. It makes clear that, according to the principles of reason, war, or indeed the use of any coercion other than within the framework of a legal order, is an illegitimate instrument of politics. Political problems cannot be settled by force, and the use of force can be sanctioned by law only when the principles according to which coercion is to be exercised by the state have been settled by rational argument. Consequently, the primary principles of politics have to be defined. Otherwise, a dogmatic approach to politics prevails, and this amounts to despotism. In other words, debate or discussion before a court of law constituted by reason makes it possible for dogmatic views and false theories to be rejected in favour of rational views and better theories so that, as Karl Popper puts it, 'we try to let our false theories die in our stead'.[2]

Discussion before the court of reason entails publicity. It must be freely and equally open to all. This implies toleration which, according to Goethe, was the watchword of the age for the best minds of the day.[3] But Kant's conception of toleration does not spring from contemporary fashion; it is rooted in the very core of his critical philosophy. It assumes that communication is—or at least ought to be—in keeping with the standards set by reason, and that it is therefore, in principle, capable of being understood by others, not merely by the initiated or by a select few, but by everyone who has attained maturity of mind. Rational thought must therefore be capable of being disseminated in

---

[1] Cf. T. J. Reed, 'The Stay-at-Home Man of the World', *Times Higher Education Supplement* (21 June 1985), No. 659, 15; cf. also Karl Jaspers, 'Kant zum Ewigen Frieden', in Jaspers, *Aneignung und Polemik. Gesammelte Aufsätze*, ed. Hans Saner (Munich, 1968), pp. 227ff., which also emphasises Kant's open, undogmatic approach.
[2] Cf. 'Conversation with Karl Popper', *Modern British Philosophy*, ed. Bryan Magee (London, 1971), p. 73.
[3] Cf. his autobiography *Dichtung und Wahrheit* (*Poetry and Truth*), III, 12; Goethe, *Werke* (Hamburg, 1949–64) IX, 512.

public. Self-scrutiny in private is never sufficient. For only if thought is publicised can it be open to criticism. As Kant puts it in *What Is Orientation in Thinking?* 'freedom of thought ... signifies the subjection of reason to no laws other than those *which it imposes on itself*; and its opposite is the maxim of the **lawless use** of reason ... If reason does not wish to be subject to the law which it imposes on itself, it must bow beneath the yoke of laws which someone else imposes upon it ...'.[1] But communication (or discussion) ought also to be based on an attempt to attain truth and to avoid falsehood. For it is not enough to communicate one's thoughts in public—falsehoods can, after all, be spread widely by shouting them loudly and repeatedly from the rooftops; the argument must be open to public criticism of the most rigorous kind, that is, to criticism in accordance with the standard set by reason. Public communication also means that any pronouncement based on an authority other than reason can be scrutinised and criticised by those who are not subject to that authority. Kant also argues against falsehood, prejudice, zealotry, misguided enthusiasm, superstition, dogmatism, confused thinking and irrationality of any kind; but he does not seek to have irrational or intolerant views suppressed. They must, of course, be rigorously and publicly criticised. On the other hand, the lawful use of reason must be protected.

There must, then, be standards for the proper use of reason. In the *Critique of Judgement* Kant sets out three maxims on which public discussion ought to be based. The first is the maxim of '*unprejudiced thought*'[2] or 'reason which is never *passive*'.[3] It requires one 'to think for oneself',[4] that is, to use one's reason independently. To do that, one must, as he says in *What Is Orientation in Thinking*, 'ask oneself, whenever one is urged to accept something, whether one finds it possible to transform the reason for accepting it, or the rule which follows from what is accepted, into a universal principle governing the use of one's reason'.[5] In other words, to think for oneself is 'the supreme touchstone of truth'.[6] It leads away from superstition to '*enlightenment*'. If we employ that maxim we proceed modestly and do not seek to know what is 'beyond our understanding'.[7] However, since we are always tempted to transgress the boundaries to which our understanding is subject and since others will always encourage us to do so, assuring us that it is

---

[1] *AA* VIII, 145; cf. p. 247 above.   [2] I, 2, § 40; *AA* V, 294.   [3] *Ibid.*   [4] *Ibid.*
[5] *AA* VIII, 146f.; cf. p. 249 above.   [6] *AA* VIII, 146; cf. p. 249 above.
[7] *Critique of Judgement*, I, 2, § 40; *AA* V, 294.

within our ability to go beyond them, we are likely to falter again and again. Enlightenment is, therefore, an arduous and slow process.

The second maxim is that of '*enlarged* thought'¹ which requires us to overcome our narrow approach to the understanding of any matter so that we may acquire 'the mental habit ... of detaching ourselves from the subjective and personal conditions of our judgement, which cramp the mind of so many others, and reflect upon our judgement from a *universal point of view* which we can do only by adopting the point of view of others'.² The third maxim is that of '*consistent* thought'. It is 'the hardest to attain'.³ Indeed, to attain it we have to combine the first two maxims and observe them so steadfastly that they become second nature to us.⁴

If these principles are observed in public discussion, the public use of reason can provide a yardstick by which we can judge whether and to what extent political arrangements are moving towards a just political society. Moreover, it is the only way in which citizens can properly debate political questions in accordance with the standards set by reason and determine whether a state is governed in accordance with (just) principles of politics.

It was natural for Kant to believe in the need for public discussion of politics. After all, he was a scholar and scientist. The very nature of both scholarship and science requires the free public dissemination of knowledge, for censorship is alien to any scholarly or scientific discourse, and criticism is essential. False theories must be eliminated if progress is to be made.⁵ Moreover, the growth of knowledge is perhaps the most striking feature of history.⁶ Hence the free public expression of opinion is essential. Similarly, political and social abuses cannot be removed unless they are exposed and shown to run counter to the right principles of politics. Since those in power only too frequently tend to cover up inefficiency and incompetence, corruption and evil conduct, unhindered public criticism is imperative. It is in fact in the ruler's interest to permit it, though he may not be aware that this is so; for it

¹ *Critique of Judgement*, I, 2, § 40; *AA* v, 294f.   ² *Ibid.*   ³ *Ibid.*
⁴ On this issue cf. also O'Neill, 'Kantian Politics, I: The Public Use of Reason', *PTh*, XIV (1986), 523–35 to which the argument in the preceding paragraph is indebted.
⁵ Cf. Karl R. Popper, *Logik der Forschung* (Vienna, 1935) (Engl. trs. *The Logic of Scientific Discovery* (London, 1959)) for the classic account of this view.
⁶ Cf. Karl R. Popper, 'A Pluralist Approach to the Philosophy of History', *Roads to Freedom. Essays in Honour of Friedrich A. von Hayek*, ed. Erich Streissler (London, 1969), pp. 183ff. and p. 200.

increases the possibility and frequency of reform and thus renders rebellion less likely, thereby ensuring stability of government, the rule of law, and peace at home and abroad.

II

THE NATURE OF MATURE POLITICAL JUDGEMENT

To be willing to accept, and engage in, the public use of reason is a sign of a mature, or rather a maturing, attitude of mind. The term 'mature' or 'maturity' is another metaphor used by Kant to great purpose (indeed, he uses a whole string of metaphors to describe the transition from immaturity to the maturity necessary to enlightenment).[1] However, maturity is not a definite condition for Kant, but a never-ceasing process of further development. Men become truly enlightened only when, in the realm of politics, they are able to stand on their own feet and make their own decisions. No one else, whether it be a parent or any other person, let alone the powers that be, has a right to treat other adults as if they were minors. Everyone is entitled to attain his own independence, i.e. to become an autonomous individual.

It is indeed a moral duty for men to learn to use their reason independently and to refrain from coercing others arbitrarily. In so far as they fail to do so, they have not yet achieved maturity and are guilty of lacking the spirit and courage to do what they ought to do. It is wrong, in principle, for anyone, particularly for a ruler, to deny anyone else the right to achieve maturity. There may indeed be practical reasons, Kant concedes, for delaying that process, but to claim that it can be put off for ever is a heinous wrong.[2] For reason—and this is the crux of the matter—is necessarily exercised within a social context. It is therefore a duty for everyone, particularly the ruler or government, to make and promote political arrangements which will allow each person to use his reason; but this is possible only in a state which is organised according to the principles of reason, that is, in a republican state (in Kant's terminology).

Undoubtedly, when Kant writes about the rights of individuals he

[1] Cf. pp. 54f. above; cf. also Reed 'The Stay-at-Home Man of the World', 15.
[2] *Religion within the Limits of Reason Alone*, IV, § 4; *AA* VI, 188. Kant calls it 'interference with the *prerogative* of the Godhead itself'.

has, like many of his contemporaries, a very narrow conception, from the point of view of our age, of what kind of individuals can be expected to achieve maturity and autonomy of political judgement. To exclude the majority of the population, wage-earners, employees of any kind (except professors and senior civil servants, and presumably ministers of the crown and courtiers), convicted criminals, and all women, reveals a regrettably myopic view of human capacities, though it must be conceded that, in principle, Kant believes that everyone should have the opportunity to achieve independence. But nowhere does he suggest that women have this innate, inalienable capacity. That this restriction is unacceptable today need hardly be stressed. Of course, the line must be drawn somewhere, as the very term 'maturity' implies; to take an extreme example, babes-in-arms are, by definition, excluded.

Kant's principal concern in politics was with the individual—and here he expresses the conviction of the Enlightenment that all individuals should have an equal right to live freely and independently. From Rousseau, he had learnt that it was a duty 'to honour mankind' and one could do so only if one set about 'restoring the rights of mankind'.[1] And that was a duty for everyone. But rights have to be safeguarded, and only the law can safeguard everyone's rights. But law implies coercion. For Kant, the problem of political theory is how to legitimise coercion, and that means discerning how law can be combined with freedom. For coercion may appear unacceptable until it is understood that freedom is not possible unless all individuals are subjected to coercion by a universally applicable system of law which is consistently executed.[2] In order to accept this system as legitimate, citizens must know that all laws are public and can be scrutinised in public by everyone without their incurring the risk of being oppressed, persecuted or even killed by the powers that be. On the other hand, we must also realise that, by not obeying the law, we violate everyone's innate and 'lawful' freedom and everyone's fundamental right to live in civil society.[3]

---

[1] *AA* xx, 44.
[2] Cf. T. W. Pogge, 'Kant's Theory of Justice', *KS* LXXIX (1988), 407–33 who emphasises the importance which Kant attached to consistency in the execution of the law.
[3] Cf John E. Atwell, *Ends and Principles in Kant's Moral Thought* (Dordrecht, Boston, Lancaster, 1986), pp. 172, 177.

III

PROPERTY AS THE BASIS OF THE LEGAL ORDER

For Kant, law is essential since everyone in this world has something or other which he can call his own and which has to be protected from interference by others. In the state of nature, any external possession is only provisional, since it lacks the protection of law. For to own something means to be able to prevent others from owning it or interfering with it. We have to live in a state in order to have this acquired right protected. It is the state's task to establish law so that whatever an individual may have owned in the state of nature can become lawfully his. However, in Kant's view, it is not the state's task to own property or to revise property rights, even with a view to achieving economic equality. Indeed, in the realm of economic life, inequalities will necessarily prevail. But economic power gives no one a right to coerce others—only the state representing the united will of the people has the right to do that. Just as feudal obligations cannot be justified, so the abuse of economic power is impermissible; for a contract to supply services ought to be freely entered into. But it is not the business of the state to secure the wellbeing or happiness of its citizens, who must be able to seek their happiness within the framework of a legal order in accordance with such 'talent, industry and good fortune'[1] as may be their share. Man does not have a right to economic wellbeing, just as he does not have a right to happiness. He has only the right to pursue economic wellbeing, just as he has a right to the pursuit of happiness.

In the light of this attitude it might be thought that Kant favours owners of property.[2] But it is important not to oversimplify Kant's attitude to the ownership of property. Admittedly, he did not grant active civil rights to everyone, but only to men of independence. He implied that everyone should have the opportunity of becoming independent. Moreover, independence for him did not rest in the actual ownership of property but could also be found in the sphere of work. Nevertheless, he does not tackle the problem of the abuse of economic power which can grant political power to men of wealth, although he does make it clear that economic coercion is wrong, for a contract to

[1] *AA* VIII, 292; cf. p. 75 above.
[2] Cf. Susan Meld Shell, *The Rights of Reason. A Study of Kant's Philosophy and Politics* (Toronto, Buffalo, London, 1980) and Mary Gregor, 'Kant's Approach to Constitutionalism', in *Constitutionalism. The Philosophical Dimension*, ed. Alan S. Rosenbaum, Contributions to Legal Studies, 46 (New York, Westcott, Conn., London, 1988), pp. 69–87 for helpful accounts of the role of property in Kant's political thought.

supply services ought to be freely entered into. But we should not expect Kant to have anticipated fully all those problems which have come to the fore only in the nineteenth and twentieth centuries. Nor does he use the term 'social justice', which would indeed have been an alien concept for him. Justice entails establishing minimum legal and political conditions which allow individuals to pursue their economic aspirations and wellbeing, but not a reshaping of society by way of allocating or redistributing wealth in accordance with a plan authorised by the state. A minimum of economic security is, however, implied, although its extent cannot be defined by an appeal to *a priori* principles; for it is bound to be a matter of empirical judgement.

IV

MORALITY AND POLITICS

Political justice implies that men can take moral decisions unhindered by government action or legislation to which they could not in principle have given their free consent. (Whether they have actually given it or not is in this context irrelevant.) Morality is essentially and exclusively a personal matter. No one can absolve a person from the burden of taking moral decisions. Politics ought therefore to be concerned with developing a legal framework which will allow individuals to lead a moral life and thus be true to their own innate humanity. Reason can be their only guide. Since they are human, they will strive for happiness, and they have a right to do so. But the goal of happiness can never be an adequate guide to political action, as reason is incapable of establishing objective criteria by which the path to happiness can be definitely mapped out.

Republicanism at home and abroad does not make men better—that would require a new creation. It merely brings about a state of affairs in which it will, in the end, be easier to perform moral actions because they come less and less into conflict with the law or with government actions. 'The Kantian republic respects the liberty ('freedom under law') that is essential to moral activity, enforces some of the ends (though never the incentives) of morality and provides a context of legal security within which acting from good will is not benevolent folly ...'.[1] Or, in other words, the right political conditions are necessary in order to create an ethical community in which all men will act

[1] Riley, *Kant's Political Philosophy*, p. 99.

morally, and in which the highest good can accordingly be realised, or rather approximated to.[1]

V

THE REPUBLICAN CONSTITUTION: REPRESENTATION AND SEPARATION OF POWERS

Moral decisions are taken by individuals and not by the people as a whole. Indeed, Kant was never a populist, and he distrusted direct rule by the people. It would conflict with the principle of the separation of powers, for it would allow the sovereign (people) both to legislate and to execute the law—and in Kant's view, this would amount to despotism. Besides, it might also interfere with the public use of reason. (Apparently he did not have any use for plebiscites, which have worked well in Switzerland, although they have been abused elsewhere by tyrants since the days of the French Revolution.)

Instead of direct rule by the people—which for Kant amounted to despotism—he advocated representation. A representative assembly can provide a forum for rational debate. However, he does not in any way define how representation is to be achieved, nor does he lay down any criteria which would allow us to judge the adequacy of such representation.[2] He appears to imply that representatives are less likely to be swayed by demagogy, empty rhetoric and zealotry, let alone fanaticism, all of which Kant abhorred as the rule of unreason, than the people as a whole. For Kant, representation should prevail only in the legislature, and not in the executive or judiciary, for otherwise there would be several masters, each claiming superior rights and therefore necessarily engaged in perpetual conflict. Separation of the three powers is, however, essential. Indeed, it is implied by the Idea of the social contract and thus by the Idea of the state; for it is based on an *a priori* principle of practical reason. Kant expresses this conception in a syllogism whose major premiss is that the sovereign legislator makes the 'law' and whose minor premiss is that the executor of the law issues

[1] Cf. Yirmiahu Yovel, *Kant and the Philosophy of History* (Princeton, N.J., 1980), pp. 196ff., who discusses this point.
[2] Cf. also my comments on pp. 30f. above about the obscurity in Kant's treatment of this issue.

the 'command' to act in accordance with the law.[1] The conclusion is that the judiciary imposes the verdict (or 'legal decision') on the rights and wrongs of each individual case. Consequently, it would be illegitimate on *a priori* grounds for any one of these three powers to usurp the function of any of the other two; only if the separation of powers is strictly observed can the rights of the citizens be safeguarded and despotism be avoided.

Kant's attested enthusiasm for the American Revolution and his criticism of Britain during the War of American Independence may well have influenced his belief that the British constitution permitted despotism to prevail. (That eighteenth-century British government, whether Whig or Tory, had in fact only too frequently manipulated elections to the House of Commons cannot be disputed, but there were checks on royal or cabinet power, though not of course so patent and decisive as those provided by the American constitution of 1787.)[2] Kant's views were broadly in agreement with the aims of the founding fathers of the American constitution, as well as with those of the French revolutionaries of 1789 and of the men who framed the French constitution of 1791. (That subsequent events in France took quite a different course in no way invalidates his theory.)

VI

KANT AND THE FRENCH REVOLUTION

It has been argued that Kant rules out constitutional change.[3] But this view calls for qualification. Admittedly, he rejects change from one outward form of the state as historically developed (be it autocracy, aristocracy or democracy) as illegitimate,[4] but he does not reject change

---

[1] Cf. p. 138 above. This point is emphasised by Wolfgang Kersting, *Wohlgeordnete Freiheit. Immanuel Kants Rechts- und Staatsphilosophie* (Berlin and New York, 1984), pp. 260ff. who also draws attention to Kant's use of the same principle of threefold division in *Religion within the Limits of Reason Alone* (*AA* VI, 139f.) when he speaks of the idea of God as a moral world ruler. Cf. also Simone Goyard–Fabre, *Kant et le Problème du Droit* (Paris, 1975), p. 200, who stresses the importance of this syllogism of practical reason.

[2] Parliamentary democracy as practised, for instance, in Britain or Canada would not, according to Kant's conception, be as close an approximation to his ideal of the separation of powers as is provided by the constitution and political practice of the United States of America. Cf. also my discussion of this problem on pp. 28ff. above.

[3] Cf. Henrich, in his perceptive and influential introduction to *Kant. Gentz. Rehberg*, p. 29, who puts forward this interpretation.

[4] *AA* VI, 340.; cf. p. 162f. above.

in the substance of the constitution. It is indeed the duty of everyone to work for the establishment of a republican constitution. This applies particularly to the government, which ought to initiate appropriate reforms from above, since these are most likely to achieve the goal in question. By convoking the States-General, Louis XVI went further than initiating reforms, according to Kant (though this was what the king had in mind). He in fact handed over sovereignty to the States-General. Thus, from a strictly constitutional point of view, no revolution at all took place in France. As I have suggested, this interpretation of the events in France may, at first sight, appear to be an exercise in casuistry, or at best an excessively legalistic and hence unrealistic interpretation. But this is not in fact the case. It is now widely accepted that the absolute monarchy had come to an end when the king, in order to solve the financial crisis, summoned the States-General to Versailles and thereby forfeited sovereignty.[1] Nevertheless, Kant did not seek to exculpate the revolutionaries. His concern was merely to spell out the character of the constitutional change involved. He knew full well that a profound change had taken place in human affairs, otherwise he would not have so strikingly referred to that spirit of the revolution which had aroused 'in the hearts and desires of the spectators who are not themselves caught up in it a *sympathy*, which almost borders on enthusiasm, although the very utterance of that sympathy was fraught with danger'.[2] This attitude of mind can be explained only by 'the moral disposition within the human race'.[3] According to Kant, the reaction of a detached philosophical observer to the events in France, particularly to the aims of the revolutionaries of 1789 and the attempt to put these aims into practice in the constitution of 1791, was an unmistakable sign which allowed him to interpret the purpose of history—namely, to lead man out of his self-incurred immaturity to freedom and independence. Thus, it was not the revolution itself nor its course, nor even its spirit, that mattered but the view which disinterested spectators like Kant himself took of these events from outside. Even the excesses of the revolution were incapable of affecting this view, and they did not make him change his mind about the event itself, just as little as a

---

[1] Cf. p. 30 above; cf. also William Doyle, *Origins of the French Revolution* (2nd. ed. Oxford, 1988) p. 115 who in this authoritative study writes that to convoke the States-General was 'as much as to announce that power had passed from the king's hands'. Cf. also his *The Oxford History of the French Revolution* (Oxford, 1989), p. 185.
[2] *AA* VII, 85; cf. p. 182 above. [3] *Ibid.*

successful uprising, even if it did not bring 'misery and atrocities'[1] in its train, could legitimise a revolution or the prospect of success confer on anyone the right of rebellion.[2]

VII

THE REJECTION OF THE RIGHT OF REBELLION

Kant's rejection of the right of resistance, rebellion, or revolution (he uses all these three terms without distinction)[3] under all circumstances, on the one hand, and his enthusiasm for the constitutional aims of the French revolutionaries, on the other, appear at first sight to be paradoxical. Indeed, his rejection of revolution seems incompatible with his own basic principles of politics. In his view, a constitution cannot contain a clause admitting a *'legal* right of revolution';[4] for that would entail a contradiction: it would permit the existence of two sovereigns, thereby destroying the very basis of sovereignty, which is indivisible. It would, in fact, lead to an infinite regress.[5]

Kant buttresses his argument against the right of revolution by invoking the principle of publicity which states that whatever in politics is incompatible with publicity, is unjust, whatever requires publicity is just, and whatever is compatible with publicity may be just.[6] He maintains that a revolution necessarily requires secrecy, or at least some measure of clandestine activity such as a conspiracy, and therefore violates the principle of publicity. However, whereas any coup d'état in an efficiently run despotic state invariably entails secrecy, a rebellion may not necessarily require it in a democracy where rebels might even have the opportunity to publicise their aims freely. But those who advocate rebellion in public would, Kant maintains, be acting on a maxim which, if it 'were publicly acknowledged, would defeat its own

[1] *Ibid.*
[2] Cf. Henrich, *Kant. Gentz. Rehberg*, p. 13 and Atwell, *Ends and Principles in Kant's Moral Thought*, p. 193, both of whom make this point.
[3] Cf. Peter Nicholson, 'Kant on the Duty Never to Resist the Sovereign', *Ethics*, LXXXVI (1976), 216, who draws attention to Kant's usage of these terms.
[4] Cf. Lewis White Beck: 'Kant and the Right of Revolution', *JHI*, XXXII (1971), 414.
[5] Cf. p. 31 above.
[6] Cf. Nicholson, 'Kant on the Duty Never to Resist the Sovereign', 224, to whose account of this issue I am indebted.

purpose';[1] for it denies the government the right to govern and claims this right for the rebels themselves. It is therefore self-contradictory and renders the existence of the state impossible. In other words, this maxim is incompatible with a rightful system of law.

VIII

THE REJECTION OF THE RIGHT OF REBELLION AND TWENTIETH-CENTURY TOTALITARIANISM

Kant's theory of law, and, hence of politics, is therefore coherent and logically consistent. But can it still be defended in the light of twentieth-century experience of totalitarian regimes? Even though he was convinced of the 'radical evil'[2] in human nature, he could hardly have envisaged the horrors perpetrated by regimes such as that of Nazi Germany. He would certainly have been an opponent of totalitarianism, given his political principles. But whether he would, in face of such extreme evil, have changed his mind and advocated active resistance or rebellion must remain a matter for speculation. One would like to think that he would have done so. At least he might have argued that the Third Reich's worst atrocities, such as the Holocaust, had never been sanctioned by law and were hence unlawful. But that would leave the problem posed by his interdiction of rebellion stubbornly unresolved.

To counter the charge of political impotence in face of so evil a system it could be argued that, in states where despotism of so extreme a kind prevails, the Idea of the social contract is violated and the civil state has ceased to exist; for in the Nazi state, the victims were patently no longer treated as human beings and, as Kant convincingly states, no one has a right to treat people thus: for no one ought to 'become a domestic animal to be employed in any chosen capacity'.[3] Consequently, in a totalitarian state, a rightful system of law has evidently ceased to operate and human beings live again in the state of nature. Individual self-help, another ideal of the Enlightenment, becomes the order of the

[1] Cf. *ibid.*, 224, where Nicholson puts the matter neatly by stating that 'the test is not whether the maxim concerning rebellion can be made public, but whether it can be made law, and rebellion fails the test'.
[2] *Religion within the Limits of Reason Alone*, I; AA VI, 17–53.
[3] *AA* VIII, 293; cf. p. 76 above.

POSTSCRIPT

day. (This view is reflected in a provision incorporated in the constitution of the German Federal Republic by a constitutional amendment of
1968 which expressly sanctions the right of resistance against anyone
who seeks to overthrow the basic (democratic) constitution by force.)
But whether this interpretation agrees with Kant's thought is a moot
point; for it could apply only if all authority had genuinely ceased to
exist and anarchy actually prevailed. (Usually, of course, totalitarian
states are particularly authoritarian and thus, at least on the surface,
anything but anarchic.) Kant does, however, appear to have considered
the circumstances which arise if a ruler destroys the rightful political
order by trampling on the basic political rights of his subjects. In a
posthumously published note he speaks of the right to resist the ruler if
the fundamental contract has been violated.[1] But since he did not
express this view in those writings which he himself published, it is
possible, perhaps even probable, that he rejected it. To suggest that he
believed in the right of rebellion under certain circumstances but
expressed the contrary view out of fear does not seem plausible, given
his character and conduct. He never published anything which he
thought to be untrue. In those works to whose publication he himself
agreed he goes no further than mentioning the possible excuse of 'the
supposed right of necessity',[2] but the latter is a pretext only, and he never
legitimises rebellion on such grounds. Nowhere does Kant suggest that
the existence of despotism, however evil and all-encompassing it might
be, can provide a rightful excuse for overthrowing a government.

Kant postulates a goal in history, namely perpetual peace based on
the establishment of states with republican constitutions; for otherwise,
he believes, history would not make sense. The prospect of the inevitable realisation of, or at least approximation to, that goal renders revolution unnecessary; for the desired effect will come about anyhow
sooner or later. But according to modern developments in the philosophy of history, such a teleological interpretation of history is mistaken. Yet even if a goal of history were not postulated, rebellion would
still not be rightful within the Kantian system. That position would not
change, even if the powers that be suppressed the public use of reason,
the freedom of the pen, which, in Kant's words, is 'the only safeguard
of the rights of the people'.[3] To suppose otherwise, however tempting

[1] Cf. the Reflection No. 8043, *AA* XIX, 590; cf. also Beck, 'Kant and the Right of Revolution', 412 and Henrich, *Kant. Gentz. Rehberg*, p. 27, both of whom discuss this issue
perceptively.,
[2] *AA* VI, 321; p. 145 above.   [3] *AA* VIII, 304; p. 85 above.

265

this may be, cannot be squared with Kant's emphasis on the overriding importance of law which allows of no exception.[1] Our duty to work for the establishment of a republican state and for perpetual peace on the basis of a federation of republican states is a conditional duty only— that is, it must be carried out only within the framework of the law— whereas the duty not to violate the law and not to seek to overthrow the government is unconditional.

Not even the monarch who has lost his throne can be exempted from this universally applicable rule and be granted the right to rebel.[2] For if he accepts his loss of power, he is bound by the law like any other citizen. If he does not accept his dethronement, he is, according to Kant, outside the state. He could then doubtless seek to regain the throne, but he would not be protected by the law. He would probably need another state's support. But no state ought, according to Kant, to interfere in the affairs of another state unless that state has already been divided into warring parts and civil war rages. If, in that case, another state or the former monarch sides with one or the other side, there is no rebellion, because there is no state. It would not therefore be illegitimate for another state to support one of the two sides. Yet while intervention would be permissible, it is always less desirable than an attempt to solve the dispute by discussion. Rational discourse is always to be preferred to the use of force.

Indeed, given our experiences of totalitarian regimes, Kant's belief in the overriding power of public knowledge and of publicity may well appear naive. The power to misuse publicity for the purpose of evil propaganda, that is of spreading lies, has developed and flourished in the twentieth century. These features of modern political life do not, however, invalidate Kant's theory. Nor does the tendency, so common in all ages, to tailor public conduct in such a way as to conceal private interests.[3] Attempts can of course be made to pervert the public use of reason, just as illogical and illegitimate arguments can be put forward

---

[1] Cf. my 'Kant and the Right of Rebellion', 190, where I put forward the opposite argument which, though it may be plausible in itself, does not agree with Kant's own views. However, I still believe that totalitarianism is 'organised lawlessness'.

[2] I regret that in my article 'Kant and the Right of Rebellion', 183, I erroneously put forward this interpretation (which is, however, not repeated in the introduction to the present volume). I have been corrected by Nicholson, 'Kant on the Duty Never to Resist the Sovereign', 225.

[3] Jürgen Habermas, *Strukturwandel der Öffentlichkeit. Untersuchungen zu einer Kategorie der bürgerlichen Gesellschaft* (Berlin/Neuwied, 1963), pp. 118–32 discusses this aspect of public life in a chapter entitled 'Publizität als Prinzip der Vermittlung von Politik und Moral (Kant)' (reprinted in *ZwBat.* (1976), pp. 175–90).

before the court of reason. In neither case can there be a guarantee that the right attitude will immediately prevail. But if reason is given full scope through public discussion, sooner or later false arguments should be exposed and the attempts to misuse publicity pilloried. Truth, as Kant believes, in the true spirit of the Enlightenment, will eventually carry the day.

Nevertheless, the problem of the right of revolution cannot be settled within the framework of Kant's political thought, because he failed to deal with the problem which any classification in the political or social spheres presents: for in these areas, distinctions like those of mathematics and logic are not always possible and borderline cases tend to arise.[1] Kant's argument involves empirical propositions, so that this problem cannot be avoided.

IX

THE LIMITS OF OBEDIENCE TO GOVERNMENT

But to deny the right of rebellion does not, in Kant's opinion, mean that obedience to the law or to governmental decrees is absolute. To observe the law is a duty, but no one should be compelled to comply with laws which require him to commit immoral acts. For instance, a government does not have the right to compel anyone to lie, to commit murder or to subscribe to religious beliefs which he does not hold. Indeed, it is our moral duty not to abide by such commands. But we must not *actively* resist, that is, we must not seek to overthrow the government by the use of force. We ought merely to resist the ruler *passively* by way of non-compliance. In this respect, St Paul's injunction in Romans I, XIII, 21–2, cited by Kant,[2] that 'we should obey the powers that be because they are ordained of God' is overridden by the command, expressly quoted by Kant,[3] in Acts V, 29 that 'we must obey God rather than men'.

Moral decisions are free decisions, but only those decisions which can in fact be performed need be taken. No one can be expected to perform impossible deeds. This does not, however, mean that moral

---

[1] I owe this observation to Stephan Körner. Cf. for instance his 'On Rousseau's, Robespierre's and Kant's Criteria of Moral Action', *The Impact of the French Revolution on European Consciousness*, ed. H. T. Mason and W. Doyle, Gloucester and Wolfeboro, N. H., 1989. Cf. also his *Experience and Theory*, London, 1966 as well as my article 'Kant und die französische Revolution', *Zeitschrift für Pädagogik*, Beiheft 24, 1989, 293–303.
[2] In *The Metaphysics of Morals*, Appendix to the Theory of Right. Conclusion, I; *AA* VI, 371.
[3] *Religion within the Limits of Reason Alone*. IV, I; *AA* VI, 154.

acts need not be performed because political circumstances are adverse or entail the prospect of physical danger.

Even if we are confronted with physical danger—be it imprisonment, torture, or death—we have no right to rebel against the government. The command to 'obey God rather than men' merely permits *passive* disobedience. However, to disobey the powers that be is always hazardous. Of that, Kant was only too well aware. He himself practised caution and cunning when threatened by the bigoted Minister, Johann Friedrich Wöllner, with the king's displeasure if he ever wrote again on religion. This was no empty threat in eighteenth-century Prussia, and it could easily have resulted in dismissal and hence loss of livelihood, or even in imprisonment. Kant acquiesced, basing his silence on the principle that it was not necessary to tell the public all that one knew.[1]

X

THE PRUSSIAN CONTEXT

Kant was realistic enough to value prudence, especially at his age—he was in his seventieth year at the time of this incident—but he kept silent with a view to future public action as a writer. Hardly anyone could have suspected that his phrase 'His Majesty's loyal servant',[2] which he used when promising the king not to write again on religion, could be used for the purpose of dissimulation. It was, after all, a standard phrase at the time for a subject to use when writing to his sovereign. Yet Kant succeeded in concealing his true intention in writing without actually being untruthful. He was shrewd enough to know that in politics one has, as he himself said, to be as wise as serpents.[3] We must not shrink from our duty to act morally, but this does not remove the need to be simultaneously astute and realistic.

Kant was silenced only in matters of religion, but was allowed to go on propounding his highly subversive political theory. Why was this so? Did the government simply fail to notice? After all, it had introduced censorship in political matters, virtually forbidding any public criticism of the monarchy and its laws, as early as 19 December 1788, very soon after instituting censorship in matters of religion on 9 July

[1] Cf. p. 2 above. [2] Cf. *ibid.* [3]Cf. *AA* VIII, 370; cf. p. 116 above.

1788. And Kant was known as the 'old Jacobin' because of his admiration for the French Revolution, which Frederick William II, together with the Austrians, had vainly sought to crush by invading France in the autumn of 1792. But the government did not even reprimand, let alone punish, Kant after he published his essay *Theory and Practice* in 1793, in which he spelt out his views on the need for a republican constitution. Admittedly, the journal in which the essay appeared was the *Berlinische Monatsschrift*, which had moved to places of publication outside Prussia, first to Jena and then to Dessau, in order to escape the censorship, so the Prussian censor would not have seen the essay prior to publication. Nonetheless, if it had wished to do so, the government could still have acted against Kant, a subject of the King of Prussia and a Prussian civil servant to boot, after the essay was published. It did so when Kant published *Religion within the Limits of Reason Alone* in the same year after the censor had forbidden publication of its second part. He had been able to circumvent the censor by making use of a professorial privilege which entitled him to publish a work provided it had obtained the *imprimatur* of a university faculty. He obtained the necessary permission by applying to a university outside Prussia, the University of Jena. Not surprisingly, the Prussian government thought it necessary to assert its authority, which Kant had, by this stratagem, called into question, and forbade him to write again on religion.

The reasons for the government's inactivity in relation to political writings can only be surmised. In the first place, it did not take theoretical discussions in learned journals all that seriously. (Indeed, one of the censors, in permitting the publication of the first part of *Religion within the Limits of Reason Alone*, expressly cited that reason.)[1] However, it would not have tolerated an overt attack on the monarchy and the laws, which Kant carefully avoided. Moreover, Kant's rejection of the right of revolution may well have been interpreted as support for the ruling authorities. At least the editor of the *Berlinische Monatsschrift*, Johann Friedrich Biester, on reading *Theory and Practice*, believed Kant to be an opponent of the French Revolution.[2] Kant does not, of course,

[1] Cf. Karl Vorländer, *Immanuel Kant. Der Mann und sein Werk* (Leipzig, 1924), II, pp. 141–7 and Klaus Epstein, *The Genesis of German Conservatism* (Princeton, N.J., 1966), pp. 265f. and 373–87, both of whom discuss the historical background. Cf. also Norbert Hinske, who writes about the intellectual climate in Berlin during the reign of Frederick William II in the introduction of his edition *Was ist Aufklärung? Beiträge aus der Berlinischen Monatsschrift*, (Darmstadt, 1973), which contains essays from the *Berlinische Monatsschrift*.

[2] Cf. *AA* XI, 456, letter of J. F. Biester to Kant, 5 October 1793. Cf. also Beck, 'Kant and the Right of Revolution', 412f., who discusses Biester's response.

rule out constitutional monarchy. Indeed, there are passages which suggest that he favours it. Furthermore, his views on the basic rights of citizens, taken over and developed from the school of Natural Law (particularly Pufendorf), and on representative government were by no means out of tune with the discussions which were taking place in government circles and the court itself in preparation for the *Allgemeine Landrecht* of 1794, the legal code which profoundly reformed the Prussian legal system.[1] (Admittedly, the king did not, in the end, surrender his autocratic powers of government, but he had tolerated free and wide-ranging theoretical discussions among his advisers and allowed his son, the Crown Prince, to become familiar with these novel constitutional ideas.) These affinities may well have been noticed; they may have affected the government's attitude to Kant's political thought and made it ignore the important differences that remained between his views and those of the authors of the Prussian code.

Thus, under the autocratic regime of eighteenth-century Prussia, Kant enjoyed the freedom to write a philosophical account of his attitude to politics which would not have been possible in a totalitarian state. It also does not make sense to compare his position, when threatened with the king's displeasure, with the situation of citizens in totalitarian states when confronted with the dilemma of either obeying a command to commit immoral acts or risking the almost certain penalty not only of imprisonment, but even of physical punishment, torture and death. There can be occasions when prudence or cunning will be of no avail.

XI

KANT'S ARGUMENT AGAINST WORLD GOVERNMENT

Kant also believed that the public use of reason, and hence of political freedom, cannot be suppressed universally. The diversity of nations should see to that. If only on account of technological developments,

---

[1] Cf. Reinhart Koselleck, *Preußen zwischen Reform und Revolution. Allgemeines Landrecht, Verwaltung und soziale Bewegung von 1791–1848* (Stuttgart, 1967), pp. 23–35, and Epstein, *The Genesis of German Conservatism*, pp. 373–88 for an account of the discussion leading up to the promulgation of the *Allgemeine Landrecht*, particularly for the views expressed by Carl Gottlieb Svarez (1746–98) in the lectures which he gave to the then Crown Prince, the later Frederick William III, in order to inform him of the ideas underlying the new law. Cf. also *ibid.* pp. 365f. for an analysis of the Prussian government's attitude towards Kant's *Religion within the Limits of Reason Alone*.

POSTSCRIPT

modern states admittedly have far greater powers of control than did those of Kant's day, and when driven by a powerful ideology, their governments usually have no compunction about using that power to the full. Yet as long as there is no world state or no ideology wholly and exclusively accepted throughout the world, the diversity of nations will permit different views to be held and published. Whether this will always be so must remain an open question, for the future is not necessarily always like the past. (It goes without saying that Kantian political principles would hardly be discussed at all if the whole world became a closed society.) We must simply hope that nature, on which Kant relied, will continue to exercise its power in the accustomed manner. It is true that the danger in question unfortunately cannot be ruled out on *a priori* grounds, but there are good empirical reasons for considering it extremely remote. Kant himself argued that the central power of a world state would find it more and more difficult to exercise control and protect its citizens the further away its territories were from the centre. The remoter territories would seek to become independent. As law would not prevail, they would probably become involved in war with their neighbours. Thus, a world state would not lead to perpetual peace at all but to further strife. Moreover, the very attempt to set up a world state would be unlawful, because it would interfere with the constitutional arrangements of existing states.[1] No one has a right to make such an attempt, nor has any state the right to surrender its own sovereignty and abandon its constitution.

XII

CONCLUSION

Kant's reflections on politics deal with perennially important problems. Many of his ideas have become an indispensable part of the armoury of modern democratic political language. That they are often paid lip-service to rather than put into practice does not invalidate them. Even tyrants, in order to succeed, have, as Machiavelli discerned, to mask their evil deeds by dressing them up as moral actions, thus proving the truth of La Rochefoucauld's aphorism 'l'hypocrisie

[1] Cf. Kenneth N. Waltz, 'Kant, Liberalism, and War', *American Political Science Review*, LVI (1962), 327, who points out some of Kant's objections to the establishment of a world state.

271

est le hommage que le vice rend à la vertu'.[1] Kant was well aware of the
need of rulers to pay respect to right, at least in public. As he wrote in
one of his posthumously published reflections: 'Thus, no government
has so far dared to declare freely and openly: that right and wrong are
mere illusions to which it need not pay any attention, and that it is
therefore entitled to make its absolute will the law of the land. On the
contrary, governments always appeal to the sense of right which their
subjects possess as free moral beings ...'.[2] Because Kant's political
principles, then, express basic human aspirations and since they have
become part of the stock of current ideas, they cannot be ignored.
Indeed, they are a powerful force; for man's desire for a freedom which
can be enjoyed by all members of a community equally, independently
and consistently has become too deeply rooted to be easily abandoned.
And no one defined those principles of politics which guarantee
freedom under the law more cogently than Kant. That is why it is
rewarding to study his political writings.

---

[1] 'Hypocrisy is the homage which vice pays to virtue', in Francois VI Duc de La Rochefoucauld, *Réflexions ou Sentences et Maximes Morales*, No. 218.
[2] Reflection No. 8077, IV; *AA* XIX, 610.

Notes to the Text

IDEA FOR A UNIVERSAL HISTORY WITH A COSMOPOLITAN PURPOSE

1   p. 41. *Idee zu einer allgemeinen Geschichte in weltbürgerlicher Absicht, AA* VIII, 15–31. First published in *Berlinische Monatsschrift*, IV (11 November 1784), 385–411. The initial reference is, as Kant says, to a passage in the *Gothaische Gelehrte Zeitungen*, 1784 (12, 11 February, p. 95).

2   p. 47. Charles Irénée Castel, Abbé de St Pierre (1658–1743). The reference is to his *Projet pour rendre la paix perpétuelle en Europe* (1712–13).

3   p. 47. The reference is to Rousseau's *Extrait du projet de paix perpétuelle* (1761).

4   p. 48. This refers to Epicurus' view that the universe was the result of a random concourse of atoms.

5   p. 50. Cf. p. 37, n. 1.

6   p. 52. 'Unknown territory.'

7   p. 52. The Septuagint, so named from the legend of its composition by seventy translators (*septuaginta* being the Latin word for seventy), or more exactly seventy-two, sent from Jerusalem to Alexandria at the request of King Ptolemy II Philadelphus (288–247 B.C.) of Egypt.

8   p. 52. Kant slightly mistranslates Hume who wrote: 'The first page of THUCYDIDES is...the commencement of real history', *Of the Populousness of Ancient Nations* (1751), David Hume, *Essays. Moral, Political and Literary* (ed. by T. H. Green and T. H. Grose) (London, 1875), I, Essay XI, 414.

AN ANSWER TO THE QUESTION: 'WHAT IS ENLIGHTENMENT?'

1   p. 54. *Beantwortung der Frage : Was ist Aufklärung?, AA* VIII, 33–42. First published in *Berlinische Monatsschrift*, IV (12 December 1784), 481–94. There is a reference in the original edition of the *Berlinische Monatsschrift* to p. 516 of the number of that journal published on 5 December 1783. This reference is to an essay by the Rev. Zöllner, 'Is it advisable to sanction marriage through religion?'. The relevant passage reads (in translation): '*What is Enlightenment?* The question, which is almost as important as the question *What is truth?*, should be answered before one begins to enlighten others. And yet I have never found it answered anywhere.'

2   p. 54. Literal translation: 'Dare to be wise'. Horace, *Epodes* I, 2, 40. Cf. Elizabeth M. Wilkinson and L. A. Willoughby (eds. and trs.), Friedrich

Schiller, *On the Aesthetic Education of Man* (Oxford, 1967), LXXIV ff.; cf. also Franco Venturi, 'Was ist Aufklärung? Sapere Aude!', *Rivista Storica Italiana*, LXXI (1959), 119 ff. Venturi traces the use made of this quotation from Horace throughout the centuries. Cf. also p. 5.

3 p. 54. 'Those who have come of age by virtue of nature.'

4 p. 55. The allusion is to Frederick II (the Great), King of Prussia (1740–86).

5 p. 58. 'Caesar is not above the grammarians.'

6 p. 58. Kant here refers, of course, to Frederick the Great.

7 p. 60. This allusion amounts to a repudiation of Julien Offray de Lamettrie's (1709–51) materialism as expressed in *L'Homme Machine* (1748).

8 p. 60. Anton Friedrich Büsching (1724–93), professor in the University of Göttingen, theologian and leading geographer of the day, editor of *Wöchentliche Nachrichten von neuen Landkarten, geographischen, statistischen und historischen Büchern*. Kant's reference is to XII, 1784 (Berlin, 1785), 291.

9 p. 60. Moses Mendelssohn (1729–86), a leading philosopher of the German Enlightenment. The reference is to Mendelssohn's essay 'Über die Frage: was heisst Aufklärung?' ('On the question: what is Enlightenment?'), *Berlinische Monatsschrift*, IV (9 September 1784), 193–200.

ON THE COMMON SAYING: 'THIS MAY BE TRUE IN THEORY, BUT IT DOES NOT APPLY IN PRACTICE'

1 p. 61. *Über den Gemeinspruch: 'Das mag in der Theorie richtig sein, taugt aber nicht für die Praxis'*, *AA* VIII, 273–313. First published in *Berlinische Monatsschrift*, XXII (September 1793), 201–84. As we know from Kant's notes for the essay (*AA* XXIII, 125 ff.; cf. also Rudolf Reicke, *Lose Blätter aus Kants Nachlaß*, I (Königsberg, 1889), 148 f. and 179), he was attacking an essay by the eminent mathematician and writer Abraham Gotthelf Kästner (1719–1800), *Gedanken über das Unvermögen der Schriftsteller Empörungen zu bewirken* (*Thoughts on the inability of writers to produce rebellion*) (Göttingen, 1793), in which Kästner satirised the apparently useless activities of theorising writers (cf. Dieter Henrich, (ed.), *Kant. Gentz. Rehberg. Über Theorie und Praxis* (Frankfurt/Main, 1967), p. 12). Kant also wished to show that the validity of a theory did not depend on its revolutionary consequences, thus dispelling ambiguities in the writing of his disciples. Cf. Henrich, *op. cit.* p. 12, who also refers to Johann Christian Gottlieb Schaumann (1768–1821), *Versuch über Aufklärung, Freiheit und Gleichheit... (Essay on Enlightenment, Freedom and Equality...)* (Halle, 1793).

2 p. 62. *Anschauung* is the term Kant uses (Translator's note).

3 p. 63. Possibly a reference to Edmund Burke's *Reflections on the Revolution in France* (1790); cf. the Everyman's Library Edition (London, 1910), pp. 55–6. It had been translated into German by Friedrich Gentz, as *Betrachtungen über die französische Revolution* (Berlin, 1793). Burke attacks those who theorise on politics without regard for experience. He uses the same quotation which Kant includes in this passage; cf. Paul Wittichen, 'Kant und Burke', *Historische Zeitschrift*, XCIII (1904), 254.

4 p. 63. 'Let him lord it there in his own court.' Aeolus in Virgil, *Aeneid* I, 140.

5 p. 63. The terms *Staatsrecht* und *Völkerrecht* are two of the numerous compounds Kant forms out of the word *Recht*, which itself occurs again and again in his political writings. For the sake of consistency, it has been rendered throughout by the English 'right', although it can often signify something more nearly equivalent to 'law' or 'justice'. Kant himself twice supplies helpful definitions of the term in the works printed in this volume: cf. p. 73 and the section *Introduction to the Theory of Right*, pp. 132–5, for the relevant passages. For further remarks by Kant on the same topic cf. *AA* XXIII, 255–6. (Translator's note.)

6 p. 64. Christian Garve (1742–98), a well-known philosopher of the German Enlightenment, whose work Kant greatly esteemed on account of Garve's sincerity. In this essay, Kant is refuting Garve's views as expressed in *Versuche über verschiedene Gegenstände aus der Moral, der Literatur und dem gesellschaftlichen Leben*, I (Breslau, 1792), particularly 111–16. The passage is reprinted in Dieter Henrich (ed.), *Kant. Gentz. Rehberg. Über Theorie und Praxis* (Frankfurt/Main, 1967), pp. 134–8.

7 p. 67. 'A matter of mere opportunity.'

8 p. 73. Kant seeks here to refute Hobbes' political theory, which found its classic expression in the *Leviathan* (1651). The actual argument is explicitly directed against Hobbes' *De cive* (1642).

9 p. 80. 'The public welfare is the supreme law of the state.'

10 p. 82. Gottfried Achenwall (1719–72), professor in Göttingen and the leading statistician of the age. His *Ius naturae in usum auditorum* was published in Göttingen, 1755–6 (7th ed. 1781). Kant used this work as a textbook for his lectures on Natural Law, held twelve times between 1767 and 1788. The use of textbooks for lectures was customary.

11 p. 82. Charter granted to Brabant by Duke John III in 1354 in which the Duke undertook to maintain the integrity of the duchy and not to wage war, make treaties or impose taxes without consulting his subjects represented by the municipalities.

12 p. 83. These remarks refer to the French Revolution.

13 p. 83. Georges Jacques Danton (1759–94), the French revolutionary leader.

14 p. 83. This remark refers to the accession of William III of Orange and Mary to the British throne in 1688 (the Glorious Revolution). After James II had been overthrown, Parliament legislated for William's and Mary's accession, restricting the monarchy to the Protestant successors of James I.

15 p. 86. 'The judgement is uncertain, and experiments are dangerous.'

16 p. 87. 'If they catch sight of a man respected for his virtue and services, they are silent and stand close with ears alert.' Virgil, *Aeneid* I, 151–2.

17 p. 87. Cf. above, p. 60, n. 9.

18 p. 87. *Jerusalem, oder über religiöse Macht und Judentum* (Berlin, 1783), one of Mendelssohn's principal works.

19 p. 87. Gotthold Ephraim Lessing (1729–81), the German writer and dramatist. These views are expressed in *Die Erziehung des Menschengeschlechts* (1780).

20 p. 88. Sisyphus, a legendary Greek King of Corinth, was punished by the Gods for his misdeeds. His punishment involved continuously carrying a heavy stone to a mountain-top in Hades always to find that as soon as he reached the top the stone rolled down again (cf. Homer, *Odyssey* XI, 593–600).

21 p. 89. 'Something certain.'

22 p. 89. 'Something uncertain.'

23 p. 92. I have been unable to trace this quotation.

24 p. 92. Cf. p. 47, n. 2.

25 p. 92. Kant's quotation is in incorrect word order. It should run: *Ducunt volentem fata, nolentem trahunt* ('The fates lead him who is willing, but drag him who is unwilling'); Seneca, *Epistle* 107, 11.

PERPETUAL PEACE: A PHILOSOPHICAL SKETCH

1 p. 93. *Zum ewigen Frieden. Ein philosophischer Entwurf*, *AA* VIII, 341–86. First published Königsberg (Friedrich Nicolovius), 1795; 2nd enlarged edition (*ibid.*), 1796. The treatise was presumably inspired by the conclusion of the Treaty of Basle on 5 April 1795. Kant offered the treatise to his publisher Nicolovius on 13 August 1795 (Letters, No. 672, *AA* XII, 35, letter to Nicolovius, 13 August 1795).

2 p. 95. This is a reference to Britain.

3 p. 98. Josef Niklas, Imperial Count of Windischgrätz (1744–1802). This nobleman invited scholars to compete in solving the problem of how it might be possible to formulate legal contracts which would be incapable of more than one interpretation and which would make all disputes over changes in ownership impossible.

4 p. 99. Αἰών, personification of eternal Time.

5 p. 101. Frederick the Great.

6 p. 102. Jacques Mallet du Pan (1749–1800), a Swiss writer born near Geneva who espoused a moderate Royalism in the period of the French Revolution. Kant here presumably refers to the *Considérations sur la révolution de France et sur les causes qui en prolongent la durée* (Brussels, 1793), by Mallet du Pan (translated into German by Friedrich Gentz as *Über die französische Revolution und die Ursachen ihrer Dauer*, Berlin, 1794). At the end of this treatise Mallet du Pan speaks of a maxim which has guided him for fifteen years and which an English poet has given us in a couplet, referring to the verse of Pope quoted by Kant in the above passage. Kant, however, translates the verses differently from Gentz.

7 p. 102. Alexander Pope, *Essay on Man*, III, 303–4.

8 p. 102. Kant alludes to the following passage, which he does not render accurately, from Swift's *Tale of a Tub* (*Prose Works of Jonathan Swift*, Bohn Library edition, I (London, 1900), 55): 'Wisdom is a hen, whose cackling we must value and consider, because it is attended with an egg; but then lastly, it is a nut, which, unless you choose with judgment, may cost you a tooth, and pay with nothing but a worm.'

9 p. 102. *Titus* Flavius Vespasianus (39–81), Roman Emperor (79–81).

10 p. 102. *Marcus Aurelius* Antoninus (121–80), Roman Emperor (161–80).

11 p. 102. Titus Flavius *Domitianus* (51–96), Roman Emperor (81–96).

12 p. 102. Lucius Aurelius *Commodus* (161–92), Roman Emperor (180–92). Titus and Marcus Aurelius are known for their beneficent government, Domitian and Commodus for their cruelty as rulers.

13 p. 103. Hugo Grotius (1583–1645), Dutch jurist and statesman. His main work is *De iure belli et pacis* (1625). He was a leading interpreter of Natural Law.

14 p. 103. Samuel Freiherr von Pufendorf (1632–94), an important theorist of Natural Law, professor in the university of Heidelberg (1661), in the university of Leyden (1670), subsequently historiographer in Berlin. His principal work is *De iure naturae et gentium* (1672).

15 p. 103. Emmerich von Vattel (1714–67), Swiss jurist and diplomat in Saxon service. His principal work is the *Droit des Gens* (1758).

16 p. 105. 'Wicked frenzy rages savagely with blood-stained mouth.' *Aeneid* I, 294–6.

17 p. 106. The full title is rather lengthy; in shortened form, it reads: *Alphabetum Tibetanum missionum apostolicarum commodo editum... Studio et labore Fr. Augustini Antonii Georgii eremitae Augustinui* (Romae, 1762). It is known as a ponderous compilation; the author was the Augustinian monk and missionary, Antonio Agostino Giorgi (1711–97).

18 p. 107. Johann Eberhard Fischer (1697–1771), historian, Professor of History and member of the Academy at St Petersburg, member of the second expedition to Kamchatka (1733–43). The reference is to his *Quaestiones Petropolitanae* (Göttingen and Gotha, 1770) (*De variis nominibus imperii Sinarum* §2, p. 81).

19 p. 107. Bukhara, city which is now in Usbek S.S.R., giving its name to the country around it.

20 p. 107. Hesychius, a Greek grammarian of Alexandria (probably fifth or sixth century A.D.), author of an important Greek dictionary.

21 p. 107. The hierophants were expounders of sacred mysteries, initiated men.

22 p. 107. This is probably an allusion to Johann Georg Hamann's ΚΟΓΖΟΜ-ΠΑΖ *Fragmente einer apokryphischen Sibylle über apokalyptische Mysterien* (Weimar, 1779) which was written in reply to the following two books: Johann August Starck, *Apologie des Ordens der Frey-Mäurer* (Berlin, 1778) and Christoph Meiners, *Über die Mysterien der Alten* (Leipzig, 1776). (Cf. J. G. Hamann, *Sämtliche Werke*, III [Vienna, 1951], 215–28; cf. also 452 ff.). Kant, according to a letter from Hamann to Herder, wrote a long letter to Hamann pointing out that this word Κογξ'Ομπαξ was derived from the Tibetan, as Kant had only very recently discovered. Hamann refused to accept this view and found it ridiculous (cf. Letter to J. G. Herder, 18 April 1783, J. G. Hamann, *Briefe*, V, Frankfurt/Main, ed. Arthur Henkel (1955), 36; Kant's letter to Hamann is not extant). The allusion would have been intelligible to those who followed the continuous battle of words between Kant and Hamann, only too frequently concealed in obscure footnotes, etc. The personal relations between Kant and Hamann, incidentally, were quite good. The word Κογξ'Ομπαξ occurs in Hesychius' dictionary. The meaning is still disputed.

23 p. 107. Fertility cult of Demeter and Persephone in Eleusis near Athens.

24 p. 107. (Abbé) Jean Jacques Barthélemy, *Voyage du jeune Anacharsis en Grèce, dans le milieu du quatrième siècle avant l'ère vulgaire*, 5 vols. (Paris, 1788). Translated into German by Johann Erich Biester, *Reise des jüngeren Anacharsis durch Griechenland* (Part v, Berlin, 1793).

25 p. 107. Mathurin Veyssière de La Croze (1661–1739), Benedictine monk, member of the Prussian Academy of Sciences.

26 p. 107. Pater Franciscus Horatius or Francisco Orazio della Penna, a missionary who lived in Lhasa (1735–47), known for his accurate description of Tibet.

27 p. 107. Epopt—one initiated into the Eleusinian mysteries.

28 p. 107. This unusual footnote indicates Kant's wide geographical and ethnological interests.

29 p. 108. 'Nature the contriver of things (i.e. of the world)', Lucretius, *De rerum naturae* v, 234.

30 p. 108. 'As soon as he has given the command, they obey without fail.'

31 p. 109. 'To harness griffins with horses.' Virgil, *Eclogues* VIII, 27, *iungentur iam gryphes equis*.

32 p. 109. 'A single cause does not suffice.'

33 p. 112. Cf. p. 92, n. 25.

34 p. 113. Presumably Friedrich Bouterwek (1766–1828), professor in Göttingen, disciple of Kant.

35 p. 115. 'Woe to the vanquished.'

36 p. 116. 'No one is obliged to do anything he is incapable of doing.'

37 p. 116. Matt. x. 16.

38 p. 120. 'Act first and justify your actions later.'

39 p. 120. 'If you are the perpetrator, deny it.'

40 p. 120. 'Divide and rule.'

41 p. 120. 'The chief among his peers.'

42 p. 121. Possibly 'Qui s'excuse s'accuse.'

43 p. 123. Literally: 'Let justice prevail even if the world perish.'

44 p. 124. 'You for your part must not give way to troubles, but confront them the more boldly.' Virgil, *Aeneid* VI, 95.

45 p. 128. Or rather its ruler (Translator's note).

46 p. 129. Cf. p. 64, n. 6. The exact title of this treatise is *Abhandlung über die Verbindung der Moral mit der Politik oder einige Betrachtungen über die Frage, inwiefern es möglich sei, die Moral des Privatlebens bei der Regierung der Staaten zu beobachten* (*Treatise on the connection of morality with politics or some observations on the question to what extent it is possible to observe the morality of private life in the government of states*) (Breslau, 1788).

47 p. 129. The beginning (in translation) runs as follows: 'A satisfactory answer to that question is beyond my horizon.'

THE METAPHYSICS OF MORALS

1 p. 131. *Die Metaphysik der Sitten*, AA VI, 203–493. First published Königsberg (Friedrich Nicolovius), 1797. The many Latin legal terms in this treatise derive from Achenwall's *Ius naturae* (cf. p. 82, n. 10).

2 p. 132. *Einleitung in die Rechtslehre*, AA VI, 229–33.

3   p. 132. Writer of Latin fables who lived about A.D. 50.
4   p. 133. This is the first of several instances in the *Introduction to the Theory of Right* where Kant uses the German term *Willkür*. The term has various meanings, but in this particular extract, it signifies the will's power of choice or freedom of choice. Since neither of these expanded expressions can be used to render *Willkür* on every occasion without undue awkwardness, the more concise English 'will' has been adopted throughout, although it is more exactly equivalent to the German term *Wille* than to *Willkür*. (Translator's note.)
5   p. 135. This passage is somewhat difficult to translate, since Kant is exploiting the ambiguity not only of the word *recht* ('right'), but also of the words *krumm* and *schief*. *Krumm*, applied to a line, signifies 'curved', but in the present ethical context, it also has overtones of 'crooked' or 'illegal'. Similarly, *schief* means 'oblique' in geometry, but in other contexts it may indicate that which deviates from the straight paths of morality or is on the wrong side of the law. (Translator's note.)
6   p. 136. *Das öffentliche Recht*, AA VI, 309–55.
7   p. 139. 'No harm is done to a man by an act when he consents to it.'
8   p. 139. 'In either the natural or the political sense.'
9   p. 140. 'Together and individually.'
10 p. 142. 'From a badly trained ruler to a ruler who is better trained.'
11 p. 142. 'The welfare of the state is the supreme law.'
12 p. 144. These remarks are specifically directed against Achenwall, *Ius naturae in usum auditorum*, §§ 203–6.
13 p. 148. Cf. p. 142, n. 10.
14 p. 156. Arthur Balmerino, 6th Baron, a Scottish nobleman who was executed on 11 August 1746 after capture in the battle of Culloden (1746) for taking part in the Scottish Jacobite Rebellion (1745–6) under the Young Pretender (Prince Charles Edward).
15 p. 157. 'To prefer life to honour', Juvenal, *Satires* III, 8, 83.
16 p. 157. Cesare Beccaria, Marchese de Bonesana (1735–94), Italian jurist, who, in his main work, *Dei delitti e delle pene* (1764), is a passionate critic of the severe penal codes of his age and argues for change, appealing to the cause of the Enlightenment.
17 p. 164. This reference is of course to Louis XVI (1754–93), King of France (1774–93), who called the Estates-General together in Versailles in 1789, after they had not met for 175 years, so that they should solve the financial problems of France.
18 p. 168. 'The laws are silent in times of war.' Cicero, *Pro Milone* 4, 10.
19 p. 171. In the later seventeenth century and the first half of the eighteenth century, The Hague was the centre of European diplomacy. The numerous treaties and conventions signed there included the Treaty of the Triple Alliance (1688), the Concert of The Hague (1710), and the Treaty of Peace between Spain, Savoy and Austria (1717). The Netherlands Estates-General (1576–1795), in which the sovereignty of the seven United Provinces of the Netherlands did not reside but whose task it was to reach a consensus of opinion among the provinces, also met in The Hague. It is not clear to which of these events or bodies Kant is referring.

20   p. 173. Cf. p. 60, n. 8.

21   p. 175. The review appeared in the *Göttingische Anzeigen von gelehrten Sachen unter Aufsicht der Königlichen Gesellschaft der Wissenschaften*, Part 28 (18 February 1797) (reprinted in *AA* xx, 445–53). The reviewer, it is believed, was Friedrich Bouterwek, professor in the University of Göttingen; cf. p. 113, n. 34.

THE CONTEST OF FACULTIES

1   p. 176. *Der Streit der Facultäten, AA* vii, 1–116. First published Königsberg (Friedrich Nicolovius), 1798.

2   p. 177. *Erneuerte Frage: Ob das menschliche Geschlecht im beständigen Fortschreiten zum Besseren sei, AA* vii, 77–94.

3   p. 177. Prophetic priestesses of the Delphic oracle.

4   p. 178. Eudaemonism usually means the teaching that all human activity is determined by a striving for happiness. It is derived from the Greek word Εὐδαιμονία. Kant does not use it in that sense, however.

5   p. 178. Originally, the belief that the millennium will be established on earth before the Day of Judgement.

6   p. 178. After a novel by Christian Martin Wieland, the eighteenth-century German writer, called *Geschichte der Abderiten* (*The Story of the Abderites*) (1774–81), in which human follies are satirised. Abdera was a city in ancient Greece whose inhabitants were alleged to be particularly foolish.

7   p. 180. Gabriel François Coyer (1707–82), French Jesuit, author of a *Dissertation sur la différence des anciennes religions* (Paris, 1755).

8   p. 180. The reference is to Tycho Brahe (1546–1601), Danish astronomer who, in order to refute Copernicus, elaborated an astronomical system of his own, the Tychonic system. He put forward the theory that the sun and the moon rotate around the earth, but that the planets rotate round the sun. His theory was well thought of by many at the time.

9   p. 182. This is, of course, a reference to the French Revolution.

10   p. 183. The reference is to the Wars of the French Revolution.

11   p. 183. Kant misquotes the first words. It should read: *Postquam arma dei ad Vulcania ventum est...* 'Now that he was faced by Vulcan's arms, his mortal blade was shattered by the blow like brittle ice.' Virgil, *Aeneid* xii, 739–41.

12   p. 184. 'Not of individuals, but of mankind as a whole.'

13   p. 184. Johann Benjamin Erhard (1766–1827), a physician and friend of Kant's, who esteemed Erhard highly. Erhard published several political treatises including an essay *Über das Recht des Volkes zu einer Revolution* (*On the Right of the People to Revolution*) (Jena, 1794), to which Kant alludes here.

14   p. 185. Petrus Camper (1722–89), a Dutch anatomist. The allusion is to a work published in German translation, *Über den natürlichen Unterschied der Gesichtszüge im Menschen...* (ed. A. G. Camper) (Berlin, 1792), §3.

15   p. 185. Johann Friedrich Blumenbach, Professor of Medicine in the University of Göttingen from 1776. He greatly furthered the study of comparative anatomy. Cf. his *Handbuch der Naturgeschichte* (Göttingen, 1779), p. 44 and pp. 474 ff.

16 p. 186. This is a reference to George III (1738–1820), King of Great Britain and Ireland (1760–1820).

17 p. 188. Atlantis here refers to the myth of a city engulfed by the sea, mentioned by Plato in the *Timaeus*.

18 p. 188. *Utopia* (1516). The exact title of this work is *De optima rei publicae statu, deque nova insula Utopia*. It was written by Sir Thomas More (1478–1535), the eminent humanist who was Lord Chancellor of England (1529–32).

19 p. 188. *Oceana*, a treatise by James Harrington (1611–77), the English political philosopher who projected the ideal state for England.

20 p. 188. A reference to the *Histoire des Sévarambes* (first published in English, London, 1675; Paris, 1677 and 1679), a political novel by Denis Vairasse d'Allais, a French writer of the seventeenth century (translated into German by J. G. Müller as *Geschichte der Sevaramben*, Itzehoe, 1783).

21 p. 189. Cf. p. 60, n. 8.

22 p. 190. The likely source for this passage is: 'I must confess, when I see princes and states fighting and quarrelling, amidst their debts, funds, and public mortgages, it always brings to my mind a match of cudgel-playing fought in a China shop.' (Hume, *Of Public Credit, Essays Moral, Political and Literary, ed.cit.* 1, 371. I owe this reference to Professor Lewis White Beck who drew my attention to the fact that he had identified this passage in his edition *Immanuel Kant: On History* (Indianapolis and New York, 1963), p.124.

23 p. 190. 'The Phrygians learn wisdom too late' (i.e. they are wise after the event).

24 p. 190. Presumably this remark refers to the war between France and Austria which was ended by the Treaty of Campo Formio (17 November 1797). It could also refer to the war between France and Prussia which was ended by the Treaty of Basle (5 April 1795). Kant probably wrote this section of the *Contest of Faculties* some considerable time before its publication (cf. *AA* VII, 338 ff. for a full discussion of the origin of the treatise by Karl Vorländer).

APPENDIX FROM 'THE CRITIQUE OF PURE REASON'

1 p. 191. *Kritik der Reinen Vernunft*: Transcendentale Logik II, Dialektik, I, 1: Von den Ideen überhaupt, *AA* IV, 201–2.

REVIEWS OF JOHANN GOTTFRIED HERDER'S IDEAS ON THE PHILOSOPHY OF THE HISTORY OF MANKIND

1 p. 201. Rezensionen von Johann Gottfried Herders *Ideen zur Philosophie der Geschichte der Menschheit* (further abbreviated as *Ideen*), Riga and Leipzig, Part I, 1784; Part II, 1785. (All references are to this edition which Kant himself used.) *AA* VIII, 43–66. Review of first part first published in

Allgemeine Literaturzeitung (Jena und Leipzig, No. 4, 6 January 1785) 17a–20b and Supplement (Beilage), 21a–22b. Kant's reply to Carl Leonhard Reinhold appeared first as 'Erinnerungen des Recensenten der Herderschen Ideen zu einer Philosophie der Geschichte der Menschheit (Nr. 4 und *Beil[age]*. *der Allg. Lit.* = *Zeit.*) über ein im Februar des Teutschen Merkurs gegen diese Rezension gerichtetes Schreiben', March Supplement (1785) of *Allgemeine Literaturzeitung*. Review of second part first published *ibid.* No. 271, IV (15 November 1785), 153a–156b. Christian Gottfried Schütz (1747–1832), the editor of the *Allgemeine Literaturzeitung*, a journal which was just about to start publication, wrote to Kant on 10 July 1784 (cf. *AA* X, 393f. and 396) inviting him to review Herder's *Ideas*. Kant accepted. He offered in a letter to Schütz of 13 September 1785 to review the second part of Herder's *Ideas* (cf. *AA* X, 406f.). He told Schütz in a letter of 25 June 1787 (cf. *AA* X, 490) that he was unable to review the third part since he intended to tackle 'the *foundations of a criticism of taste*'. Kant's reviews were published anonymously, but the authorship did not remain a secret for long. Reinhold's attack on Kant had also been published anonymously, but Reinhold admitted the authorship later (cf. letter to Kant of 12 October 1787; cf. *AA* X, 497).

2 p. 201. 'Learn to know what kind of man you should be in accordance with the command of God and where in the world you have been placed', Persius (Aulus Persius Flaccus A.D. 34–A.D. 62), *Saturae*, v, v. 71–3. These verses are the epigraph of the first part of Herder's *Ideen*.

3 p. 201. *SW* XIII, 184. Kant's quotations are frequently inaccurate in detail.

4 p. 202. *Ideen*, I, 13ff.; *SW* XIII, 19f.

5 p. 202. *Ideen*, I, 18ff.; *SW* XIII, 22f.

6 p. 202. *Ideen*, I, 23; *SW* XIII, 25.

7 p. 202. *Ideen*, I, 29; *SW* XIII, 29.

8 p. 203. A summary of sections 6 and 7 of Book I of the *Ideen*, 35–56 (*SW* XIII, 33–46), whose inaccuracy in matters of detail may in part be due to printer's errors.

9 p. 203. *Ideen*, I, 88–93; *SW* XIII, 65–70.

10 p. 203. *Ideen*, I, 94; *SW* XIII, 71.

11 p. 204. *Ideen*, I, 106; *SW* XIII, 78.

12 p. 204. A summary of Herder's views as found in *Ideen*, I, 119–34; *SW* XIII, 87–97.

13 p. 204. *Ideen*, I, 177; *SW* XIII, 112f.

14 p. 204. *Ideen*, I, 180; *SW* XIII, 114.

15 p. 204. *Ideen*, I, 185; *SW* XIII, 117.

16 p. 205. *etwas Vernommenes*. In this passage quoted by Kant, Herder is exploiting the etymological relationship between the words *Vernunft* ('reason') and *vernehmen* ('to hear', 'to perceive', 'to learn') in order to suggest that they are also semantically related. I have here translated *Vernommenes* (formed on the past principle of *vernehmen*) as 'acquired', since the more obvious rendering 'learned' is needed to translate the next word, *gelernte*. (Translator's Note.)

17 p. 205. *Ideen*, I, 205–29; *SW* XIII, 129–45.

18 p. 205. *Ideen*, I, 231; *SW* XIII, 146.

19 p. 205. *Ideen*, I, 238; *SW* XIII, 151.
20 p. 205. *Ideen*, I, 238–59; *SW* XIII, 151–64.
21 p. 205. *Ideen*, I, 265; *SW* XIII, 167.
22 p. 206. *Ideen*, I, 265–70; *SW* XIII, 167–70.
23 p. 206. *Ideen*, I, 270; *SW* XIII, 170.
24 p. 206. *Ideen*, I. 273; *SW* XIII, 172.
25 p. 206. *Ideen*, I, 274ff; *SW* XIII, 172ff.
26 p. 206. *Ideen*, I, 277; *SW* XIII, 174.
27 p. 206. *Ideen*, I, 279f.; *SW* XIII, 176.
28 p. 206. *Ideen*, I, 287; *SW* XIII, 180f.
29 p. 207. *Ideen*, I, 289–93; *SW* XIII, 182–5.
30 p. 207. *Ideen*, I, 304f.; *SW* XIII, 192.
31 p. 207. *Ideen*, I, 308–15; *SW* XIII, 194–9.
32 p. 208. *Ideen*, I, 315–18; *SW* XIII, 199–201.
33 p. 210. *SW* XIII, 102.
34 p. 211. Cf. p. 195 above n. 2.
35 p. 212. The preceding part of this sentence reads slightly differently in the original review: cf. p. 210 above. (Translator's note.) The sentence refers to the statement in *Teutscher Merkur* (February, 1785), 164.
36 p. 212. *Teutscher Merkur* (February, 1785), 165.
37 p. 213. *Ibid.*, 166.
38 p. 214. Niebuhr, Carsten (1728–1815), traveller and explorer.
39 p. 214. Parkinson, Sydney (? 1745–71), traveller.
40 p. 214. Cook, James (1728–79), traveller and explorer.
41 p. 214. Höst, Georg Hjersing (1734–94), Danish traveller.
42 p. 214. Georgi, Johann Gottlieb (1738–1802), natural scientist and geographer, or Giorgi, Antonio Agostino; cf. note 17, p. 277.
43 p. 214. Zimmermann, Eberhard August Wilhelm von (1743–1815), traveller and explorer.
44 p. 214. *Ideen*, II, 69f.; *SW* XIII, 251.
45 p. 214. *SW* XIII, 265.
46 p. 214. *SW* XIII, 265ff.
47 p. 215. Cf. p. 192 above n. 1.
48 p. 216. *SW* XIII, 270.
49 p. 216. *SW* XIII, 270.
50 p. 216. *Ideen*, II, 129; *SW* XIII, 290.
51 p. 216. *SW* XIII, 373.
52 p. 216. *SW* XIII, 342.
53 p. 218. *SW* XIII, 435.
54 p. 219. *SW* XIII, 383.
55 p. 219. *SW* XIII, 341.
56 p. 219. *SW* XIII, 342.
57 p. 220. 'The evil man' is, of course, Kant himself. Kant refers to his statement in *Idea for a Universal History with a Cosmopolitan Purpose* (cf. p. 46 above). Cf. also p. 195 above n. 1.
58 p. 220. Averroism, a philosophy propounded in the Faculty of Arts in the University of Paris under the influence of Siger of Brabant from c. 1250 onward, and which maintained that propositions could be right on rational

argument, but wrong on theological grounds. Averroes is the occidental name of the Arab physician and philosopher, Ibn Rushd (1126–98), who lived in Spain.
59 p. 220. *SW* XIII, 345f.
60 p. 220. *Ideen*, II, 212; *SW* XIII, 346.

CONJECTURES ON THE BEGINNING OF HUMAN HISTORY

1 p. 221. *Mutmaßlicher Anfang der Menschengeschichte. AA* VIII, 107–23. First published in *Berlinische Monatsschrift*, VII (January, 1786), 1–27.
2 p. 227. Rousseau, Jean-Jacques (1712–78), French philosopher, novelist, and composer.
3 p. 227. *Si le rétablissement des sciences et des arts a contribué à épurer les mœurs* (1750).
4 p. 227. *Discours sur l'origine et les fondements de l'inégalité parmi les hommes* (1754).
5 p. 227. *Émile ou de l'éducation* (1762). Kant is reputed to have forgotten his daily walk, by which the citizens of Königsberg allegedly set their watches, when first reading *Émile*, in which Rousseau expounded a theory of education that took account of the distinct needs of each individual.
6 p. 227. *Du Contrat Social* (1762).

WHAT IS ORIENTATION IN THINKING?

1 p. 237. *Was heißt: Sich im Denken orientiren?* (modern spelling: *orientieren*). *AA* VIII, 131–47. First published in *Berlinische Monatsschrift*, VIII (October 1786), 304–30.
2 p. 237. *Anschauung* is the term Kant uses. (Translator's note.)
3 p. 237. Mendelssohn: cf. p. 193, n. 9.
4 p. 237. Mendelssohn, *GS* III, 2, 81f.
5 p. 237. Cf. p. 194, n. 19.
6 p. 237. Mendelssohn, *GS* III, 2, 198 and 211.
7 p. 238. This is the first of several occasions in this essay where Kant uses the term *Schwärmerei* to denote extravagant thinking in a philosophical or religious context. Its closest equivalent in English is the term 'enthusiasm' as it was used in the eighteenth century; but since 'enthusiasm' now has different connotations—predominantly emotional rather than intellectual, and positive rather than negative—it is no longer appropriate as a translation of *Schwärmerei*. The term 'fanaticism' is scarcely adequate either, since it suggests rather the extreme emotional commitment with which a belief is held than the irrationality of the belief itself. 'Zealotry', with its implication of sectarian dogmatism as well as obsessive commitment, is perhaps the least unsatisfactory term in the present context. I have accordingly used it to translate *Schwärmerei* throughout this essay, although I am

aware that the word 'zeal' itself is more closely equivalent to the German term *Eifer*. (Translator's Note.)

8 p. 238. Friedrich Heinrich Jacobi (1743–1819), novelist and philosopher.

9 p. 238. The author was Theodor Wizenmann. Cf. Kant's description of him in the *Critique of Practical Reason*, I, 2, 2 (*AA* v, 143) as 'an intelligent and bright mind'. Wizenmann is the only philosopher mentioned by name in that work (cf. *AA* v, 508).

10 p. 238. An argument specifically directed against one's opponent as an individual rather than against his views.

11 p. 241. 'Cartesian' refers to René Descartes (1596–1650), French philosopher and mathematician.

12 p. 242. 'Wolffian' refers to Christian Wolff (1679–1754), the influential German rationalist philosopher.

13 p. 246. Spinozism is the doctrine developed by followers of the Dutch philosopher Baruch de Spinoza (1632–77). It entails the equivalence of God and nature and amounts to a form of pantheism.

Bibliography

EDITIONS IN GERMAN

The standard edition of Kant's works is the *Gesammelte Schriften* (Berlin, 1900ff.), which, since its first volumes were published by the *Preussische Akademie der Wissenschaften*, is generally referred to as the *Akademieausgabe*. Other useful editions are that by Ernst Cassirer and others (*Werke* (Berlin, 1912–22) and the *Insel-Ausgabe* (*Werke*, ed. Wilhelm Weischedel (Wiesbaden, later Frankfurt/Main, 1956–64)). On this latter edition, the paperback edition of the Suhrkamp Verlag (*Theorie–Werkausgabe*, 12 vols., Frankfurt/Main, 1968), is based.

Gablentz, Otto Heinrich von der (ed.). *Immanuel Kant. Politische Schriften* (Klassiker der Politik, 1). Cologne and Opladen, 1965.

Reicke, Rudolf (ed.). *Lose Blätter aus Kants Nachlaß* (3 vols.) Königsberg, 1889–98.

Rossmann, Kurt (ed.). *Der Streit der Fakultäten*. Heidelberg, 1947.

Schmidt, Raymund (ed.). *Die drei Kritiken in ihrem Zusammenhang mit dem Gesamtwerk*. Stuttgart (5th ed.), 1949.

Ein Reinschriftfragment zu Kants 'Streit der Fakultäten'. *KS*, LI, 1959/60.

TRANSLATIONS

Beck, Lewis White (trs.). *Perpetual Peace* (Library of Liberal Arts, No. 54). New York, 1957. We were unable to consult this volume.

Butler, Nicholas Murray (prefaced by). *Perpetual Peace*. Los Angeles, 1932.

Campbell Smith, M. (ed. and trs.). *Perpetual Peace*. London, 1903.

Friedrich, Carl J. *Inevitable Peace*. Cambridge, Mass., 1948.

(ed. with an introduction). *The Philosophy of Kant. Immanuel Kant's Moral and Political Writings*. New York, 1949.

This volume includes *inter alia*:
'Idea for a Universal History with Cosmopolitan Intent'
'What is Enlightenment?'
'Theory and Practice: Concerning the Common Saying: This May Be True in Theory But Does Not Apply in Practice'
'Eternal Peace'.

Hastie, W. (ed. and trs). *Kant: The Philosophy of Law*. Edinburgh, 1887. (ed. and trs.). *Kant's Principles of Politics*. Edinburgh, 1891.

Humphrey, Ted (ed. and trs.). *Immanuel Kant: Perpetual Peace and Other Essays on Politics. History and Morals*. Indianapolis and Cambridge, 1982.

Ladd, John (ed. and trs.). *The Metaphysical Elements of Justice*. Indianapolis, New York, Kansas City, 1965.

Morrell, J. D. (ed. and trs.). *A Philosophical Treatise on Perpetual Peace*. London, n.d. [1884].

O'Brien, Helen (trs. with an introduction by Jessie H. Buckland). *Kant's Perpetual Peace* (Texts for Students of International Relations, No. 7). London, 1927.

Schwarz, Wolfgang (trs. and ed.) *Principles of Lawful Politics. Immanuel Kant's Philosophic Draft Toward Eternal Peace. A New Faithful Translation with an Introduction. Commentary and a Postscript 'Hobbism in Kant?'*. Aalen, 1988. (We were unable to consult this edition.)

Trueblood, Benjamin (trs.). *Perpetual Peace*. Boston, 1897.

CRITICAL WRITINGS ON KANT AND HIS AGE: SUGGESTED READING

Since this volume is specifically intended for an English-speaking public, I have commented on English studies only. Since space was limited, a hard choice had to be made and a large number of valuable studies had to be left out. Together with writings in other languages, they are listed in the second part of the bibliography without comment; many of them are well worth reading by students who can muster the necessary time and energy.

a) The Enlightenment

Peter Gay, *The Enlightenment* (2 vols.) (London 1967, 1970), offers a wide-ranging general account. Ernst Cassirer, *The Philosophy of the Enlightenment*, trs. Fritz C. A. Koelln and James P. Pettegrove (Princeton, N. J., 1951) (German original *Die Philosophie der Aufklärung* (Tübingen, 1932)), is a most interesting, but demanding study. His *Rousseau, Kant. Goethe. Two Essays*, trs. James Gutmann et al. (History of Ideas, 1) (Princeton, N. J., 1945), is also most perceptive and much easier of access. There are useful extracts with helpful introductions in Isaiah Berlin (ed.), *The Age of the Enlightenment. The Eighteenth-Century Philosophers* (New York, 1956), and Jack F. Lively (ed.), *The Enlightenment* (London, 1966). Cf. also H. B. Nisbet, 'Was ist Aufklärung? The Concept of Enlightenment in Eighteenth-Century Germany', *Journal of European Studies*, XII (1982), 77–94, for a lucid account of the attempts by German Enlightenment thinkers to define the meaning of Enlightenment, which at that time had not yet been classified by intellectual historians as a movement that carried that name. For a general account of the intellectual history of the period cf. Paul Hazard, *European Thought in the Eighteenth Century from Montesquieu to Lessing*, trs. Lewis May (London, 1954). (French original *La Pensée européenne au XVIIIième siècle. De Montesquieu à Lessing* (Paris, 1946)).

b) History of Political Thought

Reinhold Aris, *History of Political Thought in Germany from 1789 to 1815* (London, 1936), deals with all the important German political thinkers of the period including Kant. Charles Edwyn Vaughan, *Studies in the History of Political Philosophy before and after Rousseau* (2 vols.), ed. A. G. Little (Manchester, 1925), provides a good general introduction to the thought of the leading late eighteenth-century and early nineteenth-century political thinkers and contains a chapter on Kant (II, pp. 64–93). A. P. D'Entrèves, *Natural Law* (London and New York, 1951), gives a concise, but perceptive general historical account of the doctrine of Natural Law, to which Kant was deeply indebted.

c) General Books on Kant

There are very many studies of Kant. Stephan Körner, *Kant* (Penguin Books, Harmondsworth, Middlesex, 1955); (German trs. Elisabeth Serelmen–Küchler and Maria Nocker, Kleine Vandenhoek Reihe 252 S, Göttingen, 1967) is excellent. There is a concise account by Roger Scruton in the Oxford Past Masters Series, *Kant* (Oxford, 1982). Fuller accounts include Edward Caird, *The Critical Philosophy of Immanuel Kant* (2 Vols.) (Oxford, 1909) and Ernst Cassirer, *Kant. His Life and Thought* (New Haven and London, 1981) (German original *Kants Leben und Lehre* in Kant, *Werke*, ed. Ernst Cassirer, XI (Berlin, 1918)).

d) Studies of Kant's Political Thought

Jeffrey G. Murphy, *Kant: The Philosophy of Right* (Lasalle, Illinois, 1970), is a useful introduction. Patrick Riley, *Kant's Political Philosophy* (Totowa, N.J., 1983), is a good full-length book. Howard Williams, *Kant's Political Philosophy* (Oxford, 1983), is a detailed account. Onora O'Neill, 'Kantian Politics I: The Public Use of Reason', *PTh*, XIV (1986), 523–51, presents a penetrating and original argument about Kant's approach to public rational discourse as the basis of his approach to politics. Other penetrating accounts are: T. W. Pogge, 'Kant's Theory of Justice', *KS*, LXXIX (1988), 407–33; Charles Taylor, 'Kant's Theory of Freedom', in *Conceptions of Liberty in Political Philosophy*, ed. J. N. Gray and Z. Pelczynski (London, 1984), pp. 100–21, reprinted in Taylor, *Philosophy and the Human Sciences. Philosophical Papers II* (Cambridge, 1985), pp. 318–37; John E. Atwell, 'Duties, Rights and Ends in the Political Order', in Atwell, *Ends and Principles in Kant's Moral Thought* (Dordrecht, Boston, Lancaster, 1986), pp. 171–207; and Robert B. Pippin, 'On the Moral Foundations of Kant's *Rechtslehre*', in *The Philosophy of Immanuel Kant*, ed. Richard Kennington (Studies in Philosophy and the History of Philosophy, 12) (Washington, D.C., 1985), pp. 107–42.

e) Kant's Conception of History

Yirmiahiu Yovel, *Kant and the Philosophy of History* (Princeton, N.J., 1980); William James Booth, 'Reason and History: Kant's Other Copernican Revolution', *KS*, LXXIV (1983), 56–71; Emil Fackenheim, 'Kant's Concept of History', *KS*, XLVIII (1956–7), 381–98; W. A. Galston, *Kant and the Problem of History* (Chicago, 1975); and Lewis White Beck (ed. with an introduction (pp. VII–XXVI)), *Immanuel Kant: On History* (Indianapolis and New York, 1963), deal specifically with this subject.

BIBLIOGRAPHY

f) Kant's Conception of Property
Mary J. Gregor, 'Kant's Approach to Constitutionalism', in *Constitutionalism.*
The Philosophical Dimension, ed. Alan S. Rosenbaum (Contributions to
Legal Studies, 46) (New York, Westport, Conn., and London, 1988), pp.
69–87; and Susan Meld Shell, *The Rights of Reason. A Study of Kant's
Philosophy and Politics* (Toronto, Buffalo, London, 1980) and 'Kant's
Theory of Property', *PTH*, VI (1978), 75–90, perceptively discuss Kant's
view of this subject.

g) Kant's Attitude to Revolution
There are many studies. The following are particularly helpful: George
Peabody Gooch, *Germany and the French Revolution* (London, 1920);
Lewis White Beck, 'Kant and the Right of Revolution', *JHI*, XXXII (1971),
411–22; Sidney Axinn, 'Kant, Authority and the French Revolution', *JHI*,
XXXII (1971), 423–32; John Atwell, 'A Brief Commentary', *JHI*, XXXII
(1971), 433–6; C. Dyke, 'Comments', *JHI*, XXXII (1971), 437–40; Iring
Fetscher, 'Immanuel Kant and the French Revolution', in *EGerr.*, 1974,
pp. 25–40 (German trs. 'Immanuel Kant und die französische Revolution', in *ZwBat.*, 1976, pp. 269–90); and Peter P. Nicholson, 'Kant on the
Duty Never to Resist the Sovereign', *Ethics*, LXXXVI (1976), 214–30. Cf.
also my article 'Kant and the Right of Rebellion', *JHI*, XVII (1956),
179–92.

FURTHER SELECT BIBLIOGRAPHY

Critical Writings on Kant

Altmann, Amandus. *Freiheit im Spiegel des rationalen Gesetzes bei Kant*. Berlin,
1982.
Ansbro, J. J. 'Kant: Limitations on Individual Freedom'. *The New Scholas-
ticism*, XLVII, 1973.
Arendt, Hanna. *Lectures on Kant's Political Philosophy* (ed. and with an inter-
pretive essay by Ronald Beiner). Chicago and Brighton, Sussex, 1982.
Armstrong, A. C. 'Kant's Philosophy of Peace and War'. *The Journal of Philosophy*, XXVIII, 1931.
Batscha, Zwi (ed.). *Materialien zu Kants Rechtsphilosophie* (suhrkamp taschen-
buch wissenschaft, 171). Frankfurt/Main, 1971. (This volume contains
extracts from Kant's posthumously published writings and from his letters
as well as twenty essays, including the introduction, by various scholars,
some of which are extracts from books cited elsewhere in the bibliography.
Lack of space prevents me from listing the individual items.)
Beck, Lewis White. 'Les deux concepts kantiens du vouloir dans leur contexte
politique'. *APP*, IV, 1962 (English original appeared as 'Kant's Two Conceptions of the Will in their Political Context'. In Beck, *Studies in the
Philosophy of Kant*. New York, 1965).
'Kant on Education'. In *Education in the 18th Century* (Publications of the

McMaster University Association for 18th-Century Studies, 7). Ed. J. D. Browning. New York and London, 1979.

Benson, Peter. 'External Freedom according to Kant'. *CLR*, LXXXVII, 1987.

Bien, Günther. 'Räsonierfreiheit und Gehorsamspflicht. Die Universität und der Prozeß der Aufklärung in Kants staatsrechtlichen Schriften'. In *AIKK*, II, 2, 1974.

Bobbio, Norberto. 'Deux notions de la liberté dans la pensée de Kant'. *APP*. IV, 1962.

Böckerstette, Heinrich. *Aporien der Freiheit und ihre Aufklärung durch Kant*. Stuttgart and Bad Cannstatt, 1982.

Booth, William James. *Interpreting the World. Kant's Philosophy of History and Politics*. Toronto, 1986.

Borries, Kurt. *Kant als Politiker. Zur Staats- und Gesellschaftslehre des Kritizismus*. Leipzig, 1928.

Bourke, John. 'Kant's Doctrine of *Perpetual Peace*'. *Philosophy*, XVII, 1942.

Brakemeier, Heinz. *Die sittliche Aufhebung des Staates in Kants Philosophie* (Campus Forschungen, 343). Frankfurt/Main and New York, 1985.

Brandt, Reinhard. 'Emanzipation und Freiheit'. *AIKK*, II, 2, 1974.

'Das Erlaubnisgesetz, oder: Vernunft und Geschichte in Kants Rechtslehre'. In *RdA*, 1982.

Brown, Stuart M. Jr. 'Has Kant a Philosophy of Law?'. *Philosophical Review*, LXXXI, 1962.

Bruns, Thomas. 'Das politische Kantbild in Frankreich. Beitrag zur Problematik wertneutraler Kantbeurteilung'. In *AIKK*, II, 2, 1974.

Burg, Peter. *Kant und die französische Revolution* (Historische Forschungen, 7). Berlin, 1974.

'Kants Deutung der französischen Revolution im "Streit der Fakultäten"'. In *AIKK*, II, 2, 1974.

Busch, Werner. *Die Entstehung der kritischen Rechtsphilosophie Kants nach den frühen Quellen 1762–1780* (KSE, 110). Berlin, 1979.

Cann, Thomas, '*Perpetual Peace*: What Kant Should Have Said'. *Social Theory and Practice*, XIV, 1987.

Carritt, E. F. 'Kant'. In Carritt, *Morals and Politics. Theories of their Relation from Hobbes and Spinoza to Marx and Bosanquet*. Oxford, 1935.

Cohen, Hermann. *Kants Begründung der Ethik nebst ihren Anwendungen auf Recht. Religion und Geschichte*. Berlin, 1877 (2nd ed. 1910).

Cohen, Morris R. 'A Critique of Kant's Philosophy of Law'. In *The Heritage of Kant*, ed. George Tapley Whitney and David F. Bowers. New York, 1962.

Deggau, Hans-Georg. *Die Aporien der Rechtslehre Kants*. Stuttgart and Bad Cannstatt, 1983.

Delekat, Friedrich. *Immanuel Kant*. Heidelberg, 1963.

'Das Verhältnis von Sitte und Recht in Kants großer "Metaphysik der Sitten (1797)"'. *Zeitschrift für Philosophische Forschung*, XII, 1958.

Delue, Steven M. 'Kant's Politics as an Expression of the Need for his Aesthetics'. *PTh*, XIII, 1985.

Denker, Rolf. 'Kant's Theory of the Three-fold Path to World Peace—or the Purposes of Nature in History'. In *EGerr.*, 1974.

Despland, Michel. *Kant on History and Religion*. Montreal, 1973.

BIBLIOGRAPHY

Dietze, Gottfried. *Kant und der Rechtsstaat* (Walter Eucken Institut Vorträge und Aufsätze, 83). Tübingen, 1982.

Dreier, Ralf. *Rechtsbegriff und Rechtsidee. Kants Rechtsbegriff und seine Bedeutung für die gegenwärtige Diskussion.* (Würzburger Vorträge zur Rechtsphilosophie, Rechtstheorie und Rechtssoziologie, 5). Frankfurt/ Main, 1986.

Dulckeit, Gerhard. *Naturrecht und positives Recht bei Kant* (Abhandlungen der Rechts- und Staatswissenschaftlichen Fakultät, Göttingen, 14). Aalen, 1973.

Ebbinghaus, Julius. *Kants Lehre vom ewigen Frieden und die Kriegsschuldfrage* (Philosophie und Geschichte, 23). Tübingen, 1929.

'Das Kantische System der Rechte der Menschheit und Bürger in seiner geschichtlichen und aktuellen Bedeutung'. *Archiv für Rechts- und SozialphilosophiM*, XX, 1964. (Both items are reprinted in Ebbingshaus, *Gesammelte Aufsätze. Vorträge und Reden*. Darmstadt, 1960.)

Enderlein, W. 'Die Begründung der Strafe bei Kant'. *KS*, LXXVI, 1985.

Engel, S. Morris. 'On the "Composition" of the *Critique*. A Brief Comment', *Ratio*, VI, 1964.

Erdmann, Karl Dietrich. *Kant und Schiller als Zeitgenossen der französischen Revolution.* The 1985 Bithell Lecture, Institute of Germanic Studies, University of London. London, 1986.

Euchner, Walter. 'Kant as the Philosopher of Political Progress'. In *E. Gerr.*. 1974. (German trs. 'Kant als Philosoph des politischen Fortschritts'. In *ZwBat*, 1976.)

Fackenheim, Emil. 'Kant and Radical Evil'. *University of Toronto Quarterly*, XXIII, 1954.

Fetscher, Iring. 'Immanuel Kants bürgerlicher Reformismus'. In *Theory and Politics. Theorie und Politik. Festschrift zum 70. Geburtstag von Carl Joachim Friedrich*, ed. Klaus von Beyne. The Hague, 1971.

Finnis, J. M. 'Legal Enforcement of "Duties to Oneself". Kant v. Neo-Kantians'. *CLR*, LXXXVII, 1987.

Fleischacker, S. 'Kant's Theory of Punishment'. *KS*, LXXIX, 1988.

Fletcher, George P. 'Why Kant'. *CLR*, LXXXVII, 1987.

'Law and Morality: A Kantian Perspective'. *CLR*, LXXXVII, 1987.

Fink, Gonthier-Louis. 'La dialectique du despotisme éclairé selon Kant'. *Recherches Germaniques*, VII, 1977.

Friedrich, Carl Joachim. *Inevitable Peace*. Cambridge, Mass., 1948.

'L'essai sur la paix. Sa position centrale dans la philosophie morale de Kant'. *APP*, IV, 1962.

Gallie, W. B. 'Kant's View of Reason in Politics'. *Philosophy*, LIV, 1979.

'Wanted: A Philosophy of International Relations'. *Political Studies*, XXVII, 1979.

Geismann, Georg. 'Kants Rechtslehre vom Weltfrieden'. *Zeitschrift für Philosophische Forschung*, XXXVII, 1983.

Gerresheim, Eduard (ed.). *Immanuel Kant 1724/1974. Kant as a political thinker.* Bonn–Bad Godesberg, 1974.

Goedecke, R. 'Kant and the Radical Regrounding of the Norms of Politics'. *Journal of Value Enquiries*, VII, 1972.

Goldmann, Lucien. *Mensch, Gemeinschaft und Welt in der Philosophie Immanuel Kants.* (Diss.) Zurich, 1945. (French trs: *La Communauté humaine et l'univers chez Kant.* Paris, 1948; Engl. trs. *Immanuel Kant.* London, 1971).

Gonzalez Vicen, Felipe. *La Filosofia del Estado en Kant.* La Laguna, 1952.

Goyard-Fabre, Simone. *Kant et le Problème du Droit.* Paris, 1975.

Grcic, Joseph. 'Kant on Revolution and Economic Inequality'. *KS,* LXXVII, 1986.

Gregor, Mary J. *Laws of Freedom. A Study of Kant's Method of Applying the Categorical Imperative in the 'Metaphysik der Sitten'.* Oxford, 1963.

Grey, Thomas C. 'Serpents and Doves. A Note on Kantian Legal Theory'. *CLR,* LXXXVII, 1987.

Gulyga, Arsenij [Vladimirovic]. *Immanuel Kant,* trs. Sigrun Bielfeldt. Frankfurt/Main, 1981.

Haensel, Werner. *Kants Lehre vom Widerstandsrecht. Ein Beitrag zur Systematik der Kantischen Rechtsphilosophie* (KSE, 60). Berlin, 1926.

Hancock, R. N. 'Kant and the Natural Right Theory'. *KS,* LII, 1960–1.

'Kant and Civil Disobedience', *Idealistic Studies,* V, 1975.

'Kant on War and Peace'. In *AIKK,* II, 2, 1974.

Hassner, Pierre. 'Situation de la philosophie politique chez Kant'. *APP,* IV, 1962.

'Immanuel Kant'. In Leo Strauss and Joseph Cropsey. *History of Political Philosophy* (2nd ed.). Chicago, 1972.

Henrich, Dieter (ed. and with introd.). *Kant. Gentz. Rehberg. Über Theorie und Praxis.* Frankfurt/Main, 1967.

Hicks, Joe J. 'Is Kant's Theory of Justice Self-Defeating?'. *The Southwestern Journal of Philosophy,* II, 1972.

Hinsley, F. H. 'Kant'. In Hinsley, *Power and the Pursuit of Politics. Theory and Practice of Relations between States.* Cambridge, 1963.

Höffe, Otfried. 'Kants Begründung des Rechtszwangs und der Kriminalstrafe'. *RdA,* 1982.

Howard, Dick. 'Kant's Political Theory. The Virtue of his Vices'. *Review of Metaphysics,* XXXIV, 1980–81.

'Kant's System and (Its) Politics'. *Man and World,* XVIII, 1985.

Ilting, Karl-Heinz. 'Gibt es eine kritische Ethik und Rechtsphilosophie Kants?'. *Archiv für Geschichte der Philosophie,* LXIII, 1981.

Irmscher, Hans Dietrich. 'Die geschichtsphilosophische Kontroverse zwischen Kant und Herder'. In *Hamann–Kant–Herder. Acta des vierten Internationalen Hamann–Kolloquiums,* ed. Bernhard Gajek. Frankfurt/Main, 1987.

Jaspers, Karl. 'Kant'. *Die großen Philosophen,* In Jaspers, I. Munich, 1957.

'Kant zum Ewigen Frieden (1957)'; 'Kants Schrift zum Ewigen Frieden'; and 'Immanuel Kant zu seinem 150. Todestag 1954'. All three essays are in Jaspers, *Aneignung und Polemik. Gesammelte Reden und Aufsätze zur Geschichte der Philosophie,* ed. Hans Saner. Munich, 1968.

Johnson, Oliver. 'Autonomy in Kant and Rawls: A Reply'. *Ethics,* LXXXVII, 1977.

Kaulbach, Friedrich. *Studien zur späten Rechtsphilosophie Kant und ihrer transzendentalen Methode*. Würzburg, 1982.
Kant (Sammlung Göschen, 2221). Berlin and New York, 1975.
'Der Zusammenhang zwischen Naturphilosophie und Geschichtsphilosophie bei Kant'. *KS*, LVI, 1965.
'Welchen Nutzen gibt Kant der Geschichtsphilosophie?'. *KS*, LXVI, 1975.
Kelly, George Armstrong. 'Rousseau, Kant and History'. *JHI*, XXIX, 1968.
'Immanuel Kant: The Rationalisation of the Chimera'. In Kelly, *Idealism, Politics and History. Sources of Hegelian Thought*. Cambridge, 1969.
'The Structure and Spirit of Legality in Kant'. *Journal of Politics*, XXXI, 1969.
Kennedy, Ellen and Mendus, Susan. 'Kant: An Honest But Narrow-Minded Bourgeois?' In Kennedy and Mendus, *Women in Western Political Philosophy: Kant to Nietzsche*. London, 1987.
Kersting, Wolfgang. *Wohlgeordnete Freiheit. Immanuel Kants Rechts- und Sozialphilosophie* (Quellen und Studien zur Philosophie, 20). Berlin and New York, 1984.
'Sittengesetz und Rechtsgesetz—Die Begründung des Rechts bei Kant und den frühen Kantianern'. In *RdA*, 1982.
'Kant und der staatsphilosophische Kontraktualismus'. *Archiv für Philosophie*, VIII, 1983.
'Neuere Interpretationen der Kantischen Rechtsphilosophie'. *Zeitschrift für Philosophische Forschung*, XXXVII, 1983.
Kojève, Alexandre. *Kant*. Paris, 1973.
Körner, Stephan. 'Kant's Conception of Freedom'. Dawes Hicks Lecture. *Proceedings of the British Academy*, LIII, 1967.
'On Rousseau's, Robespierre's and Kant's Criteria of Moral Action'. In *The Impact of the French Revolution upon European Consciousness*, ed. H. T. Mason and W. Doyle. Gloucester and Wolfeboro, N.H., 1989.
Kretschmann, Philip M.. 'An Exposition of Kant's Philosophy of Law'. In *The Heritage of Kant*, ed. George Tapley Whitney and David F. Bowers. New York, 1962.
Krieger, Leonard. 'The Philosophical Bases: Kant and Hegel'. In Krieger, *The German Idea of Freedom. History of a Political Tradition*. Boston, 1937.
'Kant and the Crisis of Natural Law'. *JHI*, XXVI, 1965.
Kühl, Kristian. *Eigentum und Ordnung als Freiheitsordnung. Zur Aktualität der Kantischen Rechts-und Eigentumslehre* (Reihe Praktische Philosophie, 20). Freiburg and Munich, 1984.
Küsters, Gerd Walter. 'Recht und Vernunft. Bedeutung und Problem von Recht und Rechtsphilosophie bei Kant'. *Philosophische Rundschau*, XXX, 1983.
Kuzniar, Alice A. 'Kant and Herder on the French Revolution'. In *The French Revolution and the Age of Goethe*, ed. Gerhart Hoffmeister. Hildesheim, Zurich, New York, 1989.
Ladd, John. 'Kant's View of the Relation of Law to Morality'. *The Journal of Philosophy*, LVII, 1960.
Langer, Claudia. *Reform nach Prinzipien. Untersuchungen zur politischen Theorie Immanuel Kants* (Sprache und Geschichte, 11). Stuttgart, 1986.

Laursen, John Christian. 'Kantian Politics III: The Subversive Kant. The Vocabulary of "Public" and "Publicity"'. *PTh*, XIV, 1986.

Lisser, Kurt. *Der Begriff des Rechts bei Kant* (KSE, 58). Berlin, 1922.

Ludwig, Bernd. 'Der Platz des rechtlichen Postulats der praktischen Vernunft innerhalb der Paragraphen 1–6 der kantischen Rechtslehre'. In *RdA*, 1982.

Kants Rechtslehre. Mit einer Untersuchung der Drucklegung Kantischer Schriften von Werner Stark (Kant-Forschungen, 2). Hamburg, 1988.

Luf, Gerhard. *Freiheit und Gleichheit. Die Aktualität im politischen Denken Kants* (Forschungen aus Staat und Recht, 42). Vienna and New York, 1978.

Marcuse, Herbert. 'Kant über Autorität und Freiheit'. In Marcuse, *Ideen zu einer kritischen Theorie der Gesellschaft*. Frankfurt/Main, 1967.

Medicus, Fritz. 'Kants Philosophie der Geschichte'. *KS*, VII, 1902.

Meiklejohn, Donald. 'Kantian Formalism and Civil Liberty'. *The Journal of Philosophy*, LI, 1954.

Moog, Willy. *Kants Ansichten über Krieg und Frieden*. Darmstadt, 1917.

Mulholland, L. A. 'Kant on War and International Justice'. *KS*, LXXVIII, 1987.

Murphy, Jeffrie C. 'Kant's Concept of a Right Action'. In *Kant Studies Today*, ed. Lewis White Beck. Lasalle, Illinois, 1969.

'Does Kant have a Theory of Punishment?', *CLR*, LXXXVII, 1987.

Natorp, Paul. *Kant über Krieg und Frieden. Ein geschichtsphilosophischer Essay.* Erlangen, 1924.

Nicholson, Peter. 'Recent Studies in English of Kant's Political Philosophy'. *Political Studies*, XXIII, 1975.

Pasini, D. 'Das Reich der Zwecke und der politisch–rechtliche Kantianische Gedanke'. In *AIKK*, II, 2, 1974.

Paton, H. J. *Kant's Metaphysic of Experience—A Commentary on the First Half of the Kritik der reinen Vernunft* (2 vols.). London, 1936.

The Categorical Imperative. A Study of Kant's Moral Philosophy. London, 1947.

'Kant's Views on International Law'. In Paton, *In Defence of Reason*. London, 1951.

Pippin, Robert B. 'On the Moral Foundations of Kant's *Rechtslehre*'. In *The Philosophy of Immanuel Kant*, ed. Richard Kennington (Studies in Philosophy and the History of Philosophy, 12). Washington, D.C., 1985.

Polin, Raymond. 'Les relations du peuple avec ceux qui le gouvernent d'après Kant'. *APP*, IV, 1962.

Popper, Karl Raimund. 'Kant's Critique and Cosmology'. In Popper, *Conjectures and Refutations. The Growth of Scientific Knowledge* (2nd ed.). London, 1965.

Psychopédis, Kosmás. *Untersuchungen zur politischen Theorie von Immanuel Kant* (Göttinger Wirtschafts- und Sozialwissenschaftliche Studien, 19). Göttingen, 1980.

Puder, Martin. 'Kant und die französische Revolution'. *Neue Deutsche Hefte*, XX, 1973.

Rawls, John. 'Kantian Constructivism in Moral Theory'. *The Journal of Philosophy*. LXXVII, 1980.

Reed, T.J. 'The Stay-at-Home Man of the World'. *Times Higher Education Supplement*, 21 June 1985, No. 659.

Reiss, Hans. *Kants Politisches Denken*, trs. Gisela Shaw. Berne, Frankfurt/ Main, Las Vegas, 1977. (Japanese translation, Masoyoshi Tarui. Tokyo, 1989.)

'Kant und die französische Revolution'. *Zeitschrift für Pädagogik*, Beiheft 24, 1989.

'The French Revolution and the "Aufklärung". Two Perspectives: Kant and Goethe'. In *The French Revolution and the Aufklärung*, ed. Gerhart Hoffmeister. Hildesheim, Zurich, New York, 1989.

Richards, David A.J. 'Kantian Ethics and the Harm Principle. A Reply to John Finnis'. *CLR*, LXXXVII, 1987.

Riley, Patrick. 'On Kant as the Most Adequate of the Social Contract Theorists'. *PTH*, I, 1973.

'Kant on Will, Moral Causality and the Social Contract'. *The Modern Schoolman*. LIV, 1976/77.

'Kantian Politics II: The "Elements" of Kant's Political Philosophy. The *Groundwork* after 200 years (1785–1985)'. *PTh*, XIV, 1985.

Ritter, Christian. *Der Rechtsgedanke Kants nach den frühen Quellen* (Juristische Abhandlungen, 10). Frankfurt/Main, 1971.

'The Politics of Law'. In *EGerr.*, 1974.

Rossi, Philip. 'Autonomy and Community: The Social Character of Kant's Moral Faith'. *The Modern Schoolman*, LXI, 1984.

Rossmann, Kurt. 'Immanuel Kant'. In *Die Grossen Deutschen. Deutsche Biographie*, ed. Hermann Heimpel et al. (2nd ed.), II. Berlin, 1956.

Ruyssen, Théodore. 'La philosophie de l'histoire selon Kant'. *APP*, IV, 1962.

Saage, Richard. *Eigentum, Staat und Gesellschaft bei Immanuel Kant*. Stuttgart, Berlin, Cologne, Mayence, 1973.

Sacksteder, William. 'Kant's Analysis of International Relations'. *The Journal of Philosophy*, LI, 1954.

Saner, Hans. *Kants Weg vom Krieg zum Frieden. Widerstreit und Einheit. Wege zu Kants politischem Denken. I.* Munich, 1967 (Engl. trs. E. B. Ashton. *Kant's Political Thought. Its Origins and Development*, Chicago and London, 1973).

Sänger, Monika. *Die kategoriale Systematik in den 'Metaphysischen Anfangsgründen der Rechtslehre* (KSE, 114). Berlin and New York, 1982.

Scheffel, Dieter. 'Kants kritische Verwerfung des Revolutionsrechts'. *RdA*, 1982.

Schrecker, Paul. 'Kant et la révolution française'. *Revue Philosophique*, XXVII, 1939.

Schulz, Uwe. *Kant in Selbstzeugnissen und Bilddokumenten* (Rowohlt Monographien). Reinbeck bei Hamburg, 1965.

Schwarz, Wolfgang. 'Kant's Philosophy of Law and International Peace'. *Philosophy and Phenomenological Research*, XXIII, 1962.

'The Right of Resistance'. *Ethics*, LXXIV, 1964.

'Kant's Refutation of Charitable Lies'. *Ethics*, LXXXI, 1970.

'The Ambiguities of Resistance. A Reply to Peter Nicholson'. *Ethics*, LXXXVII, 1977.

Seidler, Victor J. *Kant: Respect and Injustice. The Limits of Liberal Moral Theory*. London, Boston and Henley, 1986.

Shell, Susan. 'What Kant and Fichte Can Teach Us about Human Rights'. In *The Philosophy of Immanuel Kant*, ed. Richard Kennington (Studies in Philosophy and the History of Philosophy, 12). Washington, D.C., 1985.

Singh, Ratnamala. 'Kant, Morality and the Right of Resistance'. *South African Journal of Philosophy*, VI, 1987.

Strawson, P. F. *The Bounds of Sense*. London, 1966.

Struck, Peter. 'Ist Kants Rechtspostulat der praktischen Vernunft aporetisch? Ein Beitrag zur neuerlich ausgebrochenen Kontroverse über Kants Rechtsphilosophie'. *KS*, LXXVIII, 1987.

Teuber, Andreas. 'Kantian Perspectives II: Kant's Respect for Persons'. *PTH*, XI, 1983.

Van der Linden, Harry. *Kantian Ethics and Socialism*. Indianapolis and Cambridge, 1988.

Villey, Michel. 'Kant dans l'histoire du Droit'. *APP*, IV, 1962.

Vlachos, Georges. *La Pensée politique de Kant. Métaphysique de l'ordre et dialectique du progrès*. Paris, 1962.

Vollrath, Ernst. 'Kants Kritik der Urteilskraft als Grundlegung einer Theorie des Politischen'. In *AIKK*, II, 2. 1974.

Die Rekonstruktion der politischen Urteilskraft. Stuttgart, 1977.

Vorländer, Karl. *Kant und Marx. Ein Beitrag zur Philosophie des Sozialismus*. Tübingen, 1911.

'Kants Stellung zur französischen Revolution'. In *Philosophische Abhandlungen Hermann Cohen gewidmet*. Berlin, 1912.

Kant und der Gedanke des Völkerbundes. Leipzig, 1919.

Immanuel Kant. Der Mann und das Werk (2 vols.). Leipzig, 1924.

Walker, Ralph C. S. *Immanuel Kant* (The Argument of the Philosophers). London, 1978.

Waltz, K. N. 'Kant, Liberalism, and War'. *American Political Science Review*. LVI, 1962.

Weil, E. 'Kant et le problème de la politique'. *APP*, IV, 1962.

Weinrib, Ernst J. 'Law as a Kantian Idea of Reason'. *CLR*, LXXXVII, 1987.

Weyand, Klaus. *Kants Geschichtsphilosophie. Ihre Entwicklung und ihr Verhältnis zur Aufklärung*. (KSE, 85). Cologne, 1963.

Wilkins, Burley Taylor. 'Teleology in Kant's Philosophy of History'. *History and Theory*, V, 1966.

Williams, Howard. 'Politics and Philosophy in Kant and Hegel'. In *Hegel's Critique of Kant*, ed. Stephen Priest. Oxford, 1987.

Wittichen, Paul. 'Kant und Burke'. *Historische Zeitschrift*, XCII, 1904.

Wolf, Friedrich O. 'Kant and Hobbes Concerning the Foundations of Political Philosophy'. *Proceedings of the Third International Kant Congress*, ed. Lewis White Beck. Dordrecht, 1972.

Other Works

Barnard, F. M. *Herder's Social and Political Thought. From Enlightenment to Nationalism*. Oxford, 1965.

(trs., ed. and with an introduction). *J. G. Herder on Social and Political Culture*. Cambridge, 1969.

'Kantian Perspectives I: Self-Direction in Thomasius, Kant and Herder'. *PTh*, XI, 1983.

'"Aufklärung" and "Mündigkeit". Thomasius, Kant and Herder'. *Deutsche Vierteljahrsschrift für Literaturwissenschaft und Geistesgeschichte*. LVII, 1983.

Basch, Victor. *Les doctrines politiques des philosophes classiques de l'Allemagne*. Paris, 1927.

Beck, Lewis White. *Early German Philosophy. Kant and his Predecessors*. Cambridge, Mass., 1969.

Berlin, Isaiah. *Vico and Herder. Two Studies in the History of Ideas*. London, 1976.

Blackall, Eric A. *The Emergence of German as a Literary Language 1700–1775*. Cambridge, 1959.

Bruford, W. H., *Germany in the Eighteenth Century*. Cambridge, 1935.

Culture and Society in Classical Weimar 1775–1806. Cambridge, 1962.

Buchdahl, Gerd. *The Image of Newton and Locke in the Age of Reason* (Newman History and Philosophy of Science Series, 6). London and New York, 1961.

Cairns, Huntington. *Legal Philosophy from Plato to Hegel*. Baltimore, 1949.

Cobban, Alfred. *In Search of Humanity. The Role of the Enlightenment in Modern History*. New York, 1960.

A History of Modern France (2 vols., 2nd ed.). London, 1962.

Rousseau and the Modern State (2nd ed.). London, 1964.

Collingwood, R. G. *The Idea of History*. Oxford, 1946.

Cranston, Maurice William. *John Locke. A Biography*. London and New York, 1957.

Doyle, William. *Origins of the French Revolution* (2nd ed.). Oxford, 1988.

The Oxford History of the French Revolution. Oxford, 1989.

Droz, Jacques. *L'Allemagne et la révolution française*. Paris, 1949.

Dworkin, Ronald. *Taking Rights Seriously*. London, 1977.

Epstein, Klaus. *The Genesis of German Conservatism*. Princeton, N.J., 1966.

Flint, Robert. *The Philosophy of History in France and Germany*. London, 1874.

Fries, Jakob Friedrich. *Vom Deutschen Bund und Deutscher Staatsverfassung. Allgemeine staatsrechtliche Ansichten*. Heidelberg, 1816.

Politik oder philosophische Staatslehre, ed. E.F. Apelt. Jena, 1848.

Gierke, Otto Friedrich von. *Das deutsche Genossenschaftsrecht* (4 vols.). Berlin, 1868–1913. (Vol. 4. trs. Ernest Barker as *Natural Law and the Theory of Society*. Cambridge, 1934.)

Gillies, Alexander. *Herder*. Oxford, 1945.

Gooch, George Peabody. 'German Views of the State'. *The German Mind and Outlook*, ed. G. P. Gooch et al. London, 1945.

Frederick the Great. The Ruler. The Writer. The Man. London, 1947.

Gough, J. W. *The Social Contract. A Critical Study of its Development*. Oxford, 1936.

Grimsley, Ronald. *Jean-Jacques Rousseau. A Study in Self-Awareness*. Cardiff, 1961.

Habermas, Jürgen. *Strukturwandel der Öffentlichkeit. Untersuchungen zu einer Kategorie der bürgerlichen Gesellschaft.* Neuwied and Berlin, 1963.

Hart, H. L. A. *The Concept of Law.* Oxford, 1961.

Haym, Rudolf. *Herder nach seinem Leben und seinen Werken dargestellt* (2 vols.). Berlin, 1877–85 (2nd ed., Berlin, 1954).

Hazard, Paul. *La Crise de la conscience européenne (1680–1715).* Paris, 1935. (*The European Mind 1680–1715*, trs. J. Lewis May. London, 1953.)

Hendel, Charles William. *Jean-Jacques Rousseau. Moralist* (2 vols.). Oxford, 1934.

Herder, Johann Gottfried. *Sämmtliche Werke* (33 vols.), ed. Bernhard Suphan. Berlin, 1877–1913.

Hinske, Norbert (ed.). *Was ist Aufklärung? Beiträge aus der Berlinischen Monatsschrift.* Darmstadt, 1973.

Humboldt, Carl Wilhelm von. *Gesammelte Schriften*, ed. Albert Leitzmann. Berlin, 1903ff.

Irmscher, Hans Dietrich. 'Beobachtungen zur Funktion der Analogie im Denken Herders'. *Deutsche Vierteljahrsschrift für Literaturwissenschaft und Geistesgeschichte*, LV, 1981.

'Aneignung und Kritik naturwissenschaftlicher Vorstellungen bei Herder'. In *Texte. Motive und Gestalten der Goethezeit. Festschrift für Hans Reiss*, ed. John L. Hibberd and H. B. Nisbet. Tübingen, 1989.

Jacobi, Friedrich Heinrich. *Werke* (6 vols.). Leipzig, 1812–25 (Reprint: Darmstadt, 1980).

Kedourie, Elie. *Nationalism.* London, 1960.

Koepke, Wulf. *Johann Gottfried Herder.* Boston, Mass., 1987.

Körner, Stephan. *Experience and Theory.* London, 1966 (German trs. Eberhard Bubser. *Erfahrung und Theorie.* Frankfurt/Main, 1970).

Koselleck, Reinhart. *Preußen zwischen Reform und Revolution. Allgemeines Landrecht, Verwaltung und soziale Bewegung von 1791–1848.* Stuttgart, 1967.

Laslett, Peter (ed.) *Locke's Two Treatises of Government.* Cambridge, 1960 (2nd ed. Cambridge, 1967; Student Edition, Cambridge, 1988).

Mendelssohn, Moses. *Gesammelte Schriften* (Jubiläumsausgabe). Stuttgart and Bad Cannstatt, 1929ff.

Metzger, Wilhelm. *Gesellschaft, Recht und Staat in der Ethik des deutschen Idealismus.* ed. Ernst Bergmann. Heidelberg, 1917.

Nelson, Leonard. *System der philosophischen Rechtslehre*, Leipzig, 1920.

System der philosophischen Rechtslehre und Politik. Leipzig, 1924. (Reprinted in Nelson, *Gesammelte Schriften.* ed. Paul Bernays et al., VI, Hamburg, 1970.)

Nisbet, H. B. *Herder and the Philosophy and History of Science* (Modern Humanities Research Association Dissertation Series, 3). Cambridge, 1970.

Oakeshott, Michael [Joseph] (ed.). *Hobbes's Leviathan.* Oxford, 1946.

Peters, Richard. *Hobbes.* Harmondsworth, Middlesex, 1956.

Popper, Karl Raimund. *The Open Society and Its Enemies* (2 vols.), (2nd ed.). London, 1952.

The Poverty of Historicism. London, 1961.

Logik der Forschung. Vienna, 1935. (Engl. trs. *The Logic of Scientific Discovery.* London, 1959.)

'Conversation with Karl Popper'. In *Modern British Philosophy*, ed. Bryan Magee. London, 1971.

'A Pluralist Approach to the Philosophy of History'. *Roads to Freedom. Essays in Honour of Friedrich A. von Hayek*, ed. Erich Streissler. London, 1969.

Rawls, John. *A Theory of Justice*. Cambridge, Mass., 1971.

Reiss, Hans Siegbert (ed.). *The Political Thought of the German Romantics 1793–1815*. Oxford, 1955.

'The Concept of the Aesthetic State in the Work of Schiller and Novalis'. *Publications of the English Goethe Society, N. S.*, XXVI, 1957.

'Fichte als politischer Denker'. *Archiv für Rechts- und Sozialphilosophie*, XVIII, 1962.

Politisches Denken in der deutschen Romantik. Berne and Munich, 1966.

'Justus Möser und Wilhelm von Humboldt. Konservative und liberale politische Ideen im Deutschland des 18. Jahrhunderts'. *Politische Vierteljahresschrift*, VIII, 1967.

'Goethe and the French Revolution'. In *The Impact of the French Revolution on European Consciousness*, ed. H. T. Mason and W. Doyle. Gloucester and Wolfeboro, N.H. 1989. (German version 'Goethe und die französische Revolution'. *Zeitschrift für Pädagogik*, Beiheft, 24, 1989.)

Rousseau, Jean-Jacques. *The Political Writings* (2 vols.), ed. Charles Edwyn Vaughan. Cambridge, 1915.

Rousseau's Political Writings, ed. Frederick Watkins. Edinburgh and New York, 1953.

Santayana, George. *Egotism in German Philosophy*. London and Toronto, 1916.

Savigny, Friedrich Karl von. *Vom Beruf unsrer Zeit für Gesetzgebung und Rechtswissenschaft*. Heidelberg, 1814.

Scholz, Heinrich (ed. with an introduction). *Die Hauptschriften zum Pantheismusstreit zwischen Jacobi und Mendelssohn* (Neudrucke seltener philosophischer Werke, ed. Kantgesellschaft, 6). Berlin, 1916.

Schnabel, Franz. *Deutsche Geschichte im 19. Jahrhundert* (4 vols.; vol. I, 4th ed., vol. II–IV, 2nd ed.). Freiburg, 1948–51.

Valjavec, Fritz. *Geschichte der europäischen Aufklärung*. Vienna, 1961.

Venturi, Franco. 'Was ist Aufklärung? Sapere Aude!'. *Rivista Storica Italiana*, LXXI, 1959.

Walsh, W. H. *An Introduction to Philosophy of History*. London, 1951.

Watkins, Frederick (ed.). *Hume: Theory of Politics*. Edinburgh and New York, 1951.

Wilkinson, Elizabeth M. and Willoughby, L. A. (eds. and trs.). *Friedrich Schiller: On the Aesthetic Education of Man in a Series of Letters*. Oxford, 1967.

Willoughby, L. A. 'Schiller on Man's Education to Freedom through Knowledge'. *Germanic Review*, XXIX, 1954.

Index

A NAMES

Achenwall, Gottfried (*Ius naturae*), XII, 82, 275, 278 f.
Aeon, 99 n., 276
Africa, African, 25, 213
Alethophiles, 5
Alexandria, 273
Allais, *see* D'Allais
Allgemeine Literaturzeitung, 195, 211, 282
Allgemeines Landrecht, 270
Alphabetum Tibetanum, 106 n., 107 n., 277
Altai Mountains, 111
Althusius, Johannes, 10
America, American, 103, 106, 111, 166, 171, 203, 213, 217, 261
American Revolution, 3 f., 14 f., 27, 261
Arabia, Arabs (*see* also Bedouins), 230 n., 284
Arctic, 108, 110 f., 111 n.
Aristotle, 39
Asia, Asian, Asians, 203, 213 f., 215
Athens, 169, 277
Atlantis, 281
Aufklärung, see Enlightenment
Augustine, *see* St Augustine
Augustus, 97
Austria, Austrians, 269, 279, 281
Averroes, Averroism, 220, 283

Balmerino, Arthur, 6th Baron, 156, 279
Barbary Coast, 106
Barthélemy [Abbé], Jean Jacques, 278
Basle, Treaty of, 276, 281
Baumgarten, Alexander Gottlieb, 193
Beccaria, Cesare Marchese de Bonesana, 157, 279
Beck, Lewis White, X, 281
Bedouins, 106, 230 n.
Beni Haled, 230 n.
Berlin, 245

Berlinische Monatsschrift, 48, 60, 269, 273 f., 284
Bible (*Acts*) 31, 39, 52 n., (*Genesis, Acts*) 110 n., (*St Matthew*) 116, 176, 196 f., (*Genesis*) 222–6, 229, 232, (*Romans, Acts*) 267
Biester, Johann Friedrich, 269, 278
Blumenbach, Johann Friedrich, 185, 280 f.
Bouterwek, Friedrich, 113, 278, 280
Brabant, Duke John III of, 275
Brabant, Siger of, *see* Siger of Brabant
Brahe, Tycho, *see* Tycho Brahe
Britain, British, 7 ff., 29, 82 ff., 169, 186, 187 n., 261, 275 f., 281
Bückeburg, 194
Bukhara, 107 n., 277
Bulgarian, 103 n.
Burke, Edmund, 274
Büsching, Anton Friedrich 60, 173, 189, 274

Canada, 261 n.
Cameralism, 11
Camper, Petrus, 185, 280
Campo Formio (Treaty of), 281
Cape (of Good Hope), 106
Carl August, Duke (later Grand Duke) of Saxe-Weimar-Eisenach, 194
Charles I, 31, 145 n.
Charles Edward [Stuart], Prince, 279
China, 106 n., 107 n., 232
Christianity, 173
Christians, 110 n.
Cicero, 69, 279
Commodus, Lucius Aelius Aurelius, 102 n., 277
Cook, James, 214, 283
Copernicus, Nicolaus, 2, 17, 180, 280
Corinth, 276

INDEX

B SUBJECTS

INDEX

Epistemology, 17, 196, 198, 236
Equality, 25 ff., 49, 74–7, 77 n., 78, 83 n.,
    99, 99 n., 100 n., 123, 136, 139 f.,
    155 f., 168, 198 f., 226, 233, 235 f.,
    257
Equity, 135 f.
Ethics, ethical (see also Morality), XI, I,
    20, 126, 134 f., 223, 236, 259
Ethnographical, ethnological description,
    213, 215, 217
Eudaemonism (see also Chiliasm), 178 f.,
    280
Executive (see also Monarch), 24 f., 29 ff.,
    101, 141 f., 144, 146, 169, 260
Exile, see Deportation
Expediency, 35, 89, 94, 118, 122 f., 128
Experience, 8, 12, 17, 21, 28, 37 f., 47,
    50, 61 ff., 69, 70 n., 71 f., 80, 86, 93,
    102 n., 106, 117, 119, 137, 174,
    180 f., 185, 187 f., 191, 193, 196,
    198, 209, 212, 219, 221 f., 228 n.,
    237, 240, 244, 246, 246 n., 266

Federation [of states], 34, 47, 49, 90, 92,
    102, 104 f., 113, 127, 129, 165, 171,
    197, 266
Feudal system, Feudal obligations, 26,
    153, 258
Freedom, (see also Independence), 3, 11,
    13 f., 22 f., 25–9, 32 f., 36, 38 f., 41,
    43, 45–53, 55, 57 ff., 67, 70 n., 72–7,
    80, 85 f., 90, 96 f., 99, 99 n., 101–5,
    110, 112, 114, 117, 119 f., 122 f.,
    127, 129, 133–7, 139 f., 142, 144,
    148, 153, 163 f., 168, 170, 181,
    183 n., 184, 184 n., 186 f., 191, 195,
    197 f., 201, 205, 213, 221, 224, 227,
    229, 229 n., 231 f., 236, 242, 247 ff.,
    252, 254, 257, 259, 262, 265, 270 ff.

Gestalt, 197
God (Creator, Deity), 65 f., 88, 96, 99 n.,
    101 n., 105 n., 107 n., 108 n., 109 n.,
    143, 181, 197 f., 203, 205 f., 218,
    223, 227, 230, 232, 235 f., 241 n.,
    242 n., 245, 245 n., 246 f., 261 n.,
    268, 285
Government, 4, 9, 28 f., 31 f., 34 f., 39,
    51, 53, 56, 58 ff., 74, 77, 81, 86, 96,
    101 ff., 102 n., 113–7, 119, 121 n.,
    122, 141, 144, 146, 148 ff., 153, 160,
    163 f., 166, 176, 178, 183 n., 184,
    191, 199, 215, 230, 256, 259, 261–4,
    266 ff., 270 ff.

Happiness, 19, 25, 32, 43 f., 64–8, 68 n.,
    69–74, 76, 80, 83, 86, 88, 124, 130,
    142, 155, 183 n., 191, 197 f., 215,
    219, 242, 258 f.
Head of State, see Monarch
History, IX, 3, 6 f., 9, 13 f., 20, 28 f.,
    35–8, 41 f., 50 ff., 52 n., 53, 71, 79,
    82, 88 f., 122, 143, 162, 177, 179,
    181, 183 f., 192, 194, 196–9, 201,
    216, 218–21, 226 f., 229, 233, 245,
    262, 265
Hospitality, 105 f.

Idea, Ideas, 5 f., 14, 28, 31, 36, 52 f., 62,
    65 n., 68–72, 79 f., 83, 91, 94, 99,
    104, 108 f., 113, 117 ff., 130, 134,
    137 f., 140, 143, 146 n., 157, 161 ff.,
    165, 173, 187, 191, 195, 198 ff., 201,
    208, 210, 212, 220, 236, 246 n., 252,
    260, 264, 270 ff.
Immaturity, 54, 58 f., 74, 256, 262
Immortality, 205
Independence (see also Freedom), 25 f.,
    74, 77, 91, 105 n., 139 ff., 195 f.,
    198, 248, 256, 258, 262
Induction, 17
Inequality, 75 f., 229 n., 230, 258
Infanticide, 159
Instinct, 12, 42 f., 204 f., 215, 223 f., 226,
    228 n.
Intuition, 8 f., 13, 135, 237 f., 240, 245 f.

Jacobin, Jacobinism, 183 n., 269
Judiciary, 24, 29, 104, 138, 141 f., 154,
    158, 260 f.
Jurisprudence, 132
Justice, IX, 21, 27 ff., 35, 39, 46, 78, 79 n.,
    87 n., 96 f., 97 n., 112, 114 f., 123 ff.,
    137–42, 145, 146 n., 150 f., 154–9,
    166, 173, 205, 223, 230, 252, 255,
    259, 275

Language, 34, 111, 113, 196, 198, 205,
    207, 215
Law, Laws, 1, 7, 11, 13, 18–39, 41–9, 52,
    57, 59, 64–7, 67 n., 68, 72–80, 80 n.,
    81 n., 82–5, 90 ff., 97, 98 n., 101–6,
    108, 108 n., 110–18, 118 n., 119,
    121 n., 122, 127, 130–145, 145 n.,
    146 n., 147, 149, 151, 154 f., 157 ff.,
    162 f., 167 f., 171 f., 174, 176 f.,
    181, 184, 187 f., 191, 196 f., 209 f.,
    228 n., 241 f., 247, 249, 251, 253 ff.,

306

Statistics, 41
Superstition, 40, 236, 248, 249 n., 254

Taxation, 79 n., 95, 143, 149 f., 164, 275
Teleology, teleological, 36, 42, 109 n., 265
Terrorism (moral), 37, 178 f.
Theodicy, 124, 197
Theory (see also Practice), XI, 13, 15, 19 f., 39, 42, 61–6, 68, 70 n., 72 f., 83, 86 ff., 92 f., 109, 109 n., 114, 116 f., 121 n., 123 f., 132, 135, 155, 185, 173, 205, 244, 255, 261, 266, 274 ff.
Toleration, Tolerance 6, 32 f., 58, 213, 253
Totalitarianism, 250, 264–7, 270
Trade (Commerce), 50 f., 114, 172
Travelogues, 217
Treason, 144
Tyranny, see Despotism

Utilitarianism, 25

Vote, 78 f., 91, 139 f.

War, 9, 24, 27, 33 f., 38, 47 ff., 51, 79 n., 90 f., 93–8, 99 n., 100, 103–7, 105 n., 110–15, 121, 129, 153, 164–71, 174, 176, 182 ff., 187, 187 n., 189 f., 222, 230–3, 251 f., 261, 266, 271, 275
Wealth, 70, 76, 95, 231, 259
Will, 18 f., 21, 23, 25–30, 41, 43, 46 f., 58, 62, 64 n., 65–77, 65 n., 79 ff., 83, 84 n., 85 f., 91, 99 n., 101, 105, 112, 114, 117, 120, 122 ff., 127, 133 f., 136, 138–41, 143 f., 149, 152 f., 158, 161–4, 170, 176, 181, 183 n., 184 n., 186, 279
Wissenschaft (see also Scholarship), 199
World government, World state (Universal monarchy), 34, 113 f., 250, 270 f.

Zealotry (Schwärmerei), 236, 242 n., 246 n., 248, 249 n., 254, 260, 284 f.

309

Cambridge Texts in the History of Political Thought

TITLES PUBLISHED IN THE SERIES THUS FAR

Cambridge Studies in the History and Theory of Politics

STUDIES